Birth, Sex And Abuse

Women's Voices Under Nazi Rule

Beverley Chalmers (DSc(Med); PhD)

Grosvenor House
Publishing Limited

This book is published by
Grosvenor House Publishing Ltd
28-30 High Street, Guildford, Surrey, GU1 3EL.
www.grosvenorhousepublishing.co.uk

A CIP record for this book
is available from the British Library

ISBN 978-1-78148-353-4

DEDICATION

To the childbearing women and new mothers who lived
in the Nazi era,

To my husband, Bernie, who chose not to obey the rules,

To our children, their children, and their children's children,

And

To my parents, Punny and Widdie Wolfowitz, who taught me
about Judaism and about tolerance.

TABLE OF CONTENTS

Acknowledgement

Although I have endeavoured to remain detached from the often gruesome evidence reported in this text, as is in keeping with my longstanding academic and research background, I have no doubt been guilty of the plight of all scholars: to view information and to report only that which resonates with their perspective. I have striven for representativeness and objectivity in my reporting of events and in the selection of quotations from those who lived (or died) during the Nazi era. If the information contained in this book appears to reflect a preponderance of unpleasant and often cruel events, this is not because I have omitted to report the 'nice times,' but because the events that occurred during this period were mostly horrific. There is no nice way of reporting on the horrors of the Holocaust. This book reflects only the experiences of a few hundred women who lived to recount their stories. The voices – and experiences – of the millions of women who were murdered as a result of Nazi atrocities are not heard.

My sincerest appreciation goes to Prof Miriam Gillis-Carlebach, of The Joseph Carlebach Institute, Bar Ilan University, Ramat-Gan, Israel, who met with me at the start of this project. Her advice to explore *Halakhah* regarding Jewish women's experiences, led to the uncovering of evidence supporting the hitherto rejected or, at least largely discounted, idea that Jewish women were, on occasion, forced to serve as prostitutes in the brothels established by the Nazi regime. My heartfelt thanks also go to Shula and Avraham Werner, Israel, both survivors – and long time colleagues and friends – who read drafts of some aspects of this work and gave me valuable feedback, despite the enormously difficult memories these pages evoked for them. My thanks go to Yad Vashem in Jerusalem for its archives, and for the educational programs I attended, that helped me to get started on this work. My thanks also go to Boaz Tal, archivist at the Massuah Institute for the Study of the Holocaust, Tel Aviv, for the warm welcome he gave me and for the months of (most valuable) archival searching that he did on my behalf. My thanks are also due to the archivists at the Imperial War Museum in London, who were remarkably helpful, and particularly to Stephen Walton. My grateful appreciation is also due to my daughter Dana, a doctorate in Ideological Conflict and Genocide Studies, whose conceptual contributions as well as careful and critical reading of draft texts, has always been immensely valuable and to Simon Solomon for his careful checking of the manuscript. My children have all indulged my obsession with the Holocaust for the past decade and more and have furthered it by assisting me to find rare texts on the subject.

My final, and most sincere, thanks are reserved for my husband, Bernie. He has accompanied me on each step of my academic travels through the many horrors faced by women during pregnancy and birth across the globe for over forty years. In particular, I sincerely appreciate his acceptance and support for my past dozen years of work on this text, his willingness to listen to extracts recounting the most horrific events and experiences that I came across, especially during my late night reading of survivor stories, and his careful assistance with the conceptualizing of this book, as well as his critical reviews of multiple drafts of the manuscript. I am deeply grateful for his support for me and for this work, especially through some very trying periods in its creation. 'Thank you for sharing our lives' is hardly sufficient to express my immense gratitude and love.

Beverley Chalmers (DSc (Med); PhD)
Adjunct Full Professor, Dept of Obstetrics and Gynaecology, and
Affiliate Investigator, Ottawa Hospital Research Institute
University of Ottawa, Ontario, Canada.

Introduction

I have dedicated my life to studying women's experiences of pregnancy, birth and the early months of parenthood in industrialized parts of the world as well as in more difficult social, political, religious, and economic circumstances. These include: Black women giving birth in Apartheid South Africa, and in other developing African countries such as Ethiopia and war-torn Southern Sudan; women giving birth in over a dozen former Soviet countries as these moved from communism to democracy; women from Somalia and other central African countries giving birth in Canada following prior female genital mutilation; and women giving birth with unnecessarily high use of technology in the industrialized 'western' world. All of these settings reveal challenging circumstances ranging from political and economic repression in Apartheid South Africa, and in the former Soviet Union, religiously inspired cruelty of female genital mutilation, and over-medicalization of birth in the technologically developed world. None of these, however, comes anywhere close to matching the horrors experienced by those whom the Nazi regime targeted for reproductive and sexual manipulation, and, in the case of Jewish women and babies, extermination.

The Nazis used, and abused, reproduction and sexuality to achieve their ideological goal of creating a so-called Master 'Aryan' Race. On the one hand, they prohibited or prevented women and men regarded as not meeting idealized Nazi racial standards – and particularly Jewish women – from having children through legal, social, psychological and biological means, as well as by murder. On the other hand, they promoted reproductive life and sexuality to achieve the antithesis of genocide – the mass promotion of life – among those deemed sufficiently 'Aryan.'

One objective of this book is to show that targeting reproduction and sexuality was a central theme underlying many aspects of Nazi policy through both 'positive eugenics' (that could be termed 'geno-coercive') as well as 'negative eugenics' (including genocidal) policies. A second objective is to further illuminate the role played by the medical profession in particular, in manipulating reproductive and sexual lives to achieve the Nazis' goals. A third objective is to integrate the widely dispersed evidence for these Nazi policies and practices found in the writings emanating from multiple disciplines including Holocaust Studies, Women's Studies and Women's History, the History of Medicine, and Reproductive and Sexual Health Psychology. Emphasis has been placed on developing a broad social and psychological perspective on women's experiences by collating the numerous reports that inform this inter-disciplinary focus, rather than on the extensive and reductionist commentary that traditional historians favour. This is not a German history text, nor is it a history of the Holocaust. Nor is it a theoretical speculation on the academic intricacies of interpretation that could be derived from any or all of the information contained in the book. It is an integration of the reports of women themselves, written or dictated both during the Nazi period and in the ensuing years, regarding their reproductive and sexual lives. A final objective is to emphasise the climate of cruelty that pervaded not only the actions taken to implement the Holocaust by targeting reproduction and sexuality, but their sadistic and often misogynistic nature. The book reveals, by extensive reference to the voices of those who witnessed or experienced the events, a spectre of brutality that is not often recognized. The horrors of the Holocaust are legion: the misogynistic enjoyment of such actions is less well acknowledged. While a dry listing of horrific acts is sufficient incrimination in itself, the added layer of satisfaction apparently experienced by many of the perpetrators evokes repugnance.

The literature on the Holocaust gives exhaustive attention to 'direct' means of exterminating Jews, including the use of gas chambers, torture, starvation, disease, and intolerable conditions in the ghettos and camps as well as through the actions of the *Einsatzgruppen*. The manipulation of reproductive lives – as a less 'direct' method of genocide – has not yet received the same exhaustive attention. Imposing measures to prevent births is, however, included in the internationally accepted definition of genocide found in Articles II and III of the 1948 United Nations Convention on the Prevention and Punishment of Genocide.[1]

Nazi policies preventing pregnancy and birth among Jewish women were a constantly evolving combination of ideology and practice. As with other extermination processes under the Third Reich, the manipulation of Jewish reproductive life was neither static in its conceptualization nor consistent in its application. These policies were endorsed by eugenic theories and the Nuremberg Laws targeting social and sexual interactions with Jews that were emphasised from the earliest years of Nazi rule. At various times during the period of 1933-1945, and in various places in Nazi occupied Europe, the Nazis prevented those they regarded as most 'undesirable' from having offspring through forced sterilization and subsequent euthanasia of those who escaped the eugenics net. Among those allowed to live, they limited social and sexual contact between those regarded as 'desirable' and those as 'undesirable,' to avoid 'contamination.' The Nazis forbad births in some ghettos and concentration camps, and enforced abortion among those who did conceive. Reproduction was also prevented by murdering pregnant women on arrival at concentration camps or later, if pregnancy manifested after incarceration. They murdered newborns, and often their mothers, if a birth occurred. Prisoner doctors resorted to abortion or infanticide to save the mother's life. Nazis gassed Jewish children on arrival at the camps to prevent them from growing into adults who could then reproduce, or take vengeance. Over and above this, the Nazis inflicted significant humiliation on all Jews. This dehumanizing process resulted in physical, psychological, social and sexual degradation.

On the other hand, a core component of Nazi ideology was the promotion of lives deemed valuable for the generation of an idealized 'Master Race.' Numerous injunctions involving the reproductive activities of women and men deemed to be racially desirable were implemented to achieve this goal including: rewarding motherhood socially and financially; promoting interpersonal relationships and sexual practices among the racially acceptable; forbidding birth control and abortion; supporting childbirth outside of marriage and divorce on the grounds of being past childbearing age; and simply kidnapping 'desirable' children to promote the 'Aryan' racial pool. While many would have enjoyed their enhanced maternal status, many were also likely to have been sterilized, prohibited from marrying, or forced into motherhood, and felt restrictions on their Weimar period's emerging feminist freedoms. German women who were 'encouraged' to have numerous babies, or to be divorced so as to free their husbands for alternate reproductive mates, or women whose children were abducted, were also victims of Nazi ideology. Such actions reflect a disrespect and disregard for women even when they were classed as 'Aryan' and deemed 'worthy of life.' To date there is no term that succinctly encapsulates this invasive, oftentimes unpleasant, and manipulative series of actions taken to promote 'desirable' life other than 'positive eugenics,' a term that does not convey some of the negative connotations of this 'geno-coercion' adequately.

Some scholars may avoid highlighting the hardships experienced by German women in order to avoid diminishing the experiences of Jews. Jewish women, however, had no escape from the determination of the Nazis to eliminate them altogether. This book, by exposing the extent of brutality meted out to all women, clearly indicates that the disparities in treatment cannot be equalized. Analyzing both Jewish and German women's experiences highlights the diabolical intent of the Nazis to manipulate reproductive and sexual lives of all, to achieve their ideologically desired 'Master Race,' rather than to downplay the horrendous experiences of Jewish women. As Koonz writes:

> …there can be no comparison between the Nazis' drive to first ostracize and then eliminate Jewish citizens and Nazi

> social policy that relegated women to becoming bearers of children and poorly paid workers in the lowliest jobs.[2]

Under the Nazi mantle, doctors became central players in the eugenics-based sterilization program, as well as the euthanasia killings of those deemed 'unworthy of life.' They also conducted medical experiments in concentration camps, often with considerable involvement of the scientific research community, to explore – among other things – methods of mass sterilization or castration to prevent reproductive capacity among those deemed to not meet idealized Nazi racial standards or, in contrast, to promote the generation of desired biological characteristics in 'Aryan' individuals and their offspring. Nazi ideology denigrating the Jew and idealizing the 'Aryan' became imbedded in medical schools through the development of the pseudo-scientific discipline of *Rassenkunde* (racial studies) or *Rassenhygiene* (race hygiene or eugenics) which permeated Nazi society and provided a (pseudo-) scientific justification for Nazi policies.

The remainder of this introduction examines the Nazi ideology that provided the underlying justification for the actions taken by the Nazis and their collaborators. Parts 1 and 2 of the book document the experiences surrounding childbearing and sexuality, respectively, in both Jewish and non-Jewish women (and some men) during the Nazi era and provide an integration of countless testimonies and reports by women and a few men, that are currently scattered throughout the literature and in archives. Others have documented some aspects of these developments far more extensively, such as the role of the medical profession and the related eugenics and euthanasia programs as well as the family lives of German women. This book provides an overview of these programs with particular reference to the Nazi manipulation of reproduction and sexuality in order to provide a background picture of Nazi policy regarding these aspects of the creation of the 'Master Race,' in a single volume. The reader who is familiar with these aspects of Nazi history may wish to skim these sections, although viewing them through the lens of reproduction and sexuality may add hitherto less highlighted knowledge. The Epilogue provides an understanding of how the horror of these events can best be understood. While this book is by no means intended to provide a comprehensive account of the Nazi era, or of Holocaust history, it does acknowledge that events relating to reproduction and sexuality occurred within the context of far broader Nazi policy, and global warfare. An integration of women's reproductive and sexual lives into this broader agenda is, therefore, provided in the Appendix, which documents a chronology of milestones relating to medicine, women's issues, childbearing and sexuality in the Nazi era.

The book takes a multi-disciplinary perspective incorporating social science, medicine and history. To achieve this integration it focuses on social, psychological and cultural issues related to reproduction and sexuality, primarily among Jews and Germans, rather than following a strictly historical, or medical, analytic framework. It provides a gendered history in which the main players are women: to a large extent, the focus is on the voices of women as a lens through which to understand Nazi society. This approach can provide valuable insights into larger historiographical questions.[3]

Sources of Information

There are two major sources of information regarding pregnancy, birth and sexuality during the Nazi era: diaries and memoirs dating from the war years, and more recent survivor testimonies. Survivor memoirs appearing during or shortly after the war are few, and include: war-time diaries, memoirs written shortly after the war by a few women who either experienced birth in concentration camps or saw others give birth; rare accounts of prisoner doctors or their assistants who were involved in performing abortions, assisting at births while in the camps or committing infanticide to save a mother's life; and memoirs written shortly after the war that occasionally refer to births, sexuality or related events in ghettos, in hiding, or elsewhere.

In recent years, extensive efforts have been made to record testimonies of survivors before it is too late. Issues relating to the reliability of memory, the re-interpretation of events by survivors in the light of the past 70 years of life and thought about the Holocaust, and hesitancy to discuss such intimate issues as pregnancy, birth and sexual events may cloud these. Written or oral testimonies may provide different types of information, and both are influenced by the intended audience for these recollections, such as family members or children, that might inhibit the revelation of intimate experiences.[4] One of the distinctive features of testimonies and books written in the first few years following the end of World War II is that these engage directly and openly with the harsh realities of life during the war and in ghettos and camps. These 'do not beautify or soften the life of the camp and the rupture it caused. Nor do they make allowances for the survivors or their audience.'[5] Survivor reports written later, during the 1960s and 1970s, do not usually include mention of sexual exchange let alone more severe forms of abuse.[6] During these later decades however, there was a dearth of literary reports by Jewish women relating to either childbearing or sexuality possibly because survivors were too busy making new lives for themselves and also because few were interested in their stories.[7] Inhibitions regarding dealing with sexual issues may also have prevailed. Compounding the problem was the then prevalent belief that 'obsessive remembering' or 'emotional reliving of the past' would hinder rehabilitation: obliterating the memories of the past was believed to be the optimal way forward.[8] In the 1970s and 1980s Jewish women's memoirs and collections of testimonies began to emerge stimulated, possibly, by an increasing awareness of the Holocaust following the Eichmann trial in 1961 and the creation of such epic movies or television series as the American mini-series *'Holocaust'* in 1978.[9] These women, however, have been more reluctant to recall or recount their sexually related experiences and researchers have been hesitant to question women about them for fear of eliciting difficult and painful memories. Modesty too, prevented any direct exposure of these very intimate experiences, many, if not most of which, have remained secret from partners and children for a lifetime. Among the tens of thousands of testimonies held at Yad Vashem, for example, it is rare to find mention of sexual abuse or submission to male violence.[10] For these reasons, documentation derived from the war and immediate post-war years provides the primary source of information included in this text.

The book has relied primarily on English language sources. While many, if not most, of the available, and most significant, Nazi documents relating to historical events of the Nazi era have been translated into English, the voices of women who became victims of Nazi policies were rarely, if ever, documented by the Nazis. Those few who survived and who lived to record their memoirs did so, not necessarily in German but in many of the languages of the European countries overtaken by Germany, including Polish, Lithuanian, French, Hungarian, Dutch, Italian, Russian, and others, as well as in English. Testimonies have also been recorded in many of these languages, as well as in Hebrew or Yiddish. Fortunately, a number have been translated into English and provide the source for women's voices included in this book. This rich cultural and language mosaic, together with idiosyncrasies of translation, and changes in the evolution of languages such as German, over past decades, create challenges regarding spelling: as far as possible, the spelling reported in available memoirs and testimonies has been retained in this text despite resulting inconsistencies that consequently occur.

It need be noted, however, that many, if not most, women with experiences of pregnancy and birth, would not have survived to give testimony since pregnant Jewish women and those with babies and young children were selected for immediate extermination on arrival in the major camps housing women.[11] Not surprisingly, fewer women than men survived the Holocaust – in the region of a 40-60 ratio.[12]

Nazi Ideology

Nazi terminology regarding Jewish, non-Jewish and 'Aryan' identification was challenging, with the offspring of mixed marriages, and converted Jews, remaining problematic for much of their rule. In essence, people with at least three Jewish grandparents were defined as full Jews but additional categories of half and quarter Jews resulted from religious intermarriage. Religious affiliation was not, however, sufficient grounds for classification as Jewish or non-Jewish: rather genetically determined racial characteristics were considered primary identifiers regardless of the practice of, or identification with, the Jewish religion. Initial Nazi use of the terms 'Aryan' and 'non-Aryan' in 1933 led to protest on behalf of countries populated by other non-Germanic races such as Japan, Egypt, Iraq, Iran and Turkey, and led to the use of the word 'Jew,' rather than 'non-Aryan' in the Nuremberg Laws which followed.[13]

Hitler also considered Jewishness on a loftier plane.[14] He regarded the 'Jewish Spirit' as a powerful, almost supernatural force, above and beyond the physical presence of Jews. For Hitler, the Jews were responsible for many distinctive characteristics of Western civilization that he disliked. Viewed in propaganda – remarkably – as simultaneously, and in reality, impossibly, Marxist, Capitalist and Democratic they were seen as bent on world domination.[15] Such dehumanizing views of Jews were not new although the biological component of Nazi antisemitism, based on the Nazis' racially focused ideology, was a novel addition to traditional antisemitic ideas. In contrast to idealized 'Aryan' purity, the Jew in Nazi ideology was an 'embodiment of everything considered evil, impure and unwanted in the Nazi world view.'[16] As illustrated in the propaganda films *Der Ewige Jude*[17] (The Eternal Jew) and *Jud Süß,*[18] (Jew Süss) Jews were depicted as parasites, dedicated to wealth and deceit, soulless, and fit only for extermination.[19] Not only were Jews biologically impure, but they were also depicted as socially, economically, and politically contaminating and, moreover, responsible for all the world's ills, including the loss of World War 1. The Nazis' strongly anti-Jewish philosophy, grounded in racist pseudoscience, gained legitimacy during the Nazi era.

According to Hitler, and as proposed by the infamous forgery of the 'Protocols of the Elders of Zion,' Jews were involved in an international conspiracy to dominate the world. As Goebbels ranted against Jews on September 11 at the 1937 Party Congress of Labour: "Who are those responsible for this catastrophe?" His answer: "Without fear. We want to point the finger at the Jew as the inspirer, the author, and the beneficiary of this terrible catastrophe: look, this is the enemy of the world, the destroyer of cultures, the parasite among the nations, the son of chaos, the incarnation of evil, the ferment of decomposition, the visible demon of the decay of humanity."[20] Hitler believed that reviving a strong 'Aryan spirit' – developing the 'Master Race' – could oppose this Jewish spirit. He, however, did not consider the existing German population as sufficiently pure 'Aryan' but thought it should be strengthened through careful genetic selection and prevention of 'contamination.' Non-Jews who sympathized with these Jewish constructs or values were regarded as 'spiritual Jews' and were also targeted for restriction or elimination. These beliefs allowed for the destruction of not only millions of Jews but also millions of non-Jewish Europeans who supported ways of thinking that Hitler ascribed to Jewish creation.[21] 'Aryans' on the other hand were those who met racially desirable standards. Not all who lived in Germany were classed as 'Aryan' and those who were not were also subjected to restriction, segregation, internment or extermination.

Nazi ideology viewed the proposed, ideal, 'Aryan' race as the superior race – the 'Master Race' – and the ideological German nation epitomized this image. Everything good and beautiful in the world was reflected in this race.[22] As Dana Chalmers[23] writes, this image valued strength and the ability to withstand pain: a heroic image. The Nazis believed that the combination of inheritance and geography provided the founding principle of the myth of Blood and Soil – the mythical connection between the blood of the 'Aryan' race and the soil of its homeland. She notes that racial purity was associated with culturally creative forces: no other culture was thought to be able to be creative – at best, others could imitate 'Aryan' culture:

> This new Aryan who would save the community from the degeneration of the 20th century, would be able to see through the dominating, culturally destructive values and realize his or her role as a cultural leader. He would actively oppose intellectual development – a predominantly Jewish trait – and instead would promote dedication to the good of the community, self sacrifice, service and responsibility.[24]

This new 'Aryan' individual would ultimately also create a new 'Aryan' society that would promote the unity between:

> nature and man; between the Blood (*Blut*), the People (*Volk*) and the Soil (*Boden*). This philosophy of society would transcend mere citizenship, instead embodying a deep connection with the past and place, the ancestors and home… It would reawaken the self sacrificing, communal German spirit and nurture the traditional German love of nature, simple lifestyles and fellowship.[25]

This idealization of the proposed 'Aryan' race by the current Nazi regime was open to mockery: In 1938, Julian Huxley observed sarcastically:

> Our German neighbours have ascribed to themselves a Teutonic type that is fair, long–headed, tall and virile. Let us make a composite picture of a typical Teuton from the most prominent exponents of this view. Let him be as blond as Hitler, as dolichocephalic as Rosenberg, as tall as Goebbels, as slender as Goering [*sic*] and as manly as

> Streicher. How much would this resemble the German ideal?[26]

Violence of the magnitude of the Holocaust suggests that the Jews as well as others classed as not meeting 'pure' 'Aryan' standards (such as Roma and Sinti, and homosexuals) had to be intensely feared and possibly hated, as 'infected, polluted objects.'[27] Hilberg[28] describes how the belief that Jews were seen as carriers of disease was central to the system of murder. Jews were associated with lice, typhus, syphilis and infection.[29] Murder was justified, as "the Jew is a sub-human, a germ that attempts to infect the pure German blood."[30] Removing Jews from society was seen as a healing act. As Auschwitz physician Fritz Klein said, it was 'out of respect for human life' that he would "remove a gangrenous appendix from a diseased body. The Jew is the gangrenous appendix in the body of mankind."[31]

This ideology made later actions taken against Jews understandable and acceptable both by the population and by the medical profession who were particularly accountable for its implementation. For example, in the camps, Jews were dehumanized in congruence with the ideology that they were on the lowest rungs of the scale of humanity, making killing easier: tattooing of numbers removed the real vision of a person from the Nazis' perceptions, making them far easier to remove than a 'real,' identifiable person. Removing hair, clothing, and all personal belongings including names, reduced Jews to disposable 'pieces' or figures *(Figuren)* rather than individuals: they became subhumans. Franz Stangl, Commandant of Treblinka reports "I remember Wirth [who oversaw exterminations in Belsen, Sobibor and Treblinka] standing there, next to the pits full of blue-black corpses. It had nothing to do with humanity – it couldn't have; it was a mass – a mass of rotting flesh. Wirth said, "What shall we do with this garbage?"[32] Administrators and planners of the various murder programs claimed, "they were simply administering the 'public health' of the nation and were in no way directly concerned with violence and horror."[33] Deputy party leader Rudolf Hess, at a mass rally in 1934, said, "National Socialism is nothing but applied biology."[34] One Nazi supporter, interviewed after the war, observed with some indignation that his psychiatric professors "believed in euthanasia, not as Nazis, but as responsible physicians, medical ethics being defined as willingness to kill."[35]

Jews as Sexually Contaminating

Some aspects of Nazi ideology and propaganda were directed not only to the contagious ill health of the victims but specifically towards the potential for their sexual and reproductive contamination. A particularly venomous component directed against the Jew and in favour of the idealized 'Aryan' focused on the sexual proclivities of 'licentious' Jews and, in contrast, the pure qualities of 'Aryan' women. Biologically, Jews were depicted as introducing bacteria into pure 'Aryan' women through sexual contact as well as being morally corrupt through their promiscuity.[36] Hitler had popularized this conceptualization in the mid 1920s with his writing "The black-haired Jewish youth lies in wait for hours on end, satanically glaring at and spying on the unsuspicious girl whom he plans to seduce, adulterating her blood and removing her from the bosom of her own people."[37] This image was further propagated by Dr Artur Dinter's popular novel written in 1919 – *Die Sünde wider das Blut* (The Sin Against the Blood).[38] Its pseudo-scientific appendix documented the depravity of Jews who were embedded among the Germans with the aim of systematically impregnating as many 'Ayran' girls as possible. The book tells the story of a 'racially pure,' blonde, blue-eyed German woman who was seduced by a Jew. Although she later got away from him and married an 'Aryan' she and her husband produced 'typically Jewish looking' children. She had been permanently contaminated by her encounter with a Jew.[39] Such myth was further endorsed by Julius Streicher's publications including a semi-medical journal '*German People's Health*' that he edited, in which he wrote:

> It is established for all time: 'alien albumin' is the sperm of a man of alien race. The male sperm in cohabitation is partially or completely absorbed by the female and enters her bloodstream. One single cohabitation of a Jew with an Aryan woman is sufficient to poison her blood forever. Together with the 'alien albumin' she has absorbed the alien soul. Never again will she be able to bear purely Aryan children...they will all be bastards...Now we know why the Jew uses every artifice of seduction in order to ravish German girls at as early an age as possible, why the Jewish doctor rapes his female patients while they are under anaesthetics.[40]

Legal discourse repeated long held myths that branded Jewish men as pimps, pornographers, and 'white slave traders' whose sole intention was to exploit 'German women' and spread syphilis and other sexual diseases among the 'Aryan' race.[41] Hitler's observations in Vienna, prior to coming to power, nurtured his antisemitism:

> The part which the Jews played in the social phenomenon of prostitution, and more especially in the white slave traffic, could be studied here [Vienna] better than in any other West-European city... A cold shiver ran down my spine when I first ascertained that it was the same kind

> of cold-blooded, thick-skinned and shameless Jew who showed his consummate skill in conducting that revolting exploitation of the dregs of the big city. Then I became fired with wrath.[42]

A weekly paper edited by Josef Goebbels in Berlin accused the Jewish Deputy President of Police, Bernhard Weiß, of protecting 'slave traffickers' from criminal prosecution. Similarly, *Der Stürmer* claimed that Jewish and Socialist sex reformers aimed to contaminate Germany's youth with venereal disease.[43] Inspired by this belief in the licentiousness of Jews, police officers ordered Jews off the streets after 8 pm from the first day of the war in September 1939. Newspapers were instructed by the Reich press chief to justify this restriction with the explanation that "Jews had often taken advantage of the blackout to molest Aryan women."[44] Jewish employers were accused of wishing to molest 'Aryan' girls in their employ.[45] Others, including Hitler,[46] presented the image of Jewish and 'Aryan' union as unnatural bestiality.[47] Pimping, aiding and abetting prostitution and consequently syphilis,[48] spreading sexual as well as other disease[49] and indulging in homosexuality were all pornographic charges laid against Jews.[50] A highlight of this propagandistic image was reached through the release on 24 September 1940 of the film *Jud Süß*[51] depicting an 18th century Jewish money lender who extorted money from honest Germans but also abducted and raped a beautiful, young German girl. The film was popular and powerful and the lead actor's performance so convincing, that he requested, and was granted, a public announcement by Goebbels that he was not Jewish. Audience responses, particularly to the rape scene, were spontaneous, and vocally antisemitic. Himmler ordered all the SS to watch the film and it was screened particularly for non-Jewish audiences in eastern European towns in proximity to the concentration camps (where some concern over the fate of the Jews and others in such camps might have been expected), and in Germany near towns scheduled to undertake deportations of Jews.[52] *Jud Süß* was an even more powerful depiction of Nazi antisemitism than the concurrently screened *Der Ewige Jude.*[53] The latter adopted a 'documentary' flavour to depict Jews as dirty, verminous, globally pervasive, controlling and criminal.[54]

While the propaganda ministry was the primary source of antisemitic and sexually slanderous messaging in Germany, others contributed. For example, Julius Streicher, the editor of *Der Stürmer*, a viciously antisemitic newspaper, at a rally in Hamburg at which attendance was compulsory for all party comrades, led the 20,000 audience members through an increasingly emotional diatribe against Jews and their sexual proclivities. He declared that hundreds of German women had been raped by Jews, giving details of their alleged crimes and ultimately described one girl who gave birth nine months after marrying a Jew by saying: "what lay in the crib, comrades? A little ape!"[55] Sexuality has never played as important a role in politics as it did in National Socialism. The enforcement of its racial goals of preserving the 'Aryan' race made controlling the sexual behavior of men and women necessary.[56]

Jewish Doctors Targeted as Sexually Perverting

Sexual abasement of Jews in general was particularly extended to a specific group – doctors – and fuelled the persecution of this category of Jewish professionals. By the mid 1920s the right wing group of the racial hygiene movement joined with the emerging Nazi party and in 1929 formed the National Socialist Physicians League to coordinate Nazi medical policy and "purify the German medical community of Jewish Bolshevism."[57] About 3,000 doctors, six percent of the entire profession, joined the league before Hitler came to power. The coordination of all the medical doctors within the Reich began under the direction of Dr Gerhard Wagner, an old *Freikorps* (Free Corps) fighter and long time Nazi. Approximately 6,000 regional medical boards were consolidated into a central agency with district subsidiaries. From then on, physicians were regimented professionally, politically and socially while Jewish and Marxist physicians were purged from the system. By late 1935, no new Jewish doctors could be licensed and by the end of the 1930s the Nazis had expelled between 4,500 and 6,000 Jewish physicians, comprising about two-thirds of all non-'Aryan' doctors.[58] The presence of Jewish judges at beauty contests, or the 'attitude' of Jews to 'German women' revealed in 'filthy erotic literature' – promoted by the propaganda machinery – apparently justified the dismissal of Jewish gynaecologists.[59] For example, in 1942, Dr Edith Kramer still lived in Berlin but, according to a decree of July 25 1938, she had to call herself a 'Medical Practitioner for Jews' and was no longer allowed to treat 'Aryans.'[60] Some of those who stood to benefit from such expulsions voiced antisemitic statements that hastened the process.

In order to bring about the removal of their Jewish 'colleagues' and competitors in Berlin, Nazi physicians combined antisemitism and pornography, by insinuating that Jewish doctors were licentious. Jewish doctors were unjustly accused of taking advantage of their female patients or receptionists. As can be expected, obstetricians and gynaecologists were notably vulnerable to this form of attack and were depicted as performing abortions on 'Aryan' women, and as sexually abusing their female patients or taking them as mistresses.[61] Julius Streicher's popular 1938 children's book 'The Poisonous Mushroom' (*Der Giftpilz)* fuelled these flames by publishing an image of a Jewish doctor (fat, with thick lips and a hooked, fleshy nose) indecently approaching the beautiful, blonde Inge who had trustingly sought his care.[62] The powerful visual image led to increasingly common charges of race defilement as young female patients reported that their Jewish doctors had tried to kiss them or performed similar sexually offensive behaviours.[63] Kater notes that the charges were false, as were many of the 'patients' who had been set up by the Nazis to trick the doctors into compromising situations in order to catch them *in flagrante delicto.* It became increasingly common for accusations against doctors to include that of abortion. Offences against criminal code 218, which protected unborn 'Aryan' life, resulted in heavy punishment being meted out to Jews. For example, in Hamburg Dr Marin Jakobowitz was sentenced to six years in jail and in Nuremberg, Dr Ernst Seckendorf was incarcerated for ten years. After their release, they were sent to concentration camps where Jewish 'race defilers' were subjected to special tortures with little chance of survival. Not surprisingly, many Jewish doctors committed suicide.

Propaganda denigrating the Jew and particularly, the Jews' licentiousness, was pervasive throughout society: As Henry Singer reported, "The children, when they are suckling the mother's breast, are drinking in anti-Semitism."[64] In support of this sentiment, children echoed these cries: In Spring 1943, an anti-Jewish/typhus exhibit opened in Warsaw. Its primary theme equated Jews with typhus. Over 50,000 people toured the exhibit and school children were required to attend. A small boy at the exhibit was heard screaming "Jewish army! Jewish army!" Someone asked him why he was so frightened and where is this Jewish Army? He pointed to lice in an exhibit case and said "There you see it, that's the Jewish army!"[65]

In addition to their focus on eliminating racial inferiority and determining racial superiority, an insidious culture of brutality developed, in parallel, within medicine.[66] Nadav reports that as early as February 1932, Julius Moses, a Jewish physician and politician (who later died in Theresienstadt) published the following, in a periodical that he edited – with prophetical insight:

> Everything that was considered until now as the holiest obligations of medicine – to care for the sick without paying attention to their race, to deal in the same way with all diseases, to help ill men everywhere and ease their pain – all this is viewed by the National Socialists as sheer sentimental stuff which should be thrown away. The only matter of importance in their eyes is leading a war of annihilation against the less worthy (*Minderwertige*) – the incurable patients... If this line of thought will win the upper hand the German medical professional will lose its ethical norms...the physician will act as a killer, the doctor will become a murderer.[67]

Rassenkunde and *Rassenschande*

Goebbels' remarkably extensive and comprehensive propaganda campaign throughout the Nazi era corralled the power of news media, literature, theatre, film, art, and education to provide an overwhelmingly powerful, persuasive force on the German nation. Given the intensely negative and societally pervasive imagery associated with Jews in particular, the Nazis were able to persuade members of German society to tolerate, or endorse, or even to implement, their increasingly suppressive and eventually murderous programs of eugenic sterilization, euthanasia, experimentation and extermination, aimed at eliminating life depicted as threatening and undesirable. In particular, as the threat of Jewish subversion was so often depicted in a pornographic light, it is not surprising that one significant component of the programs designed to eliminate Jewish life focused on suppressing their perceived sexually destructive influence. In consequence, numerous laws were enacted to prevent social and sexual contact with Jews – so called *Rassenschande* or racial shame – and to prohibit their reproductive potential and ability. All of these actions required the direct and extensive involvement of the medical profession primarily as perpetrators (but occasionally also as rescuers). To this end, from 1936, *Rassenkunde* or the study of race was integrated into physicians' regular course of studies requiring examination, despite the lack of trained educators in this newly established medical specialty as well as the lack of theoretical conceptualization of the field. In 1936 alone, five thousand physicians attended such courses. By 1941, 32 German universities had appointed almost three dozen *Dozenten für Biologie und Rassenkunde,*[68] (Professors of Biology and Racial Science) researching the genetic health of Germans and defending against the dangers of polluted blood.

Two of the Nuremberg Laws adopted on 15 September 1935: the *Reich Citizenship Law* that removed German citizenship from Jews, and the *Law for the Protection of German Blood and German Honour*[69] together with their 13 implementation ordinances issued between November 1935 and July 1943, were part of a series of racial-hygienic laws that prevented 'contamination' of 'pure' German blood. The *Law for the Protection of German Blood and German Honour* stipulated not only that Jews were forbidden to marry or have sexual relations with 'persons of German blood' but also that marriages could not be contracted if 'offspring likely to be prejudicial to the purity of German blood' were likely to result.[70] This law forbade marriage between Germans and Jews and rendered any marriages concluded outside of Germany, in order to circumvent this law, to be invalid.[71] Such couples were then regarded as having indulged in forbidden, extramarital *Rassenschande.*[72] Violations of the marriage restriction as well as extramarital relations between Jews and Germans were punishable with prison and/or hard labour.[73] Nazi propaganda and action was replete with these prohibitions,[74] which infiltrated both Hitler's and Goebbels' speeches and writings as well as Nazi endorsed movies such as *Der Ewige Jude.*[75]

Approximately 502,000 Jews, accounting for less than 1 percent of the population, considered as completely Jewish and 250,000 persons considered '*Mischlinge*' (with some degree of Jewish heritage) were affected by the Nuremberg *Reich Citizenship Law* and the *Law for the Protection of German Blood and German Honor.*[76] Between 1870 and 1933 law in Germany had guaranteed religious freedoms. Intermarriage between members of different religions was legalized in 1875. Conversion from Judaism to Christianity and vice versa, was common. From 1901 to 1905, 15% of all Jews married non-Jews, and from 1926 to 1932, 36% married non-Jews. By 1933 44% of all Jews were married to non-Jews.[77] As Gordon continues, these figures are based on religion at the time of marriage and do not include all those who converted prior to marriage, which would make these figures even higher. With the appointment of Hitler in 1933, intermarriage reduced significantly, and was virtually eliminated in 1936 with the Nuremberg Laws. Even before the Nuremberg Laws, however, sexual relations between Jews and 'Aryans' had been informally condemned and openly punished. Only months after the Nazis came to power, 'Aryan' women were forced to walk through the streets with shaven heads and self-deprecating placards for their real or alleged sexual relations with Jews. Well before Nuremberg, families and communities halted much intermarriage.[78]

Concurrently, the *Law for the Protection of Hereditary Health of the German People*, passed on 18 October 1935, required all prospective marriage partners to obtain a certificate of fitness to marry from the public health authorities. Such rules had been applied to members of the SS for some years already: On 31 December 1931, before Hitler even came to power, Himmler's Order Concerning Engagements (A-Nr-65) required all unmarried members of the SS to obtain a marriage permit (*Heiratsgenehmigung*) confirming that the chosen partner was of racially and hereditarily sound blood.[79] Men and women had to prove unbroken 'Aryan' ancestry dating back to 1800 and, for officers, to 1700. Health certificates concerning inherited diseases, proof of potency in men and the ability to bear children in women were also required.

In addition to 'racial disgrace or racial shame,' *Rassenschande* meant 'racial pollution' or 'race defilement' or 'racial treason.'[80] The definition of illicit sexual relations was extended until it included almost any kind of bodily contact between Jews and non-Jewish Germans, including socially conventional embraces or kisses.[81] Even friendship with a Jew manifested by conversation with a Jew in the street, or visits to friends, could eventually be considered as *Rassenschande*.[82] Local prosecutors could also order the divorce of previously married Jewish-German couples.[83] From 1936 to 1939, the annual number of convictions under the *Rassenschande* laws was about 420 with two-thirds of them directed at Jewish men.[84] A total of 2,211 lawsuits were filed in Germany between 1935 and 1945.[85] Examples include a Jewish doctor being convicted of having kissed his 18-year-old 'Aryan' patient in 1936 and being sentenced to two and a half years in prison, as well as the death sentence of a Jew for having kissed an 'Aryan' woman in 1942.[86] However, many of the facts elicited in legal interrogation were irrelevant to the assessment of guilt.[87] For example, questions were routinely asked about whether intercourse had taken place with or without protection, but this information never influenced the sentence passed despite the intention of the Nuremberg Laws to prevent the birth of mixed offspring. Courts were also interested in the explicit details regarding the method and nature of sexual contact that had occurred, including activities such as masturbation or oral sex. Over time legal discourse expanded to attribute sexual meaning to even the most casual social interaction. As Szobar writes:

> This practice was later ratified by a decision of the Supreme Court which asserted that any behaviour that could serve to 'gratify the desires of at least one of the partners' was sexual and fell under the scope of the racial purity laws... local police officials began to ...[explore] whether the sexual desires of one or both partners had ... been gratified... Both male defendants and female witnesses were thus routinely asked if the man had ejaculated. In the case of women, 'gratification' was more difficult to document... Although legal discourse explicitly acknowledged the reality of female orgasm, simple participation ultimately substituted for more specific evidence of 'gratification'.[88]

Trials eventually became dramatic re-enactments of sexual scenes that became publicly titillating to the point where the Reich Ministry of Justice, in 1942, determined that the official questioning of female witnesses should only be aimed at determining if a sexual encounter had taken place without further detail being pursued. *Rassenschande* cases were treated harshly by the courts with no mitigating circumstances being considered and no need for elaborate proof.[89] The detection of individuals violating the Nuremberg Laws usually came through denouncement by acquaintances or 'busybodies,' or investigations by the police.[90]

Jewish men accused of violating the Blood Protection law were guilty of assaulting German blood. German men guilty of *Rassenschande* were regarded as traitors to their 'Aryan' blood. Interestingly, because legally, women were regarded as passive in sexual relations, or as weak, they could not be found guilty of sexual transgressions even if local community groups judged them to be so and publicly humiliated them.[91] According to

Hitler's wish,[92] Clause 5(1) of the Blood Protection law imposed penalties on both sexes for violation of the marriage ban but paragraph 2 of this clause specified that only men were to be penalized for violations regarding extramarital intercourse. Nevertheless, women who were found to have engaged in such illicit sexual relations were usually punished with detention under the protective custody provisions.[93] Gabriele Herz, imprisoned in Moringen women's prison between 1936-1937, reports unequal punishments for *Rassenschande* crimes committed by Jews and Germans: Friedel Günter, an 'Aryan' woman was imprisoned for three months for transgression of the extramarital intercourse law, while Anni Reiner, a Jewish woman, was detained for almost a year longer for the same offence.[94]

The marriage laws applied to everyone, even those of the highest social classes. Wehrmacht captain Melchior Kuno von Schlippenbach, a graduate of the prestigious Salem boarding school, wanted to marry Ilonka Dudkova, a Czech national. In order to get permission, he had to undergo an intense racial examination and submit numerous documents, which included "four photos of [his] bride in the nude, one view each side... perfectly nude for racial examination,"[95] a rather dubious demand. After 'vivid complaints' on his part the girl was allowed to wear a two-piece bathing suit in the photographs. In addition, Josef Mengele married Irene Schoenbein. Although they were given permission to marry by the *Rasse- und Siedlungshauptamt* (the Central Office for Race and Resettlement) there was some doubt about Irene's family history as her grandfather was thought to be illegitimate and therefore might possibly have had Jewish blood. Mengele therefore failed to be registered in the *Sippenbuch* or Kinship Book, for those able to prove beyond doubt that their ancestors were pure 'Aryan' back to 1750 at least.[96]

Nazi racism was not confined to Jews. As the war progressed and Germans found themselves in occupied lands or foreign workers were brought into Germany in greater numbers, the opportunities for *Rassenschande* with those of 'impure' blood increased. The Propaganda Ministry issued a guideline in 1943 warning of the dangers to the German race if Polish female workers became pregnant by German men. "Every act of sexual intercourse is a defilement of the German people and an act of treason against them and each will be harshly punished by the law." In late 1943, the Racial Political Office of the Nazi party condemned marriages between Germans and foreigners from other countries and cultures as dangerous because of the different racial and/or cultural backgrounds or foreign elements.[97]

Transgression of the Laws was generally kept out of the press. Details of court cases where German women consorted with Jews were not to be discussed. *Rassenschande* cases were especially not to be published if they occurred in German brothels and *Rassenschande* by party members was strictly taboo news for the press. Instances of mixed marriages were to be kept secret as well as annulments of mixed marriages. It was also forbidden to discuss the ancestry of German historical figures.[98]

Rassenschande Transgressions

Rassenschande occurred despite the regulations and their dire consequences for infractions. For example, Jewish women recorded incidents in which 'Aryans,' Nazis included, made advances towards them. "In daylight they reviled me as a Jewish woman and at night they wanted to kiss me."[99] Even in concentration camps, where those convicted of *Rassenschande* were sent, sexual relations between camp officials and Jewish women occurred. For example, in 1942-4, Stutthof (Gdansk) Concentration camp's chief of the Jewish section Foht, who decided which Jewish women were to be poisoned, starved to death or forced to work, "feared neither the racial regulations nor his sturdy wife [who lived on his farm not far from the camp], but maintained the most intimate relations with representatives of the Jewish women's blocks."[100] Another case occurred in Sobibor between SS *Scharführer* (troop or squad leader) Paul Groth and one of the Jewish women held in this camp. Influenced by his love, Groth changed his behavior towards the few Jewish prisoners held in this extermination camp, and acted more humanely. This relationship was viewed by the commanders of Sobibor as *Rassenschande*, and, while Groth was outside the camp, the Jewish girl was killed.[101] Also, in 1942 in Auschwitz, SS Sergeant Gerhard Palitzsch started having sexual relations with many women, mainly female guards, after his wife died of typhus. He was caught having sexual relations with a Latvian, Jewish, female prisoner, tried and found guilty by the SS court at the end of 1943 and, as punishment, 'offered' the opportunity to fight on the Russian front, where he was reported killed in action.[102]

Given the Nazi fear of biological contamination of 'pure' 'Aryan' blood by Jews, perhaps most ironic with regard to the *Rassenschande* laws was the use of Jewish blood to save German soldiers' lives during the war. As Gisella Perl, a Jewish doctor in Auschwitz, wrote in 1948:

> The sight which greeted us when we entered Block VII is one never to be forgotten. From the cages along the walls, about six hundred panic-stricken, trembling young women were looking at us with silent pleading in their eyes. The other hundred were lying on the ground, pale, faint, bleeding. Their pulse was almost inaudible, their breathing strained and deep rivers of blood were flowing around their bodies. Big strong SS men were going from one to the other sticking tremendous needles into their veins and robbing their undernourished, emaciated bodies

> of their last drop of blood. The German army needed blood plasma! The guinea pigs of Auschwitz were just the people to furnish that plasma. *Rassenschande* or contamination with 'inferior Jewish blood' was forgotten. We were too 'inferior' to live but not too inferior to keep the German army alive with our blood. Besides, nobody would know. The blood donors, along with other prisoners of Auschwitz would never live to tell their tale.[103]

Renėe Duering was given the choice of signing up for 'certain physical examinations' or being killed. She survived by having blood taken for the use of Nazi soldiers as well as being used for other experiments.[104] Tova Berger, in her post-war testimony reports being narrowly saved from such blood transfusions by her block leader.[105] Such actions were not limited to the camps: the teacher Emelia Borisova Kotlova recalled that in 1941 the Germans killed all the Jews in Fastov (Ukraine) but left the children. They ordered that villagers each take a child and fatten it up with the family being answerable for its life. After three months, when the children were in better health, they were taken to a hospital, tied to the beds and their blood drained from them for wounded Germans. The children died.[106]

Understanding the full extent of Jewish and non-Jewish women's reproductive and sexual experiences particularly with regard to the elimination of those deemed 'inferior' and its antithesis, the promotion of life regarded as 'desirable,' allows for a conceptually more comprehensive understanding of the manipulative and murderous Nazi intent behind the creation of the so-called 'Master Race.' While there were numerous groups regarded as 'undesirable,' Jews were by far the most adversely affected category of people targeted by the Nazis for extermination of reproductive women – a form of 'gendercide' – and their experiences are the primary focus of this text. The plight of the many German, Polish, Russian, Roma and Sinti, Jehovah's Witnesses, homosexuals and others regarded as 'undesirable' is fully acknowledged as worthy of considerable, further, in-depth analysis.

Part 1:
Pregnancy and Childbearing

The Eugenic Sterilization And Euthanasia Programs

Within six months of coming to power, the Nazis implemented their first steps towards achieving their goal of creating the 'Master Race' by approving laws providing for the compulsory sterilization of all those deemed unworthy to procreate due to so-called 'hereditary illness.' Both the eugenic sterilization program, and the euthanasia program that followed this from 1939 onwards and that murdered, rather than simply sterilized, those regarded as unworthy of life or of procreation, were directed at all Germans and not only Jews. The focus on eliminating the Jewish people – achieving the 'Final Solution' – became a priority sometime in 1941. What distinguishes the 'Final Solution' from other historical instances of mass murder or genocide lies in the mobilization of the scientific and professional sectors of the German population in its pursuit.[107] This was not just a delinquent approach implemented by a few disturbed individuals but a process implemented by sane people over a number of years. It was endorsed by scientists, physicians and administrators. As Glass says, "No other genocide had its major impetus in the language of science, law and administration of the society."[108]

Doctors were an integral tool used by the Nazis to implement the sterilization program, from the initial conceptualizations of the 'science' of '*Rassenkunde*" and theories of racial superiority, to the assessment of prospective victims and the performance of surgery that destroyed any prospects of marital relationships and/or reproductive ability. As Cornwall notes, "The medical doctor thus, finally, embodied the depraved Nazi vision of mass murder as a form of hellish racial therapy."[109]

As Evans writes:

> The regime was using sterilization to crush those areas of society that did not conform to the Nazi ideal of the 'New Man' or the 'New Woman'... the regime [had] the power to reach into the most intimate sphere of human

> existence, sexuality and reproduction, a power that it would subsequently extend to its dealings with Jews, and indeed, potentially at least, every adult German.[110]

Hanauske-Abel adds:

> Changes which today are interpreted as causing the downfall of the German medical community were at the time warmly welcomed by the widest segments of that highly educated biomedial and scientific elite... The changes further resulted in immediate economic benefits for physicians, rises in incomes significantly exceeding those of both the legal profession and the general population.[111]

Germany was not alone in furthering the so-called 'science' of eugenics: its position within the international setting (North America, the United Kingdom and Scandinavian countries in particular, where eugenics was enthusiastically endorsed) was significant, although other countries stopped short of developing this into euthanasia. Germany, however, combined pseudo-Darwinism and 'Aryan' supremacy mythology in its approach to eugenics. Several fundamental principles united proponents of eugenics regarding racial hygiene. The first was that character and behaviour were largely inherited. The second was that the state should manage society so as to increase national efficiency and thirdly, that the racial hygiene movement introduced a rational and scientific categorization of people into those who were 'valuable' and those who were not.[112] Endorsed by Hitler,[113] it is not surprising that this resulted in policies and practices aimed at preventing those judged to be 'racially inferior' from ever procreating.

Eugenics Pervaded Society

Eugenics was not restricted to an elite corps of medical academics. The Office of Racial Policy, with more than 4,000 employees, disseminated massive amounts of information on racial issues between 1934-8. In this period, over 64,000 meetings were organized, the office's journal, *Neues Volk* had a readership of over 300,000 and over 4,000 Nazi party members had attended week long seminars on racial hygiene.[114] Eugenics infiltrated all sectors of society. Even classrooms were converted into forums for the depiction of undesirable types and appropriate 'national comrades.' For example, a mathematics school book asked children "The construction of a lunatic asylum costs 6 million RM. How many houses at 15,000 RM each could have been built with that amount?"[115] Further arithmetic exercises included: "Every day the state spends RM 6 on one cripple, RM 4 ½ on one mentally ill person, RM 5 ½ on one deaf and dumb person, RM

5 3/5 on one feeble-minded person, RM 3 ½ on one alcoholic, RM 4 4/5 on one pupil in care, RM 2 1/20 on a pupil in a special school, and RM 9/20 on one pupil at a normal school."[116] The text asks, "what total cost do one cripple and one feeble-minded person create if one takes a lifespan of 45 years for each?" A further example is taken from a mathematics text that was widely distributed, running to several editions:

> Problem 200: According to statements of the Draeger Works in Lübeck in the gassing of a city only 50 per cent of the evaporated gas is effective. The atmosphere must be poisoned up to a height of 20 meters in a concentration of 45mg/m^3. How much phosgene is needed to poison a city of 50,000 inhabitants who live in an area of 4 square kilometres? How much phosgene would the population inhale with the air they breathe in ten minutes without the protection against gas, if one person uses 30 litres of breathing air per minute? Compare this quantity with the quantity of poison gas used.[117]

In addition, in 1932 the German Hygiene Museum in Dresden held an exhibit on *'Healthy Women, Healthy Nation,'* as eugenicists regarded maternal health as an important means of lowering infant mortality and birth anomalies.[118] Even German newspaper advertisements for mates started to incorporate eugenic values: for example, on 14 June 1935 a widowed schoolmaster, who described himself as an idealist, advertised in the *Münchner Neuesten Nachrichten* No 169, as "Fifty-two year old pure Aryan doctor, Tannenberg fighter, wishes to settle down and through civil marriage, have male offspring with healthy, devout, young virgin, modest, parsimonious, suited to hard work, thrifty, who must wear shoes with broad heels, no earrings and, if possible, with no assets. Agents declined, confidentiality assured."[119]

Sterilization Laws

As in other countries where sterilization of some whom society regarded as *'fortpflanzungsunwürdig'*[120] or unsuitable for reproduction occurred, a draft law permitting the sterilization of those considered hereditarily ill was drawn up by the Prussian government in late 1932.[121] This insisted that either the person concerned or their guardian had to consent to the operation. Within months of the Nazi party coming to power, however, the *Law for the Prevention of Genetically Diseased Offspring* replaced the voluntary principle with compulsion, using force when necessary, and was adopted on 14 July 1933 with effect from 1 January 1934.[122]

The removal of restrictions preventing the compulsory sterilization of those with hereditary mental or physical defects, or other social or racial 'undesirables,' opened the door for enthusiastic cooperation by some doctors and psychiatrists to work in collaboration with police and local government authorities through the so-called Hereditary Health Courts.[123] Kershaw notes further that not only Nazis, but also professionals in a range of fields could take advantage of this, justifying their actions through recourse to 'the wishes,' 'intentions' or 'aims' of the *Führer*, the interests or needs of the 'national community' and 'racial health.' Sterilization became a large medical industry with companies like Schering developing sterilization equipment. More than 180 doctoral dissertations exploring the criteria, methods and consequences of sterilization were written, medical experiments on methods of sterilization were conducted in concentration camps and in 1943, Carl Clauberg informed Heinrich Himmler that he could sterilize as many as 1000 women a day.[124] At the same time, however, that sterilization and abortion were instituted for those of so called 'inferior stock,' abortion and sterilization of 'healthy' German women were made illegal and punishable, sometimes by death. Access to birth control was likewise restricted to all but Jews for whom it was encouraged.[125]

Reasons for Sterilization

The law targeted both mental and physical illness.[126] Compulsory sterilization was implemented for nine diseases that were considered to be hereditary: congenital feeblemindedness, schizophrenia, manic-depressive psychosis, hereditary epilepsy, Huntington's chorea, hereditary deafness, blindness, severe deformity, or severe alcoholism.[127] Approximately 95% of the sterilizations were performed for the first four of these. The most frequent reasons given for sterilization were feeblemindedness (53%) – an extremely vaguely defined concept that included prostitution and alcoholism, as 'moral feeblemindedness' – and schizophrenia (20%).[128]

At first, definitions of these categories were narrow, although imprecise, but later became loosely defined and broadly interpreted.[129] For instance, the definition of 'mental illness' was extended to include dangerous habitual criminals and, ultimately, juvenile offenders. Eventually, even social problems like poverty were attributed to genetics.[130] In addition, persons were compulsorily sterilized who were unaffected by any of the illnesses that were specified by the Law and who were perfectly capable of passing the intelligence tests which were required for selection.[131] For instance, many victims simply deviated from 'normal' behaviour, as judged by their apparent social 'superiors.' For example, people who failed to be monogamous, thrifty, clean, efficient, tidy, responsible and striving upwards were designated 'socially feebleminded' on the basis of 'intelligence tests,' spurious diagnoses' or, more usually, gossip or hearsay. Also, far more women were accused of 'social feeblemindedness' than men because of either the frequency of their changes of sexual partner or their having illegitimate children. Social and gender specific prejudices undermined the so-called 'objective' scientific selection criteria employed. Some criteria were arbitrary such as those exempting Nazi party members of obviously low intelligence who might otherwise have been labeled as 'feebleminded.'[132] One major criterion focused on procreation and sexuality: sterilization had to be performed especially on people with a mild degree of illness, as they were perceived as more likely to indulge in sexual intercourse, either voluntarily or against their will, than those who were seriously ill. Female feeblemindedness was, consequently seen as a particular danger.[133] As early as 1929, a widely known book '*Sterilization on Social and Race Grounds*' suggested that 'the number of degenerate individuals born depends mainly on the number of degenerate women capable of procreation. Thus the sterilization of degenerate women is for reasons of racial hygiene, more important than the sterilization of men.'[134] In line with these arguments, and as reported in the *Frankfurter Zeitung* of 30 January 1937, those that were sterilized were not permitted to marry, and the pregnancies of those who evaded this restriction and became pregnant could be legally aborted, otherwise a most heinous crime in the Nazi statute book.[135]

A considerable number of the victims were from the poorer sections of society or were discharges from asylums.[136] Regardless of their actual state of health, the latter were alleged to have recessive genes. Roughly two-thirds of those sterilized were the inmates of mental hospitals. Sterilization was attractive to asylum directors because it meant that in many cases the patients could be discharged into the community afterwards. The better the chances of recovery the more likely they were to be sterilized. This reduced the running costs of the asylum, which directors of such institutions were under heavy pressure to do.

Eventually even children considered uncooperative in orphanages were included in the sterilization program, although there was some consideration of age: sterilizations of children under the age of eleven were prohibited, as was forcible sterilization of juveniles under fifteen.[137] 'Mentally deficient' children were, however, sterilized. Instructors in schools for these children were given the task of explaining to the parents the necessity for the state's laws on sterilization.[138] The Nazis' sterilization guidelines[139] included the importance of converting parents to the value of sterilization. They expected intelligent parents to recognize this as a necessary offering for the Fatherland and a blessing, while less intelligent ones would think of it as a welcome measure of help from the state. Education of parents was given at parent evenings and on an individual basis, including at home visits. Only those convinced of the value of sterilization were allowed to teach: they needed to be familiar with the mental standpoint of parents and could not be too young as they would be less convincing for parents.

The actual criteria for sterilization are documented in court records.[140] These include mentally and physically defective kin – ranging from quarrelsome aunts, alcoholic grandparents, spendthrifts, to sexual deviance, particularly alleged promiscuity of women and the resulting illegitimate births, currently ill and recovered schizophrenics, backward students, and so-called promiscuous women, 'asocials' and prostitutes. Intelligence tests called for the ability to read, write and do arithmetic as well as for knowledge of history, geography and the names of Nazi leaders. Questions reflecting 'general ethical concepts,' a further criterion for sterilization, included: Why does one study? Why and for whom does one save money? Why should one not burn even one's own house? If you won the lottery what would you do with the money? How do you plan your future? What is the meaning of fidelity, piety, honour, modesty? What is the opposite of bravery?

Selecting Candidates for Sterilization

About 250 special sterilization centres in hospitals or clinics were established and race hygiene experts along with judges decided on the desirability of sterilizations.[141] Even though the concept of hereditary degeneracy was being challenged in academic eugenic literature, doctors in Germany had to undergo training in recognizing such degeneracy (for example though the shape of the patient's earlobes, the patient's gait, or the configuration of the half moon at the base of the patients' fingernails).[142] Doctors were required to record all cases of serious alcoholism and what were termed incurable hereditary or congenital diseases such as imbecilism, and highly contagious diseases like venereal diseases, except in women over forty-five (who were regarded as less of a threat to the potential racial pool), and could be fined for failing to do so.[143] Directors of institutions such as hospitals, schools, prisons, workhouses and concentration camps as well as welfare authorities were responsible for selecting candidates from their charges.[144] The courts included three judges, two of whom were doctors. Virtually all the better-known eugenicists and psychiatrists, thousands in all, sat on these courts at one time or another, or were involved in providing 'expert' advice.[145] Most applications came from newly established State Medical Officers who got their information from institutions, mayors and private doctors, and less often, from employers and neighbours as well as through the medical examination of all recipients of state funds. Hardly anyone applied to be sterilized him/herself.[146] Some patients agreed to be sterilized but most did not. In 1934, the first year of the law's application, 4,000 people appealed against the decision of the sterilization authorities, but 3,559 – almost 89% – of the appeals failed: 90% of sterilization applications from doctors, nurses or other 'legitimate' sources were approved.[147] David et al. provide different figures with, however, the same conclusion. According to them, of the petitions heard by 205 hereditary health courts (against sterilization) 94% resulted in sterilization, and only 6% were denied. Also, they report that only 377 (5%) of 8,219 appeals to the 26 superior hereditary health courts were upheld.[148] Paragraph 12 of the *Law for the Prevention of Genetically Diseased Offspring* allowed that sterilization "must be performed even against the will of the person to be sterilized. The attending surgeon may request any assistance from the Police authority. If other measures are insufficient it is permissable to use direct force."[149] Force was used on about 30% of those sterilized in some regions.[150] Insurance companies and the person being sterilized were billed for the costs of the operation.[151] On 29 July 1933, the *Deutsches Ärzteblatt* (today still a most respected and widely read continuing medical education and professional medium in Germany) reprinted the entire sterilization act and commented: "Since sterilization is the only safe method to prevent the inheritance of mental disease and serious genetic disorders, the law must be looked upon as an expresion of loving care for the coming generations, and as an act of altruism."[152]

Numbers Sterilized

The Nazis implemented a ruthless sterilization program that ultimately victimized 350,000 to 400,000 Germans divided equally between men and women, including an unknown number of Jews.[153] Also included were 'gypsies,' classed as 'disorderly wanderers,' and approximately 500 'Rhineland bastards' – children of liaisons between German women and black French soldiers.[154]

The techniques of sterilization employed included vasectomy for men as outpatients and tubal ligation for women with full anaesthesia. Complications sometimes occurred: The overall death rate, overwhelmingly among women (90%), is variously estimated to be about 2,000[155] to 5,000[156] people. The ensuing deaths led to public outcry – which according to the Nazis – came from the 'Jewish Press.' From 1935, Hitler urged the use of x-rays instead of surgery, which was then introduced for women over 38.

The Impact of Sterilization on Non-'Aryan,' German Women

The impact of the sterilization program on German women who did not meet idealized Nazi racial criteria was marked. In 1936, the Protestant welfare office circulated a questionnaire to evaluate its impact.[157] Social workers who three years earlier had welcomed the introduction of eugenics measures, reported the dire impact of sterilization on morale and social relations, although minimal physical after-effects. Social workers watched their clients' reactions and expressed shock at the psychological cost. In reality, the 'Aryan' community turned against its 370,000 'genetically unworthy' members as if they belonged to inferior races. Despite official statements that 'genetic damage is no one's fault, and sterilization does not change a person's character,' and that 'genetically ill people have suffered a hard fate and should not be mocked' public opinion persisted in treating sterilized women as second-class citizens. Sterilized women, often without their advance knowledge and almost always without their consent, felt the double stigma in a society dominated by racial-biological thinking. Raised to believe that motherhood would be their only calling in life and that they belonged to a superior race, sterilization, and its consequent social stigma, was a shock. A second source of conflict emerged. The eugenics courts that ordered sterilization swore total secrecy, but that promise contradicted a second provision: A specialized *'Law of Matrimonial Health'* (*Ehe-Gesundheitsgesetz*) prohibited marriage for people who had been sterilized, for people who had been under guardianship because of mental incompetence and for severe psychopaths and syphilitics.[158] Sterilized persons could not marry because the primary goal of marriage could never be achieved. To enforce this prohibition, every sterilized person's records followed him or her throughout life. Rumours, too, spread scandal. Social workers were instructed not to inform prospective candidates for sterilization that the Nazi marriage law prohibited sterilized persons from marrying even other sterilized people, and they felt betrayed when they found out. Propaganda urged them to act patriotically and submit to sterilization in the interests of the community. But Nazi law prevented them from ever leading the life that propaganda described as normal and healthy. In late 1936, Catholic bishops reversed their earlier decision to comply with this prohibition and allowed sterilized people to marry other infertile people.[159]

The Euthanasia Program

In 1939, the Nazis moved from sterilizing those deemed unworthy of reproduction to murdering them. Although the question of how few or many doctors resisted either the sterilization or euthanasia programs[160] is unknown, Evans notes that virtually the entire medical profession was involved in the sterilization program and for an unknown number, moving to involuntary euthanasia was but a short step.[161] The methods of killing involved gassing, starvation and chemical abuse, all of which were the responsibility of the medical profession. Many of these doctors spoke with pride about their work after the war, maintaining that they had been contributing to human progress.[162] One argument favouring euthanasia was that as so many healthy men were being killed in the war it was necessary to balance this with the removal of the unfit, so as not to allow them to become dominant.[163] Alternatively, the purification of the 'Aryan' race in preparation for the Thousand Year Reich remained a driving force endorsing euthanasia. A fundamental reason given for implementing the euthanasia program was, however, economic.[164]

Sterilization, the first approach taken to prevent the further propagation of those regarded as having unwanted characteristics, was seen as an insufficient measure and (in Nazi Germany only) annihilation became a preferred option. As early as the 1920s, some physicians and lawyers proposed medical killing of those with genetic defects.[165] In 1920, the lawyer Karl Binding and the forensic psychiatrist Alfred Hoche coined the phrase 'life unworthy of life' in a document entitled '*The Sanctioning of the Destruction of Life Unworthy of Living*,' and argued that what they called 'ballast existences' (*Ballastexistenzen*)[166] – people who were nothing but a burden on society – should be killed.[167] They proposed that as the incurably ill and mentally retarded were costing millions of marks and were taking up thousands of needed hospital beds, doctors should be allowed to put them to death. In the Weimar Republic, this idea still met with hostility on the part of most medical men.[168] Originating in the 'simple' idea that a dying person may be helped to die, the concept developed into the notion that life not worth living may be unworthy of life. Concern for the individual was replaced by preoccupation with society and was accomplished by representing retarded or malfunctioning persons, especially those with problems perceived to be congenital, as sick or harmful cells in the healthy body of the nation.[169] These ideas were not originally racial in character but were easily incorporated into Hitler's and the Nazis' racist policies. For Hitler, euthanasia and the war were as interrelated as the 'Final Solution' and the war.[170]

Books and movies alluding to euthanasia were popular in Germany. These included '*Was du erbst*' (*What you inherit*) and '*Erbkrank*' (*The Hereditarily Ill*) (1935), both silent movies showing images of the most severely mentally handicapped patients. '*Das Erbe*' (*The Inheritance*) (1935) used fiction and documentary footage to support the idea that the weak should not survive. *Opfer der Vergangenheit* (*Victims of the Past*), produced under Hitler's direct order in 1937 was shown by law in all 5,300 German movie theatres.[171] '*Dasein ohne Leben*' (*Existence Without Life*) (1939) was made to reassure those involved in the euthanasia program that this was an ethical and humane procedure, as did '*Geisteskrank*' (*The Mentally Ill*) (1939).[172] The film '*Ich klage an*' (*I Accuse*), made in

1941, was based on a novel '*Sendung und Gewissen*' (*Mission and Conscience*) by doctor and writer Helmut Unger, and was of professional quality. It portrayed an innocent physician who killed his incurably sick wife.[173] In addition, organized tours of mental institutions were arranged to demonstrate the freakish appearance of mental patients and the unnecessary costs that their upkeep entailed.[174] For example, the Munich asylum Eglfing-Haar was toured by members of the SA Reich Leadership School, by local SS race experts, by instructors of the SS regiment 'Julius Schreck' and by several groups from the *Arbeitsfront* (Labour Front).

'Mercy Killing' Begins

By May 1939, Hitler had already made arrangements for the killing of mentally ill children under the aegis of the Reich Committee for Hereditary Health matters, renamed in the summer of 1939 as the Reich Committee for the Scientific Registering of Serious Hereditary and Congenital Illnesses.[175] Seizing an opportunity, Hitler personally ordered Karl Brandt, one of his personal physicians, to travel to Leipzig to examine the request of some parents for the mercy killing of their child by some accounts born blind, with one leg and part of one arm missing and suffering from convulsions.[176] Hitler ordered Brandt – by means of a signed note dated 1 September 1939[177] – to kill the child himself after confirming the diagnosis and consulting with medical colleagues. Shortly afterwards Brandt reported that he had had the local doctors kill the child on 25 July 1939. In October 1939 Hitler signed an order, backdated to the start of the war to give it the weight of a national crisis, charging Brandt as chief of the medical division of the program and Philipp Bouhler (Chief of the Chancellery) as head of the administrative division of the program, to "extend the power of doctors to be specified by name, so that sick people who by human estimation are incurable can, on the most critical assessment of their illness, be granted a merciful death."[178] At about the same time, a decree dated 31 August 1939 officially 'ended' the sterilization program and although it was heavily curtailed, it continued. According to Weinberg, there is some significance in the fact that Hitler backdated the authorization of the Euthanasia program from late October to 1 September. In public speeches, he similarly misdated his speech of 30 January 1939 in which he threatened to kill the Jews, as occurring on 1 September. Weinberg suggests that his similar dating of the two murder programs – the killing of children and that of adults[179] – was integrally related to the war. Further support for this concept comes from the report that when asked to authorize the killing of handicapped and disabled persons in the 1930s, he replied that this could only be done in wartime.[180]

Children's Euthanasia and the T4 program

The Nazi 'children's euthanasia' measures were launched first, directed by Hitler's private chancellery.[181] According to Leo Alexander, an order of the Ministry of the Interior for the Reich and Prussia dated 26 June 1940 (but noted by Burleigh and Lifton as being issued on 18 August 1939[182]) established compulsory registration of all children who were suffering from "severe congenital illness such as (1) idiocy and mongolism, especially cases associated with blindness and deafness; (2) microcephaly; (3) hydrocephalus of severe and progressive type; (4) malformations of every type, especially absence of limbs and severe cleft formations of the head and spine; (5) palsies, including Little's disease."[183] Nearly 100,000 children were registered with the Reich Committee, of whom an estimated 5,200 severely handicapped children were killed outright.[184] – called variously 'special treatment', 'cleansing', 'therapy' and 'disinfection' – between 1939 and 1941.[185] The program began by targeting newborns and then children up to three years old as their deaths appeared more natural.[186] Gradually the upper age limit for murder was raised, first to 8, then to 12, then to 16.[187] Many more children were retained in institutions and some were used for research purposes, including testing of vaccines for tuberculosis and scarlet fever.[188] At first, the authorization of the euthanasia program was kept secret and narrow in scope but later it became extensive and increasingly known.[189]

Hitler expanded this operation to include the killing of adults – also administered by his private chancellery – ultimately murdering over 200,000.[190] So began the *Aktion T4* program.[191] Within a few months, virtually the entire German psychiatric community was involved: The Nazis justified the killings on economic grounds but for scientists the attraction was the scientific goal of perfecting the 'Aryan' race.[192] The principal objective of the whole program was the elimination of '*Ballastexistenzen*' (burdensome life), or *Nutzlose Esser* (useless eaters) (and coincidentally, the prevention of their having any progeny).[193] The adult euthanasia program became known under the administrative name T4 (named after the address of the project's offices in Berlin at 4 *Tiergartenstrasse,* a confiscated Jewish villa[194]).

The T4 program was a complex organization.[195] Three 'front' organizations were established to implement the plan: (1) the *Allgemeine Stifftung für Anstaltwesen* (General Foundation for Affairs of Insane Asylums), which employed the staff in the killing institutions, (2) the *Reichsarbeitsgemeinschaft Heil- und Pflegeanstalten* (Reich Working Group of Asylums and Nursing Homes) which distributed questionnaires to institutions regarding patients eligible for T4 and obtained the appropriate judgments; and (3) the *Gemeinnützige Krankentransportgesellschaft* (Public Benefit Patient Transport Society) which transported patients from their institutions to the killing centres. The Charitable Foundation for Institutional Care was charged with the financial arrangements[196] that consisted of, among other activities, collecting money to cover the expenses from the families of patients.[197] A significant portion of the personnel, medical and nonmedical, was drawn from the SS. Himmler himself was familiar with all these operations and appraised of all their problems.[198]

The T4 program targeted adults including senile persons, the feebleminded, epileptics, sufferers from Huntington's chorea and other neurological disorders, individuals who had been treated at institutions for at least five years and 'criminally insane persons', especially those involved in 'moral crimes'.[199] Adults, however, were not murdered through fatal injection or starvation as children were, but by gassing.[200] Although the criteria used to determine who should be killed expanded over time and were subject to local interpretations, in April 1940 a proclamation from the Reich Interior Ministry determined that all Jewish patients in institutions were henceforth to be inventoried for extermination regardless of illness.[201]

Doctors and midwives were paid 2 Reich marks for every case they reported.[202] In December 1939, questionnaires were sent to hundreds of hospitals and clinics in Germany and Austria that participated in the euthanasia program to be completed for each inmate.[203] Inmates with stays of five years or longer were at particular risk.[204] At first concerned with physical issues, the reports were considerably expanded in June 1940 to include: details about the birth, family history, especially concerning such things as hereditary illness and excessive use of alcohol, nicotine or drugs, expectations for improvement and life expectancy, prior institutional observations and treatment, details of physical and mental development, and descriptions of convulsions and related events.[205] After this time, the questionnaires also inquired about the ability of the patients to work.[206] Eventually, all physicians were allowed to complete the questionnaire and not only psychiatrists. The lists of selected victims were sent to a post box in Berlin next to Bouhler's office. Three doctors in the chancellery including two paediatricians and one physician director of a psychiatric institute[207] processed the reports, without examining the patient, and marked the registration forms with a + if the child was to be killed. They were then sent to the nearest public health office which ordered the child's admission to a paediatric clinic.[208] The first doctor recorded his judgment (kill, or not kill or postpone decision/observe) on the questionnaire before forwarding it to the next, so that the last was able to see the judgments of each of the prior two. A unanimous decision was needed before euthanizing the child. Children requiring observation were sent to the same institutions where the killings took place until further information was made available favouring eventual killing. The completed forms were either assessed by the central assessors themselves or were contracted out to individual physicians some of whom handled vast numbers of forms in remarkably short time periods, spurred on by payment for the number of forms processed with added incentives for speed. Hermann Pfannmüller, one of the doctors involved, evaluated 2,109 patients between 14 November and 1 December 1940 or an average of about 131 a day while at the same time carrying out his duties as director of a state hospital.[209] Another expert, Josef Schreck, completed 15,000 forms from April 1940 to the end of the year sometimes processing up to 400 a week in addition to attending to his other hospital duties.[210] As Evans writes, it could not have taken more than a few seconds to determine the life or death in each case. Some doctors at institutions tried to protect their inmates by sending them home or finding them local employment, while others were quick to assign them for euthanasia.[211] According to Burleigh, the T4 directors tolerated argument over a few patients whose lives they could then claim to have saved, while the majority were sent to their deaths.

Killing Centers

Initially, in Germany, 30 killing centres were established[212] for the extermination of children. Six centres were equipped with gassing facilities for the killing of adults: Brandenburg, Bernburg, Sonnenstein, Hadamar, Grafeneck in Germany and Hartheim in Austria including some of Germany's most prestigious hospitals which were set up as medical schools conducting classes, not in curing, but in killing, mental and genetic 'defectives.'[213] The remainder used lethal injections, drug overdoses and starvation as methods of killing. The gassing facilities were established in selected locations that combined remote areas with good access to rail or road connections.[214] Fences and signs warning 'danger of disease' surrounded these.

The first killing center opened in 1939 at Görden, a large hospital complex just outside Brandenburg that became the training ground for doctors sent to handle the euthanasia cases in other centres.[215] Parents were informed their children would receive improved treatment in these institutions and this allowed parents to believe they were acting in the child's best interests: in addition, the government would often force the mother into the war industry so that home care was no longer possible.[216] 'Treatment' included injections of morphine and cyanide, or carbon monoxide gassing in sealed chambers, chemical agents including luminal and veronal in addition to morphine and scopolamine, and occasionally the injection of phenol directly into the heart.[217]

Families received fraudulent death certificates listing the cause of death as pneumonia, typhus, meningitis, bronchitis, carbuncles, seizures, and other natural causes.[218] Brothers and sisters were not sent on the same transports for killing so that families receiving simultaneous receipts of death notices from disease or accident would not become suspicious.[219] Families received an urn purportedly containing the ashes of their loved one although the urns contained the ashes of many people from the crematorium.[220] At Hartheim, for example, about 400-500 urns were turned out each month, indiscriminately filled with ashes scooped from a large pile.[221] Mistakes were also made. For example, one family received two urns in error while for another, a death notification gave appendicitis as the cause, but the victim's appendix had been removed 10 years earlier. In a third case the cause of death was given as a spinal ailment but the family had visited the patient who was in perfect good health a week earlier. In a fourth incident, a family received a death notice while the woman was living in an institution in good physical health.[222] Broaches and hairpins sometimes appeared in the urns of males.[223] Relatives and organizations inquiring about patients were told that the person had been sent to an unknown destination and they could inquire further from the transport company – often a futile exercise.

The Scope of the Program

The killing program of people in mental institutions, in hospitals and in old age homes was not confined to Germany but also occurred in territories outside Germany targeting those considered unworthy of life.[224] From the summer of 1941, it extended to the parts of the Soviet Union conquered and occupied by German troops as part of Operation Barbarossa. For example, on 29 July 1941, 58 mentally ill persons were taken from the hospital in Łódź ghetto for lethal injections.[225] As well as killing Jews and Communist Party officials, the *Einsatzgruppen* sought out psychiatric hospitals and systematically killed the inmates by shooting, poisoning, starvation or leaving them outside to freeze to death. The *Einsatzgruppen A* report covering June 23 1941 to October 15 1941, specifies that 748 'lunatics' were executed in White–Ruthenia and the Baltic States.[226] About 10,000 people were exterminated in this way.[227]

The Euthanasia program included not only the killing centers but also research institutes that provided morphological analysis and dissection of the bodies of such 'undesirables'. Glass reports on the direct association of 11 hospitals/extermination centres with 14 research institutes.[228]

Resistance

There was little resistance from the medical profession regarding the program although some institutions refused to complete the questionnaires and got away with it.[229] Religious protest was first heard from Protestant Bishop Theophil Wurm in July 1940, although in 1941 protest from some Catholic Bishops, in particular, became embarrassing for the Nazi administration.[230] Catholic Bishops Konrad von Preysing of Berlin and Clemens August von Galen of Münster protested with the latter creating the most attention by publicly exposing the program in sermons delivered on 6, 13 and 20 July and 3 August 1941. He said, "If so-called unproductive people can be killed like animals, then woe to us all when we become old and feeble."[231] This statement emerged from a general feeling of insecurity created by the euthanasia program among the population. Galen's sermons were printed and read out in Church parishes. The British obtained a copy, broadcast them on BBC, and dropped copies over Germany and (after translation) over France, Holland, Poland and other parts of Europe.[232]

At almost the same time, on 29 August, the Nazis released the film *Ich klage an* (*I Accuse*) showing a young girl with MS who expresses a wish to end her life. 18 million people viewed the film and saw it as a response to Galen.[233] Nevertheless, on 24 August 1941 Hitler gave Brandt a verbal order to end or at least to 'stall' operation T4 partly because of the public outcry but also, debatably, because the T4 program had achieved its numerical objectives.[234] The formal, centrally organized euthanasia program was discontinued and instead, from about August 1941, euthanasia became part of normal hospital routine: handicapped infants, and persons requiring long-term psychiatric care and judged incurable were routinely murdered.[235] Only the visible aspects of the T4 program were discontinued – the large scale gassing of victims that resulted in obvious smoke from burning bodies in the crematoria – while the killing by other means continued.[236] A policy of starvation in the state institutions without transfer to special killing centres was substituted.[237] This policy had the advantage that the deaths were more spread out and masses of patients did not die simultaneously. Lifton asserts that most of the killing of children occurred after the T4 program had been officially ended.[238] The program continued on a lesser scale for the remainder of the war[239] with killing now by drugs, lethal injection or by starvation.[240] The last transfers to Hadamar for starvation occurred in June 1944 although killing by starvation continued in other centres until the Nazi administration collapsed in 1945.[241]

Although Catholic Bishops Konrad von Preysing and Clemens August von Galen had protested against the euthanasia program in August 1941, the Vatican only voiced its concern and protested against the killing of physically deformed people, mentally disturbed people and hereditarily ill people in an encyclical *Mystici Corporis* (On the Mystical Body of Christ) on 19 June 1943.[242]

The 14f13 Program

From August 1941, the focus of the T4 program changed from the formal German institutional level to concentrate on camp inmates and continued until the winter of 1944-45.[243] These prisoners were removed from their camps to the euthanasia centres and murdered there. This program was code named 'Special Treatment 14f13': special treatment meant killing, 14 referred to reported deaths in camps and 13 to the cause of death, namely gassing (other file series were labeled 14f16 – suicide, 14f7 – natural death, etc.).[244] Alternatively it was called 'Operation Invalid' or the 'prisoner euthanasia' program.[245] Under the 14f13 program doctors from the euthanasia organization visited the camps from September 1941 onwards. After inspecting the inmates as they paraded in front of them, (rather than medically examining them), they filled out forms of the kind usually employed in the T4 program for those they targeted for killing. Nonmedical diagnoses were often arrived at including 'antisocial Communist psychopath,' 'fanatical Germanophobe', or in the case of Jews 'parasite on the nation.'[246] Estimates suggest that as many as 20,000 camp inmates died during the two and a half years of this program, from spring 1941 to the end of 1943.[247]

From Eugenics and Euthanasia to the 'Final Solution'

Although the sequence of events from eugenics to euthanasia and ultimately to the concentration and death camps appears, on the surface, to be clear cut, it was by no means so. Although the exact date is uncertain, the decision to implement the Final Solution was probably made sometime during 1941 and steps were already taken to slaughter Jews by the *Einsatzgruppen* during Operation Barbarossa (commencing June 22 1941) and at Chelmno (opened in December 1941).[248] A milestone in the coordination of the 'Final Solution' was reached at the Wannsee conference on 20 January 1942. The T4 program, with its killing centres supervised by physicians, efficient, and with a minimum of resources, was a forerunner of the methods followed to achieve the Holocaust. The various aspects of this program, from initial selection to transportation to incarceration and extermination centres provided the model for the elimination of other 'undesirable' elements in Germany and German occupied Europe.[249] The physicians trained in the T4 program became the top level administrators of the death camps and moved from killing tens of thousands to hundreds of thousands.[250] About 90 of the T4 program's personnel were subcontracted, following the occupation of Poland and the establishment of the 'Operation Reinhard' death camps of Sobibor, Belzec and Treblinka, to work in these camps, beginning in about spring of 1942 and ending in the fall of 1943.[251] T4 men made up almost the entire German personnel of the Operation Reinhard camps.[252] Dr Irmfried Eberl who led the Euthanasia centre at Brandenburg and

Franz Stangl who was stationed at Hartheim were sent, at the end of 1941, to advise and supervise the construction and operation of gas installations in the first death camps of Chelmno, Belzec, Sobibor and Treblinka. Eberl and Stangl served as the first SS commandants of Treblinka and Sobibor.[253] This move provides an intrinsic link between the T4 program and the Final Solution.[254] Opposition to the euthanasia program, however, did not transfer to opposition towards the killing of Jews. One reason for this is that the euthanasia program affected every German family while the killing of Jews – who were separated and stigmatized – did not.[255]

Responsibility for Implementing the Final Solution

The role of top level officials in implementing the 'Final Solution' was diffused and dependent on local functionaries' personal initiatives when faced with differing realities in the field.[256] For example, the head offices of the Nazi party in Berlin, of the SS, of the *Einsatzgruppen*, functional elites of the party, and other social groups all contributed in their own ways, and not always in concurrence with each other, towards the goal of a 'Jew-free' Germany and Europe. The relative importance of ideology, including racism and antisemitism, as well as such factors as German perceptions of 'the East,' societal norms, or the perpetrators' mindsets, is as yet unclear although all probably contributed to the multi-causal nature of Nazi genocidal actions.[257] Hilberg[258] provides a possible explanation for how the process functioned. He notes that Nazi Germany was anarchic – organized chaos. It had three centralized groups – the civil service, the army, and the party – each operating under a leadership principle and each with legislative, administrative and judicial powers of its own, as well as a fourth group, industry. In 1933 there was no blueprint for action against the Jews although there was a program of action that became ever more intensively directed against Jews: what Hilberg calls 'the destructive process.' Jews were initially marked, then separated, divested of all their property, deported and, after 1941, gassed. Steps taken as part of this process included the definition of Jews, their concentration into geographically isolated areas and then their annihilation. An economic process of segregation occurred concurrently, including dismissal from jobs, transfer or liquidation of their property, special taxes and wages, forced labour after ghettoization or marking, and confiscation of their estate after their murder. These processes were accompanied by an evolution in the decision making process: laws gave way to decrees, and these in turn to announcements. Written orders gave way to oral orders and finally to no order at all, but simply the ability of a functionary to sense the purpose of the operation and to devise ways of implementing it. Although complex and sometimes contradictory, the process proved to be highly effective.

As with other aspects of Nazi functioning detailed by Hilberg, there was also a steadily progressive process of suppression of reproductive ability of all deemed unworthy of procreating through sterilization and later euthanasia, restrictions on social and sexual interactions of those escaping the eugenics and euthanasia nets, restrictions on the childbearing freedoms, particularly of Jews, through forced abortion, segregation of the sexes in many camps accompanied by sexual humiliation, degradation and abuse, as well as murder of pregnant women or their newborns until, ultimately, the extermination of all.

Motherhood In Germany

As early as the late 1920s, the Nazis gave enthusiastic support to groups such as the Reich League for Child Rich Families that called for measures to regain the health of the '*Volk*'[259] and to promote marriage and childbearing among approved 'Aryan' women. The First World War had decimated the numbers of young men in Germany. Only one in four women between 25 and 30 could hope to find a husband.[260] The consequence was a huge drop in the birth rate aggravated by economic concerns including the Wall Street crash of 1929, the spread of birth control and the emancipation of women. According to Nazi party statistics, the German population of 37 million in 1885 had produced the same number of children as the population of 67 million in 1935.[261] German birth rates in 1900 were 36/1000 population while in 1932 this figure had dropped to 15/1000.[262] As early as 1914, Fritz Lenz blamed this on women's emancipation and advocated putting a ban on women's higher education.[263] Walter Darré, the Nazi minister of Agriculture, believed that the desire for emancipation among women was the result of malfunctioning sex glands.[264] The lack of will to have children was also traced back to the growth of the market for contraceptives and the threat this posed to the birth rate.[265]

The Ideal Aryan Woman

The Nazis made every effort to return women to their former subservient roles and particularly to their childbearing role. The independent, intellectual, childless, emancipated woman was to be forced back to the home, to the traditional principles of *Kuche, Kinder und Kirche* (Kitchen, Children and Church). Some racial hygienists thought that a woman should give birth to eight or nine children in her lifetime: Lenz thought they should give birth every other year over a 30-year period, and therefore, have 15 children.[266]

The desirability of motherhood for all German women became a central issue for the Nazis.[267] In their view, just as men served the state by fighting, so women served by bearing children. The theme of childbirth as an analogy to battle was common in Nazi ideology: "Every child that a woman brings into the world is a battle, a battle waged for the existence of her people"[268] referred to as the "birth war."[269] There was great emphasis on women's health, strength and grace: she was not frail and helpless but strong, vigorous and athletic.[270] The peasant woman who laboured in the fields, cared for the garden and poultry, cooked the meals, cleaned the house, and bore numerous strong, healthy children was a prime example of the ideal Nazi wife and mother.[271] This image encompassed broad-hipped women who could easily bear children.[272] Mothers were depicted as "wanting nothing more than to toil from morning to night in caring for their families and household: this was her strength through joy!"[273] For the Nazis, there was no task more beautiful than a mother educating her offspring "making the developing soul of her child receptive to all the goodness and beauty of the *Volk*."[274] As Goebbels said in 1929, "The mission of the woman is to be beautiful and to bring children into the world."[275] For Himmler, the ideal Nazi woman would be a brood mare to produce blonde and blue-eyed children as well as being a strong and purposeful woman like the Roman vestals.[276] Grunberger writes, "Women basked in public esteem between marriage and the menopause after which they imperceptibly declined into a twilight condition of eugenic superfluity."[277] Himmler dreamed of setting up 'Women's Academies for Wisdom and Culture' in which women chosen for their natural grace of mind and body – and Nordic appearance – would receive the best possible education. As Waller writes:

> The fair, latter day Rhine maidens would be steeped in Nazi philosophy, history and foreign languages. Daily games of chess would be part of the curriculum to sharpen their minds, while training in fencing would condition their bodies. But cookery and housekeeping would also be part of their curriculum....While careers in government and diplomacy would ultimately be opened to the 'chosen women' their initial purpose would be to provide proper wives for Germany's leaders, who would be 'honourably' separated from their present 'inferior' wives so that they might marry such proper paragons. Others would watch such elite couples and 'follow their example.'[278]

Not surprisingly, the Hitler regime curtailed university admission for women to a strict 10% quota and denied women opportunities for factory employment leaving them few alternatives for self support.[279] Before a woman could enter university, she had first to complete six months labour service where she was assigned tasks to prepare her for marriage and motherhood – cooking, sewing and learning to care for children. The

Washington Post, 17 February 1934, called Germany's labour camps 'bride factories.'[280]

Ernst Kaltenbrunner, Chief of the Gestapo and Police (SS-*Obergruppenführer und General der Polizei und Waffen-SS*) and Chief of the Reich Main Security Office (*SS-Reichssicherheitshauptamt)* also believed that all German women of fertile age must produce children – if not sired by their husbands then by other proven fathers. The father of three children himself, he followed his own advice: he had twins with his titled mistress Countess Gisella von Westhaup (neé Wolf) towards the end of the war. Nazi ideology granted women importance in the family but also as guardians of racial purity. They had to choose their partners carefully which involved understanding the value of health, recognising secondary racial characteristics and exploring the ancestry of their intended spouse.[281]

The Women's Movements

One of the regime's first targets for eradication on coming to power was Germany's active feminist movement, which was seen as an obstacle to the birth rate.[282] Any aspirations that women had for emancipation, autonomy, and liberation were smothered under Hitler's, and the Nazis' views that: "Marriage is not an end in itself but must serve the greater end, which is that of increasing and maintaining the human species and the race. This is its only meaning and purpose."[283]

Hitler equated the emancipation of women as a depravity similar to parliamentary democracy.[284] Women were regarded as unworthy, and in January 1921, one of the earliest Nazi party ordinances excluded them from holding any leading Party positions.[285] During the Weimar years, a number of women's groups had emerged, striving for emancipation, independence and freedoms for women. Within weeks of coming to power the Nazis quietly eased all the leaders of these women's groups out of power.[286] In May 1933, Lydia Gottschewski was appointed to integrate Germany's 230 civic and religious women's organizations into the Women's front (*Frauenfront*). She ordered all the groups to comply quickly or face closure. Her leadership was challenged and a series of leaders followed until Gertrud Scholtz-Klink was appointed in February 1934 to become the national women's leader of the Third Reich. She was a Nazi compliant leader willing to follow the party's dictates.[287] Although her title sounded impressive she was, in keeping with Nazi party rulings, awarded the rank of little more than an office manager with no direct representation in the party leadership and subject to the Welfare Society's scrutiny.[288] She organized thousands of courses, programs, outings, lectures, and radio programs oriented towards practical activities. By 1939, 1.7 million women had attended maternity schools that educated them in childcare and home economics including warnings regarding the dangers of smoking or excessive drinking during pregnancy.[289] A one-year course gave instructions regarding everything women would need to know as future mothers regarding correct behavior, diet and dress of pregnant women in order to ensure healthy babies – although they did not include sexual education.[290] Make-up was frowned upon and women wearing powder and lipstick could be excluded from meetings. Smoking in public was not allowed. Slimness was seen as incompatible with childbearing and women were persuaded not to worry about their figures. They were to sleep on hard beds, dress simply and not be vain.[291] All of these courses indoctrinated women in race, National Socialism, and national aims. In 'racial science' courses, for example, every young woman memorized the 'Ten Commandments for Choosing a Partner:'

1. Remember you are a German!
2. Remain pure in body and spirit!
3. Keep your body pure!
4. If hereditarily fit, do not remain single!
5. Marry only for love!
6. Being a German, choose only a spouse of similar or related blood!
7. When choosing a spouse, inquire into his or her forebears!
8. Health is essential to outward beauty as well!
9. Seek a companion in marriage, not a playmate!
10. Hope for as many children as possible![292]

Fourteen year olds – girls and boys – leaving school were provided with copies of this 10 point eugenic list.[293] There was also a service providing second hand cots, prams and children's clothing.[294] In 1936, Himmler decreed that prospective SS brides would be required to attend Reich Bride Schools (*Reichsbräuteschule*) prior to obtaining a marriage certificate. Lasting two months, and organized by Gertrud Scholtz-Klink they were held in nine state sponsored villas in Berlin and elsewhere.[295]

German women read magazines like *Die Deutsche Hausfrau* (The German Housewife) published by a popular middle-class housewives' organization, or visited one of the many travelling health exhibitions organized by the Dresden Hygiene Museum, held even during the Weimar period, in order to ensure the 'fitness and the physical and mental health of future generations'. For example, over seven million people visited the *Ge-So-Lei* (*Gesundheit, Soziale Fürsorge und Liebesübungen* / Health, Social Welfare and Exercise) exhibition, with its prominent publicity for the League of Child-Rich Families held in 1926.[296] Most German women considered the maternity cult a good thing and did their best to conform to the image of the ideal Nazi woman: a striking blonde with generous hips, hair tied back at the nape of the neck or in braids piled on top of the head, and without makeup.[297] From 1933 onwards, large families of German stock were entitled to numerous benefits including decoration with the German Mother's Honour Cross – bronze for 4-5 children, silver for 6-7 and gold for 8 or more.[298] Magda Goebbels, wife of propaganda minister Joseph Goebbels, was the first to receive the Honour Cross for the large number of children she had: six with Joseph and one with her former husband, Gunther Quandt, all of whose names began with the letter H – Helga, Hilde, Helmuth, Holde, Hedda, Heide and Harald.[299] Hitler himself on August 12, a new national holiday and the new date for Mother's Day – his mother's birthday – pinned on gold medals.[300] These women were entitled to salutes from members of the Hitler Youth organizations while wearing their decorations, as well as to other special allocations, allowances and privileges such as jumping queues in stores.[301] Initially, women who bore their fifth child could make a nationally prominent man the godfather of that baby: Hindenberg, however, outran Hitler in popularity, and the plan was suspended before the president's death.[302] Mothers with 10 children, however, had the honour of having Hitler as godfather to this child, which meant naming the child Adolf.[303] Such rewards for motherhood were not initiated in Germany but followed the examples already set in other European countries including Britain, Russia and France. Pronatalist policies in Germany, however, exceeded those in other countries in terms of funding, extent and ingenuity. Whereas policy makers in the USA and Europe justified such programs in terms of people's happiness, Nazi pamphlets told women:"Your body does not belong to you, but to your blood brethren [*Sippe*] and your …*Volk.*"[304]

Despite the Party protestations of women's childbearing role, few of the elite members of the Nazi party followed these recommendations themselves. Decorative women were a welcome part of Hitler's personal entourage and few were further from the Nazi ideal of a peasant-like field worker than the women, spouses and mistresses of elite Nazis.[305] With the exception of the Bormann and Goebbels families, they did not bear the required number of children either.[306] Only Gerda Bormann, wife of the party secretary Martin Bormann, met all the party ideals: She was the daughter of Walter Buch, a long-time Nazi party member, married Martin Bormann, a convicted accomplice to murder, in a wedding decorated by swastikas. She had seven children and idealized both Hitler and her husband. She went so far as to devise a system that would allow her, and their children, as well as her husband's mistresses, to live in the same house. In a letter to her husband dated 24 January 1944 she wrote "…put all the children together in the house on the lake and live together, and the woman who has not just had a child will always be available for you."[307]

Encouraging Marriage and Births

Encouraging marriage went hand in hand with encouraging an increase in the birth rate. The marriage loan program introduced in 1933, promised interest free loans of RM 1,000 to young, racially fit couples about to marry – of 'Nordic' ancestry, certified as 'Jew-free' for two generations[308] – as long as the woman promised not to work until the loan was repaid.[309] After 1938, however, as labour scarcity increased due to the war, marriage loans were only granted if the women continued to work.[310] To ensure they did not waste this money, the grants took the form of coupons that could only be used for the purchase of household goods. By 1939, 42% of all marriages were assisted by a loan.[311] The loans were to be repaid at the rate of 1% per month, but for every birth that ensued in this marriage, 25% of the debt was reduced, so that four children cancelled the debt altogether – known as 'paying off with children.'[312] In the short-term, the impact was impressive. Five hundred thousand marriages created jobs for men by forcing wives' exits from the labor market. The coupons stimulated consumer spending and created more jobs.[313] Demographic trends facilitated the increase in marriages as the post World War I generation reached adulthood, and as marriages deferred during the great depression were assisted by the loans.[314]

The Nazis, however, wanted more children and not only more marriages and the marriage loans had little effect on the number of babies born.[315] In 1920, marriages produced 2.3 children on average while in 1940 they produced 1.8. This was because the loans covered a mere 20% of the costs of having a three-child family and were not accompanied by a commensurate housing policy that would have made larger families viable in an urban environment. New furniture made little difference to people living in tiny apartments. In addition, as the loans were based on racial criteria it became dangerous to be examined in case of not meeting these and being forced into sterilization. Also, while there was an attempt to force women back into the home to provide jobs for men, this mainly influenced professional women as female labour was generally paid two thirds less than men and remained an attractive work force for employers.[316]

For those that qualified by having four children under 16 (the Nazi norm[317]), there were advantages such as work for the father, priority training and better housing for the whole family.[318] Additional grants were made for those with five or more children. From 1938, the benefits were extended to children up to 21 and later to 25. Like the marriage loans, the child allowances were paid to the father and not the mother.[319] Despite these concessions, the number of families with four or more children continued to decline. Nearly half of all marriages in 1900-1904 had four or more children: for those married between 1926 and 1930 the proportion was only 20%. In 1931-5, this reduced to 18% and in 1936-1940 to 13%.[320] The better off, the upwardly mobile, those pursuing hard work and women seeking emancipation all limited the number of their offspring. The economic, social and cultural costs of having more than one or two children were simply too high to overcome.[321] Even within the Nazi party's senior echelons, considerable deviations from the party ideal occurred: the Speers' and Goebbels' had six children each and, by the end of the Nazi era, Martin Bormann had nine. Göring and Himmler, however, had only one legitimate child each and Hitler had none. Himmler, however, had two illegitimate children who were concealed from the public and his wife.[322] The most 'valuable,' the families of SS members, had on average only 1.1 children in 1939 and 61% of the SS were unmarried.[323] There was, in fact, an inverse relationship between the social position of a family and its size: in the highest professional group, 31.3% had no children and only 3.4% had five or more children. These numbers reversed as one progressed lower on the socio-economic scale.[324]

One factor did, however, contribute to an increase in births: From the outbreak of war in 1939, under the command of Fritz Sauckel, unemployed (mostly middle class) women were encouraged or forced to join the war effort in the munitions industries and employed women (mostly lower class) were forbidden to quit their jobs. Hundreds of thousands of women used the only alternative to forced employment open to them: pregnancy. These women were called '*Sauckelfrauen*' and their children '*Sauckelkinder*' while Nazi leaders accused them of 'lack of comprehension for the necessity of war.'[325]

Abortions and the Birth Rate

Birth rates did increase from 12.8 births per 1000 population in 1934 to 20.4/1000 in 1939. The official report on German Fertility Trends in 1940, suggests that the increase in the birth rate from 1933 to 1938 was probably largely due to the economic recovery following the Great Depression of 1929.[326] Tauber and Tauber report that the 1938 rate was approximately the same as that for 1926, and that the increase in births reflected the decrease in abortions.[327] Nazi anti-abortion policy was strong and legislation made sterilization and abortion of 'Aryan' women 'crimes against the body of the German people'[328] or "acts of sabotage against Germany's racial future."[329] Additional births possibly reflected the greater difficulty women had in obtaining abortions, contraceptives or birth control advice all of which were banned.[330] In addition, from 1935 onwards doctors and midwives were obliged to notify the regional state health office of every induced abortion or miscarriage before the 32nd week of pregnancy and every preterm birth had to be reported to the authorities in writing within three days.[331] Women's names and addresses were then handed over to the police who investigated the cases suspected of being, in actuality, induced abortions. This meant that women who had previously sought illegal abortions feeling secure that complications could be attended by a doctor without being reported as an abortion might now be deterred from terminating unwanted pregnancies by the fear of possible legal proceedings. The guidelines consequently increased the likelihood of morbidity or mortality arising from unsafe abortions.[332] As a result of these rules, the number of requests for pregnancy terminations decreased from 34,690 in 1932 to 4,391 in 1936, and 2,275 in 1939.

Women having abortions and the abortionist could be punished by imprisonment or what was considered worse, penitentiary. If the perpetrator was a repeat offender, s/he could be sentenced to death. In the years prior to the Nazi era fines on abortionists did not exceed 40 marks. In contrast, Nazi courts imposed jail terms of 6-15 years on doctors found guilty of performing abortions. In 1935, 85% of these charged with performing illegal abortions were imprisoned.[333] For example, at Nordhausen, as reported in the Frankfurter Zeitung of 2 September 1937, a doctor was imprisoned for 6 years for four completed abortions and a number of attempted ones. At Gittingen, a colleague of his was jailed for 15 years for 15 completed abortions (*Frankfurter Zeitung*, 16 June 1939).[334] The majority of physicians arrested on abortion charges were women although women comprised only 5% of all physicians. This imbalance resulted because, firstly, a disproportionate percentage of women were gynaecologists in the first place. Secondly, since legislation prevented them from practicing except in their husband's practices and then excluded them (along with Jews) from receiving public health insurance payments, many might have chosen to continue their profession clandestinely.[335]

At the start of the war, the fight against abortion intensified. A Police Ordinance of 21 January 1941[336] prohibited the importing, manufacture or sale of methods, materials or instruments likely to prevent or interrupt a pregnancy. The ordinance prohibited not only vaginal specula and intrauterine devices but also, 'such substances and preparations embodied in manufacturers' products as are intended for introduction into the vagina and are capable of preventing pregnancy.' Irradiation, injections, or any other medical treatment administered for the purposes of preventing conception were also forbidden. Some 23 brands of paste, vaginal tablets, emulsifying agents, powders, suppositories, and other contraceptives produced by specific companies in Germany, Austria, Czechoslovakia, England, France, the Netherlands, Romania, and Switzerland were prohibited. Condoms, not mentioned in the Ordinance, were exempt at the request of the military authorities to help prevent venereal disease. By Police Ordinance of 9 February 1941, reports about each case of abortion had to include names, occupations, addresses of everyone involved, detailed description of the technique used (with samples of instruments if possible) payment demanded and received, exact time, and a short summary of events. Cases brought to the court for offences against the ordinance for '*Safeguarding of German National Military Potential*' rapidly increased from 1,909 in 1940 to 4,345 in 1941 and 9,108 in 1942. The rate of 'racially undesirable' pregnancies also increased, however, because of the anti-abortion laws. Abortion of 'defective' pregnancies was, however, secretly practiced from 1934, on the initiative of Gerhard Wagner, the Reich Medical Doctor's Leader, and allowed with Hitler's approval.[337] This was introduced into law on 26 June 1935 but required the woman's consent. After she was declared 'of inferior value' she was sterilized as well. Reich Health leader Leonard Conti in a secret decree of September 1940, granted health officers permission to perform eugenic abortions and sterilization on prostitutes, women of inferior character and those of alien race.[338] In 1942, Hitler, together with his secretary Martin Bormann and his physician Karl Brandt, issued an extreme policy statement:

> In view of the large families of the native Slav population, it could only suit us if girls and women there had as many abortions as possible. We are not interested in seeing the non-German population multiply...We must use every means to install in the population the idea that it is harmful to have several children, the expenses that they cause and the dangerous effect on women's health...It will be necessary to open special institutions for abortions and doctors must be able to help out there in case there is any question of this being a breach of professional ethics.[339]

In 1942, however, no more sterilizations and abortions were permitted for Jewish women: they would now be killed.[340] Eugenic sterilization was called a *Hitlerschnitt* thereby linking it to an anti-abortion policy that refused abortions even to women who had gone through two previous *Kaiserschnitte* (Caesarean sections).[341] Only after three Caesarean sections did a woman have a right to an abortion and then only on the condition that she also be sterilized.[342] The severest abortion prohibitions were incorporated into law on 9 March 1943.[343] Surviving court records indicate that the death penalty for performing abortions was in fact implemented in Mannheim, Vienna and Innsbruck in 1944.

Anti-abortion policy infiltrated the world of entertainment as well as the real world of medicine.[344] For example, a 'Blood and Soil' play called '*Schwarzmann and the Maid*' was widely performed in 1937. In it, Schwarzman, a rich farmer's son seduces a maid with false promises of marriage. Rather than abort the subsequent pregnancy as he wishes, the maid chooses to continue the illegitimate pregnancy but finally dies in childbirth. Critics in the Hakenkreuze Banner likened her death on 27 May

1937, to a soldier's death on the field of honour. Another play endorsing similar values was '*Peter Rothman's Maid.*' Farmer Rothman's marriage of ten years was childless and ultimately breaks down. A young and healthy maid presents him with a long hoped for son following which his wife commits suicide leaving the way clear for the maid to become mistress of the farm. Nevertheless, extramarital sex in movies or in plays, such as in '*Peter Rothman's Maid*' had to be carefully balanced, especially after war began as public dismay rather than appreciation was the likely response.

Divorce

Over time, infertility in marriage was seen as political opposition to the regime.[345] Divorce on the grounds that a woman was sterile or unable to bear children (even after decades of marriage and bearing previous children) was facilitated and the divorce rate leapt. In 1938 a major divorce reform incorporated *de facto* trends and officially defined new grounds for divorce including: adultery, refusal to procreate, immorality, VD, a three year separation, mental illness, racial incompatibility, and eugenic weakness.[346] Divorce rates increased more rapidly than marriage rates.[347] Within two years of this law, there were 30,000 divorces: men initiated 80% of these in the absence of any due cause related to their wives. In the majority of cases (60%), the wives were women over 45 who had been married for at least 20 years. Innocent ex-wives had to forego any alimony or maintenance claims unless they were old, infirm or had minor children.[348] The Christian view of monogamous marriage came to be seen as an enemy of fertility and the taking of younger partners (in addition to the first wife) was encouraged by the state and, reportedly, often welcomed by the first wife in the interests of Germany.[349] The Nazi poet Hans Johst wrote approvingly of a *'ménage à trois'* including a farmer, his barren wife and his pregnant maid. The *Schwartzes Korps* endorsed a similar situation of a craftsman in a childless marriage who has a child with his wife's sister.[350]

The Impact of Nazi Procreation Policies

Relatively little of the increase in the birth rate could, however, be ascribed to Reich policies.[351] In fact, by emphasizing the themes of 'duty' and 'responsibility' the State made parenthood sound like a burden.[352] During the war years, with husbands away, women were less likely to get pregnant and less willing to become what were in effect single mothers. Births fell from over 1,413,000 in 1939 to just over a million, on average, during the war years while the number of new marriages dropped from almost 775,000 to less than 520,000.[353] Hitler became increasingly worried about Germany's demographic future. On 15 August 1942, he ordered the last surviving son in every family where more than one son had been killed, to return home because he said, "in view of the obviously strong hereditary strain of bravery and self-sacrifice in such families, nation and state have an interest in your families not dying out."[354] Both Evans and Noakes note further that in January 1944, Martin Bormann issued a memorandum warning of the catastrophic position of Germany after the war following the mass death of the bravest young men. He suggested a variety of postwar remedies including educating women in the benefits of having children, and relaxing the laws on illegitimacy in a situation where there would be a large surplus of women over men.

A campaign to reduce infant mortality provided another avenue for possibly increasing Germany's future racial stock.[355] Prior to the war the program appeared to be successful and infant deaths in the first year of life reduced from 6.6% in 1936 to 6.0% in 1938. In 1943, however, the trend was reversed, with infant mortality rates reaching 7.2%. In the same year, British rates were 4.8% and American 4.0%. One contributory factor for the lack of success of this campaign in the war years was the reluctance of pregnant women to stop work at the recommended 6 weeks prior to their date of confinement because of the 25% loss of pay that this would incur. Instead pregnant employees frequently worked until their labour pains began. For the same reasons they nursed their infants for only a few days before handing them over to others to care for them – both actions likely to increase risks for their newborns' health.

Himmler was concerned about the predicted post-war surplus of women. The Scientific Statistical Institute calculated that with one million wartime deaths there would be a post-war ratio of women to men of 100-94. With two million dead, this ratio would be 100-86.[356] Statistics suggested that the male to female, newborn birth ratio was higher in SS marriages but this information proved false. Other figures provided to him had suggested that the mortality rate of infants in the SS maternity homes was 2% lower than in others, but this too proved false, with their rates being 2% higher than the norm. He became concerned with the production of male offspring and ordered a file to be opened on 'The Question of Producing Boys or Girls.' His Central Office Chief, Gottlob Berger, had told him of a custom from his native Swabian Alps which Himmler placed on record:

> Having like his wife, consumed no alcohol the week before, the husband sets out at 12 noon and tramps the 20 kilometers to Ulm and back. He must not stop at an Inn on the way. The wife does not work for a full week prior to the day in question, eats well, sleeps a great deal and

> refrains from exerting herself in any way. Copulation takes place when the man returns from his march. This is said to invariably result in the birth of a male child.[357]

The SS Reich Medical Officer-in-Chief Ernst Grawitz made no comment on this.

In addition to promoting childbearing among so called 'Aryan' Germans, Himmler also adopted two less conventional approaches to encouraging childbirth and racial expansion among those deemed 'worthy of life.' These were the *Lebensborn* program and the kidnapping of 'desirable' children in occupied countries.

The *Lebensborn* Program

The *Lebensborn* program was part of Himmler's plan to 'Breed the SS into a biological elite' and to combat abortion.[358] He had numerous concerns about the trends that pointed to an insufficient growth of the racially fit population of Germany. He was anxious about the falling birth rate especially prior to 1933. While WWI fatalities were accepted as contributing to this low birth rate, Himmler considered that other factors were also playing a role, including rampant homosexuality, widespread venereal disease, frequent abortions and an increase in illegitimate children. He blamed Weimar period 'bourgeois mentality' that valued liberal sexual enjoyment and endorsed contraception, as well as religious admonitions for chastity and marital fidelity that delayed marriage until economic security was obtained.[359] He did, however, endorse Catholic teaching that a childless marriage was a great sin.[360] He believed that rampant venereal disease would lead to the birth of mentally retarded and physically handicapped children, and that the multiple abortions that women were getting were injurious to their reproductive health. He was concerned about the plight of racially valuable illegitimate children. He estimated that 3 million homosexuals existed in Germany who corrupted other men and made them unwilling or unable to have children. He claimed that when they did marry to hide themselves, they made poor fathers and their sexual neglect made their wives unfaithful and led them to seek abortion.[361] He was concerned that racially eligible couples who were professionally and economically successful tended to limit their family size. The *Lebensborn* program was an experimental solution to some of these problems: it would provide financial support to SS families, offer maternity care for unwed mothers, would result in fewer abortions, and by providing good medical care would minimize infant mortality and morbidity. He informed SS leaders of the founding of *Lebensborn eingetragener Verein* on 13 September 1936, reminding all that they must fulfill their 'duty': "We have fought in vain if political victory is not followed by victory of births of good blood. The question of multiplicity of children is not a private affair of the individual, but his duty towards his ancestors and our people."[362]

The *Lebensborn* (Spring of Life) Registered Society (*Lebensborn eingetragener Verein* or *Lebensborn e.V*) came into existence on 12 December 1935 although the first home was not opened until December 1936.[363] Its obligations were to (1) support racially, biologically and hereditarily valuable families with many children, (2) support racially, biologically and hereditarily valuable pregnant women, who can be expected to produce equally valuable children, (3) care for the children and (4) care for the children's mothers.[364] It provided a maternity home and *crèche* for children and facilities for the confinement of wives, fiancées and girl friends of the (racially valuable) SS and police whether married or unmarried.[365] In addition to providing ante- and post-natal care, *Lebensborn* defined the financial obligations of fathers and acted as an adoption service for party members.[366]

Because of the heavy penalties for abortion, many women availed themselves of *Lebensborn* facilities to get rid of unwanted children through adoption, although recipients of this program still had to meet the criteria for racial desirability. The marriage decree required that both parties undergo a thorough physical examination and to submit a detailed history of their ancestry. Racial experts in the *SS-Rassenamt* examined these documents for evidence of genetic inheritance looking especially at trends in family longevity, causes of death, incidence of disease, infant mortality rates, and mental health data.[367] The first homes opened – usually large castle-like structures in spacious grounds situated in very pleasant surroundings[368] – at Steinhöring near Munich, Wernigerode in the Harz, Klosterheide near Lindau in the Mark and Bad Pölzin in Pomerania, although numerous others followed.[369] The premises were acquired on 'favourable' terms: The municipality of Pölzin had in 1937 presented Heim Pommern to the Führer who passed it on to the *Lebensborn* project's Health Insurance Fund; Klosterheide in Brandenburg was leased by Berlin; Heim Wienerwald was expropriated from Jewish owners by Himmler's Gestapo; Schloss Oberweis had likewise been 'made over' to the association. By the beginning of 1939, the list included the maternity homes Hochland in Bavaria, Friesland at Hohehorst near Bremen, and Neulengbach in the Wienerwald, which was planned as a *crèche*. The homes had complete administrative and financial autonomy, maintaining their own registry offices, which issued birth certificates for the newborns so that the children could later have access to standard services such as medical care, education and welfare.[370] The documents did not give any indication that they were born out of wedlock.[371] No expense was spared in furnishing or equipping the *Lebensborn* homes. The SS drew the monies from a fund made up of confiscated Jewish holdings. In addition, one-quarter of the millions of marks taken from the Jews in compensation for the damage of *Kristallnacht* went to *Lebensborn*.[372] In addition, membership dues were obligatory for all SS leaders[373] and were based on income and number of children for which the SS member was responsible.[374]

The babies were kept in nurseries separate from their mothers under the watchful eyes of nurses, who proudly reported that diapers were changed six times a day. Not only was this seen as efficient but also the nurses could examine the children carefully and any 'unworthy' child could be detected and reported. If the defect was not too serious, both mother and child were simply expelled. Otherwise, both parents were likely to be sterilized. The child would be sent to an institution with an uncertain future. Babies were taken to their mothers for breastfeeding, which was compulsory but according to Nicholas, was often resisted as mothers wished – in keeping with the then current, erroneous belief – to preserve the shape of their breasts. SS paediatric theory believed that babies could not remember anything until two years of age so that they could be kept in communal situations until then without harm. After two, family life was considered important and if the mother could not keep her child when it reached that age, it was sent to a foster home.[375] As Monika (a pseudonym) who had been born in a *Lebensborn* home reported in the 1980s, her mother had got her back at the age of three – 'a finished child' – but emotionally disturbed and needing therapy to overcome her anger at her mother's actions.[376]

Courses in parenting and childcare as well as Nazi ideology were held for mothers.[377] Within the homes, discipline was strict and the atmosphere was chaste: women were addressed only by their first names with the honourable prefix of '*Frau*,' even if they were unwed. They were expected to clean their own rooms and keep them tidy with regular room inspections. Squabbles, however, broke out: The wives of senior SS men were quick to complain that the staff treated unmarried fellow patients preferentially or that they had been neglected. The ratio of wives to unmarried mothers was 60-40.[378]

A newborn would be given a name in a special 'Germanic cultic' ceremony: The baby was placed on a pillow before a swastika emblazoned alter, surrounded by Nazi flags, a bust of Hitler and a portrait of Hitler's mother. Staff, the residents and a few family members would be invited to attend. SS officers were chosen as 'godfathers.' The celebrant, usually the director of the home, gave a speech clarifying that the concept of original sin and the Church teaching that unwed motherhood disgraced a woman should be rejected as 'un-German'. After a musical interlude, the celebrant asked the 'German mother' if she promised to bring up her child in the spirit of the 'Nationalist Socialist worldview' and the 'godfather' if he would supervise the child's education in the ideas of the 'SS Clan.' The director then held an unsheathed SS ceremonial dagger over the child (if it was a boy) and said "I take you into protection of our clan and give you the name so-and-so. Carry this name with honor!" The names suggested were ancient Nordic ones such as Freya, Gerhild or Sigurd, and were not popular. For a girl the SS leader would simply make a brief speech and the ceremonial name giving would conclude with singing.[379]

The SS guarded the homes. Only those with special passes could enter including the staff, *Lebensborn* directors, SS leaders on 'official business,' concentration camp inmates working on repairs and gardening, and sometimes groups of young women as recruits for staff. The latter were – not always known to them – both potential staff as well as potential mothers.[380] Engelman reports that it was mainly the student nurses working in the homes that became pregnant: The girls chosen had to be of pure 'Aryan' ancestry as far back as 1750, at least 5' 4" tall, blonde and blue eyed, and fully convinced of Nazi ideology and racial doctrine. One of four places in Munich was given as their home addresses. At least one of these places served as a meeting place for young girls and SS officers. The girls would stay for a few days or several weeks and then move on. Other young women were forcibly recruited by being called up to serve at the eastern front where they were quartered among the SS in the hope that they would conceive.

Lebensborn also developed foster care and adoption agencies. A baby born in a *Lebensborn* home could either be handed over to become an SS child through adoption, or the mother could keep it and raise it herself. It would not release an infant unless the mother met certain criteria suitable for motherhood. *Lebensborn* housed the infant for the first year and rather than give the child to adoptive parents, would wait, in the hope that the unwed mother's situation would improve and the child could live with at least one of the parents. SS families that could not have children were called upon by Himmler to accept one or more children from the *Lebensborn* homes and either to raise or adopt them.[381]

Himmler enjoyed working on the *Lebensborn* program: 'The *Lebensborns* were his hobby' said Paula H, one of the nurses from a *Lebensborn* home.[382] He became involved with the details of its administration including advising on the dietary habits of pregnant women, lavishing gifts on the children on his birthday, examining the records of unwed mothers personally and deciding which were eligible for admission and even corresponding with reluctant fathers urging them to do their 'honourable duty' and marry the compromised woman.[383] He expected reports on the milk production of nursing mothers in the homes and gave prizes for those who established records such as being allowed to stay in the home for another year. He also ordered that a file be set up for those with Roman noses or the suggestion of one.[384]

The increase in the number of children during the war years caused the expansion of the number of homes to 15 by mid 1944. At that time, the number of nurses staffing them was only 139: Heim Taunus 23 nurses, Hochland 18, Sonnenwiese 18, Wienerwald 15, Pommern 14, Kurmark 12, Harz 10, Schwarzwald 9, Ardennen 9, Westwald 4, Moselland 3, Friesland

3, Alpenland 1.[385] *Lebensborn* officials claimed that no more than 700 employees were ever connected with it although some estimates place the totals somewhere in the thousands.[386] One explanation for this discrepancy may be that the *Lebensborn* used staff employed by other SS units (such as doctors and the party Welfare Organization) and that children were placed in foster homes relatively quickly. In addition, most of the staff came from mothers who wanted to stay with their children or who feared to return to their families.[387]

Unmarried Mothers

Hitler Youth girls were encouraged to bear "racially and biologically flawless children for the continuation of a pure Volk."[388] An order given to the SS and the police on 28 October 1939 says, "it will be a high duty of German women and girls of good blood to become mothers, outside the boundaries of marriage."[389] As Bleuel reports, Hitler argued in favour of unmarried women and illegitimate children:

> How healthy, argued Hitler on the subject of family policy, was the peasant custom of the 'trial'! (It was, and still is, customary in many rural districts of Germany for a bride to prove her fertility before marriage by becoming pregnant.) How many great men, he said, stressing the spiritual aspects of the matter, had emerged from foundlings' homes? How ignoble it was, he lamented, demonstrating his human understanding, to pour scorn on an unmarried mother and her child when their status was the result of authentic passion![390]

In consequence, unmarried mothers enjoyed protection: illegitimacy was no disgrace and adultery ceased to be valid grounds for disciplinary proceedings. Hess published an open '*Letter to Unmarried Mothers*' on this subject at the beginning of the war: The unmarried mother whose 'betrothed' was killed in the war would be treated with regard to a widow's pension exactly as if the marriage had taken place. When her child's birth was recorded at the registry office the designation '*Kriegsvater*' (war father) would either replace or supplement the father's name. The party would, if so required, provide the child with a guardian. Bleuel describes how Nazi institutions supported Himmler's call for babies. The woman superintendent of a training camp for girls wrote gleefully to the mother of a participant to say that her daughter and five other girls were going to 'present the Führer with a child.' The German Girls League alerted young women to their responsibilities: a senior party official announced to them that 'You can't all get a husband but you can all be mothers!' Bleuel adds that bachelors on leave from the front were provided with female companions who were instructed to wear attractive clothes and not uniforms, socials and dances were arranged and excursions, sightseeing trips and factory tours were arranged to facilitate matches. Physicians expert in genetics were instructed to bring suitable mates together based on their genetic horoscopes. Bleuel goes on to say that Leonard Conti envisaged that an artificial insemination scheme would be provided which would allow single women to choose whether they had children by their lovers, by genetically tested strangers or by artificial insemination. In each case, *Lebensborn* would assume responsibility for the child. Himmler further proposed that childless marriages should not be supported by the State and should be dissolved if lasting longer than five years without offspring. He believed that men failed to produce more children with their wives because of personal distaste and did not dare to do so with their mistresses for fear of social disapproval. Bleuel notes that Himmler further told his masseur that he planned to legalize bigamy after the war as a reward for war heroes: "This would encompass the majority of those with proven fighting qualities, it being of vital importance to the Reich that they should transmit these to their children."[391] He believed wives would compete for their husband's favour and would satisfy men's polygamous disposition while women would accept such a situation for the benefit of the state. In 1942, Himmler proposed, in a letter to SS Lieutenant General Oswald Pohl, that because Germany faced a shortage of men due to the war, women whose husbands had been killed should be put up in a home accommodating some forty thousand women, where they would be expected to bear children sired by appropriate 'Aryan' men. This mass breeding exercise would thus strengthen Germany.[392]

Although much debated, and usually denounced, it has been suggested that some babies born within the program were the result of facilities provided for SS men to have sexual relations with racially acceptable women without the hindrance of such matters as marriage or commitment, and in so doing to produce desirable offspring to strengthen the idealized 'Aryan' race.[393] Himmler made it known that any unmarried women wishing to have a child could turn to the organization, which would then recommend racially flawless males as 'reproduction assistants'.[394] A number of memoirs and testimonies do indicate that SS members served women in the Lebensborn homes. For example, Heck, a Hitler Youth leader, confirms that SS members with Nordic appearances served as 'studs.'[395] Ernst Kaltenbrunner's testimony[396] before the International Tribunal in Nuremberg also reported that women up to the age of 35 would be obliged to have four children with racially pure men. After this, the husband was to make himself available for the program of impregnating other women. In similar vein, Erna Hanfstängel in Munich, April 1967, reported that in the autumn of 1937, while travelling on a local Bavarian train, a girl passenger suddenly announced, "I am going to the *SS Ordensburg Sonthofen* to have myself impregnated."[397]

Hildegard Trutz also reported that the procedure for mothers was:

> At the Tegernsee hostel, I waited until the tenth day after the beginning of my period and was medically examined; then I slept with an SS man (for three nights) who had also to perform his duty with another girl. When pregnancy was diagnosed, I had the choice of returning home or going straight into a maternity home...The birth was not easy, but no good German woman would think of having artificial injections to deaden the pain.[398]

The SS newspaper – the Black Corps – discussed the theme in long articles before the war. It did not always agree with this approach and in 1934, it ruled that non-marital liaisons are as a rule 'frivolous or the selfish exploitation of one party of the other, and that the illegitimate child is, as a consequence, generally racially inferior.' Support for Himmler's approach, however, grew as the war progressed, and from 1940 advertisements in newspapers displayed support for such illegitimacy.[399] Friendly foreign countries published cartoons and commented 'Himmler wants breeding establishments for Nordic men – the German woman is to be only a birth machine.'[400] The Waffen SS was to have the task of breaking the moral ban on unwed mothers – 'using whisper propaganda.'[401] Himmler's post-war planning included the idea of settlements of peasants in the Slavic lands that would serve as both defense outposts as well as 'Aryan' stud farms[402] as well as allowing 'double marriage' among large deserving groups of German men such as Party officials or soldiers decorated for bravery.[403] His dream was that all women over 30 who were still childless should be statutorily enabled, if not compelled, to contribute to the Reich's racial assets in this manner.[404] Hitler approved of these plans, as did Gerda Bormann, wife of Martin Bormann.[405] USA propaganda films such as Frank Capra's '*Prelude to War*' of 1942, asserted that the *Lebensborn* program provided stud farms, emphasizing this socially unacceptable image.[406] In addition, rumours that the homes were simply sanitized brothels where chosen SS men could produce children or where Nazi fanatical women could produce a child for their Führer were, according to post-war German reports, perpetuated by sensationalizing journalists after the war.[407] According to Jutta Rüdiger, the slogan 'Give the Führer a Child!' was the work of a few fanatics during the war.[408] Certainly unwed mothers were treated well according to the testimony of Frau Weber:

> Frau Weber told of her sister, Gussi Hohlbaum, who was pregnant by Jochen who died in an ambush by Polish Partisans. One of Himmler's officers came to visit her and suggested she go to an SS home near Bremen (Hohehorst

> Castle) where she could have the baby and recuperate under excellent medical supervision and care. The very next day an SS car and driver picked her up… She gave birth not only to Jochen's baby but to another one the following year. She probably would have had four or five more babies but her health wasn't good. In 1941 after her second birth, they advised her to stay in the home and help take care of the other mothers. When she decided against that she was transferred to an armaments factory in Prague.[409]

Because of the secrecy initially offered to women, the *Lebensborn* program could not be advertised widely. With war, Himmler seized the opportunity to advertise it. On 28 October 1939, he issued an order to the entire police and SS force:

> it may prove to be a noble duty – even outside marriage – for German women and girls of good blood to become, not irresponsibly but in a spirit of profound moral solemnity, the mothers of children fathered by departing soldiers of whom fate alone knows whether they will return home or die for Germany.[410]

Reproduction was held not to be a private matter but a sacred duty to ensure a racially valuable reservoir of good blood to lead Germany into the future. Himmler, however, was criticized for encouraging licentiousness and adultery in the SS and *Wehrmacht.* He defended himself by saying that he did not want to encourage illegitimacy or adultery but simply to assist mothers who became pregnant out of wedlock whose parents might normally marry but who were prevented from doing so by the vicissitudes of war.[411] *Lebensborn* records, however, show that many men were filled with guilt for adulterous behavior and marriages were threatened by the wives of some unfaithful SS men. In addition, attempted and successful suicides by frustrated and guilt ridden, unmarried parents were frequent when marriage was disallowed or not possible, and the *Lebensborn* refused them custody of their child.[412]

Outcomes of the Program

The results of the SS *Lebensborn* birth promotion program were, nevertheless, disappointing. In January 1939 the *Lebensborn* society reported 13,000 members of whom only 8,000 of the 238,000 SS had joined although close on two-thirds (61%) of the SS in 1939 were bachelors. The 93,000 married SS men had only 100,000 children between them: 1.1 children per family. Even officers did not set good examples: 23% were single while the more than 10,000 officers had slightly over 15,000 children: about 1.5 children per family. In addition, SS men married relatively late – on average at 27. In 1937, a backlog of over 20,000 marriage requests for the SS existed in the Race and Settlement Department, delaying their marriages. However, Himmler also forbad his SS officer candidates to marry before the age of 25, unless they had attained certain ranks before then.[413] He ordered his men to marry once they reached 30, and urged them to seek medical advice if pregnancy did not occur soon after marriage. If they did not comply, they risked losing the chance of further promotion: he was responsible for promotion above the rank of major.[414] In 1943 when SS casualties were increasing, he ordered men to plan for their leaves with their wives, so that they might optimize the possibility of conceiving. If they were unable to return home, their wives were ordered to join them at appropriate rest areas.

While exact numbers of births in the *Lebensborn* homes are not known, some estimate there to have been about 12,000[415] with 6,000 being illegitimate and the remainder SS children.[416] According to other historians, up until 1938 the seven functioning *Lebensborn* homes received only 653 mothers[417] although Koonz reports 1,436 mothers giving birth between 1936 and 1939, 823 of whom were unmarried.[418] Bock reports that 1,371 children were born before 1939 in ten homes in Germany but that most of the children were born during the war and outside of Germany.[419] Neither the total numbers of unwed mothers who sought admission or were accepted are known, but illegitimate children of SS fathers were relatively rare: some reports suggest that only 200 were fathered by the SS.[420]

Himmler's attempts to increase the rate of births through condoning illegitimacy failed, possibly because the majority of Germans (95% in 1939) described themselves as either Catholics or Protestants and still adhered to religious morals regarding unmarried motherhood.[421] In addition, the program exacted such racial requirements that only 40% of applications qualified for admission:[422] potential rejection and its possible adverse consequences might have deterred many from applying.

Abduction of 'Aryan' Children

The *Lebensborn* program was extended further in its efforts to increase the offspring of the 'Aryan' race. In some situations, children were removed from families where political or religious convictions of parents were judged unsuitable. Youth Officers could apply to Guardianship Courts to remove children from 'nonconformist' homes and to place them in 'politically reliable ones.[423] Parental offences punishable by judicial kidnapping were friendships with Jews, refusal to enroll children in Hitler

Youth programs and membership of the Jehovah Witnesses. The program extended beyond Germany's borders. In France, for example, the SS estimated that several thousand French women were pregnant by German soldiers, SS and civilian occupation personnel. Himmler ordered the French women to be seized – when German paternity could be proved – and racially examined. Provided both parents received racial certificates, the women were forcibly taken to *Lebensborn* homes in their own areas or in Germany to have their babies. These practices extended to both the occupied and unoccupied areas.[424] The Nordic peoples had also long provided a model of racial superiority and following the occupation of Norway, relations between SS and police with the local population were encouraged, and facilitated through the establishment of maternity homes staffed by Germans and under Nazi instruction regarding their operation. The Norwegian legal code was revised so that these children would not automatically have Norwegian citizenship but could be adopted in the Reich.[425] The mothers, who might have encountered censure in Norway for their relationships with Germans were encouraged to move to Germany and between 400 and as many as 2,000 are reported to have done so. Estimates suggest that 60,000 Norwegian women married German men and between 6-12,000 babies were born to Norwegian mothers.[426] Similar programs were implemented in Denmark, Holland, Belgium, France and Luxembourg with, however, less success.[427] In occupied territories, women giving birth to an illegitimate child of a German soldier were left to raise these children alone following the war. These women endured the censure of their neighbours who condemned them as 'Nazi whores' or collaborators while their children experienced ostracism and abuse as they grew up.[428]

From 1939, the *Lebensborn* program also extended to kidnapping of 'biologically valuable children' in occupied countries, usually between the ages of 2-6 but not older than 8 or 10, some of them fathered by German occupiers.[429] The Nazis ordered that in occupied countries there was to be no education of children above the fourth grade. Parents wanting a higher education for their children, could, if the child met superior racial standards, apply to allow their child to be removed to Germany and educated there or to move with them and become loyal German citizens.[430] Parents' permission was not always sought, and hundreds of thousands of children (some estimates suggest as many as 1.8 to 2 million) in occupied countries, including Poland, were simply abducted from their parents, sometimes under threat of physical or economic reprisal if they did not cooperate, and sent first to selection centres, where they were examined for racial purity, and then, if found acceptable (about 10%), to Germany for education and upbringing. Some children were simply identified on the streets by German police, SS patrols or by women volunteers from the Nazi People's Welfare Organization.[431] They were given German names and German foster parents. Those found unfit were often not returned to their parents but were sent to nearby concentration camps or were sent to 'eastern centres for foreign children' where they were starved to death.[432] Their corpses were packed into cardboard boxes and incinerated. Many of the children were orphans whose parents died during military operations, or were executed by the occupation authorities.[433] For instance, when the village of Lidice was leveled as reprisal for the assassination of *Obergruppenführer* Reinhard Heydrich, 13 out of over 100 children were allowed to survive because they were blonde.[434] Teams of SS doctors acting under Himmler's orders examined the racial suitability of children, including those in orphanages or in public care. The *Lebensborn* program was responsible for the 'Germanization' of these children.[435] Stefan Przybylski, after his liberation from Gusen (a subcamp of Mauthausen) was in charge of food distribution in a number of Displaced Persons camps near Salzburg. He encountered a little Polish girl whose parents had been killed by the Germans and who had then been given to Austrian foster-parents as part of the *Lebensborn* program. Further investigation led to his finding 187 children mostly between 8-9 years of age, throughout Austria and Bavaria, some of them deeply traumatized through having witnessed their parents' murders.[436] About 80% of the abducted children were never returned to their parents.[437] The full scope of the project is, however, unknown as the renaming of its victims obliterated its traces.[438] According to Beer, after the war the Russians searched the country for children of Germans and slave labourers and took them to the Soviet Union in retaliation for the heartless kidnapping of thousands of Russian children by the Nazi forces for 'Aryanization.'[439]

German Women as Victims or Perpetrators

In the late 1980s, there was considerable debate about whether German women in the Nazi era were supporters and perpetrators of the regime, victims of it, or perhaps both.[440] Simplified, the debate focused on Claudia Koonz' proposition that non-persecuted German women ('Aryans') were complicit in perpetrating National Socialism. For Koonz, privileged German women benefited from social benefits, profited from 'Aryanization,' were offered more professional opportunities, slave labour, and war booty. In contrast, Gisella Bock contented that even racially privileged classes of women could be classified as victims of Nazism: they were also subject to limited reproductive autonomy, burdensome demands of multiple children or, alternatively, potentially botched, unsafe abortions, and limitations on any personal emancipatory desires.

In support of Koonz' argument, Ute Frevert[441] remarked that by 1939 over 1 million of the approximately 3.3 million women in the *Frauenschaft* and *Frauenwerk* held some kind of official position and therefore identified significantly with the regime's social and political goals. Multiple memoirs and oral testimonies from former friends and acquaintances also testify to 'Aryan' women's willingness to accept racial dogma and actions. In addition, Troger's pioneering oral history project at the Institute for Comparative Research in Fascism of the Free University of Berlin reported that young researchers were disconcerted by the depth of women's happy memories of the Third Reich.[442] Interviewees burst into old League of German Girls' songs while remembering their youth movement days as a time of solidarity, adventure and empowerment.

In contrast Bock argues that all German women were victimized as they were oppressed and disciplined by the threat of forced abortion and sterilization if they did not live up to the required standards of fitness and social behavior. For Bock, depriving these women of motherhood was a crime. In addition, she sympathizes with women in that over 90% of the fatalities resulting from involuntary sterilizations occurred in women and the resulting childlessness was devastating for women. Notwithstanding the above, approximately one half of the sterilizations performed were on men, although the death rate from these was less due to the relatively simple procedure involved.[443]

There is little value in debating a binary opposition argument: German women, even if privileged, were likely to have both benefitted from and been harmed by Nazi policies. As Bock clearly enunciates, Nazi policy was both racist and sexist. Both Koonz and Bock, however, agree that racism was primary rather than gender. The Nazis aimed to establish a new European order based on a hierarchy of racial criteria and manipulating women's lives to do so was clearly viewed as fair game. While gender issues played a role in victimizing women in the realm of reproductive life, it was the racist element of this prejudice that was dominant in determining who would live, procreate or die.[444]

German Women's use of Pregnancy to Oppose Nazi Policy

Not all German women identified with and admired the Nazi regime. Some resisted, especially in the early years of Nazi rule, and in so doing manipulated the Nazi system relating to marriage and motherhood for their subversive activities. Such resistance sometimes occurred but is poorly documented.[445] Koonz reports that Gestapo records identify 12 major resistance groups existing in 1935 with 6,100 members but these had thinned to a few hundred within two years. They needed paper to disseminate their views but this was in short supply. Women would take their babies for a stroll in their carriage and in large cities would purchase small amounts of paper from as many as fifty stores in one day. At night, they would print their resistance pamphlets. The pamphlets and handbills had to be distributed and the news sent abroad, but paper was heavy and difficult to hide. Carola Karg, disguised as a pregnant, peasant woman made dozens of border crossing at different checkpoints, each time chatting informally with the guards while carrying pounds of illegal printed material beneath her maternity dress.[446] In another incident reported by Koonz, Gertrud Staewen, told about a circle of women from all backgrounds who used to collect motherhood medals in order to pin them on Jewish women who then (accompanied by their own or borrowed children) would escape across the Swiss border. Koonz reports that:

> Everywhere in Germany women with babies and buggies would take strolls, chat amiably with Gestapo officers, and drop forged identity papers and illegal printed matter at pickup points... Some of these papers have survived. Sometimes the corners of a resistance pamphlet have dozens of pinpricks in the margins. In order to maintain anonymity yet provide one another with a feeling of solidarity, each reader made a tiny hole before passing it on.[447]

To what extent German women were perpetrators or victims of Nazism is a challenging issue. Even though some may have been forced to bear more children than they would have wanted, to endure unsatisfactory marriage arrangements, or even to be sterilized, others were happy to do so. In neither situation, however, can these 'hardships' be equated with the horrors faced by Jewish women for whom pregnancy, if detected, almost invariably spelled death.

Ghettos, Hiding, And Elsewhere

Ghettoization and transport of those incarcerated in them to 'the east' became an integral part of the Nazi Holocaust of those it deemed less 'valuable' and particularly the Jews. While such actions are despicable enough, it is the reports of some Nazis' apparent enjoyment of the horrific actions taken against the victims, and particularly those directed towards pregnant women or new mothers and their babies that emerges from the eyewitness reports as particularly shocking and unfathomable. To shoot and kill a heavily pregnant woman, to laughingly murder a newborn, to boastfully shoot a mother and her baby with a single bullet, or to make a public spectacle of a mother giving birth in a town square, are shocking examples of the depths of inhumanity to which some Germans sank in the process of implementing Nazi ideology. Sadly these are only a few of the instances that are recorded regarding marriage, pregnancy and childbirth in ghettos and other places of confinement, and while being transported to their deaths, that reveal this facet of Nazi mentality.

Marriage

Nazism in Germany prior to the war influenced every aspect of Jews' intimate relationships, from whether to marry, have children or even adopt children. These normally joyful occasions became fraught with difficulties. In the pre-war years, conditions determined that some marriages were rather unorthodox: in some instances, the marriage ceremony was held with the bride and groom in different countries as travel restrictions did not allow one to return to Germany safely. In others, bridal *trousseaux* were bought and put into storage until the couple could decide where they might be able to live.[448] In yet others, women married or announced their engagement before emigrating. Some married in order to emigrate using the same travel documents that granted two people safe passage.[449] Local Jewish newspapers carried advertisements seeking emigration partners: one businessman offered a 'pretty, healthy and young woman' the opportunity to emigrate to Palestine together since two people could enter on one certificate.[450] In Poland, there was a rash of weddings as parents of young women were loath to have their daughters try to emigrate alone to the Soviet controlled region.[451]

Mixed Jewish/non-Jewish couples (*Mischlinge*) were affected as well as couples where both partners were Jewish.[452] Jewish women married to 'Aryans' were viciously tainted as 'Jew whores' by Gestapo agents and sometimes brutally assaulted. In some mixed marriages, the German male partner refused to have sexual relations with the spouse even though he would remain with her and support their child. Some spouses committed suicide believing that the other would survive better without them.

The relationships between parents and foster or adopted children were also affected: 'Aryan' children could be removed from families where even one parent was Jewish. Adoption of racially different children was forbidden. Marriages between 'Aryans' and Jews had to withstand enormous pressure from government, employers, friends, and families to split. Some, like Ilse Koehn's parents, divorced formally in order to protect their child (who was not told of her second-degree *mischling* status and remained successfully immersed in German society, including being a member of the Hitler Youth) but nevertheless remained totally supportive of each other and reunited after the war.[453] Those marriages that remained intact – the majority – faced ostracism and deprivation (well described by Viktor Klemperer[454] and his non-Jewish wife Eva), although most Jewish spouses' lives were spared.[455]

Pregnancy created increasing pressure for women and couples. Pregnant women would lie about in the Vienna Consulate Office hoping they would have their babies on British territory. On one occasion, a couple went away and committed suicide: there was nothing the consul could do for them.[456]

Conditions in Ghettos

Numerous authors have documented the pitiful conditions prevalent in the ghettos[457] from the time the first was established in October 1939 (Piotrkow Trybunalski) through to the last in 1943 (Upper Silesia) for those Jews of Europe who had not managed to emigrate – or had chosen to stay during the earlier years of Nazi rule.[458] Suffice it to say that ghettos played a valuable role for the Nazis as part of their plan to isolate and stigmatize Jews, and later to facilitate their transport 'to the east' for extermination. Ghettos were usually centered in the poorest and least serviced areas of a city where living conditions were dismal even prior to their establishment. Overcrowding, and lack of food and basic hygienic services, exacerbated these conditions. As Lucy Dawidowicz reports, "three and four families lived in space adequate for one. Toilets, running water, all plumbing and sewage facilities were taxed beyond capacity and beyond repair. The mephitic exhalations of latrines and broken toilets poisoned the air. In the long winters of bitter Polish cold, the water in the pipes froze."[459] Hunger was a constant companion in ghettos:

> Hunger killed, but first it wrought disabling change – mental, psychological and physical. Loss of weight and the disappearance of subcutaneous fat aged and withered its victims. Hunger destroyed the normal rhythm of existence, affected the physical capacity to work and the mental ability to think. Nutrition deficiencies caused anaemia, suppressed the menses. Fatigue and dizziness, apathy and depression were part of the general sense of malaise. Nausea, vomiting and diarrhea were the daily complaints of the hungry.[460]

Hunger drove people to extremities, for example, one mother hid her dead child under the bed for eight days in order to receive a larger food ration,[461] another mother was seen nursing a baby at a dried up breast and next to her the dead body of an older child,[462] and sometimes a mother could be seen cuddling a child frozen to death, trying to warm the inanimate little body. Sometimes a child huddled against his dead mother, thinking that she was asleep and trying to waken her.[463] Adibna Szwajger reported leaving a hospital in the Warsaw ghetto where she worked and standing on something soft: a baby's corpse, swollen, covered in newspaper.[464]

Moorhouse cites an eyewitness account of the poverty and desperation of a family in the Warsaw ghetto:

> One well known case involved a family from Łódź, which at first numbered eight people. Their entire belongings consisted of two baby strollers: the father pushed three children in one, while the mother kept two others in the top of the second. They rolled the strollers along the curb and sang old Yiddish songs. They had beautiful voices. He sang and she sang accompanied by six children's descants. After a while there were only four voices; then there were three, then one stroller disappeared, along with the family's shoes and what was left of their outer garments. Finally only two people remained. The father pushed while the mother lay in the stroller, singing to accompany her husband. She was thirty-nine years old but looked one hundred.[465]

Love and Marriage in Ghettos

Despite the abject poverty, despair and abnormality of life in ghettos, flirting, romance and marriages still occurred together with theatrical performances, concerts, education and other semblances of normal life.[466] People fell in love in the most improbable places; they married whether or not they could create a home for themselves and regardless of whether either of them might survive. For example, Krysia married Salomon (Salek) Kucynski in the Sosnowiec Ghetto They were later sent to Annaberg Camp together. Then Salomon was transferred to Blechhammer Camp and Krysia to Peterswald Camp. Salomon died during the death march to Buchenwald, Krysia survived and later remarried.[467] Sally H. testified "people had hope things would go on."[468]

Marriage patterns changed over time in the ghettos from traditional ceremonies to those that defied custom. In Łódź ghetto, Mary Berg, (Miriam Wattenberg), in her diary (23 November 1939), reports the wedding of her uncle Perry despite the official German order forbidding Jews to marry. She writes:

> in defiance of their order, the number of Jewish marriages is increasing. It goes without saying that all the marriage certificates are antedated...To attend this wedding, we slunk one by one like shadows down the few blocks that separated us from the place of the ceremony. A guard stood at the door on the watch for Nazis.[469]

In most cases, the bride would be required to wear a Star of David on her wedding dress.[470] Weddings were often small, improvised events, with makeshift *chuppas* (wedding canopies) and wedding cakes made out of potato peels.[471] By 29 October 1941, however, Berg reports that the number of marriages in the ghetto had decreased significantly, due not to the Nazi prohibition, but to the shortage of apartments available for the newlyweds.[472] In August 1942, she reports the marriage of her friends Edzia and Zelig attended by many of their friends at the exact time the Nazis were blockading their street.[473] Traditional marriage norms, however, began to crumble at this point. On 30 March 1942, Mary Berg reports that her friends Harry and Anka wore rings on their fingers:

> Harry said...'The rabbi refuses to marry us because Anka is not of age and we must have permission from her parents...but her parents are opposed...But that doesn't matter,' said Anka, laughing. 'We're married anyway. We don't need witnesses. No rabbi will ever be able to express in a document a union as strong as that which joins us now and forever.'[474]

The reasons for marriages also changed from marriages of love to those of convenience. Marriages like that of Anka and Harry resulted from love. Some were the hurried decisions of young people who felt they had little time left; in some cases, parents withdrew earlier objections to the match. Sometimes marriages were conveniences for sharing cramped ghetto space or gaining the protection of labour cards, such as those of Irene S. in Warsaw, Solomon K. in Kovno, and Freda P. in Plonsk ghettos.[475] Marriages of convenience became common after the seizure of many women without male support in the Kovno ghetto. By October of 1942, Mary Berg reports that, in Łódź, "Husbands whose families have been deported try to escape their loneliness and ask the first woman they meet to stay with them. A woman makes life somewhat easier for a man, and two people together feel more secure amidst the terror."[476] As Oskar Rosenfeld wrote in his notebooks in the Łódź ghetto, "Some people marry out of need, some from having extra. Two weak people together can become strong: their rations are equal and the double measure of coal and firewood expands their possibilities."[477] As Mary Berg continues reporting, "thousands of people are sleeping wherever they can find a place,"[478] all seeking solace and support from others in similar situations. Mary herself was asked by numerous men to stay with them and she reports, "all the girls are doing this. Very few women are left in the ghetto, and young girls, especially, receive daily proposals to live with men who have jobs and rooms near the factories."[479] Gertrude Schneider, a survivor, reported that "There were many songs about girls who did and girls who didn't…There were songs that those who did, you know….sometimes will get pregnant."[480] Oskar Rosenfeld noted that the decrease in marriages in the later years of the Łódź ghetto's life could be attributed to a loss of sexual interest rather than to the difficulties of life and shortage of accommodation: He wrote (18 January 1943) "Women without periods, complete death of the erotic, especially among the Western Jews. Thus no marriages."[481] A few months later, on 11 November 1943 he wrote, "Lovemaking has on the whole withered away. As the finer more tender aspects of life – music, literature, springtime, flowers and the rest – have vanished, so too has love."[482]

A few weddings were permitted in Theresienstadt (a unique mixture of ghetto and concentration camp, also used as a 'show-camp' to obscure the realities of concentration camp life from observers). As, Vera Schiff reports, weddings were "part of the sham of social and recreational activities of the camp."[483] Schiff notes that people decided to marry in order to leave the camp together (on transports to 'the East'), or in the usually futile attempt to prevent the partner from being deported, as occurred in the case of Ruth Baeck, niece of the Rabbi of Berlin Leo Baeck, whose newly married and sick husband was shot the day following the ceremony.[484] The Germans allowed these marriages and permitted the couple to choose a civil or religious ceremony. The civil marriage was an official declaration of the intent to marry: both names were placed on the card system of the camp together and they were deported together. Some couples had a mistaken belief that in another camp they might be able to live together. Religious weddings took place under a *chuppah* (canopy) with an officiating rabbi. Vera Schiff herself married in Theresienstadt on 6 March 1945. She wore a borrowed black designer dress, which a new arrival at the camp still had with her. She married under a *chuppah*: a thin blanket fastened to four wobbly sticks. Dr Friediger, a Danish rabbi presided while Hambro, a Danish violinist played.[485] Her marriage was founded on mutual attraction. As she writes, "it would be preposterous to pretend that when young men and women are thrown together, even if interned, that they are not attracted to one another. In fact, perhaps the opposite was true. The imminent danger intensified every feeling and tolerated little delay of gratification. Which one of us really believed to have a tomorrow?"[486]

Some existing marriages became stronger in Theresienstadt, in part because of the separate living quarters, which prevented everyday bickering and made the brief daily encounter a special occasion. Others did not withstand the strain of ghetto/camp life, and both women and men found new partners until virtually all were sent to concentration camps, or murdered.[487]

Statistics support the stabilizing effect of the ghettos on family. Divorces ceased, but all ghettos recorded a rash of marriages and widows and widowers married more frequently in the ghettos than in prewar days.[488] Religious traditions surrounding marriage had to adapt in the ghettos, to accommodate Nazi restrictions. In the Łódź ghetto, in March 1942, because the rabbinate was abolished and divorce, marriage and funeral rites were all forbidden by the Nazis, a rabbinate consisting of seven *dayonim* (scholars in the administration of justice, Talmudic Law and certain rituals) would meet regularly in an apartment to supervise the religious life of the ghetto.[489] Marriage ceremonies were conducted by the ghetto Elder (Chaim Rumkowski).[490] The groom would place the ring on the finger of the bride as Rumkowski uttered the traditional blessing. The father and one other Jew served as witnesses and the ceremony was conducted in the House of Culture. The marriage was regarded as just as valid as any rabbinical marriage. About ten couples a week were married in this way. The Nazi prohibition of *mikvehs* (ritual baths), that were a prerequisite prior to a wedding, had implications for marriage and for survival. Each ghetto dealt with this differently. In Łódź, for example, the rabbis gave permission to proceed without a ritual bath, because weddings were often for the sake of *pikuahk nefesh* (saving an endangered life) when a woman without a work permit married a man who had one, and was thus exempt from deportation. In the Warsaw ghetto, the ritual baths were sealed and boarded up, but occasionally were used secretly.[491] In Vilna ghetto, in contrast, rabbis ruled against performing weddings, since the brides could not take the prescribed bath.

Childbirth in Ghettos

In the early years of ghetto existence, pregnancies and births still occurred. 'Aryan' women had many babies: German propaganda showed laughing babies everywhere. Jewish women shared this ideal, and some became pregnant.[492] Most families in ghettos, however, lived under grievously crowded conditions so that normal conjugal life was difficult to maintain under the circumstances, and family tension often ensued. Hunger and disease caused most of the women to stop menstruating and rendered many men impotent.[493] This factor, coupled with unwillingness to bring children into a world so unstable and cruel, contributed to a lowered birth rate.[494]

Lack of contraceptives also made prevention of births difficult.[495] The most common form of contraceptive was *coitus interruptus*, renowned for its unreliability.[496] While Muller[497] reports that French Letters (condoms) were found among the clothing of those sent to the gas chambers of Birkenau, Adam Czernaikow in the Warsaw ghetto reflects on the Jewish inventiveness of the ghetto: contraceptives were made from baby pacifiers, confirming their lack of availability.[498] Amenorrhea (cessation of menstruation) provided a further obstacle to conception. Preiss reports on the understanding of amenorrhea in a number of ghettos.[499] Dr Yaakov Nakhimovsky, chairman of the medical committee in the Kovno ghetto, surveyed workers in the Kovno ghetto during 1942 and 1943 and found that amenorrhea was common especially when women first moved to the ghetto. Dr Aharon Peretz, also in the Kovno ghetto, believed that the widespread incidence of pregnancy in the ghetto was the result of amenorrhea among women who were unaware that they could still conceive. He claimed that emotional stress, worries and hard labor caused changes in the functioning of the endocrine system resulting in amenorrhea. Dr Yaakov Nakhimovsky believed that hormonal disturbances affected the thyroid glands of women and had consequences for fertility. He also reported instances of false pregnancies with symptoms of pregnancy, including amenorrhea, but no fetus. Dr Mark Dworzecki, a physician in the Vilna ghetto, said that the explanation of amenorrhea caused heated arguments among the doctors. Some believed it was irreversible and others that it was temporary. Dworzecki found that with improvement in nutrition and with fewer *Aktions* (Actions) menses returned for some. In the Łódź ghetto, starvation and disease were believed to cause amenorrhea. In the Warsaw ghetto, amenorrhea was common as well but here Vitamin A deficiency was believed to be the cause.

The Nazi ban on births in ghettos, enforced in 1942, was a most disruptive influence on the procreation of Jewish families.[500] Hitler had said, "There are many means by which a systematic and completely painless extinction of undesirable races can be attained, at any rate without blood being shed."[501] Banning births was one of these. That the Nazis banned births in ghettos is well documented, primarily from diaries and from documents written at the time. On 11 December 1961, an Israeli court convicted Adolf Eichmann on all counts of his indictment including "directing that births be banned and pregnancies interrupted among Jewish women" in Theresienstadt.[502] The order to ban births in ghettos such as Shavli, Kovno and Vilna in Lithuania, among others, followed a statement made in December 1941 by Karl Jäger, commandant of the third *Einsatzkommando* Unit regarding the Jewish labour force that remained in Lithuania after the mass murder actions. He wrote, "I believe that we should begin sterilizing male Jews from among the Jewish laborers to prevent future increase. If a Jewish woman should become pregnant, she should be killed."[503] Reports on the ban on births in various ghettos reveal both similarities and differences in its impact and the ghetto residents' reactions to it. Some of these are considered below.

Births in Shavli Ghetto

The Shavli ghetto Judenrat posted a notice – Security Police Order signed by 'The Delegation' – to inhabitants on 13 July 1942. It read:

> In accordance with the Order of the Security Police, births are permitted in the ghetto only up to August 15, 1942. After this date it is forbidden to give birth to Jewish children either in the hospitals or in the homes of the pregnant women. It is pointed out, at the same time, that it is permitted to interrupt the pregnancies by means of abortions. A great responsibility rests on the pregnant women. If they do not comply with this order there is a danger that they will be executed, together with their families. The delegates [the Shavli *Judenrat*] are making this matter widely known. In warning the women of the possible consequences, they believe that the women concerned will remember it well....and will take the necessary measures during the registration of pregnant women which will take place during the next few days, and subsequently.[504]

According to the Nazi order, in the event of a birth taking place in a Jewish family after this date the whole Jewish family would be 'removed' (exterminated) and the responsibility would rest with the Jewish delegates. The decision to enforce the Nazi order to ban births in the ghetto was only taken following immense soul searching by the ghetto *Judenrat*. The arguments debated at the meeting of the Shavli *Judenrat* held on 24 March 1943 follow as these clearly reveal the 'choiceless choices'[505] faced by the leaders of this ghetto (and other ghettos faced with similar demands):

> ... There was a birth recently in Kovno and all members of the family were shot and killed... Can the pregnant women be forced to have abortions performed? ... there are about 20 pregnant women in the ghetto, most of them in the first few months, but some who are already in the fourth or fifth month and one even in the eighth month. Only two of the pregnant women refuse to have an abortion; for one of them this would be a third abortion and she is threatened by the danger of subsequent childlessness, and the other is the one who has reached the eighth month ... They must be persuaded to have an abortion. They must be told what happened in Kovno and Riga. If necessary one must make use of a white lie in this emergency and tell them that the Security police is already looking for these cases... the whole medical team, including the midwives, should be forbidden to attend births ... all cases of pregnancy should be registered and the pregnant women persuaded to have abortions ... We must not make propaganda against births in public! The matter could reach ears that should not hear it. ... the pregnant women [should] ...be warned in the presence of the doctor and a representative of the Delegation, and the full danger that awaits them be explained. ... How can one perform an abortion on a woman who has already reached the eighth month of her pregnancy? Surely we must understand the feelings of the mother. It will surely be impossible to convince her. And what will happen to the infant if we cause a premature birth? We cannot carry out an operation like that in a private home, and it is forbidden to leave the child at the hospital. And what will happen if despite everything the child is born alive? Shall we kill it? ... very difficult in a case like this for no doctor will take upon himself the responsibility of killing a live child, for that would be murder ... Perhaps we should let the child be born and give it to a Christian? ... We cannot allow the child to be born because we are required to report every case of a birth ...What can we do when the ghetto is in such danger? If the danger were only to the family of the

> infant we could leave the matter to the responsibility of the person concerned, but it endangers the whole ghetto. The consequences are liable to be most terrible...[506]

The council decided that in the case of the woman in her eighth month, a doctor would induce premature birth and a nurse would kill the child.[507] The nurse would be told to proceed in such a way that she would not know the nature of her act. In Shavli ghetto at least one woman defied the order to abort her pregnancy. Regina Gotz testified in 1957 that she became pregnant in 1943. Her husband was a member of the Jewish council that enforced abortion of pregnant women – she refused to have an abortion resulting in him having to resign from the council. Her friends and family hid her successfully and she gave birth and cared for her baby for a few months. When they received warning that children would be sent away she arranged for a local priest to give the baby to a Lithuanian Catholic woman who had agreed to care for him. She managed to smuggle her baby out of the ghetto and gave him away. Soon after, she was sent to Stutthof camp and her husband to Dachau. Both survived as did the baby. They were eventually reunited as a family when the boy, Ben Zion, was a 12 year old. The years of separation had taken their toll and their relationship remained strained for many years, until he himself had had a family.[508]

Births in Kovno Ghetto

Similar reports exist relating to the ban on births in Kovno ghetto in Lithuania. Tory, in his diary written while in the ghetto, reports that births as of September were forbidden by the Gestapo on 24 July 1942 and that after this time pregnant women would be put to death. On 29 July, the *Judenrat* issued a letter to all physicians and midwives announcing the need to terminate pregnancies.[509] On 7 August 1942, his diary records that Rauca (the commander of the SS in the ghetto) noticed a pregnant woman in her 7th month. He said, "This embryo must perish. If not, it will be taken away from its mother right after birth."[510] Dr Aharon Peretz, a gynaecologist in the Kovno ghetto, testified about the same or a similar incident at the Eichmann trial.[511] In Kovno ghetto, Rabbi Oshry was asked whether *Halakhah* (Jewish Law) would allow a woman to use a diaphragm to prevent pregnancy given the decree that had been issued forbidding pregnancy on pain of death. He agreed to its use because the woman's life is in danger and the fetus would never live either. In addition, the wrath of the SS might extend to the family and community as well.[512] Similarly, on 9 August 1942, Rabbi Oshry agreed that, in the light of the Nazi decree to murder any pregnant women in the ghetto, a pregnant woman could have an abortion to save her life.[513] Yet another circumstance occurred in the ghetto which challenged Jewish laws: On 7 May 1942, the day the Nazi directive was promulgated, an SS officer saw a heavily pregnant woman and fired at her, killing her. She was taken to the hospital where the surgeon asked Rabbi Oshry for permission to do an emergency caesarean section to save the baby. He agreed and a live baby was delivered. But this contravenes another law, which forbids disfigurement of the dead, and also the possibility that if the woman were not dead but only close to death, the surgery would kill her. As events transpired, the outcome was disastrous. The Germans returned to the hospital to record the name of the dead woman, found the baby had lived, and were furious. They picked up the baby and dashed its head against the walls of the hospital room.[514]

Peretz testified that as the hospital had been burned down by the SS a while earlier, abortions were performed under very difficult conditions "in kitchens, in small attics, amidst terrible congestion, and understandably there were fatalities."[515] On 8 September 1942, the Germans declared that from then on any pregnant woman would be killed on the spot.[516] On 6 June 1943, Tory reports that no births had taken place in the ghetto for the past 22 months on pain of death.[517] At about the same time, (9 June 1943) he reports bargaining with the SS for the life of Dr Shlomo Nabriski who had tried to escape from the ghetto with two other men but had been caught. The ghetto council pleaded for his lenient treatment by explaining that as a gynaecologist he was very useful to the ghetto, as, in line with Gestapo orders to terminate all pregnancies, his skills were needed. The terminations were being carried out by inexperienced physicians, which resulted in work absenteeism by the women – arguments appealing to the SS.

Not everyone complied with Gestapo rules. Tory records on 25 June 1943, that Hela Aronovski Voschin, a Christian woman married to a Jew, who had followed her husband to the ghetto, later disappeared from sight for a long while. It emerged that after becoming pregnant she had refused to have an abortion. Despite the danger to herself and her husband, she carried the baby to term and gave birth. Hela and her baby survived the war although her husband was murdered in the Ninth Fort (near Kovno, Lithuania) for refusing to tell the Germans the location of hiding places in the ghetto.[518] Tory recorded another birth in Kovno ghetto: on 18 February 1943, a couple who refused to leave their names brought a baby to the hospital and left it there. The baby had just been born. It was taken care of but there was no guarantee that it would survive. The baby was named the second Gideon. A baby left near the ghetto gate a year before had also been named Gideon.[519] Chasia K. also gave birth in the Kovno ghetto in a small smoke filled room. Her mother and a nurse were with her for the birth. She had no milk and fed the baby scraps. Her mother cooked *kasha* (porridge) for her although the doctors had warned that the baby's intestines could not take it. The baby – *Tikvah* (hope) – grew and was talking before it was killed in an *Aktion* in 1944.[520] In a rare father's report relating to birth,

Benesch T. told of his wife's childbirth in Kovno on 4 March 1941. They did not have a crib so he put chairs together and a board on the side of the chairs to make one. His wife gave birth at home helped by a doctor who was a friend of theirs. His wife nursed the baby but did not have enough milk because she did not have enough to eat. He gave her whatever he could. Luckily, the baby was healthy. He was able to hide the baby with a Christian woman and he and his wife were reunited with the baby after the war.[521]

Births in Vilna ghetto

In the Vilna ghetto, the Nazi decree forbidding births was issued on 5 February 1942, but deliveries were conducted in secret and newborns hidden.[522] A secret delivery room functioned in the gynaecology department of the hospital. Newborn infants were hidden in an area outside the hospital where the mothers could nurse their babies. When the children grew older, they were registered in the *Judenrat* offices as having been born prior to the date of the ban. Abram Gerzevitch Suzkever reported at the Nuremberg Trials that the decree banning births had been issued 'at the end of December 1941.' He related that after his wife had given birth to a baby boy, he went to the hospital in the evening, after the Germans had left and found her in tears. After the Jewish physicians had received the order that Jewish women were not to give birth, they had hidden her child as well as other newborns. When members of the German commission returned to the hospital, however, they heard the newborns crying. Suskever continues: "She saw one German holding the baby and smearing something under its nose. Afterwards he threw it on the bed and laughed. When my wife picked up the child there was something black under its nose. When I arrived at the hospital I saw that my baby was dead. He was still warm."[523] This rarely mentioned method of killing children was also reported by Lazar Lagin in the Crimea,[524] although it is not known what substance was used to cause the infant death.

Rachel D. in the Vilna ghetto faced abortion, with her mother warning her that if she had an abortion she would never conceive later.[525] Nechama Tec tells the story of Dobka Freund-Waldhorn in the Vilna ghetto.[526] From a wealthy Jewish family, Dobka married Julek Fröhlich in 1939 against her parents' wishes as he was not Orthodox. The war and her family's objections to Julek pushed the couple away and they ended up in the Vilna ghetto. She was transferred to a nearby estate where she realized she was pregnant. Her husband and a Polish doctor at the estate pleaded with her to end the pregnancy but she loved her husband and wanted his child. When she was about seven months pregnant, at her husband's request, she went to the ghetto hospital to learn of her options. Although sympathetic, the ghetto doctor urged her to give birth and then dispose of the child. Under existing laws, unless she followed that advice both she and the baby would be killed. The doctor tried to induce delivery: "They gave me medicine to break the water but there was no birth."[527] She stayed in hospital for about a month and they tried 'all sorts of things' but nothing worked. Eventually she developed a high fever and a live baby girl was born. She was shown her beautiful baby who looked just like her husband and then they took her away. The doctor tried to console her that she was young and that she could have other babies…that this had to be… Her husband also told her they would have other babies. But he died in Klooga concentration camp later. After the war, she remarried and had two sons. Following the birth of her second son she dreamed of her first husband and that they would be reunited.

Birth was not easy, safe or pleasant in the ghettos. Macha Rolnikas, 14 years old, witnessed a horrifying scene from within the Vilna ghetto and recorded this in her diary, which she managed to save, in June 1941:

> A woman is crawling on all fours. Her hair is all tangled, her clothes dirty because of dragging herself along the ground. Covered with sweat, she stops every few minutes and like an animal, pricks up her ears: is danger awaiting her somewhere? She is losing her strength. With every passing moment she feels a bit weaker. A great pain seizes her, shoots pain into her breast. She knows that her last moments are approaching, she is going to give birth.
>
> All night long, rolled up like a ball, exhausted, full of pain, she felt the approaching delivery. She continues to advance on all fours. She flops down in the middle of the street, very close to the entrance [of the ghetto], crawls to the sidewalk so as not to get run over. She won't ever get up again. She turns over and over in pain, in a kind of convulsion, writhing like a snake. She startles and death comes to interrupt her anguish at the same moment as her little girl comes to this world of pain and shadows. She is found next to her and is taken into the ghetto and named Ghettala. Poor little girl.[528]

Births in Theresienstadt

Giving birth in Theresienstadt was also problematical. Rules regarding giving birth or terminating pregnancies changed from time to time. The

Theresienstadt daily bulletin of 21 August 1943 carried a formal notice instructing doctors to abort all pregnancies, otherwise both parents would be transported.[529] Anna (sometimes Anka) Bergman, a young Czech woman in Theresienstadt in 1943-4 reported that everybody lost their menstruation and thought they were pregnant but in her case, it came back after two months or so.[530] She, and another five couples, became pregnant. At first, they wanted to abort her baby, but she was too far gone and instead had to sign a document giving permission for euthanasia for the child. It never happened, however: her child was born and lived although it died two months later of pneumonia.[531] She became pregnant for the second time intentionally:

> When my first child died we decided to have another – this was after the invasion of June 1944 – we thought that if we returned to Prague after the war there would be nothing there for us and we would think twice about having a child to care for; but if I returned pregnant, or had a baby, that child would be *there*.[532] [Italics original]

Ruth Reiser who worked as a nurse in a hospital in Theresienstadt recalls many abortions being done.[533] Ruth Bondy records that the parents had to agree to an abortion in writing in Theresienstadt.[534] Dina Gottlieb-Babbitt was one of those who had an abortion in Theresienstadt: she said, "no-one wanted to have a baby there."[535] She testified that another woman had an abortion at eight months of pregnancy: the baby was born alive but the mother refused to care for it. Hana Muller Bruml recalls that Drs. Hahn and Pollak from Brno who were gynaecologists who worked in impossible situations and who tried to be as humane and kind as possible performed abortions in Theresienstadt very skillfully. Not all abortions were safe, however. Nobody talked about the abortions, but it was a necessity because it meant survival for the mother.[536] Ruth Elias, on the other hand, also became pregnant in Theresienstadt in about December 1943, but was unable to find a doctor skilled enough to be both willing and able to abort her baby. A new regulation changing the recent August 1943 directive to abort all pregnancies, now prohibited abortion in the ghetto. She made desperate appeals for help to one doctor after another, but none wanted to take the risk: "if the authorities had found out about a doctor performing an abortion, he would have been on the next transport east….All of them were afraid."[537] A further notice of 18 March 1944 warned room elders in Theresienstadt that they would be held accountable if a pregnancy was not reported. Shortly after her marriage in Theresienstadt in March 1945, Vera Schiff discovered she was pregnant. She had stopped menstruating three years before and was assured by her doctor (Dr Klein) that this would be unlikely to return even if normal diet and lifestyle were restored. Nevertheless, the slightly better rations she had recently been able to obtain were sufficient to restore her fertility. She was admitted to the 'endometritis ward' (a cover for the pregnancy termination ward) and the baby was aborted with little medication. She writes, "The excruciating pain of the procedure was nothing in comparison to the emotional anguish it caused me."[538]

As many as 230 births occurred in Theresienstadt, and about 350 abortions.[539] The babies were housed in a special nursery where their mothers were allowed to come and feed them once a day.[540] Ellen Eliel-Wallach was assigned to caring for and washing babies born in Theresienstadt: she reports that all were later sent to Auschwitz.[541] Theresienstadt also had some mothers who had been forced to leave their babies with their non-Jewish spouses. One of these, 'Fisherova', managed to have sufficient milk to nurse the weakest babies in the Theresienstadt nursery for almost two years, thus saving their lives.[542] Conversely, the presence of babies in Theresienstadt may have saved the lives of some women: Anna Lenji testified that in March 1945 she was sent to *Dresdner Kaserne*, a part of Theresienstadt that was for soldiers. There were babies there and she was entrusted with their care. With German precision, the same allocation of food was made to everyone, including the babies, so she was able to eat whatever the babies did not finish.[543]

In addition to aborting pregnancies, some babies were murdered at delivery. Vera Schiff reports that Dr Freund delivered a baby for a woman whose pregnancy had not been detected on arrival in Theresienstadt. He asked Vera to kill the baby but she was unable to do so. He grabbed her hand, pushed the syringe into it and with his hand wrapped around hers forced the needle into the baby's thigh. She writes, "It hardly took a second, but the memory of that moment has followed me my entire life."[544]

Births in Other Ghettos

Reports of Jewish births in other ghettos are also recorded. Adibna Szwajger delivered a baby in the Warsaw ghetto during the Yom Kippur bombings of 13 Sept 1939: "luckily it delivered itself."[545] Luba L. gave birth in a bathroom in the Warsaw ghetto in April 1941. A midwife put a handkerchief in her mouth during labour to stop her screaming. The baby lived and both she and Luba escaped to Czestochowa but were then caught by the Nazis and placed in a forced labour camp. She hid her child with other children in a bunker under her barracks but six months before liberation, the children were discovered and executed.[546]

In Łódź ghetto, in 1941, a woman was taken to the hospital in the night to have her baby. She died but the baby lived: an orphan with nobody to care for him except his paralyzed grandmother. Neither was able to wait in the long lines to submit a written application for help at the Department of Relief and nobody in the family was willing to take on the responsibility of caring for them in addition to caring for their own families.[547] Nellie A. also became pregnant in the Łódź ghetto: when she started to show she was hidden in a cold and dark cellar. She reports, "It was like being buried alive." Eventually a woman helped her bring her baby into the world. She was able to nurse him. She stayed in the cellar until liberation by the Russians.[548] Josef Zelkowicz in his surviving 345 page manuscript from the Łódź ghetto writes on 6 September 1942, of a Yiddish poet who wrote poems about Blimele, his 6 or 7 or 8 year old daughter. The poet's wife, Blimele's mother, had just given birth to a newborn, not yet named, when ghetto Jewish police took Blimele away. The father tried to comfort the weak and feverish mother by not telling her and by assuring her that they would not take the older child away….He hid his own fears from her until a few hours later they too, father, mother and newborn were also taken away.[549]

One (unnamed) participant at the 1983 Conference on 'Women Surviving the Holocaust' told of having given birth in a cellar in a Lithuanian ghetto (unspecified) in 1942. She traded her excess breastmilk for food and soap for her baby. She eventually developed a breast infection and had 'surgery' by a doctor, in secret, alone, with no anaesthetic, no medication and with a razor blade to make the incisions. Although she survived, she had to surrender her baby to the Germans when she was transported to the camps.[550]

A few stories have happy endings. A participant at the 1983 'Women Surviving the Holocaust' Conference reported that she met a woman who had decided to get pregnant and have her baby in the ghettos. She had said, "…I am going die anyway so I want to know the feeling what it means to be pregnant, what it means to give birth and what it means to be a mother; then I will die with everybody else."[551] The day after she gave birth, an '*aktion*' took place. Her family left her in the bunker where they had hidden her because 'in those days they believed that if you moved a woman who just gave birth, she would die immediately.' An SS German found her:

> He said, "What are you doing here with a son?" She said, "Please sir, come kill me tomorrow. Let me enjoy my son for a little while more." So he asked, "How old is your son?" She said, "I don't know, four hours, five hours." Well even in a Nazi you know, sometimes you can touch a human point. He said, "Well remain in bed." He called for a guard to be put around the house and he told them not to let anyone in. The family [hidden] in bunkers survived too. The whole family survived the war.[552]

In most cases, women wished to abort their pregnancies given the obstacles facing them. Abortion was life saving for some: Helen Stone, a young Polish Jewish woman, sent to the Kamionka Ghetto when Bedzin was made *Judenrein* (Jew free), got pregnant and if she had not had an abortion her child would have been three weeks old when she arrived in Auschwitz. Both she and the child would have been killed.[553] For many, having an abortion was a traumatic event: Irene S. recalled having a hazardous abortion in a ghetto basement while Rena G. noted that the termination of her pregnancy was her most difficult memory of the Holocaust.[554]

Occasionally some women wished to continue to create new life. Eva Wysbar, the Jewish wife of an 'Aryan' film director, had an increasing desire for children: "The more danger I saw.....the more strongly I wanted to fortify the family and to support the tiny being who already existed with a second one."[555] Likewise, Becker-Kohen gave birth to her baby sometime around Christmas 1937. Despite fears for her child, the pregnancy and anticipation period had been "the most solemn, most beautiful' of her life."[556]

Obstetric Services in Ghettos

In the Vilna, Shavli and Kovno ghettos in Lithuania the banning of births affected medical services significantly.[557] In all three, gynaecological services were largely dedicated to terminating pregnancies. In the Vilna ghetto, Dr Shadowsky[558] documented that in 1942, 429 women were hospitalized in the gynaecology department: of these 60 were for abortions. Because of the large number of pregnancies, the Vilna Health office helped with various forms of birth control: in the beginning, they evaded the decrees banning births by falsifying birth records, later they provided lectures by ghetto doctors on how to avoid pregnancy, and provided a counseling centre where women could obtain contraceptives made by a local physician. In Kovno ghetto, the medical staff informed people of the ban and warned women of the consequences of ignoring it. They also helped women who refused to comply by delivering their babies in secret. Dr Aharon Peretz noted that deliveries were performed in secrecy, mainly by specially trained midwives, while doctors were called only in cases of severe complications. In Shavli ghetto, Dr Josef Luntz, the senior gynaecologist in the ghetto, created a method of terminating pregnancies and speeding deliveries by mechanical means and using special medications. According to Dr Luntz, these methods worked: women did not become ill, and babies were born without harm. In contradiction, Dr Aharon Pick, a senior physician in the same ghetto, reported in his journal that many women submitted complaints to the ghetto court about severe complications they had suffered because of negligence in abortions. Some women testified about terrible conditions that they had had to suffer when giving birth or having abortions.

Deportation of Pregnant or New Mothers

As desperate as marriage, pregnancy and childbirth conditions were in the ghettos they became worse as Jews were rounded up and deported 'to the east' to concentration camps. Pregnant women and those giving birth or recently confined were not shown any sympathy and were sometimes targeted for particularly sadistic acts by the Nazis. For example, Abel Herzberg wrote:

> Deportation to Poland [from Westerbork, Netherlands] might at best be postponed – for a week, perhaps, or for a few weeks at most. Husbands were powerless to protect their wives, parents had to watch helplessly as their children were torn away from them forever. The sick, the blind, the hurt, the mentally disturbed, pregnant women, the dying, orphans, newborn babies – none was spared on the Tuesdays when the cattle-trucks were being loaded with human freight for Poland. Tuesdays, week in, week out, for two interminable years.[559]

T Van Reemst-de Vries relates a paradoxical tale from the Westerbork camp. After she gave birth to a preterm infant Commandant Gemmeker ordered an incubator from Groningen and sent for a Professor of Paediatrics to assist. She relates:

> Gemmeker frequently came to have a look, whenever I was tending the baby....To us this meant that the child would stay alive, and that they were fighting for its life.... We clung to this hope... And this little human did stay alive...One day he could drink from a bottle. And when he weighed five and a half pounds, he was even let out of the incubator into a cradle.....We thought that we had made it, that this proved that there was hope, that there was a future. But when Michael weighed six pounds, he was transported to a labor camp.[560]

A twelve-year-old boy described the destruction of a maternity ward in Łódź, shortly after his sister had given birth, during a German roundup:

> ...as the next group of patients was being escorted to a waiting truck we saw Esther....She was pale and frightened as she stood there in her pink nightgown...Soon the truck drove off and we knew we would never see our beloved Esther again... Suddenly two Germans appeared in an upper story window and pushed it open. Seconds later a

> naked baby was pushed over the ledge and it dropped to its death directly into the truck below...The SS seemed to enjoy this bloody escapade...The young SS butcher rolled up his rifle sleeve and caught the very next infant on his bayonet. The blood of the infant flowed down the knife onto the murderer's arm.[561]

Similarly, Esther Brunstein, a young Polish, Jewish woman in the Łódź Ghetto saw newborn babies being thrown out of second and third floor windows onto big lorries. She could see the blood spattering and the Germans laughing and joking.[562] On 5 November 1942, an SS man at Ciechanów, Poland, politely asked a Jewish woman to hand him her baby. When she complied, he smashed the baby to the street head first, killing it.[563] Hilberg also reports that during the dissolution of the ghettos, children were thrown on the floor and their heads trampled with boots.[564] Many report similar incidents.[565]

In Tata, Hungary, a young mother who had just given birth to twins and who was unable to move, was taken by the hands and feet and tossed into a truck. Her newborn babies were flung in after her.[566] Sick people, those who had recently undergone operations, women in childbirth and the insane were all crammed into the trucks. On 8 November 1944, Jews being rounded up from Hungary for deportation to the camps were marched from Budapest to Germany due to a lack of transport. Witnesses reported that, *en route*, they were put in barracks where newborn babies were bitten by lice and would die within hours. In one of these barracks, an SS officer placed a woman who was about to give birth on the floor under a big spotlight, saying he wanted to see how a human being comes into the world.[567]

In the Warsaw ghetto an eyewitness – Alexander Donat – reported:

> I saw a young mother run downstairs into the street to get milk for her baby. Her husband, who worked at the Ostbahn, had as usual left earlier that morning. She had not bothered to dress, but was in bathrobe and slippers. And empty milk bottle in hand, she was headed for a shop where, she knew, they sold milk under the counter. She walked into Operation Reinhard. The executioners demanded her Ausweis. 'Upstairs... Ostbahn.....work certificate. I'll bring it right away.'
>
> 'We've heard that one before. Have you got an Ausweis with you, or haven't you?'
>
> She was dragged protesting to the wagon, scarcely able to realize what was happening. 'But my baby is all alone. Milk...' she protested. 'My Ausweis is upstairs.'

> Then, for the first time, she really looked at the men who were holding her and she saw where she was being dragged: to the gaping entrance at the back of a high-boarded wagon with victims already jammed into it. With all her young mother's strength she wrenched herself free, and then two, and four, policemen fell on her, hitting her, smashing her to the ground, picking her up again, and tossing her into the wagon like a sack.[568]

Some mothers tried to hide from roundups: Edyta Klein-Smith: a Polish, Jewish child in the Warsaw ghetto, in 1942, remembered that she and her stepfather ran into a building and hid in a small hiding place together with a woman with a baby. The Germans started banging on the doors and shooting and the baby started to cry. The mother smothered the baby.[569] Lucille Eichengreen reported that her roommates Eta and Julek hid their baby Rachel in a drawer during a roundup: the baby suffocated.[570] Matylda Gelenter reported a gruesome story of Mrs Greenberg in Katowice:

> The Ukrainians and Germans who had broken into her house found her giving birth... she was taken from her home in a nightshirt and dragged into the square in front of the town hall...when the birth pangs started, she was dragged onto a dumpster in the yard of the town hall with a crowd of Ukrainians present, who cracked jokes and jeered and watched the pain of childbirth and she gave birth to a child. The child was immediately torn from her arms with its umbilical cord and thrown – It was trampled by the crowd and she was stood on her feet as blood poured out of her with bleeding bits hanging and she stood that way for a few hours by the wall of the town hall, afterwards she went with all the others to the train station where they loaded her into a carriage in a train to Belzec.[571]

Desperate mothers would leave their children on the doorstep of a non-Jewish home or institution in the hope that somebody would be kind enough to take them into care or look after them.[572] Michelle Donet testified that when her family was moved to the ghetto in Otwock, Poland, her mother left her in the middle of the street outside the ghetto thinking that "with G-d's will, at least this is the last hope for me to survive, not to stay with her...I was just few years old child, so I have been picked up."[573] She was placed in orphanages and cared for by nuns, ensuring her survival. In Grodno, a heartbroken Mrs Kovitzka also left her child near a Christian orphanage, but this child was not so fortunate as to survive.[574] In Berlin, Jewish mothers ordered to assemble for deportation, left their infants at a Catholic hospital in the hope that the babies, at least, would be spared.[575] Many parents did not know where the resistance had placed their child. "Many of those who hid children did not even know they were Jewish. Few of the parents could keep in touch with their children."[576]

At the railroad station in Berlin, victims were herded onto vans and into trains. Some babies were in cardboard suitcases because the Gestapo had confiscated their carriages as a 'luxury.'[577] Further tragedies awaited those pregnant women who were packed into deportation trucks or trains. Hubert Pfloch a young Austrian draftee whose train was just behind a transport to Treblinka watched as it was loaded and reported later: "mother jumps down with her baby and calmly looks into a pointing gun barrel – a moment later we hear the guard who shot them boast….that he "managed to do them both with one shot through both their heads."[578] Franciszek Zabecki a Polish railway worker at Treblinka railway station "saw a pregnant Jewish woman who had managed to break away from the train seek sanctuary in [Willi] Klinzman's [a German railwayman] quarters. But the Germans were without charity: Klinzman and an SS man who was with him killed her. They kicked her to death."[579] Other alternatives were also tried: On the eve of an *Aktion* Jewish girls who wanted to save their lives offered themselves to policemen. As a rule, women were used during the night and killed in the morning.[580] Some mothers threw their babies out of the trains on the way to the camps. This was an ultimate endeavour to save the child.[581] Women also gave birth while on the trains,[582] and some tossed their babies from a window in the hope of saving them.[583]

Remarkably, love occasionally managed to flourish even under such disastrous conditions. Rudolf Vrba reports that:

> Monsignor Tiso, puppet President of Slovakia, Quisling Extraordinary had…promised that families would never be separated when they were deported. The result was a rash of teenage marriages throughout the country as those in love strived to stay together…
>
> A young couple, just married, had to have a bridal suite; and this was not easy because the wagon was packed so tightly that only a few could lie down to sleep at a time while the rest stood.
>
> Still we managed somehow. We shifted the luggage. We reorganized ourselves. Though the Tomasovs protested vigorously, we contrived to give them very special sleeping accommodation and as much privacy as possible.[584]

Pregnancy, Abortion and Childbirth While in Hiding

Some women and men chose to go into hiding rather than be confined to ghettos. Some women became pregnant during this time, with ensuing difficulties. One of these was obtaining or having an abortion. Some, like Trees Soetendorp, had an abortion before going into hiding in Amsterdam, in May 1943 as she thought it would have been impossible to have a baby while hidden.[585] Zwia Rechtman-Schwartz,[586] hiding as a gentile in the countryside, heard of her mother's deportation and execution. Her mother had been arrested in the office of a Polish gynaecologist to whom she had turned for help. Zwia suspects that the doctor betrayed her mother when she asked him to abort her fetus.

Adibna Szwajger became pregnant while hiding in Warsaw. A 'trusted' doctor did an abortion for her for a large sum of money. "It was not nice at all. And the very idea was not nice either. The doctor was skillful but terribly vulgar. Obviously he did the operation without anaesthetic, and it was a terrible experience for me…"[587] She also reports:

> taking three other young girls for the same operation each of whom might, as a consequence, never be able to have children. Especially as I couldn't guarantee them anything except the operation itself. There were no facilities for convalescence. … I had to be present at every operation. I had to hold the girls by the hand and make sure they didn't scream….He blackmailed me saying that he knew who I was bringing and raised his fees accordingly, and I blackmailed him with the fact that he was carrying out illegal operations. It was disgusting![588]

Strange coincidences also occurred, for example, at the end of November 1942 an abortion was performed on a Jewish woman in hiding, by a Jewish doctor passing for a gentile, in a hospital in Cracow, Poland.[589]

Jews in hiding avoided medical personnel or hospitalization whenever possible.[590] Kaplan relates the story of a couple in Berlin who gave birth in hiding with only her lover to assist her. Similarly, Ruth Abrahams, in hiding in Germany, was also attended by her husband: a doctor only arrived as the head was crowning and then fled before the afterbirth emerged as an air raid warning sounded.

Margot Dränger married Jurek in Kraków ghetto.[591] At the end of 1943, the couple was hiding in a bunker on a farm in Bochnia. When she felt the baby's movements, the couple collected a few rags, cotton and scissors. A few months later, her labour began. She kept silent through the labour and her husband helped deliver the baby and cut the cord with scissors. It was a little girl, but the infant lived only a few hours.

She believes it was because of a poorly tied umbilical cord. Two days after the birth the farm where they were hiding was raided by the Polish police and they were asked to leave. Rhodea Shandler, a Dutch Jewish woman, also reports giving birth while hiding on a farm. Following this, she and her husband were not fed as well as before and they were moved to the barn rather than being allowed to stay in the house: a baby in hiding was dangerous. She gave birth, assisted by a nurse (who was also in hiding in the house), to a breech-positioned baby girl, who lived despite their poor surroundings. Rhodea, however, developed severe post-partum depression.[592] Others fared better: Cyla Menkes-Fast gave birth to a baby in the fall of 1941. She could not part with her child and managed to stay hidden on farms in Poland during the war, together with her child. She reports "At dangerous times my child would distract a murderer's attention from me to herself. Occasionally, too, the compassion people felt for her made them invite us both into their homes during our horrible wanderings."[593] Nina Mogilevskaya,[594] wife of a welder in Ukraine, was pregnant and being hidden by her husband's relatives. She did not want to endanger those who were hiding her if her child cried so she left in the night and took to the road. Desperate, she was about to throw herself and the baby under a train when she was told of a sugar beet farm where she was able to work, keeping the baby with her. She could not take time to feed her baby and it died by her side although she survived.

Wiktoria Balul, and her husband Wincenty, a devout elderly Polish, Christian couple (later honoured as 'Righteous Among Nations' by Yad Vashem) hid a Jewish couple, Moshe and Chawiwa Flechtman, and another 13-year-old Jewish boy, in the home of her son Antoni. The couple provided those in hiding with food from Polish farmers outside the city. Chawiawa Flechtman was pregnant and after the baby was born, the Baluls made sure that it was safely hidden. All four of those in hiding survived.[595]

A father of a newborn daughter, his fourth, while in hiding, recorded another touching story of survival as a letter to his baby. Separated from his wife and newborn, who were also being hidden, he expressed his emotions by writing a diary which he began on the day of her birth (14 March 1943) and then written intermittently over the next couple of weeks.[596] A Dutch woman 'juffrouw Liesje' hid Leo Markus and his wife Hilde in Holland. Their three older daughters Fran (11), Fien (7) and Judith (almost 5), were also hidden but apart from them. Juffrouw Liesje managed to take Hilde to a safe place for her confinement and Leo, unable to visit her or the newborn often, wrote a letter/diary for his newborn in case she would live and they, her parents, and her sisters, did not. The document introduced the members of the family to the little girl while at the same time documenting ongoing events of the war as well as her parents' brave optimism throughout their period of hardship. At four weeks old, the baby, Leonie, was left on the doorstep of a Dutch doctor and his wife, Dr and

Mrs Aalders, who registered her and managed to avoid the Nazi ruling that all foundlings should be considered as Jewish and handed over to them. Ultimately, all the family survived and were reunited in 1945 although the baby, Leonie, lived only until 1950 when she died suddenly of meningitis. The father's document remained in the family's hands.

Women rather than men provide most of the memoirs and testimonies reporting reproductive life events during the Nazi era.[597] The moving account by Leo Markus, separated from his wife and newborn while in hiding, as well as comments by the occasional male survivor such as Ernie Weiss, who reflected on the impact of his mother's sometimes traumatic childbearing experiences, in his presence, on the birth and illnesses of his own family later,[598] are rare. Men's perceptions regarding birth experiences is an aspect of the Holocaust that has not been (and might never be) thoroughly explored.

Women in hiding faced enormous challenges when facing menstruation, childbirth and infant care.[599] The full extent of their difficulties – ignorance, being alone, pain, concealing materials, illness, and the decision to let the baby live or not – is portrayed in the story of Frania who gave birth in hiding in Poland assisted by her husband Israel and her friend Zofia:

> … they put flashlights into the straw, and they tied my mouth with a towel, I shouldn't be able to yell. And the child got born, and I heard crying. So Israel got old that night, because even today, if he sees blood, he could faint – but what could he do? After the baby was born comes the afterbirth, so he didn't even know what it is. Naturally we were very naïve – what do you think, Poland is like here? – children now know everything. Israel said to me, 'Frania, it's still coming something.' So I said 'If it's coming, take. What do I know?' And the child was born, but Israel didn't know how to cut the cord. I think Zofia knew, but she didn't want to do it. I'm sure she knew, because when she had Maniek, she gave birth to him in the field, and she did everything herself. Well she said she doesn't know what to do. Israel really didn't know what to do….Anyway the child was overcome with blood, because they didn't cut the cord, so naturally the child died, and Zofia buried it.
>
> In the meantime I was very sick, because when Israel saw a little head, he had to pull fast, so he tore me probably in six places – and how can you heal this? And this was burning and hurting. Zofia said there was a herb you brew like tea, and from this it's good to make compresses. First of all I was bleeding a terrible amount. All right, I had a lot of absorbent cotton, that was good, but later you

> had to bury it somewhere. Zofia did it, and Israel, they went down at night, and buried it outside. But this torn place was burning, terrible. Terrible aches. You see, I just couldn't take it. Zofia brewed that tea in the house, and she brought it up. Israel put compresses on all the time, to heal. So it healed like this and it was never sewn together, you understand. When I came to Canada years after, the doctor in Montreal said he doesn't have to do anything, it's OK...
>
> After three, four days, the milk starts to get into your breasts. ....on the right side, it went away by itself, but on the left side......and I had there the milk .....I was so sick, that I was already dying......started to get boils [abscesses]...and the pains were so terrible I would bite my finger through to blood. I couldn't cry, I couldn't yell, I couldn't scream. And this was going on like this for three months. ...And after that, all these boils burst, and the pus was just running out.[600]

Perhaps one of the most awful hiding places in which a woman gave birth was the sewers of Lvov. Leopold Socha, had been a thief prior to the war and had used the sewers as a hiding place for his stolen goods. During the war, he and his fellow sewer worker, Stefan Wroblewski, hid twenty Jews in one of these underground hiding places managing to feed them every day by entering different manholes to reach them without arousing suspicion. One of the people sheltered by Socha was a pregnant woman, Weinbergowa. While she survived childbirth, her baby did not and died shortly after birth. Ten of Socha's group survived the war by remaining in the sewers. Yad Vashem later honoured Socha as a 'Righteous Among Nations.'[601]

One young woman, her husband and two children hid in the woods for months.[602] She was holding one child by the hand with another clutched to her breast when a stray bullet killed the infant in her arms, saving her. Unable to bury the infant in the frozen winter ground they had to leave it lying on the ground. As a survivor she was unable to leave her memories of this behind, a state described by William Niederland,[603] as '*Seelenmord*' or the death of a soul – the state you are reduced to when you can no longer escape from the outrage committed to your psyche. This, surely, describes the experience of many.

Babies in Hiding

In Holland, midwives delivered babies for women in hiding and tried to place them in foster families. This was most important as a crying infant in a walled-up bunker in a house, which might hold a number of people, would betray them all, and such babies were often killed, accidentally or deliberately, by their own parents by smothering or sedative overdose.[604] Jerry Koenig, a Polish Jew in hiding, related that two women were pregnant in the group with which he was hiding. One gave birth to a baby that died at birth. The second gave birth a few days later. The baby however cried, endangering the lives of the 11 people in hiding:

> Everyone realized it was impossible to keep the baby in the shelter. The conclusion was that the baby had to die. They made a potion of poppies – opium – which the mother had to spoon-feed to her baby. The baby simply dozed off and died, never regaining consciousness. The whole thing had a tremendously traumatic effect on everyone in the shelter.[605]

Whether to smother a child while in hiding in order to save the lives of others became a debated issue especially for religious Jews. Rabbi Shimon Efrati (formerly rabbi of Bessarabia and deported to Siberia during the war) was appointed as rabbi of the surviving community of Warsaw. While there, he was asked whether a Jew in hiding from the Germans in a ghetto bunker must pay respect for having inadvertently smothered a crying infant to avoid detection. His *responsum*, published in 1961, concluded that *Halakhah* (Jewish law) does not require that the infant be killed: rather it is optional. If one chooses to die rather than the infant be killed, they shall be called holy. However, the individual who did inadvertently suffocate the child should not have a bad conscience for he acted lawfully to save Jewish lives. Rabbi Efrati was probably influenced by the fact that his own brother had been hiding in a bunker during such a search when a baby burst out crying. The rabbi then had ordered that no one should risk harming the child and, as a result, all twenty people were discovered and murdered by the Nazis.[606]

Pregnancy and Childbirth in Forced Labour Camps

Jews were generally confined to ghettos before being transferred to concentration camps. Some were selected to work as labourers both in Germany and in other parts of the Reich. The number of forced labourers – Jews and non-Jews – in the Third Reich is unknown with estimates ranging from 8-12 million, mostly drawn from eastern Europe.[607]

Skarżysko-Kamienna munitions factory was taken over from Poles 1939 and became a forced labour camp managed by the HASAG company (Hugo Schneider AG of Leipzig).[608] About 12,000 Jews were sent there from

1942 of whom about 6,000 died. It had three units, each with its associated camp. One of these had underwater mines filled with picric acid that turned the workers' skin, hair and nails a yellowish-red colour: life expectancy was three months. Work conditions in the other two camps were not quite as bad but out of an estimated 30,000 labourers, 23,000 perished from starvation and diseases, selections and executions.[609] Skarżysko-Kamienna was particularly well noted for its sexual abuse of women prisoners: some women became pregnant. Abortions were reportedly done by a doctor from the nearby town and babies born were immediately taken from their mothers.[610] Executions of pregnant women ceased in 1944 but birth meant the immediate death of the baby. Many testimonies relate finding the bodies of infants in carts of dead bodies, the latrine or under a pallet.[611]

Births occurred in other forced labour camps as well. One of the participants at the 1983 'Women Surviving the Holocaust Conference' recalls a pregnant woman who gave birth without anything to help her in their (unspecified) labour camp. She had placed the child by a window, purposely, to let it die as the woman would otherwise have been killed. They bribed a boy with some bread to bury the child.[612] Phyllis Young, also recalled a baby being born in Walzel labour camp in Czechoslovakia.[613] Ada, a factory worker, was six months pregnant in January 1944. Following a rumour that the Jews would be sent to Auschwitz, she paid '$1,200' to a Polish doctor to come to the factory (unspecified) and to abort her by Caesarean section. On 20 January 1944, she was sent to Auschwitz: as she expressed it 'her convalescent home'.[614] Anna Bergman, a young Czech woman, found herself in a forced labour camp when she was five months pregnant: "a pregnant skeleton with a baby moving inside me."[615] She could not be sent to Auschwitz as the Germans had already evacuated it on 18 January 1945. Instead, she was given lighter work: sweeping the three stories of the factory for 14 hours a day. In Kaiserwald concentration camp near Riga, Latvia, Jews and others were forced to work in factories producing electrical goods. Gertrude Schneider related that many women came to the camp pregnant: the Germans killed their children by injection at birth. She reported:

> And suddenly there were big signs in the ghetto saying that sex is henceforth forbidden. I swear, Verboten, [forbidden] sexual intercourse. It is not very funny. On the other hand, it is funny because we lived in families. How are you going to control this? You can't. So people made lots and lots of jokes about it. The famous gallows humour came up.[616]

In response, the Jewish doctor and his wife opened up a small abortion clinic where a gynaecologist performed the procedure. The girls would go there for a few days under the pretense of being sick. Pretty soon this became known as 'appendicitis with little feet' although as Schneider remarks, this must have been the most crushing thing for many of them.

Pregnancy and Childbirth Among Partisans

Nechama Tec[617] reports that partisans did not want babies, and pregnancy, whether terminated or completed, meant facing painful and difficult choices. In the Bielski *otriad* (a Jewish partisan group in Poland) abortions were common and were performed in difficult circumstances. Dr Hirsch, the camp physician performed abortions for women from this group as well as for the surrounding Soviet partisan units. Nothing happened to those who did give birth and in the Bielski *otriad* there were 2-3 babies born. Many of the women who were sexually active had one or two abortions. One died. After the war, some of these women had trouble becoming pregnant and many were bitter about this decades later, blaming the men for not practicing birth control. "I paid with my body; did I need pregnancies too? It depended on him, not on me."[618]

Not all attempted abortions were successful: Szwajger reports trying to abort a pregnancy of a partisan woman without success. A second attempt by a colleague also failed and the woman was eventually taken to the nearest city where she gave birth in a makeshift delivery room in a cellar.[619] On the other hand, Eva Kracowski, a partisan, reported to Tec, that she had no sexual drive during the war. For a year, she stopped menstruating and felt that something within her had died.[620]

Some women joined the partisans in advanced pregnancy. If this happened, the newborns were often killed. Bronka K. assisted a woman who gave birth in a partisan camp. A man smashed the baby's head with a piece of wood: when it continued to cry he strangled it and wrapped it in a potato sack. Several days later, the woman's placenta delivered leaving the mother with an infectious fever.[621] In another partisan group, no woman was supposed to keep her baby. The commander of the group, Heinia Dobrowski, was very strict about this rule, but when she herself became pregnant, she ignored the rule, gave birth and kept the baby. The baby, her lover and she all survived.[622] Not all were so fortunate: Anda Luft, a Jewish co-leader of a partisan group gave birth to a baby girl on 11 July 1943. In November 1943, German police attacked the group. She fought with her baby strapped to her back up until the last moment when both she and her baby, riddled with bullets, fell.[623]

Birth in Prisons

Dr Edith Kramer-Freund was a doctor in Auschwitz and Theresienstadt.[624] She reports that, while being held for a short period in a Gestapo women's prison in Berlin, she was called to assist a young Ukrainian woman prisoner give birth on the dirty floor. As a reward, she received half a loaf of bread.[625] Olga Benário-Prestes was a Jewish,

German member of the Communist party who gave birth to a daughter in a Berlin prison (Moabit) for women on Barnimstrasse in 1936. She was told that she could keep her baby as long as she had milk for it and as soon as the child was weaned, it would be placed in an orphanage. According to Kina Haag[626] this was their idea of a joke as she was fed so little ensuring that her milk supply would fail. The SS kept threatening her, demanding proof of her milk. The child was rescued by a family member and reunited with the father after the war. Olga was gassed at the Bernberg euthanasia centre in March 1942.[627]

Pregnancy as Resistance?

While a full discussion of resistance during the Holocaust is beyond the scope of this book, the question of pregnancy as a form of resistance can be considered. Von Kellenbach, for example, suggests that Jewish women who chose to become pregnant and to carry their pregnancy to term were actively resisting the Nazi regime.[628] Peled, however, disagrees strongly arguing that:

> Pregnancy and childbirth are such personal and intimate experiences for women, and the price of being pregnant or having a baby in the Holocaust was so high (it usually resulted in the murder of both mother and baby) that resistance or politics or any other external agenda is irrelevant.[629]

As was hotly debated during a 1968 conference on Jewish resistance[630] almost every action taken by a person, such as simply breathing, stealing food to live despite the Germans' attempts to exterminate them, could be seen as resistance. Peled asks, were women who became pregnant by accident unintentionally resisting? Was choosing to abort a pregnancy, in order to live, resistance? Or was carrying the baby to term resistance?[631] Some, like Ruth Elias, could not find someone willing to abort her pregnancy: is this resistance? It is likely that while a few women might have deliberately embarked on pregnancy as a form of resistance, most were simply victims of circumstance and were guided in their actions to either continue or terminate their pregnancies, by factors including hope, lack of alternatives, ignorance, external pressure or desperation.

The issue of whether pregnant women in ghettos, hiding, forests or elsewhere, should be viewed as resisters is closely allied to the question of whether they were heroes or victims. As Sara Horowitz notes, some writers, like Inbar,[632] seek to present women as heroes, focusing on their ability to cope with the hardships they experienced, while others concentrate on exposing the atrocities they, as victims, experienced.[633]

In narratives of atrocity, pregnancy and motherhood leave women particularly susceptible to Nazi cruelty while in narratives of heroism these experiences allow women to be perceived as resistors. As heroes, women are portrayed as resisting Nazi terrors by persisting with pregnancies, saving a newborn child, or hiding a Jewish baby with strangers. Such stories idealize motherhood and reflect a feeling of optimism as they have potentially happy endings – in reality a rare outcome of the Nazi era. They are easier to listen to and stories which the listener wants to hear.[634] In contrast, in narratives of atrocity, the woman is not able to save her baby. The fetus may be aborted, the infant stillborn or killed soon after birth. Mothers may kill their babies themselves while in hiding, to preserve their own or other's lives. These stories contradict the symbol of hope that pregnancy usually conveys and reinforce the tragic and overwhelming losses that were experienced.[635]

For most women, pregnancy brought with it overwhelming concerns for their own, their baby's and their family's lives. It forced difficult moral dilemmas onto those caring for them including the doctors in ghettos or camps, who chose to deliver them, induce abortion or commit infanticide. It also rendered women susceptible to sadistic acts of violence perpetrated by the Nazis. While their condition might have given hope (albeit false) to their ghetto or prisoner companions, it was by no means a heroic or – probably in most cases – a deliberate act.

Concentration Camps

Pregnant women faced particularly difficult experiences when transferred to concentration camps. They were specifically targeted for extermination, as they threatened the creation of the 'Master Race' by their ability to procreate those deemed to be less 'valuable'[636] who might later seek revenge.

A multitude of institutions of differing origins and purposes are incorporated into the category of Nazi camps. The United States Holocaust Memorial Museum[637] website notes that over 42,000 sites have been identified. These include slave labour camps, Jewish ghettos, concentration camps, prisoner-of-war camps, brothels and other camps used for such purposes as euthanizing victims, performing forced abortions, 'Germanizing' prisoners, or transporting victims to killing centres.[638] The spread of sub-camps became so prolific that there was hardly a town or community of even a modest size in the Reich or in the occupied territories that did not have a concentration or some form of labour camp in or near it.[639] The two largest camps to which Jewish women were sent were Ravensbrück (opened on 15 May 1939) and Auschwitz-Birkenau (opened on 26 May 1940). Jewish women (and men) were the minority – estimated at 20% [640] – in Ravensbrück. Unlike Ravensbrück, about half of Auschwitz' inmates were Jews.[641]

Conditions in Camps

Conditions in the camps were appalling, particularly for Jews, who were treated far worse than animals. While utter starvation was the norm, in Buchenwald for example, even as late as 1944, the bears, birds and apes in the falconry received meat every day taken from the prisoners' rations: "the bears received honey and marmalade, the monkeys mashed potatoes with milk, oatmeal, zwieback, white bread, etc. Even in times of greatest shortages in the camp, the falconry was maintained to its fullest extent while the prisoners received only one sixth of a loaf of bread a day and cooked rutabagas for lunch. The resulting hunger and deprivation caused fights to the death over food."[642] Cannibalism was reported by many in different camps.[643] According to Yehuda Bacon, a prisoner in Auschwitz, Mauthausen and Günskirchen, it seemed natural. A simple friend from a village, who had eaten human flesh told him; "Yehuda, you won't believe my luck. I went into the *lanzarett* (sick bay/hospital) just after the bombing raid, and it was unguarded, and there was a dead body in there, and I managed to cut off some thigh where there was most meat before the others came up and tore up the rest between them."[644] Cannibalism was not always voluntary: in Neuengamme in November 1944, Robert Darnau found a human jawbone in his soup.[645] The kitchen Kapo had agreed to sell the meat from the kitchen and to feed the prisoners on corpses. These human rights abuses, reflected in the starvation of prisoners, were matched by conditions relating not only to pregnancy, birth and sexuality, but to hygiene, accommodation, work, psychological manipulation and abuse, punishment, torture, and ultimately extermination.

On Arrival in Camps

Pregnant Jewish women were generally sent to their deaths immediately on arrival in concentration camps, unless they became the subjects of heinous 'medical' experiments. This was in accordance with a decree of 6 May 1943: *Erlass zum Verbot der Einweisung schwangerer Häftlinge in die Frauenkonzentrationslager Ravensbrück bzw. in die Frauenabteilungen der Konzentrationslager Auschwitz und Lublin* [Decree forbidding the admission of pregnant inmates into the women's concentration camp Ravensbrück or the women's section of the concentration camps Auschwitz and Lublin[Majdanek]].[646]

Unlike Jewish men, Jewish women were killed not only because they were Jews but also because they were able to reproduce another generation to replace those being exterminated by the Germans or able to take revenge.[647] Heinrich Himmler offered special justification for the killing of women (no justification was needed for the killing of men):

> We came to the question: what about the women and children? I have decided to find a clear solution here too. In fact I did not regard myself as justified in exterminating men – let us say killing them or having them killed – while letting avengers in the shape of the children…grow up. The difficult decision had to be taken to make this people disappear from the face of the earth.[648]

On arrival in Auschwitz, mothers who stayed with their children under the age of 14, or whose pregnancies were obvious, were sent directly to the gas chambers, although a few were sent to the experimental block

– mainly Block 10.[649] Liana Millu confirms this: one woman in her block, whose daughter had been ready to give birth on arrival in Birkenau, had been sent directly to the gas chambers. Her mother had virtually lost her mind in consequence.[650] Children were consigned to the fire either alive or following gassing.[651] Meir Sosnowicz, himself a child at the time, recalled that when mothers did not want to be separated from their children the SS simply snatched the children from the mothers and smashed them against the wall so that their brains spilled out.[652] Stanislawa Mlodkowska-Bielawska, Krystyna Cryz-Wilgat, Stanislaw Michalik and Pelagia Mackowska, testified that if women arrived in Ravensbrück in early pregnancy, and were not killed on arrival, doctors would kill the fetus and sterilize the mother: those arriving in later stages of pregnancy would be induced and if the child was born alive a German prisoner named Gerda would drown it in a bucket of water.[653] In Treblinka, even a German shepherd dog that licked the face of a Jewish baby was savagely beaten by his SS master before he trampled the baby to death.[654] In this camp also, guards shot and killed a Jewish woman and her child when she was found hiding the child under a bedsheet that she was wearing.[655]

Josef Mengele provided his own explanation for the killing of Jewish mothers and babies on arrival:

> When a Jewish child is born, or a woman comes to camp with a child already...I don't know what to do with the child. I can't set the child free because there are no longer any Jews who live in freedom. I can't let the child stay in the camp because there are no facilities...that would enable the child to develop normally. It would not be humanitarian to send a child to the ovens without permitting the mother to be there to witness the child's death. That is why I send the mother and child to the gas ovens together.[656]

Testimonies reveal that Jewish prisoners from the 'Canada commando' – where the belongings of those sent to the gas chambers were sorted – also met the arriving trains and tried to warn mothers to give their children to older women to save the mother's life, or to adjust the ages of younger children upwards or older women downwards to avoid their selection for immediate gassing.[657] Most mothers, however, chose to go with their children.[658] One mother who helped her friends look healthy by using rouge on their cheeks but did not do so for herself as she chose to go with her two children. Another woman hid from her child while the SS guard walked with the child seeking the mother. The German became outraged and sent the child to its death anyway, leaving the mother distraught.[659]

The testimony of Hadassah Becker regarding the separation of mothers and the killing of their babies on arrival at Majdanek reveals the emotional horror of the sadistic procedure followed. She reported:

> ...the Jewish mothers wouldn't give up their babies, so the beating and the clubbing of the babies and the Jewish mothers was a very major occupation of these guards and they became very bestial, very bestial...[SS] Frau von Orlov went to the Lagerkommandant and said she could do the job better... she... organized Polish and Russian workers dressed them as nannies and got beautifully decorated perambulators...So she came among the women ... and said, 'Only babies who cannot walk are eligible for our nursery...' So when the mothers saw how beautifully this was arranged they tried to smuggle kids who could walk already...older babies...Then she said, 'Look this is such an expensive and beautiful nursery, you have to pay for it. So with a diaper and with the formula and with whatever you need for the baby, you must also put your valuables so we can pay for it...' And she would collect two babies to a perambulator ... she would take these perambulators...across the road ...[to] a laundry... up above there was a disinfection area. ...she would take these babies up to the disinfection area, ...undress them, and put them in and kill them and she would throw the white baby shoes, ... right out the window, and as we came out from the sauna, ... we saw a pile of white baby shoes. Now the mothers of these babies deluded themselves for a long time that this couldn't possibly be....they're probably giving them other shoes. Since they can't walk, maybe they don't want to use the shoes...
>
> Later Becker had an opportunity to see a suitcase filled with jewels that [Orlov] had stolen from the Jewish babies under her bed... Orlov came away from the war a very wealthy woman and she got herself legal representation and nobody could touch her.[660]

In similar vein, a number of writers comment on the painful sight of hundreds of baby carriages without babies.[661] Roth cites Danuta Czech who writes:

> Empty children's strollers are taken away from the storerooms of the personal effects camp, known as 'Canada', which is located behind Camp B-IIf between crematoriums III and IV. The strollers are pushed in rows

> of five along the path from the crematoriums to the train station: the removal takes an hour.[662]

For some, being allowed to take a baby carriage on the transport to the camps was a sign of hope. For Egon Redlich, in Theresienstadt, sending the child and leaving the pram meant death. He was authorized to take the pram along and for him this allowed for optimism: "Why else would they permit us to take a baby carriage along?"[663] Both Redlich and his infant son Dan were murdered on arrival.

Those Sent Directly to the Gas Chambers

Mothers who suspected or knew that they were going to their deaths were reported to still manage to play with their children and talk to them lovingly despite their own terror.[664] Others gave their breasts to their babies to keep them from crying.[665] Vrba testified that the SS guards ensured that no space would be left in the gas chambers by firing a few shots at the entrance. 'This encouraged those already inside to press away from the doors and more victims were ushered in. Then babies and very small children were tossed onto the heads of the adults and the doors were closed and sealed.'[666]

Following a gassing, the corpses were hosed down both to neutralize the gas crystals still lying around but also to clean the dead bodies:[667] "Almost all of them were wet with sweat and urine, filthy with blood and excrement, while the legs of women were streaked with menstrual blood... Among them lay the bodies of pregnant women, some of whom had expressed the head of their baby just before they died."[668] Sometimes when the doors were opened, some people were still alive:

> Once, to the horror of the men of the Sonderkommando, they found a tiny baby alive when all others were already dead. It lay sucking its dead mother's breast and probably sucked all the time and so had not inhaled the deadly fumes. SS man Wagner, who was there, was furious and picking up the little baby, threw it into the blazing oven.[669]

Venezia, a *Sonderkommando* worker, similarly reports finding a barely two-month-old baby still clinging to her mother's breast and vainly trying to suckle. He took the baby and brought it out of the gas chamber. As he reports "as soon as the guard saw the baby, he didn't seem at all displeased at having a little baby to kill. He fired a shot and that little girl who had miraculously survived the gas was dead. Nobody could survive."[670]

Rudolf Höss, (Commandant of Auschwitz) reported that many of the women tried to hide their babies among the piles of clothing before going into the gas chambers/showers. "The men of the *Sonderkommando* were particularly on the lookout for this, and would speak words of encouragement to the woman until they had persuaded her to take the child with her. The women believed that the disinfectant would be bad for their smaller children, hence their efforts to conceal them."[671] Some mothers, however, succeeded in hiding their babies. "Sometimes we would open a suitcase in 'Canada' and find a baby inside, just barely alive. We never knew what to do. A mother had tried desperately to give her child a chance at life. We agonized but we could never conceal them. The Kapos came."[672]

Pregnant Women Admitted to Auschwitz-Birkenau

Women admitted to Auschwitz-Birkenau, had to undress and the SS inspected their breasts and their bellies for signs of pregnancy.[673] As Sima Vaisman, a Jewish doctor in Auschwitz testified, women with stretch marks on their bellies were at risk of being sent to the gas chambers.[674] Judith Jagudah – a twin in Auschwitz – reports that so were those who were overweight and had bellies that were mistaken for pregnancy.[675] SS doctors asked pregnant women to identify themselves with promises of clean housing and added food while they await birth.[676] As Gisella Perl, a doctor in Auschwitz-Birkenau, testified in 1948:

> one of the SS chiefs would address the women, encouraging the pregnant ones to step forward, because they would be taken to another camp where living conditions were better. He also promised them double bread rations so as to be strong and healthy when the hour of delivery came. Group after group of pregnant women left Camp C. Even I was naïve enough, at that time, to believe the Germans, until one day I happened to have an errand near the crematories and saw with my own eyes what was being done to these women.
>
> They were surrounded by a group of SS men and women, who amused these helpless creatures by giving them a taste of hell, after which death was a welcome friend. They were beaten with clubs and whips, torn by dogs, dragged around by the hair and kicked in the stomach with heavy German boots. Then, when they collapsed, they were thrown into the crematory – alive.[677]

Perl was so horrified that she determined to save pregnant women by helping them to abort their pregnancies. "I ran back to camp and going from block to block told the women what I had seen. Never again was anyone to betray their condition." As she wrote:

> First I took the ninth-month pregnancies, I accelerated the birth by the rupture of membranes, and usually within one or two days spontaneous birth took place without further intervention. Or I produced dilatation with my fingers, inverted the embryo and this brought it to life...After the child had been delivered, I quickly bandaged the mother's abdomen and sent her back to work. When possible, I placed her in my hospital, which was in reality just a grim joke...I delivered women in the eighth, seventh, sixth, fifth month, always in a hurry, always with my five fingers, in the dark, under terrible conditions...By a miracle, which to every doctor must sound like a fairy tale, every one of these women recovered and was able to work, which, at least for a while, saved her life.[678]

Camp inmates were not the only ones to have abortions: Gisella Perl was forced to perform an abortion on Irma Grese (sometimes Greze or Griese), the infamous camp guard, at gunpoint. Although she fully expected to be killed afterwards as she knew too much, she was spared.[679] Olga Lengyel's memoir confirms this experience reporting that she assisted Dr Perl throughout the procedure.[680]

Other doctors in Auschwitz-Birkenau made similar decisions: Lucie Adelsberger saved whatever poisons she could find to kill newborns in order to save their mothers. They did not have enough. "It's amazing what newborns can bear. They simply slept off otherwise lethal doses of poison, sometimes without any apparent damage. We never had enough for them."[681] As she wrote, "Doctors who had been trained to preserve life had to become killers to help their patients survive."[682]

It is impossible and inappropriate to judge doctors' actions regarding pregnant women or newborns during the Holocaust. Yet society and some historians have sometimes done so. Amesberger notes that doctors who conducted abortions or those who took the newborn babies away and killed them to save the mothers' lives were sometimes stigmatized as morally reprehensible after the war.[683] Ben-Sefer, for example, while acknowledging the difficulty of understanding doctors' dilemmas during the Holocaust, criticizes Lucie Adelsberger, for performing abortions on women in Auschwitz. Ben-Sefer argues that Adelsberger was acting in direct contradiction to the Hippocratic Oath 'to do no harm.' She writes:

> She not only did harm by aborting the fetus, but she selectively applied personal interpretation of medical

> ethics to pregnant women. Furthermore, at no point did she make sure that all of the women agreed to the procedure. On the contrary, she admitted that some of the women never forgave her for killing their babies. Nor is it clear if gestational age was a consideration for her. Early term pregnancies would be considered an abortion but late-term pregnancies involved labour and delivery and therefore can be considered infanticide. Nor did Adelsberger discuss the attitudes of Orthodox Jewish women with regard to abortion, and the question must be raised whether she gave any of them a choice or proceeded irrespective of their personal wishes[684]

While it is difficult to accept Ben-Sefer's retrospective judgments of conditions beyond imagination, or of conversations that might or might not have occurred, it is worth noting that despite the Hippocratic Oath's injunction to "not give to a woman an abortive remedy"[685] Jewish law does allow for preference to be given to the life of the mother when it is threatened by pregnancy.[686] The situation in camps faced by pregnant women is surely one such setting.

The doctors involved in saving women's lives through inducing birth or committing infanticide were under no delusions of heroism regarding their murderous actions. As Ben-Sefer herself notes, Rochelle Saidel states that the birth of a baby in concentration camps should really be termed 'childdeath' rather than childbirth.[687] Nor did Lucie Adelsberger, or any of the other doctors or their assistants, who later reported they had contributed to the deaths of babies *in utero* or after birth – Gisella Perl, Olga Lengyel, Sara Nomberg-Przytyk – believe they were committing anything other than murder. Their decision – usually taken with extreme difficulty[688] – was to preserve the lives of mothers who would otherwise certainly have been killed. Should they have always obtained 'informed consent' – a postwar concept – but nevertheless perhaps a valid question to ask? To what extent did they involve the women in the decisions? Little is known about this other than a few existing memoirs and testimonies. Historians are unjustified in criticizing them from the comfort of post-war perspectives. Auschwitz-Birkenau barrack doctors were ordered to report pregnant women. Lengyel, however, reports that she saw some of them – particularly 'Dr G.' (possibly Dr Gisella Perl with whom she was imprisoned) – defy every danger including deceiving Dr Mengele himself, and certify that a woman was not pregnant when she was.[689]

At selections pregnant women tried to drape their clothes to hide their pregnancies.[690] Edith Polgar was four and a half months pregnant on arrival in Auschwitz-Birkenau, but escaped Mengele's selection.[691] Dvora Rosenbaum-Fogel was in the early stages of pregnancy when she was deported from Hungary to Auschwitz in the summer of 1944. Her life was saved by the old large black dress that she was given to wear which covered her growing pregnancy. The camp authorities never discovered her condition and she gave birth to a boy on 12 May 1945 assisted by a Soviet physician. Dvora was not alone: a close friend also escaped detection and gave birth to a son at about the same time.[692]

Women whose pregnancy was detected could also be sent to the medical experiments block. Laura Varon, a Greek Jewish woman in Auschwitz reported that a friend of hers who was four months pregnant identified herself as pregnant when asked and was taken to the experimental block:

> But the second week we saw a woman came all bent in two and like she was in terrible pain and she was our friend, the pregnant woman…she told us that they took her in this barrack where doctors there and nurses, they cut her stomach and they took the baby and they placed the baby in a jar. Everything was done without anaesthesia. They did other things to her…She died that night of infection.[693]

Mengele and Birthing

Mengele reputedly showed a peculiar interest in pregnancy and birthing. He ordered Gisella Perl to interrupt a two-month-old pregnancy and to preserve the embryo, whole, in formalin.[694] Mengele never missed an opportunity to ask women improper questions relating to sexuality and pregnancy.[695] He hunted down a 15 year old whose pregnancy dated from her arrival in the camp. He questioned her at length and asked her the most intimate details before sending her to the gas chambers.[696] He asked pregnant women dozens of detailed questions that were "more personal than scientific, more voyeuristic than impartial."[697] Magda Spiegel – one of Mengele's twins – reported that he wanted to be present at every birth.[698] Mengele also fluctuated in his policy regarding killing pregnant women. Some weeks he ordered that pregnant women be kept alive and be given every consideration, other weeks he ordered them killed immediately.[699] Perl reports on the birth of twins and Dr Mengele's excited interest in them:

> Dr. Mengerle [*sic*] seemed to be very polite and thankful to the mother of the twins. He provided a basket for the twins; they received baby shirts; they were even given a blanket to cover their frail bodies… from day to day, the French twins were taken away every morning and carried to a special laboratory where Dr. Mengerle performed his satanic research on them. For fourteen days this…

> continued. And then one morning we found one of the twins dead…A few days later, the other little Frenchman followed his brother…When Dr. Mengerle appeared again and found that the twins had died, he became furious, and laughingly threw Jeanette [the mother] into the crematory.[700]

Mengele also supervised a birth with meticulous care and then sent both mother and baby to the gas chambers within an hour.[701] Judith Becker heard a story told by the daughter of Dr Senderovich from Radom who worked in the '*revier*' (infirmary), regarding an event that occurred when she had arrived in Auschwitz-Birkenau:

> as we left the train there was a blond young woman, very pregnant, who insisted that she speak to the *Lageraeltester* and she had a letter that she is carrying the child of a high–ranking German and that she must be protected And when they were trying to drag [her] to the crematorium …she kept insisting and screaming that she be treated separately…when Mengele finally came …she … told him her story…He says, 'Ach I know the man and I think it is such a thoughtful thing that he gave you this letter.' And he ordered her to be taken to the '*revier'* …and to be given very preferential treatment… He instructed the doctor that he must be there at the delivery. And they did a very careful delivery and they had the pail there for, you know, the afterbirth and after the baby was born he inspected the baby, 'what a beautiful baby' and as they were stitching her up, he put the baby in the pail with the afterbirth and sat down on it. And she kept trying to get up…the nurses were holding her down because they were working on her, so she says, 'But Dr. Mengele, my baby, my baby,' 'Oh he says, it's a beautiful baby. It's a gorgeous baby. It looks like a German baby.' And all this while he is sitting on top of the pail and this goes on – she's trying to get up and he's telling her 'You relax, you relax' and 'you have a beautiful baby.' Doesn't change the tone, he doesn't get angry. 'Ach, you have such a beautiful baby' until of course it is too late at which point she goes crazy, you know, she goes completely kaput, so he claps his hands and he says, 'Okay, now you can send her out.' To the crematorium.[702]

One story of Dr Mengele's involvement in birth in Auschwitz stands out: that of Ruth Elias. She arrived in Auschwitz-Birkenau in early pregnancy and escaped detection on arrival and in a later selection.[703] She had been unable to find someone who could abort her in Theresienstadt and she was forced to hide her pregnancy.[704] Fischer, the Jewish hangman, helped her by providing her with extra food. She eventually gave birth to a healthy baby girl with the help of a midwife but little else. Mengele saw that she had given birth. "He looked at the baby for a long time, and after some reflection he directed one of the woman doctors to tightly bandage my breasts…when I heard him give the order that I was not to breast-feed my child I was horrified."[705] One of the prisoners told her that this was one of Mengele's experiments: to see how long a newborn can live without being fed. Her breasts became swollen with milk, the baby cried and cried but she was forbidden to feed her. Elias writes eloquently of her feelings as though she were speaking to the child:

> My child you were born with such a lovely little body. Your legs are soft and pudgy, and they have tiny creases. What beautiful clear features you have. Dark hair and little fingers with such small fingernails. When you first saw the light of day you were a pretty baby. Now, for three days, your crying has not stopped. Your pale skin turns red when you scream, and your lovely little face is distorted. Am I imagining it or is your face getting smaller? Your legs thinner? Oh why, my child, are you not allowed to drink your mother's milk? If you could, you would fill out and not wither so quickly. Is your voice getting weaker, your crying and screaming gradually turning into a whimper? My child, how can I help you in your suffering? How can I keep you alive? Please don't leave me.
>
> …How can we put an end to this misery? Is there anything that I as your mother can do? Do I have the right to even think about ending both our lives? How can you and I live through this? When will the pain end?
>
> Here, my child, take this pacifier made of bread soaked in coffee; maybe it will alleviate your hunger. You have scarcely any strength left to suck on it. You're already six days old, and still I see no way out of this terrible plight. Oh God, please let us both die.
>
> My child, you've turned ashen-grey, just a tiny skeleton covered with skin. You can't even whimper anymore. And all those bedsores. Are you still breathing? Come, Mengele, examine my child. Feast your eyes on her! Is your medical curiosity finally satisfied? Now do you know how long a newborn child can live without food, you devil in human form![706]

Ultimately, Maca Stenberg, a Czech Jewish dentist and fellow prisoner, brought Ruth a syringe with morphine and instructed Ruth to inject it into the child: Her own Hippocratic Oath would not allow her to inject it for Ruth. Ruth did so: she killed her own child. A fellow prisoner Berta gave birth a few days later. This time Maca provided the morphine syringe and the baby was killed shortly after birth. Mengele was told that it had been a stillbirth.

Mengele's cruelty regarding pregnancy and childbirth was well acknowledged. According to Moser, although he was never brought to trial, the legal charges laid against Mengele, in addition to the murder of millions at Auschwitz, included standing on the stomachs of pregnant women until the baby was expelled.[707]

Births in the *Revier*

Both Madame Valliant Couturier, a French political prisoner in Auschwitz-Birkenau and Stanislawa Leszcynska, a Polish midwife, testified at the Nuremberg trials that the treatment of Jewish women in the *revier* changed at different times during the war[708] although each of these changes and precisely when they were introduced is not known. Margarita Schwalbova reports that until spring of 1943 both 'non-Jewish' and Jewish mothers and babies were murdered on arrival in Auschwitz-Birkenau: from then on 'non-Jewish' mothers and babies were not killed, only Jewish women and their newborns. Different approaches were implemented at different times including aborting pregnancies, allowing births but either starving the newborns to death or drowning them immediately, sending both the newly delivered woman and her newborn to the gas chambers, or allowing both mothers and their infants to live. Pregnant women from mixed marriages who gave birth were generally spared the gas chambers.[709]

At one stage, pregnant women were forced to abort. SS doctors performed abortions but with perhaps less concern for outcomes than prisoner doctors. Margarita Schwalbova[710] reports that in 1942, SS Dr von Bodmann aborted every pregnancy, regardless of whether it was in the early stages or advanced to even the eight month. In this series about 20 women were affected who all died of blood poisoning while in the hospital. Later, women in early stages of pregnancy were aborted under conditions that were more hygienic and they survived.

Those in advanced pregnancy were allowed to deliver but, until May 1943, Schwester Klara, and Schwester Pfani, a German midwife and a nurse who had been imprisoned for having performed illegal operations and for child murder, respectively, drowned all the newborn babies in a bucket of water.[711] Stanislawa Leszcynska reported, "After each delivery there could be heard from the room occupied by these women a loud gurgle and the splashing water, which lasted quite a long time. Soon afterwards the mother who had just given birth could see her baby's body thrown out of the block and torn to pieces by the rats."[712] Lillian Steinberg also testified to babies being drowned after birth in the *revier*: she reports the birth of one baby that took about 'an hour' to drown.[713]

It was the fate of other babies to die slowly of hunger "It was a principle that the babies received no food rations, not even a drop of milk."[714] A directive was issued in April 1943 in Auschwitz allowing for a special ration of half a litre of milk or pap with sugar and butter to be given to infants, but this was used for Dr Mengele's experimental twins and children in the gypsy camp, when the guards did not misappropriate it.[715] After a short while it was stopped. SS guidelines at Auschwitz required that babies allowed to live (temporarily) were to have a prisoner number tattooed on their thigh "because the arm of the infant is too small."[716]

Sometimes both mothers and babies were sent to the gas chambers as occurred with twenty-two year old Selma Haas from Bratislava after she gave birth to a healthy boy,[717] and to Esther, in Auschwitz-Birkenau.[718] When the gas chambers were inadequate the SS forced prisoners to dig large pits in which fires were lit and bodies thrown in. She described one occurrence in which the gas had run out and children were thrown into the fire alive.[719]

Olga Lengyel and Lucie Adelsberger confirm that at other times, pregnant Jewish women were put to death immediately, or both mothers and babies were sent to the gas chambers:[720] Only if the infant was not likely to survive or the baby was stillborn was the mother allowed to go back to her barrack.[721] Judith Rubenstein testified that a woman, for fear of being sent to the gas herself, begged her to provide an aspirin to kill her baby, which had been born during the night in the *revier*.[722]

Perl reports that in September 1944, Jewish women were allowed to have their babies in the 'maternity ward' of the '*revier*' (Block 20) where Polish, Ukrainian, Greek and Yugoslav woman gave birth, and their babies would be permitted to live. However, twenty-four hours after Eva Benedek gave birth there to a son, a new order came depriving Jewish mothers of the additional food, a thin, milky soup mixed with flour, which helped them produce breastmilk. For eight days, Eva had to watch as her baby slowly starved to death.[723]

Births in the Barracks of Auschwitz-Birkenau

Katerina Grünstein said that pregnant women concealed their pregnancies and preferred to give birth alone in the barracks rather than in the '*revier,*' and threw the babies under bunks, into the sewer and latrines in order to save themselves.[724] Nomberg-Przytyk and Vaillant-Couturier confirm that births that took place in secret in the barracks had to be in total silence and the babies were either killed by injections or drowned soon after delivery. After dark, the babies were thrown on a pile of corpses.[725] Janis Szasz, the director of the film '*Eyes of the Holocaust*' reported the testimony of a Hungarian woman in Auschwitz regarding a Jewish woman who gave birth but whose baby was left on the central divide running through the barracks and left to die. The mother was not allowed to touch it or feed it as its cries, strong at first, gradually became weaker. In the same film, survivors testified to another woman who was heard singing while holding a bundled, dead child.[726] Silvia Gross Martin in Auschwitz-Birkenau reports seeing a young Greek woman, naked, sucking the milk from her own breasts. She had given birth, smothered the infant before the Germans could kill it and was deliriously, but insanely, happy and giggling while she did so.[727] Arina B. gave birth to a boy on the central oven going through the barracks. A midwife in the barracks helped her and took her baby away to kill it. She reported, "And till now I don't know where's my baby."[728] Lengyel reports that:

> ...if a woman's labour pains started in the day, we... stretched her out on a blanket in one of the bottom koias of the barrack... in the night we ventured to take the woman to the infirmary, for at least in the dark we could proceed comparatively unobserved... we had our examination table. Still we lacked antiseptic, and the danger of infection was enormous, for this was the same room in which we treated purulent wounds.
>
> ...the fate of the baby always had to be the same...we pinched and closed the little tike's nostrils and when it opened its mouth to breathe, we gave it a dose of a lethal product... An injection might have been quicker, but that would have left a trace and we dared not let the Germans suspect the truth ...As far as the camp administration was concerned, this was a stillbirth...To this day the picture of those murdered babies haunts me...without our interventions they would have endured worse sufferings, for they would have been thrown into the crematory ovens while still alive.[729]

Liana Millu[730] reports a case of childbirth in the barracks of Birkenau. Maria's pregnancy was not detected on her arrival in the camp. She hid the pregnancy by binding her stomach with torn up blankets and worked harder than most to escape detection. Eventually, when close to term she was discovered but was protected by her barrack companions until she ultimately gave birth assisted by an older woman inmate. From the description provided, the baby was born alive and well but no mention is made of cutting or tying the umbilical cord and the mother is described as bleeding profusely after the birth. When the mother's absence was discovered at roll call shortly afterwards a German officer entered the barracks seeking her out. Millu reports that both mother and baby were dead but whether this was due to haemorrhaging of both mother and baby, or whether the German officer killed them, is unclear. Mollie Stauber, Susan Rubin, Masza Rosenroth and Matilda Klein all testified babies were born in the barracks of Auschwitz-Birkenau: In all cases, the mothers lived while the babies were killed.[731]

While most births that occurred in barracks appear to have occurred with minimal, if any, complications, Perl reports that one woman, Yolanda, experienced severe convulsive seizures (most likely eclampsia) for two days and nights before giving birth to a healthy boy. She hid the baby for two days unable to destroy him, before strangling him.[732]

The above listing is not exhaustive of births in the barracks of Auschwitz-Birkenau. Friedman[733] reports a number of additional testimonies that recall pregnancy and birth: Toby K. took newborns, wrapped them in blankets and put them in a pile outside the barracks to die; Fanny L. reported that her cousin gave birth to a stillborn baby. She took the baby to the latrine and buried it in the excrement. Eva S.'s cousin Lilly was pregnant and the block elder suffocated the baby when it was born. Shary N. gave birth in Auschwitz-Birkenau: the doctor took the baby boy and reported the next day that it was dead. Magdalena V. who worked in the hospital reported that a woman gave birth alone without a doctor or nurse assisting. The Nazis took the baby away, said it was dead and put it on the fire; Lola Goldstein Taubman testified that a woman gave birth to a stillborn baby in the bunk next to her: as they did not have scissors, they tore the umbilical cord and threw the baby away.[734] Eva Galt also gave birth in Auschwitz-Birkenau although no further details of her birth are reported.[735]

Few maternal deaths in childbirth or infant anomalies are reported by survivors. Marion Gottesman testified that Elfie Eiman gave birth in Merzdorf labour camp (a subcamp of Auschwitz) but both died. Marion was required to dig the grave and bury both mother and newborn.[736] Testimonies of both Maria Scheffer[737] in Dunderstadt camp in Germany and Zsoka Prochazka[738] in Auschwitz each report that infants with an imperforate anus were born: both babies died.

Births in Ravensbrück

Pregnant women were sometimes transported from various camps to give birth in Ravensbrück. Yehudit Harris recalls women who had been sent to Ravensbrück from Hungary to have their babies: they showed her their milk-laden breasts.[739] Before 1942, women sent to Ravensbrück to give birth were sent to a nearby hospital in Templin, and returned to Ravensbrück without their babies.[740] After that year, births were allowed in the camp.[741] Stennie Pratomo-Gret recalled the birth of a baby that survived in Ravensbrück.[742] In 1943, women were pressured into having abortions, even in late pregnancy. Alternatively, newly born babies were killed.[743] The prisoner nurses strangled the babies. One eyewitness account by Germaine Tillion reports that women were forced to witness their infants being smothered or drowned in a bucket after birth.[744] Marie-Jo Chombart de Lauwe was present when a newborn baby was killed in Ravensbrück.[745] Charlotte Müller, a German political prisoner who worked as a plumber in Ravensbrück described the reason for a drainage blockage that she was sent to correct. After days of pumping, the body of a dead newborn baby was pulled out of the sewage drain adjacent to the tent of the Hungarian Jewish women.[746] By October and November 1944 there were so many babies being born that Dr Treite created a maternity ward and assigned a prisoner nurse Hanka Houskova to be the midwife there. It was essentially the only concession the SS made to mothers and their infants. Shortly after giving birth, the new mothers returned to work and to roll calls. The newborns had to go the whole day without being fed. Most of the mothers were so malnourished they were unable to produce much milk[747]– and minimal feeding would have further diminished their milk supply. Between October 1944 and March 1945 an estimated 850 infants were killed in Ravensbrück.[748] A similar statistic is reported by Wanda Kiedrzynska[749] who notes that if not killed at birth the babies died within a month of birth from starvation, cold and neglect. In February and March 1945, orders were received to ship all children and pregnant women out of Ravensbrück.[750]

Births in Bergen-Belsen

By the beginning of 1945, Bergen-Belsen had intentionally become a camp for receiving pregnant concentration camp inmates together with transports of sick camp prisoners who were no longer able to work. Pregnant women fell into this category as they were regarded as unable to be used for forced labour.[751] There they were starved to death.[752] This was the final destination of women with small children as well, and they had little hope of surviving there. Yehudit Harris testified that she was a child when she was sent from Ravensbrück to Bergen-Belsen. She recalls seeing 13 dead babies laid out on a table when the train arrived.[753] Eichengreen reports the birth of a stillborn, eighth month gestation baby weighing only about two pounds, on the first night she arrived in Bergen-Belsen in March 1945. The mother had not known she was pregnant. The baby was dropped into a huge open pit of decaying bodies near the latrine.[754] Shortly afterwards they were liberated by the Russians.

Block II was the 'maternity block' of Bergen-Belsen. Perl describes it in April 1945:

> ...German, Hungarian, Dutch, French, Gypsy, Russian, Polish, Czechoslovak women lying in the cages along the walls, two in each. Their tremendous stomachs, swollen to a bursting point with child and hunger, did not permit them to move, and their moans, their screams, their helpless cursing, filled the building with a constant deafening cacophony. Lice covered their bodies in thick layers – hungry persistent, insufferable lice sparing nobody, not even the faces and hands of the doctors.[755]

Eva S.[756] remembers a cousin who gave birth in Bergen-Belsen and washed the baby in her own spit. Fania Fenelon witnessed the birth of a baby in Bergen-Belsen in the very last days of the war. As they had nothing to wrap the child in she took off her cloak and tore out the lining. "I'd been living in that cloak day and night for months now, and it was this bit of cloth, rotten with sweat, grimy with dirt, covered with stains, in which we wrapped the baby, a solid marvelous child."[757] Perl recounts her experience of assisting at the birth of the first free baby to be born in Bergen-Belsen on 15 April 1945:

> ...a tremendous shout of joy coming from thousands of throats shook the entire camp. The British have come... We are free...free... A moment later there was between her legs the first free child born in Belsen-Bergen... But her mother's blood would not stop flowing. She grew paler and weaker and wide streams of blood came gushing out of her womb...I ran out of the barrack and stopped the first British soldier I saw. Water! Get me water and a disinfectant... Half and hour later I had water, the disinfectant, and could wash my hands and perform the operation, not as a helpless prisoner, but as a doctor... I saved the life of Marusa and of little Marusa, her daughter. The tall, hardened soldier looked on, with tears rolling down his cheeks...He was Brigadier General Glen Hughes, head of the Second British Army.[758]

Births in Other Camps

The policy of drowning newborns was not confined to Auschwitz-Birkenau: Joly Z.'s testified that a newborn was drowned in Hamburg: "the

SS man brought out the baby holding him or her upside down. And put it under the sink, and opened the water, and he said, 'Here you go little Moses, down the stream.'"[759] Births are also reported from other camps. Ester Lebenswold testified to two babies being born in Bremen camp: both mothers and babies were sent to Bergen-Belsen and murdered.[760] Phyllis Young testified to a baby being born in Walzel labour camp in Czechoslovakia,[761] Wladyaslawa Tracz[762] and Estelle Laughlin[763] report babies being born and killed in Skarżysko-Kamienna labour camp and Edith Reifer[764] reports a baby being born in Markkleeberg camp before both mother and baby were transported to Auschwitz. In Mühldorf camp, one woman gave birth towards the end of the war and the camp commandant knew and hid the child.[765] Handa Stark testified that one woman gave birth in Ruzanberak camp in Czechoslovakia where pregnant women had been allocated a special room as the Germans were trying to make a good impression prior to the camp being liberated, in the last days of the war.[766] Anna K. was pregnant in Buchenwald but was saved by the liberation of the camp.[767] Anna Bergman was pregnant when deported from Theresienstadt to Auschwitz in October 1944 and was transferred to a subcamp of Flossenbürg at Freiberg and later to Mauthausen. On 29 April 1945, she gave birth on a cart on the way to Mauthausen just a few days before the American liberation of the camp. She testified:

> she [my baby] wasn't moving or crying for about ten minutes, until we got there [to Mauthausen], and it was cold, and these women with typhus. The lice were running around in millions, And I was sitting up and not having been washed for three weeks and not having eaten properly for three weeks. And just sitting there. And I couldn't care less really at the moment when the baby came out if it cries or doesn't cry.[768]

Her baby was wrapped in paper and survived.[769] Her daughter (Eva Clarke) testified decades later that her mother had weighed five stone (90 pounds) at the time of her birth and that she had weighed just three pounds at birth.[770] Rachela Schlufman testified that Helen Herlig gave birth in Leipzig camp shortly before the war's end: she was saved from death as the truck transporting women to the gas chambers was full and the camp was liberated before it could return to collect her.[771] Halina Strnad in Stuthoff camp reported a stillbirth.[772]

Miriam Rosenthal was transferred together with six other pregnant women from Auschwitz-Birkenau to Augsberg, a subcamp of Dachau, when she was eight months pregnant. She was the last to deliver. She had a 48 hour labour and delivered a healthy 10 pound baby but the placenta was retained and she became ill with fever. Consequently, her milk dried up and another woman fed her baby. As the Americans were approaching, the Germans tried to move her (and the others) to nearby Dachau, but as they tried to move her she started to haemorrhage. The doctor came to help her as she eventually began to expel the placenta. The doctor did a manual removal of the placental remains: –"with his bare hands he made a cleaning."[773] She was then sent to Dachau: both she and her baby survived.

Edith Serras' 1946 testimony tells of five non-Jewish Yugoslavian women prisoners giving birth on a 'death transport' from Auschwitz to Ravensbrück in an open railroad car on 18 January 1945:

> ..snowed all over them for three days and nights. Five women gave birth in the car during this time. Women would lie stretched out half naked to give birth to their babies. She says one woman was frozen and had not strength to give birth…the woman was so weakened and said 'I can't. I …we are cold.' We saw the baby emerging with a half-head outside and it goes back. The baby is… cannot come out. Finally it lasted three days and three nights, and the women gave birth to their children – live children on the snow…All alive. It lasted three days and three nights. And in a corner of the car little children were lying and saw how women have children.[774]

Rachel Gleitman[775] was on the death march from Auschwitz together with four sisters. The eldest had told her sisters that her periods had stopped (like most other women's) when she arrived in the camp. But on the death march they stopped in some abandoned houses in Poland where the oldest sister felt 'something coming out.' She gave birth to a stillborn baby that they buried in the snow before moving on.

Survival Rates

What is remarkable is that any woman, living under camp conditions, could have given birth to live, apparently 'healthy' babies, yet this is frequently attested to by survivors' testimonies. Babies showed a remarkable ability to resist the hardships they were exposed to, at least *in utero*. Nomberg-Przytyk was told by a doctor in the camps, "I want so much for babies to be born dead, but out of spite they are born healthy. I simply don't know why the children are healthy. The pregnant women do heavy work till the last day; there is no food; and in spite of it all, the children are healthy."[776] As Bluhm wrote shortly after the war, "Death in a concentration camp requires no explanation. Survival does."[777]

According to Stanislawa Leszcynska, 3,000 babies were born at Auschwitz-Birkenau and in spite of the filth, the state of the mother's health and the appalling conditions all the babies were born live and were well until they died of murder, starvation or forced neglect. Only 30 babies (1%, according to these estimates) survived Auschwitz.[778] Margarita Schwalbova, a doctor in Auschwitz-Birkenau, says that no one actually knows how many babies were born[779] or whether babies that died did so due to pregnancy or birth complications rather than by murder or starvation.

Figures that are somewhat more reliable are available from Ravensbrück. Between 19 September 1944 and 22 April 1945, 551 children were born in Ravensbrück and entered into the Book of Births (*Geburtenbuch*) a registry kept by a prisoner official, Lisa Ulrich, which has survived.[780] The registry also gives the date of death, and many of the newborns lived only a few days. For example, one of these babies, born to the wife of Walter Winter, a surviving German Sinto, died at birth, to be followed three days later, on Christmas eve 1944, by its mother.[781] Walter, in the men's camp at the time, never saw his newborn. The registry indicates that 23 women delivered prematurely (23/551 = 4.2%), 20 had stillborn babies (20/551 = 3.6%), and 5 suffered miscarriages (5/551 = 0.9%). For 266 children a date of death is given in the same book that records their birth (infant death: 48.3%). According to these records, 22 Jewish women (from Hungary, Poland, Slovakia and stateless) gave birth in the Ravensbrück delivery block. Most of these women came to Ravensbrück in the last months of 1944 or the beginning of 1945, some from Auschwitz. 11 newborn babies definitely did not survive (11/22 = 50%), most of them died after 2-4 weeks. The fate of the others is not known. In total, perhaps about 100 infants survived (100/551 = 18.2%) thanks to the solidarity among the prisoners and the timing of the births during the last weeks of the war.[782]

In the texts and testimonies reviewed in this book, 45 births occurred in concentration camps with 4 being reported as stillbirths – or 8.8%. This figure is not dissimilar to the combined proportions of preterm births (4.2%) – that would likely not have survived without specialist medical care – and stillbirths (3.6%), totalling 7.8%, reported in the Ravensbrück registry.

Both the births reported here, and the Ravensbrück registry figures provide an interesting, although unreliable, insight into neonatal mortality rates in the especially horrendous camp setting: A 7.8% or 8.8% newborn death rate is not remarkably different from that found in modern times and in good conditions. It is apparent from these limited figures that childbirth outcomes were apparently far less affected by camp conditions than infant survival. The poor rate of infant survival on the other hand, is not surprising, given the murder of newborns, or their inadequate feeding, housing or care facilities. Rates of direct maternal mortality (due to pregnancy related causes rather than Nazi extermination policies) are unknown: only one woman's death in childbirth has been noted in the testimonies reviewed here. The scanty but telling data available from

Ravensbrück in the final months of the war confirms the remarkably protective environment of the womb. In contrast, the inability of newborns to survive after birth in the camps reflects the extremely debilitating world into which they were delivered.

The sample of births reported in this review is by no means exhaustive. There are likely many additional women who gave birth and lived even though their babies died or were killed, as well as some, perhaps, who lived together with their newborns. In addition, there are probably many women who gave birth and died, whose experiences were never recorded or recalled by others. Little, if any, information is available regarding the number of miscarriages that took place during pregnancy although reference to this occurrence in Theresienstadt and Bergen-Belsen is made by at least one survivor of each camp.[783] There is also no record of the number of pregnant women who were killed immediately on arrival in camps, as these women were not registered in camp records.

Impact of Birthing on Later Experiences

The enormously high marriage and birth rate among the Jewish Displaced Persons (DP) camps after the war was in stark contrast to the declining rates among the non-Jewish population. In Berlin, for example, in 1946, divorce rates escalated and 25,000 divorces were registered with about 1,700-2,000 occurring each month until the end of 1947.[784] In contrast, Jews in DP camps married, sometimes within days of meeting others who were past neighbours or distant kin or acquaintances from home. Many of the newlyweds hardly knew each other.[785] Celia K. reports marrying her husband three weeks after meeting him, because "everyone was out there raping girls."[786] Bertha married her husband eight weeks after meeting him to avoid being sent to work by the Russians.[787] Eichengreen tried, unsuccessfully, to marry a relative stranger just to be able to move to Palestine and escape the DP camps.[788] Marriage in the DP camps after the war posed a challenge to *Halakhah (*Jewish Law) especially for those women previously married. Surviving *Halakhic* scholars in Europe were directed to finding ways to grant permission to marry *(heterim)* without having the usual required proof of the death of their spouses.[789] According to existing religious laws, those women who were *agunoth* (women whose husbands have disappeared without divorcing them) would be condemned to remain widows until the end of their days. Eventually allowing a two-year period to elapse before granting permission to remarry became one solution to this problem.[790] Brenner reports that in Belsen DP camp there were over a thousand marriages between 1945 and 1947.[791] Only in rare cases were surviving family members present at the wedding and the ceremony under the traditional wedding canopy usually began with the memorial prayer for the murdered parents of the couple. According to Schiff, many of the survivors married soon after the war's end and almost none intermarried, although a 'greater part' of them renounced their Jewishness for the safety of belonging to a national majority. She reports that there were fewer divorces among these marriages: not because the partners were very compatible but because they shared ties to a powerful past that led them to believe that others would never understand.[792] Women brought memories of rape and sexual violation, or the humiliation of nudity and forced shaving with them into the marriage, with many of them never sharing these experiences with their partners or children.[793] Yael Danieli, a psychiatrist specializing in Holocaust survivor trauma, refers to some of these marriages as 'marriages of despair.'[794]

In 1945, the birthrate of the Bavarian population (South-Eastern Germany) was 5 births per 1,000 persons,[795] and abortion rates were high as Germans, demoralized, were unwilling to bear children.[796] In contrast, the birthrate of 1,000 Jewish DPs in Bavaria a year later was 14.1 per 1,000.[797] A Joint Distribution Committee survey reported that 750 babies were born every month in the US zone DP camps alone and that by the end of 1946 nearly a third of all Jewish women of reproductive age (18-45) were either pregnant or had recently given birth. The number of Jewish babies reached about 8,000 at this time.[798] Children born on land that had been declared '*Judenrein*' (Jew free) to women intended by the Nazis to be exterminated were called 'Children of the Messiah' (*Maschiachskinder*).[799] Reasons given for marriage and giving birth included: to overcome the damage done, to create life again after so much death, to recreate a family, to be loved, and to belong to someone, or even to get revenge.[800] For some, loneliness, coincidence, emptiness, social norms, the insistence of the partner and lack of contraceptives might have played a role.[801] Tova Flatto Giladi who had been in Ravensbrück said that "If you are not going to have children it's like Hitler would win."[802] On the other hand, her own experiences of parenting were so difficult that she also reflected "Maybe we should not have had children because we are too damaged." Even after the children were born, some parents worried that their children might have inherited the damage that had been done to them.[803] Helen Epstein reports one woman's fear that:

> Any child it [her body] produced would be deficient in calcium, in vitamins. Her baby would be born with soft bones, or no arms, or blind. Or she would be like some of the women in Terezin and Belsen. She would be pregnant for a few weeks and then begin to bleed, and the baby would be lost.[804]

Gertrude Schneider had similar fears: "The doctor I chose, a German Jew of advanced age, promised me that if my children were totally defective he would do away with them so that I would not have to face this problem in addition to all my other problems."[805] Olga Grossman – one of Mengele's twins – was so worried during her pregnancy that what had been done to her by Mengele would cause her to have an abnormal baby. When she was told her baby was healthy she collapsed: she had a nervous breakdown and had to be institutionalized. She was hospitalized after every childbirth and required shock treatment as she was reliving the terror.[806] Women who gave birth soon after the war, while still in DP camps, experienced fear of non-Jewish German doctors and German hospitals.[807] In at least one setting, this fear was well grounded: Gina Roitman reports that a Nazi midwife in the DP camp of Pocking-Waldstadt near Passau, Germany, murdered 52 babies by exerting pressure on the newborns' fontanelles. Her mother, afraid of giving birth in the camp, chose, instead, to give birth in Passau resulting in Gina's survival.[808] Notwithstanding this, infant mortality among the offspring was extremely low (5.3/1,000 in 1948), lower than almost all other countries at the time (for example New Zealand with 26.1/1,000 in 1948-9): these babies were 'precious' and afforded the utmost care and attention.[809]

Traumatic birth experiences in which newborns were murdered during the Holocaust also took their toll on mothers in later years. Ruth Elias gave birth in Israel in 1950: the delivery was fine until the nurse wrapped her baby and started to walk out the room with him. Horrific memories of babies being taken from mothers and killed in Auschwitz flooded over her and she began to scream and cry inconsolably. Only then did a doctor ask her, and talk to her, about her wartime experiences. When her second son was born no emotional concentration camp associations were triggered.[810] Raisa also recalls being afraid after giving birth in the USA, that the hospital would take her baby and would sell him to cover the costs of the delivery.[811] Feinstein too, reports some women's overwhelming fear after giving birth that a Jewish baby would not be allowed to live.[812] Luba Gurdus became pregnant, was confined to bed for four months but gave birth to a child that died. She was told that the mental and emotional stress she had experienced was so great that she should not have another child.[813] Charlotte Delbo recounts the story of Mado whose joy on giving birth after the war was suffused with sad memories of her friends killed during the Holocaust.[814] Epstein reported women forever wondering if the child they had given birth to in the camps, and that had been taken away from them, had perhaps survived "and they were growing up in Poland somewhere not knowing they were Jewish."[815]

Circumcision of newborn boys also aroused fear in women giving birth after the Holocaust. Vera Schiff gave birth to a baby boy in May 1947: the impending *brith milah* (circumcision) threw her into emotional panic because of her memories of how the Nazis had used this physical distinction to identify Jews.[816] Similarly, Maria, a non-Jewish Polish woman gave birth to a second son after the war in the UK. The baby was taken from her briefly in the post-partum period. When she asked where he was being taken, she was told to be circumcised, as was common at that time. This sent her into a total panic attack because to be circumcised in Poland was a death sentence. She rushed down the corridor and had a tug-of war with the doctor to retrieve her son, refusing to have him circumcised. Emotionally she had reverted to the camps.[817]

Fear of having children that might be killed also followed Holocaust experiences. Arina B.[818] was afraid to have a child although her husband wanted one. She managed to give birth to one baby in Germany but aborted her next pregnancy. Her fear of her children being killed was too great. She did manage to have another baby six years later after moving to America. Anka Bergman was so afraid that the same fate might befall her children that she had her Jewish daughter who was born in Mauthausen baptized by a priest and educated in Catholic schools.[819]

Other women reported having abortions in DP camps, rather than giving birth on German soil although the number of abortions was low in comparison to the high birth rate.[820] Abortions were also obtained due to unintended pregnancies resulting from little knowledge regarding sexuality, a lack of contraception, and with few if anyone to confide in or from whom to obtain advice.[821] Sandra Brand reported that she had left her four and a half year old child Bruno with her husband during the war and had never reconnected with him: she did not want to forget Bruno by having another child, and deliberately aborted two later pregnancies.[822]

Some women could not have children after the medical experiments that had been performed on them. Trees Soetendorp of Amsterdam was one of these. Her husband was murdered at Auschwitz. She remarried out of loneliness in 1949. During an argument, her second husband blurted out, "Why did I marry you anyway? You can't even have children."[823] She divorced him and never married again requiring professional psychological help over years to keep going.

Holocaust experiences led to over protectiveness of children in later years. A number of Mengele's surviving twins including Hedvah and Leah Stern, Judith Yagudah, and Peter Somogyi, report being exceedingly anxious and overprotective about their children as they were growing up.[824] Alizia, another survivor, reported being excessively fearful and communicated her fears to her own daughters who had to seek help for their own fears as well.[825] Gertrude Schneider testified that she and her husband were overly anxious about their children until such time as they were old enough to have passed through a selection: their fears returned with the birth of grandchildren.[826] For some, having a child substituted for their many great losses and brought joy, others could not find happiness in their children because of their memories of their losses or of murdered children: some thought it had been a mistake to have a child, and these suffered serious psychological scars.[827] Women who had left their children behind when being transported to camps tell of difficulties being accepted as the mother of the child on their return. Some children never forgave their mothers for abandoning them.[828]

Ignorance about birth and the lack of parental guidance about pregnancy and birth was felt deeply by couples who faced childbirth without family support after the war. Even if emotional support was available knowledge of childbirth was scarce among surviving women as the Nazis had targeted older women and those with children for the gas chambers. Very few women survivors had first-hand knowledge of childbirth.[829] In addition, the topics of sex, pregnancy and physical hygiene were not included in school curricula: it was believed that if sex was handled in hushed silence it would somehow preserve a girl's virtue.[830] Early in 1948, Itka Zygmuntowicz became pregnant. When her waters broke neither she nor her neighbor knew what this meant. As she recounted:

> I was thirteen when Poland was first occupied, nineteen at liberation. I spent my teenage years in a camp. I didn't see a normal pregnancy carried to term in a normal situation. I didn't know what you were supposed to do…And I had no one to tell me this, to advise me, because my mother was killed at Auschwitz. [831]

On Friday afternoon, with the baby not yet born, a friend warned Zygmuntowicz's husband, 'The baby's not going to live.' Such cases, the friend told him, where the water breaks too soon and the baby is not born immediately, do not auger well. But at 1 in the morning on Saturday, October 3 1948, Zygmuntowicz gave birth to a healthy son. Soon after her husband stepped into the hospital room where she lay recuperating. She recalls him standing with his hands behind his back, looking sad. He didn't speak. His sorrow puzzled her. "I said to him, 'You know we have a son,'' and he broke down crying. Only then did he offer her the flowers he had hidden behind his back. "Because he didn't know if we had a baby or if the baby had died."

It was not only women who had birthing related wartime experiences who suffered post-war trauma in this regard: men did too, although this is mentioned less often. Ira never forgave himself for not being able to save his brother Chaim: he had undertaken this responsibility during the war years. When he married he chose never to have children as he said, "I don't want to be responsible for anybody."[832] Ernie Weiss, the eldest of seven siblings, had witnessed his mother giving birth in the confined living conditions of their home in Hungary, following years of anti-Jewish restrictions, and was deeply traumatized by this. One childbirth resulted in a stillborn infant and his mother's grief remained with him all his life. One of his own children reported him being exceedingly concerned whenever they became ill.[833] Gill also reports on a 32-year-old son of a Holocaust survivor who after the war, agreed to be present at the birth of his first child. The labour was very difficult and his wife's screams invoked feelings of overwhelming helplessness. A severe panic attack followed associated with extreme fears of death and terrifying destructive death imagery that were related to his own mother's stories of her Holocaust experiences. He required emergency psychiatric hospitalization and treatment.[834] Rubinik also reports on the grief expressed by a man who was unable to have children following medical experimentation during the war.[835]

Doctors also suffered after effects. Szwajger reports, "For forty years after the war I was a doctor…I felt I had no right to carry out my profession. After all, one does not start one's work as a doctor by leading people not to life but to death."[836]

A number of Jewish women raise questions in their testimonies (recorded some decades after the war's end), regarding the childbirth care they had received in the DP camps after liberation. Some report that they were not given pain relief as a deliberate continuation of former antisemitic attitudes on the part of the (frequently) German doctors who cared for them.[837] While antisemitism did not disappear because the war was lost, and many reports of antisemitic acts in the immediate postwar period exist, (for example the massacre at Kielce[838]) it is not clear that women were further victimized by their German health care providers while in DP camps. The use of pain medications during delivery was not routine medical practice as it was much later when the testimonies were provided. Schiff, for example reports that in Czechoslovakia, after the war, deliveries occurred without painkillers or anaesthesia except for Caesarean sections, which were performed under general anaesthetic.[839] Many medications were not available after the war and unmedicated birth was likely to have been standard. It is easy to see how women speaking decades later when pain management in labour and birth was common, interpreted their postwar care as a continuation of pre-war antisemitism, but possibly unjustly so.

Pregnant women or those with newborn babies posed an immediate threat to the creation of the 'Master Race' by their procreation, and/or care for, those regarded as less 'valuable'. While all women were targets of the Nazi genocide those who were pregnant, gave birth or who had children were the most vulnerable targets of the Nazi genocide. Ideologically fuelled fear and hatred of them, as threats to Nazi superiority, contributed to the sadistic and misogynistic actions taken against them. Understanding the experiences of survivors, as well as the second-generation children of survivors, has been the subject of much study. The long-term reproductive health consequences of those women who gave birth during the Holocaust, whose newborn babies had been killed, or whose children had been murdered or separated from them, raise issues of particularly severe concern.

The Medical Profession And Reproduction

In some circles, the term 'Holocaust' has become the ultimate description of horror or horrific events. The Nazi medical experiments and practices are an example of these. Nazi medical science played a central and crucial role in creating and implementing practices designed to achieve the objectives of eliminating those deemed as not meeting idealized Nazi racial standards, and, in contrast, promoting the achievement of the ideologically pure, 'Aryan' race. Doctors interfered with the most intimate and previously sacrosanct aspects of life in these medical experiments – reproductive function and behaviour – in addition to implementing eugenic sterilizations, euthanasia, and extermination programs.

As the commandant of Auschwitz, Höss, revealed in his memoirs, doctors fulfilled numerous roles during the Holocaust that contributed significantly to achieving Nazi goals.[840] For instance, their role in the eugenic sterilization and euthanasia programs was extensive. In the camps too, they: selected prisoners from the incoming transports; supervised the extermination process in the gas chambers by supervising the application of Zyklon B and ensuring that the extermination process had been carried out once the doors were opened; supervised that the 'dentists' removed all valuables that might have been hidden in bodily orifices, and gold teeth, from the gassed victims, and supervised the melting of the teeth and their safekeeping until delivery to the SS; selected prisoners who could no longer work for gassing; or those with infectious diseases for extermination; decided which bedridden inmates they would kill with lethal injections or which would be sent to gas chambers; certified that the prisoners to whom they administered lethal injections had died from an illness which led to a quick death; had to be present at executions and certify that the executed were dead; had to examine prisoners sentenced to receive corporal punishment for reasons which might prevent this punishment, and had to be present when this was carried out; and had to perform abortions on foreign women at least up until the fifth month of pregnancy. In addition, many doctors and medical institutes were directly involved in ghastly medical experimentation and some like Profs Clauberg, Schumann, and Mengele worked on medical experiments involving reproductive function.

Each of these events evokes traumatic images that are best described in the words of those who witnessed them. Alexander O, a French trained, prisoner doctor writes of only one of these doctor's roles – the selection of patients in the infirmary for death:

> All, in turn – naked – go before the [SS] doctor, running past him, chest out, in a very military fashion... Whoever has not seen this military bearing in a skeleton does not know what degradation and contempt are...If a skeleton walks stooped over, slowly, slowly, that is a skeleton presenting a normal appearance, one might say even a decent appearance. But to see this procession of skeletons marching at a military pace, chest out, shoulders thrown back, and coming to a stop abruptly – well, it is something saddening, debasing, beyond description. A skeleton marching this way- the edema [fluid] in the scrotum swinging, the completely emaciated scrotum swinging – that is something one cannot forget.[841]

Not all German doctors relished their role. Some like Dr Ernst B,[842] at Auschwitz, went further than anyone else in assisting prisoner doctors. A few are remembered by prisoners as having moments or even longer of humanity towards inmates. Some were able to assist other doctors or treated inmates respectfully rather than brutally while still implementing Nazi requirements.[843] Other German doctors, like Dr Herta Oberheuser in Ravensbrück, went beyond the call of Nazi duty by deliberately inflicting pain for example, when tearing off bandages and dressings from unhealed wounds, as reported by numerous Polish women who were used as guinea pigs in medical experiments at this camp.[844] Notwithstanding the few exceptions, the ready internalization of Nazi ideology by a number of Nazi doctors into their daily medical practice remains a blot on the hitherto esteemed, German, medical reputation.

In contrast, prisoner doctors had to deal with the overwhelming consequences of Nazi ideology: As Lengyel writes there were 30-40,000 internees in her camp in Auschwitz-Birkenau with only five women serving in the infirmary. She writes:

> We rose at four in the morning, the consultations began at five. The sick, of whom there were as many as fifteen hundred in a day, had to wait their turn by rows of five. ...we operated as late as eight in the evening. Sometimes we had accouchements during the night. We were literally crushed by the burden of work. Sometimes there were

several accouchements in succession resulting in sleepless nights...[845]

The workload, combined with the totally inadequate medical facilities and medications available, added to the impossible decisions that had to be made, were an overwhelming burden for any medical practitioner to carry. These choices may have involved who should receive the limited supply of medications, whether the behaviour of one patient who was endangering the lives of others meant s/he should be killed, and killing newborns or aborting fetuses to save the mother's life.[846] For example, Elie Cohen, a Dutch Jewish doctor in Auschwitz, reported giving an intractable, raving, violent prisoner insulin to kill him as he was endangering the entire ward. On another occasion he refused the request of a Dutch university professor to give him a medication that would render him unconscious when he entered the gas chamber as such medication was scarce and desperately needed by others. He admits that he was scared to do so in case he was found out. He reports the legacy of such decisions as "a lifetime of remorse."[847]

Some, like Dr Adelaide Hautval (a French, Christian, psychiatrist) in Auschwitz, refused to collaborate on some of the medical experiments and escaped harm, although narrowly. Expecting to be punished, a medical assistant, Orli, gave her a sleeping draught, admitted her to the infirmary, exchanged her body for that of a corpse, and smuggled her back to Birkenau.[848] Less fortunately, Dr Samuels was murdered for his secret protection of women's fertility when operating on them. Those prisoner doctors or assistants who survived, including Gisella Perl, Olga Lengyel (a university qualified surgical assistant), Sima Vaisman, Lucie Adelsberger, and Sara Nomberg-Przytyk (an attendant in the *revier*), lived uneasily with the memories of their actions, including aborting pregnancies or killing newborns to save life. While the actions of Nazi doctors involved in every aspect of the genocide against the Jews cannot be condoned, it is also important to recognize the remarkable care and concern provided by prisoner doctors and their assistants, and the occasional SS physician, who did what they could to help their fellow inmates under horrendous conditions.

Medical Experiments

The period between the arrival of prisoners in the camps and their ultimate murder provided the Nazis with an opportunity to conduct medical experiments on them – mostly hidden from public view. These experiments gave the Nazis the opportunity to implement both of their ideological goals – the refinement of the 'Master Race' and the elimination of the sub-human Jews and others categorized as 'undesirable.'

Medical experiments were designed to enhance the survival of Germans (e.g. survival in freezing conditions or at high altitude, or treatment of illnesses), or the refinement of hereditarily desirable characteristics (e.g. the eye colour experiments), or to facilitate the prevention of reproduction of 'undesirable' peoples (e.g. the sterilization experiments). The writings of Eugen Fischer, the director of the highly prestigious Kaiser Wilhelm Institute that trained researchers/SS personnel on racial theory and racial traits and diseases, encouraged such experimentation.[849] Researchers at this institute and others, working in collaboration with their protégés like Mengele in Auschwitz, experimented on: sterilization in Auschwitz and Ravensbrück; the eyes of 'gypsies' and twins to discern colour abnormalities and their refinement in Auschwitz; survival in conditions of high altitude, sea water or freezing (and re-warming through physical and sexual contact) at Dachau; malaria tolerance and treatment after forced infection, at both Dachau and Buchenwald; treatment with sulfanilamide following deliberate infection of wounds with bacteria, as well as bone, muscle and nerve regeneration and bone and limb transplantation at Ravensbrück; infection with typhus and manipulating treatments for this in Buchenwald and Natzweiler; injection and 'treatment' for tuberculosis at Neuengamme, poisons and their effect in Buchenwald and Sachsenhausen; development of a cellulose based food at Mauthausen; simulation of battlefield injuries through infection and inflammation (phlegmon), polygal (blood coagulation) and phenol (gas oedema) in Dachau and Auschwitz; incendiary/phosphorus bombs in Buchenwald; and hepatitis, epidemic jaundice, mustard and phosgene gas at Sachsenhausen and Natzweiler.[850] Many were conducted without appropriate anaesthesia, or proper surgical technique or conditions. Other 'studies' harvested fresh brain tissue and examined organ transplants. Further, a skeleton collection for the Reich University in Strasbourg, France, was collected at Natzweiler camp including more than 100 Jewish prisoners,[851] while a similar collection of brains was created for Dr Julius Hallevorden at the Kaiser Wilhelm Institute for Brain Research, primarily from euthanasia killings at Brandenburg.[852] Dr Hallevorden stated after the war that "where they came from and how they came to me was none of my business."[853] Intolerable suffering and pain was induced without consent or concern for the subjects' experiences.[854] Hundreds, if not thousands of prisoners – Jews and non-Jews – died in these experiments.[855]

Sterilization Experiments

A great deal of scientific attention was dedicated towards determining ways of mass sterilization. At postwar Nuremberg trials, defendants

Karl Brandt (executed 1948), Karl Gebhardt (executed 1948), Rudolf Brandt (executed 1948), Joachim Murgowsky (executed 1948), Helmut Poppendick (sentenced to 10 years, later reduced to time served), Viktor Brack (executed 1948), Adolf Pokorny (acquitted), and Herta Oberheuser (sentenced to 20 years, later reduced to 10) were charged with special responsibility for and participation in these sterilization crimes.[856]

Sterilization experiments were conducted from March 1941 to January 1945 in Auschwitz, Ravensbrück and other camps.[857] Women subjected to such experiments were called 'rabbits' or 'guinea pigs'.[858] Carl Clauberg requested permission from Himmler to conduct sterilization experiments in Auschwitz on 30 May 1942. Himmler agreed, through his assistant Rudolf Brandt, on 10 July 1942, indicating that he would be "interested to learn …how long it would take to sterilize a thousand Jewesses."[859] He also advocated a practical follow-up experiment "locking up a Jewess and a Jew together for a certain period and then seeing what results are achieved"[860] and whether the sterilization procedures had been effective in preventing conception. Viktor Brack also submitted a proposal to Himmler for the sterilization of 2-3 million Jewish workers on June 23 1942:

> According to my impression there are at least 2-3 million men and women well fit for work among the approximately 10 million European Jews. In consideration of the exceptional difficulties posed for us by the question of labor, I am of the opinion that these 2-3 million should in any case be taken out and kept alive. Of course this can only be done if they are at the same time rendered incapable of reproduction. I reported to you about a year ago that persons under my instruction have completed the necessary experiments for this purpose. I wish to bring up these facts again, The type of sterilization that is normally carried out on persons with genetic disease is out of the question in this case, and it takes too much time and is expensive. Castration by means of X-rays, however, is not only cheap, but can be carried out on many thousands in a very short time. I believe that it has become unimportant at the present time whether those affected will then in the course of a few weeks or months realize by the effects that they are castrated.
>
> In the event Mr.Reichsführer, that you decide to choose these means in the interest of maintaining labor-material, Reichsleiter Bouhler will be ready to provide the doctors and other personnel needed to carry out this work. He also

instructed me to inform you that I should then order the required equipment as quickly as possible.[861]

Himmler gave his permission for these experiments on June 30 1942. The aims of the experiments were reiterated in a statement made by Rudolph Brandt at the Nuremberg Trials: "Himmler was extremely interested in the development of a cheap and rapid sterilization method which could be used against enemies of Germany, such as the Russians, Poles and Jews…The capacity for work of the sterilized persons could be exploited by Germany, while the danger of propagation would be eliminated."[862] Three methods were tried: sterilization by medication, by x-rays and by chemicals.

Sterilization by Medication Experiments

The first approach involved using drugs that were designed to induce infertility developed from a South American plant c*aladium seguinum* (American arum) and tested on animals by the firm Madaus and Co., Dresden-Radebeul. Dr Karl Tauboeck at the University of Vienna (later a consultant to the USA CIA under the Paperclip project[863]) was ordered by Himmler in 1942, to produce sizeable quantities of a drug obtained from the Brazilian plant of the same family, d*ieffenbachia seguina* (Dumb cane), which he was informed was to be used for the mass sterilization of the mentally ill, Polish and Ukrainian populations.[864] The drug was believed to reduce sexual excitation and to induce impotency in males at least: for females, the effect appeared to be temporary. Dr Tauboeck reported destroying all the available plants by allowing them to freeze as he thought the research unethical. In addition, Dr Adolf Pokorny testified after the war that he had worked on a second series of experiments using these plants, and had also used delaying tactics to prevent such research from being successful: he was acquitted at the Nuremberg trials.[865] Mitscherlich and Mielke report that a sworn statement of Rudolf Brandt, Himmler's personal adjutant, explains that experiments with c*aladium seguinum* were actually made on concentration camp inmates, but all efforts to discover the details proved fruitless at the time of the 1947 Nuremberg trials.[866]

In contrast to these experiments designed to reduce fertility, Dr Tauboeck was also ordered by Himmler to produce a drug that would excite the sexual desires of women to facilitate the actions of spies in cases where women might have desired information.[867] This manipulation is yet another manifestation of the Nazi's willingness to use or misuse women, as sexual and reproductive beings, to facilitate their cause.

Sterilization by X-Rays Experiments

A second method tried to provide a method of mass sterilization, explored the use of x-rays in both men and women. Dr Horst Schumann's experiments were directed towards castrating Jewish men by means of x-rays to the genital organs. Schumann was the director of Grafeneck euthanasia centre and later Sonnenstein. Following this he became active in project 14f13 as a member of the medical commissions visiting camps.[868] Victims of his experiments reported having their sperm collected, being forced to masturbate, having their prostate glands brutally massaged by means of wooden or iron instruments inserted into the rectum to induce ejaculation, and having operations to remove one or both testicles, or even a portion of a testicle. They were questioned about the result of the 'treatment,' their desires, nocturnal emissions, and loss of memory. Brutality and minimal anaesthesia made their experiences disastrous. Haemorrhage and septicaemia often followed as well as absence of muscle tone from wounds so that the men died rapidly.[869] Lifton also reports castration experiments on a group of healthy Polish men to whom unusually high doses of x-rays were given causing their genitals to rot away. After long suffering, the men were sent to the gas chambers.[870] Mitscherlich and Mielke report the testimony of a former Jewish prisoner at Auschwitz during the Nuremberg trials regarding his castration experience:

> We were taken to Birkenau, to a labour camp for women… We had to strip and our sexual organs were placed on a machine and kept there for 15 minutes. The machine heated up the sexual organs and the surrounding parts, and afterwards these parts turned black. After this performance we had to resume work at once. In the course of the next few days the sexual organs discharged pus with most of my comrades, and they had great difficulty walking. Nevertheless they had to go on working until they dropped. Those that fell were taken to be gassed.
>
> I myself experienced only a watery discharge, but no pus. After about two weeks, about October 1943, seven men of our group were taken to Auschwitz I. This distance had to be traversed on foot. They had great difficulty in walking, because of pain in the sexual organs. We were taken to the hospital buildings in Auschwitz I. There we were operated. We received an injection in the back which turned the lower part of the body numb while the upper part remained quite normal. Both testicles were removed. There was no prior

> examination of the seminal fluid. I was able to watch the proceedings in the mirror of a surgical lamp. No consent for the operation was obtained. We were merely told 'Your turn' and sent to the operating table without a word. The director of the sterilization and castration experiments at Auschwitz was Dr Schumann...Excuse me for crying, I can't help it. I was at the Auschwitz hospital for three weeks. Afterwards there was a muster and sixty percent of our group was taken to be gassed. I got scared and though still half sick I went back to work.[871]

Victor Brack reported that high doses of x-rays destroyed the inner secretions of both the testicles and ovaries. Lesser dosages only suspended the procreative activities for a time.

Prof. Schumann's experiments on women involved the use of x-rays of the pelvic organs to induce sterility. He forcibly sterilized women by positioning them between two x-ray machines aimed at their sexual organs. Ovariectomies were later performed – often by a Polish prisoner Dr Wladyslav Dering. Most women died after suffering greatly.[872] Posner and Ware report that Schumann and his co-workers performed 90 sterilizations in one day on at least one occasion.[873] The method of operation used most often was a horizontal incision above the pubic area that carried the greater risk of infection as opposed to a median laparotomy (abdominal opening).[874] He notes that Dering also administered spinal anesthesia in a most painful way – without first anaesthetizing the track of the main injection – often while patients were forcibly restrained. Operations were done without sterile procedures for hands or instruments and executed extremely rapidly – in about 10 minutes – followed by hasty and rough suturing. Lifton continues that Dr Wanda J. who looked after the women during recovery observed him doing ten operations in one afternoon under conditions that were not sterile. Dr Wanda J noted that Dering failed to take the ordinarily obligatory step of applying a portion of the peritoneum (the membrane lining the abdominal cavity) as a flap to cover the stump of the tube from which the ovary had been removed, contributing to later complications of bleeding and severe infection. She observed extensive tissue destruction and infection arising from the combination of deep X-rays, crude surgery and the general Auschwitz conditions. She had to struggle to find ways to protect these women – who often stayed in bed for nine months – from official scrutiny as they were 'bearers of secrets' (the surgical experiments) and were in danger of being sent to the gas chambers. Lifton reports further that Dering had a tobacco pouch made from the scrotum of one of the testicles he had removed from a Jewish prisoner and he sometimes displayed it for other inmates.[875]

In women, symptoms induced by X-rays included the cessation of menstruation, changes in body hair, and changes in metabolism. As it was not possible to prevent irradiation of other body parts, irradiation sickness also ensued together with burning of the skin.[876] Danuta Czech testified that 15 of the girls experimented on by Dr Schumann on 2 November 1942 were between 17 and 18 years of age: only a few survived. Because of the experiments, the girls completely changed in appearance and resembled old women.[877]

Aliza Barouch gave testimony regarding her experiences of being sterilized in Block 10 of Auschwitz.[878] Schumann put a wooden board on her back and abdomen, connected to many wires. Then she had to stand naked between the two x-ray apparatuses. After 20 minutes, they let her go. It did not hurt. It caused continuous vomiting. Afterwards the women stayed in bed for 18 days. They lost all their hair, and after the second irradiation, their bodies were burned and turned black: they had blood in their stools. She and one other girl were irradiated three times, the others only twice. Ovariectomies were ordered for all the girls. A Jewish prisoner, Dr Samuels, did hers and those of two others who survived. Dr Dering did Dora's. In Aliza's case Dr Samuels removed only one ovary and part of the uterus and she later went on to have 2 children – although in between the first and last she had four babies that died within days of birth. Two other girls cared for by Dr Samuels also had children later. He was sent to the gas chambers when it was discovered that he was protecting the women. Trees Soetendorp also testified to these brave acts of kindness.[879] A week after their operations the stitches were removed, but because of the radiation the skin did not grow together and there were suppurations. The abdomen opened and pus came pouring out. They put paper on the wounds instead of a bandage and closed the skin with a safety pin. Aliza lay there for 11 months in excruciating pain and with a terribly high fever. She did not know what they had done to her.[880]

Victor Brack reported to Himmler, on the basis of Schumann's experiments, that men or women could step up to a window where they could be asked questions or have to complete a form thus detaining them for the desired time needed to expose them to the x-rays. The official behind the window could operate the x-ray tubes. He reported that "a two-tube installation could thus sterilize 150-200 persons a day, twenty installations some 3,000 to 4,000 persons a day."[881] Schumann himself, however, reported on 29 April 1944, that castration of men by this method was not feasible and probably too expensive. He suggested that castration by surgical means was cheaper and took no more than 6-7 minutes but that this method was not fast or inconspicuous.[882]

It is interesting to note what the consequences of their actions during the Holocaust were for those who perpetrated the experiments targeting reproductive function. Dering was released from Auschwitz and went to work for Clauberg at his private clinic. After the war, he fled to the UK where he was held in a British prison until a decision was reached not to extradite him. He worked in Africa as a physician with the British Colonial

Medical Service and then returned to London where he practiced medicine. In 1959, Leon Uris published '*Exodus*' in which he accused Dering of conducting 17,000 sterilizations without anaesthetic.[883] Dering initiated a libel suit against Uris in which surviving prisoners and prisoner physicians revealed his atrocities. Although the verdict was technically against Uris as he had incorrectly asserted the number of operations and technique used, the award to Dering was 'one half penny' – a severe indictment of his crimes. He became ill and died shortly after the trial.[884] Schumann fled after the war and spent about seven years working as the head of a hospital in Khartoum, Sudan. Identified by a survivor he fled again to Ghana from where he was eventually handed over to West Germany. After spending some years in custody, he was released on the grounds of ill health and died in Frankfort in 1983, without having stood trial.[885]

Experiments on Sterilization with Chemicals

Prof. Clauberg, an SS Brigadier-General and MD from Köningshütte, working under the supervision of the chief SS physician Dr Eduard Wirth, was particularly involved in a third approach to sterilization: the injection of chemical irritants into the uterus.[886] On 1 April 1943 Commandant Höss, put Block 10 at Auschwitz at his disposal for these experiments. By 5 May 1943, there were 243 women prisoners housed in Block 10 who were to be used for this research. There were also 22 nurses who were prisoners assigned to the Block.[887] Both Jews and Gypsies were subjected to these experiments.[888] In addition to wards, Block 10 had an elaborate x-ray machine and four experimental rooms, one of which served as a dark room for developing x-rays.[889] Clauberg's program began on 18 December 1942 with about 350-400 Greek and Dutch women. He injected 'iodiprin,' F12a, which was diluted Novocain, and 'citobarium' or barium sulphate into the uterus and subjected the women to x-rays. This resulted in peritonitis, inflammation of the ovaries, and high fever, causing closure of the fallopian tubes and permanent sterility. Sometimes the belly of the woman was opened to observe the lesions. The ovaries were then removed, usually in two separate operations, and sent to Berlin for analysis. Clauberg reassured women that he would not return them to Birkenau but would send them to his private research clinic in Königsshütte a few kilometers from Auschwitz. After the successful experiment Clauberg planned that every one of the female prisoners at the end of a year undergo sexual intercourse with a male partner chosen especially for this purpose in order to carry out a practical test of Clauberg's sterilization method. This test was never performed 'because of the course of the war' and most of the women were later sent to the gas chambers.[890] On 7 June 1943, Clauberg reported to Himmler – under whose direct orders he was working – that he could sterilize, without an operation, as many as a thousand women a day. He suggested that a single injection into the cervix was sufficient and it could be administered during the 'usual gynaecological examination familiar to every physician.' He reported that "*One* adequately trained physician in *one* adequately equipped place, with perhaps ten assistants (the number of assistants in conformity with the speed desired) *will most likely to be able to deal with several hundred even if not 1000 per day.*" [Italics original].[891] X-ray photographs made during certain preliminary tests performed at Ravensbrück showed that Clauberg's injections "penetrated to the end of the ovarian duct; in several cases even to the abdominal cavity."[892]

Dr Zdewnka Nedvedova-Nejedla, a woman prisoner who practiced at Ravensbrück reports on sterilization by injection into the uterus from her own experience:

> I saw gypsy women inmates going into the x-ray room and coming out again – there they were sterilized by a method which so far as I know, was tested at Osviecim. The method was based on the injection into the uterus of an irritant fluid, most probably silver nitrate, together with a contrasting fluid in order to permit an x-ray check of the operation. All sterilized women were x-rayed immediately after sterilization. I examined these pictures together with Dr. Mlada Taufrova and can therefore testify that in most of the cases mentioned the injection penetrated to the end of the ovarian ducts; in several cases even to the abdominal cavity. Only the ten last cases were given anaesthesia, by the intervention of the SS nurse Gerda. I took care of the children the whole night after the operation. All these girls bled from the sexual organs and were in such pain that I had to give them sedatives secretly. In the morning, before roll call, I took the children to their blocks, with the help of girls working in the hospital.[893]

The primary targets of the sterilization experiments were Jews and 'Gypsies' (Roma and Sinti). This text has made no attempt to examine the plight of the Roma and Sinti as this requires a dedicated work to do it justice. Suffice it to say that the concentration camps had done much to violate gypsy customs and cultural sensitivities in addition to their physical degradation and elimination. Those who had been sterilized, like Walter Winter's brother and eldest cousin,[894] also lost much of their self worth as their standing within their communities depended heavily on fertility.[895]

According to Hájková and Housková, Clauberg left Auschwitz with over 5,000 scientific photographs in his briefcase.[896] While overall statistics are uncertain it is estimated that approximately 1,000 prisoners, male and female, underwent x-ray sterilization or castration and about 200 of these were subjected to surgical removal of ovaries or testes.[897] Clauberg was captured by the Russians on 8 June 1945.[898] Lifton reports that he was imprisoned in the Soviet Union for 3 years before being tried, and was then convicted of war crimes and sentenced to 25 years. Following Stalin's death in 1953, and various diplomatic agreements, he was repatriated to Germany in October 1955. He was not repentant but boasted of his achievements in sterilization and spoke proudly of his work in Auschwitz. He was arrested again in November 1955 but the German Chamber of Medicine resisted efforts to divest him of his title of doctor of medicine. Only after an impressive declaration from a number of former prisoner physicians condemning his Auschwitz activities was his license finally revoked. He died mysteriously in his prison cell on 9 August 1957, amidst rumours that he was in the process of naming names at the top of the Nazi medical hierarchy and that consequently colleagues helped bring about his death.

Other Experiments on Reproductive Organs

A further series of experiments were conducted on menstruation and the menstrual cycle in women, largely using the bodies of women to be executed by the Gestapo. German scientist Hermann Stieve of the University of Berlin was notified of the date of execution of women of reproductive age. During her period, the prisoner was also informed: "You will be shot in two days."[899] Stieve then studied the effects of the impending trauma on the woman's menstrual cycle. Upon her death, her pelvic organs were removed for histological examination. Stieve also followed the migration of sperm in the women's bodies following their rape before execution. Stieve continued to lecture on his research in Berlin after the war and was sought after by Russian scientists.[900]

A series of additional experiments involved the reproductive organs and behaviours of prisoners. Lengyel reports that experiments on artificial insemination were tried although the experiments yielded no results.[901] In alternative experiments, a Dr Treite (who committed suicide after the war[902]) performed surgical tying of the oviducts.[903] Further experiments in Buchenwald and Neuengamme attempted to counteract homosexuality by gland implants and synthetic hormones. These experiments were suggested and executed by the Danish SS Major Dr Carl Vaernet.[904] In Buchenwald, 15 inmates were treated of whom two died. No positive findings emerged.[905] Dr Franz Blaha testified at Dachau during the war trials that the infamous freezing water experiments conducted by

Dr Sigmund Rascher utilized either a heating apparatus to re-warm frozen prisoners or – at Himmler's suggestion – the person was placed in a bed between two women.[906] In eight cases the subject was placed between two naked women: they were supposed to nestle close to the subject to warm him up. All three were then covered with blankets. Consciousness returned earlier than with other methods of warming (hot baths, blankets). The temperature rose rapidly in four of the experimental subjects who engaged in sexual intercourse. Additional experiments involving re-warming by one woman indicated that return to consciousness and re-warming occurred even more quickly compared to when two women were involved, possibly due to fewer inhibitions.[907] Himmler considered these experiments as entertaining and, on occasion, brought friends to view them.[908] Kogon in his post-war report includes similar findings.[909] Photographic evidence reveals other experiments of an unknown nature resulting in gross disfigurement of women's breasts.[910]

Medical students were allowed to 'learn' surgical techniques using camp prisoners. A surviving woman reported on an event that took place in the female hospital block in Birkenau:

> the sudden appearance of many young doctors in white coats (later identified as students)…[who] walked through the wards and looked us all over, who through orders to the prisoner doctor, chose certain women, put anaesthesia masks on them, and had them taken to an operating area, from which they returned hours later to wake up in their beds, each with wounds differing from the others.[911]

The women concluded that "each of the students performed an operation as an experiment in his specialty: throat, eyes, stomach or gynaecology." The woman who gave the testimony later discovered that her uterus and ovaries had been removed.

Mengele's Twin Studies

Twins, Mengele's primary concern were, in addition, regarded as the ideal experimental subject with which to examine eugenics: how people developed, how they resisted or became ill, and how they reacted to demands were questions that could be answered through twin studies, as they were often identical siblings. Twins were also valued because of their potential in promoting multiple births, in order to create the 'Master Race.'[912] In that respect Mengele's twin studies were not simply about increasing fertility through multiple births but also about perfecting the replication of the ideal features of the desired 'Aryan' race: blue eyes, blond hair and strong bodies.[913] To this end, Mengele tried to change the pigmentation of eyes by injecting them with substances such as methylen blue. The procedure did not cause any permanent change in eye colour but did cause considerable pain, vision damage and on occasion death.[914] Mengele was also believed to have experimented with sexuality among his twin subjects:[915] Several twin survivors believe that Mengele had twins mate although no twins have elaborated on what they knew about this. Some female twins were, however, sterilized and some males castrated. In addition, Moshe Offer reported that his twin brother had several operations following which his sexual organs were removed. Rumours suggest that Mengele wanted to use twins' sperm to impregnate German women to see if they would also bear twins and to see if male twins who had intercourse with female twins would again bear twins.[916] At the end of 1944, a new block was being built in Auschwitz for experiments with artificial insemination, for the greater population of Germany; but the evacuation of Auschwitz prohibited their implementation.

The Value of this Experimentation

Referring to these experiments as 'research' credits them with some scientific validity. There is however, considerable doubt as to whether any research conducted on starving prisoners living under appalling concentration camp conditions and without consistently following appropriate medical standards is of any value. In addition, some of the activities of camp doctors under the guise of 'research,' and later testified to by survivors, raise images of sheer morbid curiosity rather than science. For example, in 1985, at a mock trial of Mengele held at Yad Vashem, thirty surviving twins and dwarfs testified to a six-man tribunal of world dignitaries including General Telford Taylor (of Nuremberg trial fame), Gideon Hausner (who had successfully prosecuted Adolph Eichmann), and Simon Weisenthal. At this 'trial' a former nurse at Auschwitz testified that she had watched Mengele 'sew' two twins together in an effort to make them Siamese. Black reports these twin brothers as Guido and Nino – sewn together at the wrist and back with interconnected veins.[917] The boys screamed all night until their mother was able to give them a fatal shot of morphine. A pair of dwarfs – also twins – testified that they had been forced to dance naked in front of Mengele (before the war they had been circus performers).[918] Such instances – and many others documented by Lifton[919] – suggest less than scientific standards, or principles, of research.

Prisoner physicians were not always compelled to work on the medical experiments.[920] A few refused to do so including Adelaide Hautval, a French, Christian, physician prisoner who was ordered to work on sterilization experiments with SS physician Edward Wirth. She refused, but nevertheless survived. "He was surprised," she later recalled, "that a doctor practicing psychiatry could condemn a method which aimed to improve and preserve the race. I answered that it brought grave abuse. He talked to me about the Jewish question and I answered that we have no right to dispose of the life and destiny of others." Later she was asked to sterilize a seventeen year old Jewish girl from Greece. When she refused, Dr. Wirths said to her, "Cannot you see that these people are different from you?" To which she replied, "There are several other people different from me, starting with you!"[921]

Those who did participate often saw this as a research opportunity and as a service to the nation's health. Findings of these experiments were presented at scientific meetings and conventions and published in the most respected journals.[922] German industry too, benefitted enormously from these activities: Glass[923] reports that Behring-Werke employed concentration camp prisoners in testing new vaccines against typhus and Bayer Pharmaceutical Company developed a contract with Auschwitz that allowed the company to purchase Jewish female subjects for 700 Reich marks each for experimentation. Bayer's parent company IG Farben was a major financial supporter of Auschwitz and some of its research.[924] At the Nazi doctor's trial following the war commencing on 25 October 1946, none of those charged with the most heinous of these programs expressed remorse or regret: they remained convinced of the value and normality of their actions.[925] At the Dachau war crimes trial, Dr Schilling appealed to the court to be able to finish his report on the experiments he had conducted on Jewish concentration camp inmates.[926] He had infected over 1,000 prisoners with malaria.[927] Such research appeared, to them, to have achieved the highest goals of purifying and removing degeneracy from the superior German /'Aryan' race and they believed they should be honoured for their achievements rather than criminalized.[928] He said, "It would be a terrible loss if I could not finish this work... I need only a table and a chair and a typewriter. It would be an enormous help for science, for my colleagues, and a good part to rehabilitate myself."[929] Estimates suggest that between 200 and 350 German doctors, including university professors and lecturers, had been direct participants in research, while hundreds or perhaps thousands had stood silently by.[930] Among these doctors, the power of ideological conviction, combined with selfish achievement motivation, clearly outweighed the humanitarian underpinnings of their Hippocratic Oath.

The Aftermath of the Nazi Medical Experiments

The so-called medical experiments conducted in the camps in association with many of the top research facilities in Germany at the time were horrendous. They have, however, stimulated a process of developing and refining ethical guidelines for research on human subjects that commenced shortly after the war and is still in progress. While this in no way justifies their occurrence, it is, at least, one optimistic outcome of these disastrous events.

Ethical guidelines protecting animals from research involving freezing, drowning, burning and poisoning were passed in Germany on 24 November 1933. This law was explicitly designed to:

> ...prevent cruelty and indifference of man towards animals and to awaken and develop sympathy and understanding of animals as one of the highest moral values of a people. The soul of the people should abhor the principle or mere utility without consideration of the moral aspects.
>
> The law cites further that all operations or treatments which are associated with pain or injury, especially experiments involving the use of cold, heat, or infection, are prohibited...
>
> Medico-legal tests, vaccinations, withdrawal of blood for diagnostic purposes, and trial of vaccines prepared according to well established scientific principles are permitted, but the animals have to be killed immediately and painlessly after such experiments.[931]

It was also forbidden to allow animals to look on during the slaughter of other animals.[932] Similar ethical guidelines for human research were not, apparently, considered. In fact, in some cases, the intended death of the experimental subject was the stated aim of the Nazi doctors' research protocols: so-called "terminal experiments."[933] Rascher's research group presented findings of the freezing experiments to conferences in Nuremberg in October 1942 and in Berlin in December 1942, without any protest being voiced by delegates at these meetings.[934] Yet other bizarre situations arose which indicated that a clear moral code was operating among these researchers: it was just not one to which the scientific community would now, or even subsequent to the war, adhere. Dr Sigmund Rascher, for example, reported to Himmler on his freezing and re-warming experiments that one of the prostitutes sent to him from Ravensbrück to serve as a body-warmer/sexual contact had impeccable Nordic racial characteristics:

fair hair, blue eyes, corresponding skull shape and physical build, age 21 ¾. He wrote:

> My racial conscience is outraged by the prospect of exposing to racially inferior concentration camp elements a girl who is outwardly pure Nordic and who might be led on the right path by proper employment.[935]

He refused to use her in his experiments. Such outrage was, perhaps, sadly misplaced.

Unwillingness to Examine Nazi Medicine

Debates around issues related to the medical experiments of the Nazi era are difficult. Using the 'Nazi analogy' is a persuasive argument and tends to result in the moral argument winning.[936] In the medical world, a lack of understanding of Nazi medicine results in the 'Nazi analogy' being a powerful force preventing careful examination of the merits and demerits of current medical developments such as cloning, or the use of stem cells, or assisted dying. It is only in recent decades that bioethicists have analyzed the ethical issues raised by the brutal experiments in the camps and the eugenics and euthanasia programs.[937] The German medical community in particular has been reluctant to confront its role in the Nazi era: Mitscherlich[938] was rejected by German medical bodies for editing the documents produced at the 1946-7 Doctor's Trial at Nuremberg. Of 422 articles on Nazi Medicine published between 1966 and 1979, only two originated in Germany.[939] The reluctance of post war scientists to examine the Nazi experiments and to dismiss them as irrelevant has led to a disregard for their implications for our current medical and scientific activities.[940] Exposing the extent and horror of the Nazi era is important if a balanced view of current medical developments can be obtained in relation to the faulty science underlying Nazi ideology. This is important because what took place in Germany was grounded not only in racism (as occurs in many current day conflicts and genocides) but also in science and medicine. Nazi racism was implemented using scientific and engineering technology administered by doctors and other health care providers. As Caplan writes,

> Whether it was building a gas chamber, running a transportation network, or selecting who would die based on a psychological, physical or anthropological examination, science permeated the Holocaust. And for those who see medicine and science as bound by a higher moral code, that is a very difficult fact to accept.[941]

Consequences of Not Examining Nazi Medicine After 1945

Our unwillingness to examine Nazi Medicine in the decades following the end of World War II might have contributed to the ability of scientists to proceed with research that was, on occasion, questionable. For example, Katz reports that the mustard gas experiments conducted by the US armed forces between 1950 and 1970 continued patterns of abuse and neglect where subjects were recruited through lies and half-truths for experiments using chemicals known to cause debilitating long-term effects.[942] Similarly, Katz asserts that the Tuskagee Syphilis studies conducted between 1932 and 1972, by the US public health service allowed for the monitoring of the natural history of untreated syphilis from its inception until death in 400 African-Americans, denying them treatment. Katz further reports that as recently as 1994, consideration was given to the use of Alzheimer patients – who were unable to give consent – in research that would expose them to greater than minimal risk. In addition, he indicates that some studies have been approved by the US National Institute of Health, with doubtful informed consent protocols. As he elucidates, these studies share a common disregard of the human subjects' interests for the noble, scientific purpose of alleviating the pain and suffering of others. Nazi doctors might well have used the same argument. It need be noted, however, that while these questionable research instances have occurred in the decades since the end of World War II, these are nowhere near equivalent to Nazi era experiments and are not in any way representative of North American research in general.

A Code of Medical Research Ethics

What is most remarkable is that these studies were conducted long after a medical code of experimental ethics emerged from the ashes of the Holocaust. The Nuremberg Code of 1947, emerging from the Nuremberg trials, had as its first and most significant clause that the voluntary consent of human subjects in research is absolutely essential.[943] Remarkably, the World Medical Association Helsinki code of 1964 removed this requirement and emphasised the importance of the scientific research instead. Later versions of the code, in 1975, 1983 and 1989, did once again include informed consent but this was listed as principles 9, 10 or 11 respectively.[944] As George Annas points out, judges and lawyers devised the Nuremberg Code, while physicians developed the Helsinki Code for their own guidance.[945] In conflict here is the principle of doing the best for the individual versus the broader population good. As Jay Katz mentions we are now more concerned with the science of medicine than the art of healing.[946] In 1982, the World Health Organization together with the Council for International Organization of Medical Sciences (WHO/CIOMS) developed further guidelines, which, to an extent, may replace the requirement for individual consent with an independent 'impartial perspective' review of all protocols. A 1992 version from this same body continued moving away from an individual rights approach to a prior group review approach.[947] To compound the problem, the Nuremberg Code, the Helsinki declaration and the WHO/CIOMS guidelines are advisory only: they have no legal standing in most countries and do not carry any ability for sanction of researchers who disregard them.[948]

As Michael Grodin points out, economic pressures are currently forcing doctors to make research related decisions based on economic constraints (including lucrative sources of research funding and pharmaceutical companies' interests) and not necessarily in the best interests of patients – pressure that might well lead physicians down a wrong path.[949] Grodin also emphasises that the fundamental relationship between physician and patient must not become subordinate to the needs of the state, as it did in Nazi times. As Katz notes, medical ethics should never allow research experiments on persons whose lives the state considers expendable including those in prisons, serving as soldiers or in hospitals or similar institutions.[950]

Drawing analogies between present actions and Nazi Holocaust behaviour arouses strong emotive reactions and may result in the moral argument discounting any possibility of logical analysis as to when, where and why some lives might be terminated. Donai O'Mathúna notes that James Watson (winner of the shared Nobel prize for discovering the structure of DNA; the first director of the Human Genome Project) believes that society needs to eliminate defective genes. Such thinking might justify embryo selection, abortion and infanticide.[951] Debates about the ethics of such actions continue: while many countries allow for abortion on some grounds, and embryo selection in particular circumstances, emotional and religiously based arguments abound decrying these steps and making constructive development of guidelines for the appropriate use of these techniques difficult. O'Mathúna further notes that prenatal caregivers and women worldwide have long accepted the value of routine prenatal screening with the intention of terminating some pregnancies. Even infanticide – which is, emotionally, perhaps the most difficult to accept of the three methods – needs consideration with regard to when, where and if it should be supported. According to O'Mathúna, Prof. John Harris, a member of the British Medical Association ethics committee, notes that there is widespread acceptance of infanticide in some countries and he questions the difference between aborting late term fetuses and infanticide. The acceptability of giving lethal injections to patients with terminal and debilitating or painful illnesses is also currently debated in many countries with varying degrees of approval of this action.[952] Seen as merciful by some it runs contrary to the religious or moral beliefs of others. While we have the technological ability to implement many such actions we currently still lack the guidelines that determine when, how and under what circumstances such actions are acceptable. The importance of discussing and determining ethical guidelines for the implementation of such actions remains a challenge for today's world.

Distinctive in almost all of these situations, however, is the requirement for patient consent for any of these procedures, which is in stark contrast to the practices of the Nazi era that imposed forced experimentation and killing. These sensitive issues reinforce the importance of maintaining the requirement of 'informed consent' in all research and clinical practice medical guidelines. Unfortunately, 'informed consent' is also open to abuse. To be truly ethical, informed consent should be both evidence-based and unbiased by the traditional 'superior doctor-inferior patient' hierarchy that is commonly prevalent in both society and in medical care.[953] Yet not all doctors are fully aware of the most up-to-date evidence underlying their advocated practices, and not all provide information to their patients in a manner that is truly non-coercive, thereby diminishing the high moral grounds underlying the requirement to obtain 'informed consent' for procedures.

Whether we examine childbearing today, matters of life and death, or Nazi medicine, it appears that lessons from the Nazi Holocaust have yet to be learned.

Part 2:
Sexuality And Sexualized Abuse

Sex And Sexuality Among Germans

Medical theories of the late 19th and early 20th century drew a firm distinction between reproduction and sexuality.[954] It was believed that the development of reproductive powers and of maternal instincts could only occur when sexuality was suppressed. Women were told that sexual feelings were "unnatural, unwomanly, pathological and possibly detrimental to the supreme function of reproduction."[955] A change in this way of thinking in Germany began with the establishment of the Society for Sex Reform (*Gesex*) in 1913 by Felix A Theilhaber who documented the use of a vaginal sponge as a contraceptive. The society was dedicated to the improvement of birth control and the legitimization of abortion. In 1919 Magnus Hirschfeld was given a large grant to develop his informal Scientific Humanitarian Committee into a state funded Institute for Sexual Science, with its premises in the grand Tiergarten district in the centre of Berlin.[956] The Institute offered sexual counseling and provided information on such questions as 'what is the best way to have sex without making a baby?' In 1929, Hirschfeld's Berlin clinic was the first to focus on sexual deviation and in 1930, Lehfeldt and Hirsch opened a Marriage and Sex Advisory Centre under the patronage of the Society for Sex Reform. Hirschfeld campaigned for a reform of all the laws regulating sexual behaviour. He built up a wide range of international contacts, organized the World League for Sexual Reform, and his institute became its effective headquarters in the 1920s. In the Weimar Republic, he and his institute became the leading force behind the spread of public and private birth control and sex counseling clinics. Hirschfeld's Institute was known in Berlin, not only for championing the legalization of homosexuality and abortion, and for its popular evening classes in sexual education, but also for its enormous collection of books and manuscripts on sexual topics. By 1933, it housed between 12,000 and 20,000 books – estimates vary – and an even larger collection of photographs of sexual subjects.[957]

By 1927, contraceptive advice clinics were operating in most larger towns with travelling services being provided to less populated areas.[958] Over 100 centres gave contraceptive advice at little or no cost. Beginning in 1928, postgraduate courses in birth control were offered to physicians in Berlin. By 1933, more than 15 organizations had merged with the National Association for Birth Control with a combined membership of over 50,000. This development was in accord with the Weimar Republic's reputation for modernity and a high standard of living. Laws restricting the sale of condoms were eased in 1927, and by the early 1930s there were more than 1,600 vending machines in public places, with one Berlin firm producing 25 million condoms a year.[959] Abortion was a more controversial issue both because of the medical risks it entailed and on moral grounds. Nevertheless, in 1927, the law was relaxed, and the offence reduced from a felony to a misdemeanour. Concurrently, however, between 1929 and 1932, prostitution among both males and females became more widespread and noticeable as a product of both Weimar's sexual tolerance and its economic failure.[960]

Under the leadership of Helen Stöcker a parallel development emerged during the 1920s called the *League for the Protection of Motherhood and Sexual Reform* (*Bund für Mutterschutz und Sexualreform*). Rather than escaping from motherhood as many of the feminist movements were advocating at that time as women's liberation, she advocated strengthening motherhood through its liberation. She claimed that eugenic education, birth control, legal abortions, divorce reform, and aid for mothers, whether or not they were married, were every woman's birthright. She worked closely with the sex reform movement, which sought to make sexuality freer and more satisfying. Inspired by Magnus Hirschfeld and Helen Stöcker, sexologists applied scientific measures to the study of sexual behaviour. Proclaiming sexual pleasure as every person's right, they chartered orgasmic curves of men and women, evaluated sexual preferences, analyzed arousal patterns, and dispensed contraceptives. They discovered a new ailment that they claimed pervaded the culture: female frigidity, and suggested that if women found fulfillment with their husbands, they would not resort to adultery, lesbianism, or masturbation. Women's emancipation meant the right to sexual pleasure.

Nazi Attitudes to Sexual Liberation

Once the Nazis came to power, the trend towards more liberal views regarding sexuality and homosexuality, seen as a Jewish movement to subvert the German family, ended.[961] Hirschfeld's group had made significant progress on liberalizing laws against homosexuality with Reichstag recommendations, on 16 October 1929, to legalize homosexuality among consenting adults.[962] Reforming paragraph 175 of the Reich Criminal Code condemning homosexuality had, however, been strongly opposed by the Nazi party. An article in the *Völkischer Beobachter* on 2

August 1930 had said, "We congratulate you Herr Kahl and Herr Hirschfeld, on this success! But don't you believe that we Germans will allow such a law to exist for one day when we have succeeded in coming to power."[963] True to these words, on 6th May 1933, students from the Berlin School and members of the National Socialist German Students' League raided the Institute for Sexual Science for Physical Education. They drew up in military formation, took out their trumpets and tubas and started to play patriotic music, while others marched into the building.[964] The Nazi students who stormed into the Institute poured red ink over books and manuscripts, played football with framed photographs, and ransacked the cupboards and drawers, throwing their contents onto the floor. Four days later stormtroopers arrived carrying baskets, into which they piled as many books and manuscripts as they could and took them out into the Opera Square where they set fire to them. About 10,000-12,000 books contained in this collection are said to have been destroyed.[965] Hirschfeld himself was both Jewish and homosexual, factors probably lending weight to the Nazi's opposition to his work. While destruction of Hirschfeld's institute reflected Nazi disapproval of sexual liberation and homosexuality in particular, it was also part of the larger Nazi program targeting 'Jewish intellectualism,' 'decadence' and 'moral corruption.' In all, upwards of 25,000 books were burned on 10 May 1933 in the *Bücherverbrennung* (book burning) instigated by the Propaganda Ministry and implemented by the National Student's Union that destroyed so-called 'un-German' writing.[966]

Movements towards sexual liberation were not the only targets. In the same month, with conservative and Catholic approval, the Nazis banned Helen Stöcker's organization for its insistence on women's rights and integrated the hundreds of existing women's organizations into a unified Nazi Women's front (*Frauenfront*), ultimately under the leadership of Nazi enthusiast Gertrud Scholtz-Klink.[967] They closed all marriage and sex counselling centres and destroyed related research papers, books and educational materials. Sex education associations were dissolved including the League for Social Physicians and the Institute for Social Gynaecology and its Journal. Leading persons in the birth control movement were arrested, pushed into retirement or 'persuaded' to emigrate.[968] Those who dispensed birth control information or treated sexual dysfunction were also criminalized. Germany, and Berlin in particular, which had been the centre for the international movement for sex research and reform in early 1933 immediately lost its status in this field. The practitioners and advocates for this movement for sexual enlightenment and female liberation, many of whom were Jewish and/or women, emigrated or were arrested.[969] The Nazis eliminated Weimar's sexual freedoms, including the reform of the abortion law, the decriminalization of homosexuality, and the public dispensing of contraceptive advice.

Assaults on the Church

The Catholic Church signed a "Concordat" with the Nazi party within six months of Hitler coming to power, granting the Church freedom to operate in Germany independently, in exchange for not opposing Hitler's political and social aims. In particular, Nazi suppression of birth control, abortion and homosexuality gained support in Catholic circles. Hitler soon lashed out against the Church, however, with some actions specifically directed towards sexually related issues.

Nazism, while restricting some aspects of sexuality as 'degenerate' also promoted healthy sexuality. *Das schwartze Korps* (The Black Corps), one of the most popular weeklies of the Third Reich and an official SS journal, mocked Christian efforts to defend the sanctity of marriage and what it called 'the pathological tendency to Catholic virginalism' as early as 19 June 1935.[970] Goebbels and his propaganda ministry fuelled sexual scandals revolving around the Catholic Church and its priests.[971] Fifteen monks were taken to court for homosexual offences committed against the mentally ill in an institution in western Germany: they had held the penises of patients while urinating.[972] Other priests were tried for sexual offences against minors in children's homes and institutions. A trial of 267 Franciscan monks (out of a total of 500) on similar charges occurred in May 1936.[973] These stories combined the Nazi's dislike of the Catholic Church and homosexuals. Sexual offences of priests against girls received less attention (or occurred less often). According to Evans, by April 1937 over a thousand priests, monks and friars were said to be awaiting trial on such charges. The accused were supported by the Church and were treated as martyrs while the propaganda ministry portrayed the Church as sexually corrupt and not to be trusted with the education of the young. In contrast, reporting of other sexual offences in Germany including the homosexual crimes committed by Hitler Youth leaders was suppressed leading to the impression that such crimes only occurred in the Church as a result of celibacy requirements.[974] According to Evans:

> In one particularly serious case in 1935, just as Goebbels was beginning his exposure of sex scandals in the Church, a boy was sexually assaulted by several others at a Hitler Youth camp then knifed to death to stop him talking. When his mother found out what had happened and reported it to the Reich Commissioner Mutschmann, he immediately had her arrested and imprisoned to prevent the scandal coming out into the open.[975]

The Papal encyclical – *Mit Brennener Sorge* (With Burning Anxiety) – published in March 1937, condemned the hatred of the Nazis towards the Church. Nevertheless, the result of the negative propaganda against the Catholic clergy was the withdrawal of most children from Catholic schools (down from 84% in 1934 to 5% in 1937 in Munich).[976] The Nazi campaign was successful in achieving its goal of turning all denominational schools into community schools and closing down all private schools by 1939. Instead of traditional religious prayers, young children learned this Hitler deifying, bedtime prayer:

> Führer, my Führer sent to me from God, protect and maintain me throughout my life. Thou who has saved Germany from deepest need, I thank thee today for thy daily bread. Remain at my side and never leave me. Führer, my Führer. My faith. My light. Heil, mein Führer![977]

In addition, children at school were required to learn this parodied version of 'The Lord's Prayer' (also called the 'Pater Noster' or 'Our Father'):

> Adolf Hitler, you are our great Führer. Thy name makes the enemy tremble. The Third Reich comes, thy will alone is law upon earth. Let us hear daily thy voice and order us by thy leadership, for we will obey to the end and even with our lives. We praise thee! Heil Hitler![978]

Nazism and Sexuality

As Timm notes, Nazism was, however, not just sexually repressive.[979] Sex was used to serve national goals. Sex and reproduction were crucial elements of population policy and most Nazi propaganda related to sexuality was focused on childbearing – to promote larger, desirable, 'Aryan' families and to ensure the survival of the racial state that the Nazis wished to establish even by having illegitimate children. Children were taught that part of their future duty was to perpetuate the race for the Reich. As Paris notes, "some couldn't contain their patriotism and forests and fields sheltered zealous young bodies getting a head start on their duties."[980]

Somewhat paradoxically, while the regime branded prostitutes as 'asocials' and sent thousands of them to concentration camps, the Nazis also created a formal widespread system of brothels. Prostitution was eventually seen as a necessary sexual outlet to satisfy productive men's needs that if left unsatisfied would lead men into homosexuality, dampen their fighting spirit or reduce their productivity, although fear of contracting syphilis and consequent sterility may also have been a concern.[981] A coveted award for heroism among German fighter pilots was a few nights in Hamburg's red light district.[982] The Nazi sponsorship of prostitution complicates the Nazi imagery of a 'nation of chaste families.'[983] Sexuality was, however, a means to an end: 'desirable' families should produce more children and not be 'contaminated' by the ready availability of prostitution, while brothels could enhance the productive capacities and fighting spirit of the men engaged in warfare. The ideological goal was sexual activity with a national purpose and not individual pleasure. Within this, male sexual needs took preference over those of women.

Nazi Sexual Policy

According to Timm, there were three stages to Nazi sexual policy. In the first few years of the Nazi era the leadership created the appearance of chastity depicting the new social system as devoted to the foundation and maintenance of healthy, racially fit, families. Articles in medical journals, newspapers and educational literature stressed the positive benefits of eugenic controls and organized youth activities e.g. the Hitler Youth, the League of German Girls, and the labor organization Strength Through Joy. Hitler preferred to think that physical training would provide an alternative for sexual indulgence:

> The extravagant emphasis laid on purely intellectual education and its consequent neglect of physical training must necessarily lead to sexual thoughts in early youth. Those boys whose constitutions have been trained and hardened by sports and gymnastics are less prone to sexual indulgence than those stay-at-homes who have been fed exclusively with mental pabulum.[984]

Some historians believe this to have been the case. Mosse,[985] for example, argued that the nudes and other similar printed materials of the Third Reich were, in fact, emptied of eroticism.[986] During this stage, 'asocial' behaviours for women (but not for men) included such categories as becoming too easily sexually aroused (*sexuelle Erregbarkeit*) or creating 'strongly erotic impressions.' 'Oversexed' women along with those who infected soldiers with venereal diseases were immediately placed in one of three categories; promiscuous individual, prostitute or sterilization candidate.[987] Errant sexual behavior could earn a woman a label of 'asocial' or 'feebleminded' both of which might make her eligible for sterilization. Inappropriate sexual deportment could result in denial of the award of a Mother's Cross to an otherwise qualified woman, but worse still, it could result in her being punished.[988]

Large youth group meetings provided an opportunity for sexual exploration among the young. As Victor Klemperer reported in his diary on 19 October 1935:

> Annemarie Kohler tells us in despair, that the hospitals are overcrowded with fifteen-year-old girls, some pregnant, some with gonorrhoea. The BDM. [The League of German Girls] Her brother has vehemently refused to allow his daughter to join.[989]

Similarly the physician Walter Gmelin, in a widely discussed 1936 essay, reported that:

> in his work evaluating couples' 'racial' and 'hereditary' suitability for marriage, less than 5 percent of the men and women he interviewed turned out to have been virgins. Most had begun to have intercourse in their late teens and early twenties, approximately seven years before they had married. ...the majority had had more than one premarital partner.[990]

The *Deutsches Ärtzeblatt* of 12 December 1936[991] reported that premarital sexual intercourse was widespread in the Third Reich, estimated at 51% in Saxony to over 90% in Munich. In 1936, when about 100,000 members of the Hitler Youth and the League of German Girls attended the Nuremberg rally, 900 girls between 15 and 18 returned home pregnant.[992] The Hitler youth gave young people an excuse to be out at night and the German Labour Front gave many young adults a chance to be away from their parents' homes and their first unsupervised contact with members of the opposite sex.[993] Sexuality among teenagers in Germany also became more prevalent during the war years and there was a growing incidence of pregnancies, births and venereal diseases among the 14-18 age group.[994] Bleuel notes further that a Munich court identified a number of causes including: inadequate parental control in war time, substandard Hitler Youth leaders and evening Hitler Youth parades, youth camps and employment of youth labour, a flood of trashy and obscene literature, and the reduction of police patrols for the supervision of juveniles. In addition, young people began to affiliate in their own social groups and gangs and not only in the Hitler Youth or its affiliated groups. These gangs evolved their own rules, leaders, uniforms and code names. Most members also belonged to the Hitler Youth or the *Bund Deutscher Mädchen* or German Girls League. The initials of the BDM (*Bund Deutscher Mädschen)* became corrupted into both '*Bald deutsche Mutter'* – soon to be German mothers – and '*Bubi drück Mich'* – squeeze me, babe.[995] Ilse Burch-Lennartz tells that in the BDM the demand for 'children for the Führer' left its mark:

> My sister was in a camp for girls, and right beside it was a men's camp. Then one night, after the girls had gone to sleep, the commandants of both camps opened the doors and

> windows and sent the lads over to the girls' camp. Needless to say they leapt on the girls. My sister fled in tears.[996]

Among the youth gangs, the BDM acronym took on additional meanings: the *Bund Deutscher Matratzen* (German Mattresses league) or *Baldur, drück mich* (Balder, squeeze me) referring to Baldur von Schirach who was the leader of the Hitler youth.[997] As is implied by these unofficial names, members indulged in active and indiscriminate promiscuity.[998] Both boys and girls experienced sex soon after puberty. By the end of the war an estimated 23% of all young Germans were infected with venereal diseases.[999]

In 1938, Nazi physician Ferdinand Hoffmann published evidence of how unpopular Nazi sexual conservatism was:

> ...approximately 72 million condoms are used in Germany each year and that 'in the surroundings of the big cities, evening after evening, the roads into the woods are covered with automobiles in which, after the American pattern, so-called love is made. 'Premarital intercourse was nearly ubiquitous,' Dr Hoffman complained. 'A young man who does not have a girlfriend is a priori a dummy; a girl without a boyfriend is a 'homely Gretchen type.' The idea that one should stay chaste until marriage 'possesses absolutely no more validity.' At best 5 percent of women entering marriage were still virgins; many had already had numerous boyfriends. Even after marriage German girls were hardly faithful to their spouses.[1000]

Herzog notes that the Jews were blamed for leading Germans astray.[1001] For example, Hoffman linked liberated sexuality with Jews who had proposed that the purpose of sexuality is simply pleasure: nothing more or less. One Berlin physician, Dr P Orlowski, blamed Jewish doctors for what he saw as unfortunate pressure being put on men to please women sexually. According to him, Jewish doctors and psychoanalysts had put the idea into women's heads that they were capable of orgasm. He warned that concern for women's needs would only result in erectile dysfunction and prostate problems for men and that they should return to 'automatic-egotistical sexual intercourse.' Nevertheless, although the population had largely adopted both Nazism and antisemitism, they were unwilling to abandon their emancipated sexual lives.

Stage Two

Timm's second stage of Nazi sexual policy promoted tolerance of extramarital sex, particularly prostitution, as long as it did not offend public opinion.[1002] Consideration of what constitutes a prostitute led to complex classification systems. As Timm explains, the venereal disease control forces in Germany had labeled promiscuous individuals as hwGs – *häufig wechselnder Geschlechtsverkehr* (people with frequently changing sexual partners) – since the 1920s. Married women who had illegitimate children while their husbands were off fighting the war were frequently labeled hwG or prostitute. In 1936, a new category of 'alternating intercourse' was used to describe occasionally promiscuous individuals – wG (*wechselnder Geschlechtsverkehr*) – whose behavior verged on but did not constitute prostitution or hwG. The distinction between wG and hwG was crucial as it determined the level of surveillance imposed on the individual. However, the exact definition of these terms was left to local workers. The outcomes were therefore unpredictable and dependent on such factors as appearance, gender, race, job status and education.[1003]

By 1941 Nazi thinking about sexuality had changed somewhat. Dr Hans Endres, a leading Nazi racial theorist had told an audience of high-ranking Nazis and their guests "our younger generation…must become proud of their bodies and enjoy the natural pleasures of sex without being ashamed."[1004] Ideas about the unnaturalness of prudery and the 'transcendental, quasi spiritual' qualities of sexuality were made generally available through the official, weekly, SS journal, *das schwartze Korps*, printed in hundreds and thousands of copies and enthusiastically endorsed by the Nazi regime. It mocked Christian defense of the sanctity of marriage, and aligned itself with young people's rejection of traditional mores. It attacked "the denominational morality…that sees in the body something to be despised, and wants to interpret what are natural processes as sinful drives."[1005] The paper defended both illegitimacy and non-reproductive heterosexual intercourse. It also printed numerous pictures of nudes – paintings, statues, and photographs – and defended nudity as pure and life enhancing. As Herzog writes:

> In 1938 two full-page photo spreads showed the 'beautiful and pure' nudity advocated by Nazism (beautiful naked women luxuriating in sun, sand and sea) and juxtaposed this with the 'shameless money making 'of the 'previous cultural epoch' (illustrated by photos of titillating half clothed and excessively made up women from what looked like Weimar dance halls). Not only the continual labeling as 'pure' and 'clean' then, but also the fiercely hyperbolic attacks on Jews, Marxists and Weimar-era cultural arbiters for their purported advocacy of extramarital sex, pornography, and nakedness served to distract attention from the Nazis advocacy of these very same things.[1006]

Udo Pini's *Leibeskult und Liebeskitsch* book (*Cult of the Body and Love Kitsch*)[1007] argued that the erotic had a firm place in Nazi culture by citing hundreds of examples from everyday outlets such as dancing, fashion, and picture postcards.[1008] While the regime denounced 'degenerate' sexuality it promised opportunities for 'healthy sexuality:' The German labour front offered courses in cosmetics and the 'Strength through Joy' cruises *(Kraft durch Freude)*, hinted that travel may bring sexual adventure. At its peak, in 1938, 10 million German workers and their dependants enjoyed minimal cost vacation trips through this program.[1009] On some ships, the lifeboats were said to be filled with couples every night. Not surprisingly, these cruises were also known as *Kind durch Freund* or Child by a Friend.[1010] Young, single women travelled on these cruises in large numbers. As Evans reports:

> Flirtations, dalliances and affairs with men on board or, even worse, with dark skinned young Italian, Greek or Arab men on shore aroused frequent critical comment from Gestapo spies. Known prostitutes were sometimes on the passenger list. A popular nickname for Strength Through Joy was 'the 'bigwigs' knocking shop (*Bonzenbordell*).'[1011]

Stage Three

Timm's Stage three – support for brothels in the military zones – was an apparently logical next development. Eight days after the invasion of Poland, in September 1939, an order was given to establish brothels in the military zone. In March 1942, these services were extended as rewards for productive camp inmates. After the beginning of the war, brothels were also created in Germany for foreign labourers, to protect German women from sexual defilement.[1012]

The establishment of brothels in the military zone was important for additional reasons. German men often stayed in the same region of the military rear and in occupied territories for lengthy periods.[1013] They lodged in private homes, operated amidst the population and developed friendships and intimate contact with local women. The military became concerned that these relationships could lead to emotional conflicts; they might cease to view the enemy as the enemy and might also develop conflicting experiences with their home lives. Some soldiers in Norway had been known to commit suicide because they felt unable to handle both their families in Germany and their girlfriends in Norway. The military tried to prevent this problem by evicting all the inhabitants of a house that they occupied and by creating the image that the female enemy spy would take advantage of their friendships. Despite this, relationships continued. Ultimately the Nazis became interested in the children of these relationships and women were required to undergo racial inspection to assess the possibility of Germanization of their offspring. As the regulations enforced to control sexual encounters with foreign women and German men varied from place to place and over time, so too did their assessments of racial value of the offspring.[1014]

At home too, it was difficult to prevent sexual contact with 'foreign' prisoners of war. As Bleuel notes, "It was easy to persuade her that the old Jew living near her was inferior and beneath her notice, besides which her husband was with her. But the young Polish prisoner of war working alongside her while her husband was at the front was more appealing."[1015] Sexual relations between German women and foreign workers or prisoners of war began from their first arrival in Germany and increased in frequency as more arrived.[1016] The war resulted in millions of Germans being separated from their wives for years: 1,909 cases of sexual relations between German women and foreigners were brought under Paragraph 4 of the Ordinance for the Safeguarding of German National Military Potential in 1940, 4,345 in 1941, and 9,108 in 1942.[1017] These official figures from the Reich Bureau of Statistics do not, however, include the numerous denunciations of women suspected of crimes of indecency who were sent directly to concentration camps without trial. Evans notes that the Social Security report of 1944 laid the blame for women's infidelities at home on female idleness. The high family benefits given to soldiers' wives made this possible. Some women thought that if soldiers were having 'a bit on the side' they too were entitled to amuse themselves. Sex also became a commodity with which to barter for luxuries. In addition, the frequent air raids led to a feeling that life was easily cut short so why not live it to the full while you could.[1018] The Nazi encouragement of illegitimate children may also have contributed to increased sexual freedoms among wives left at home.

The Nazis became concerned about these sexual relations, as they were believed to endanger the stability of the family and were detrimental to children.[1019] Soldiers blamed the state for their wives' infidelity and felt that their masculinity was being undermined. Further, these relationships challenged the Nazi ideal of sexuality only within racially 'pure' couples. After the start of the war, German women having sexual relationships with prisoners of war had their heads shaved and were paraded in public. These acts, however, had the effect of rousing sympathy and pity for the women rather than acting as the intended deterrent:

> Female observers became repelled by the double standards in evidence: in early 1942 in the town of Ebern, for example, a crowd watched while women whose hair had been shaved off were paraded through the streets with a sign that said "I sullied the honor of German womanhood" A number of women in the crowd ventured to ask whether

> the same would be done to a man who had an affair with a French woman while in France.[1020]

In October 1941, in part as a concession to public opinion, Hitler issued a directive prohibiting all public punishment.[1021]

Prostitution

Prostitution became an integrated part of the Nazi endeavour particularly during the war years, but this was largely restricted to non-'Aryan' women. So-called 'Aryan' German women were exempt from forced prostitution: the ideological image of the 'pure German woman' allowed them to escape from this form of coerced abuse although they were still exhorted and encouraged to voluntarily have intercourse with 'pure' Aryans to bear progeny for the Reich. They were not, however, forced to become prostitutes.

Prostitution was seen as fulfilling a number of purposes including satisfying the sexual needs of German soldiers and thereby avoiding their contact with forced labourers in the occupied countries, as well as serving as a means of 'therapy' for homosexual male prisoners.[1022] Lengyel[1023] suggests they were provided as an acceptable sexual outlet for SS and other camp guards who were continuously exposed to vast numbers of women who were paraded naked before them in camps. Access to prostitutes was also used as an incentive for increased productivity among both senior camp personnel and privileged prisoners in camps or, occasionally, in ghettos.[1024] On occasion, prostitution served as a punishment for an errant female prisoner.[1025]

Himmler was shocked by a report that there were two hundred cases of gonorrhoea in the Adolf Hitler SS guards, and, in consequence, ordered medically supervised brothels to be established for all units of the Waffen-SS.[1026] Two directives were issued by the Reich Minister of the Interior on 9 September 1939 and 16 March 1940 authorizing their establishment.[1027] As part of these directives, prostitutes were to be registered and those acting independently were detained or sent to concentration camps as 'asocials.' The brothels were to be situated away from places where juveniles could be corrupted and no private landlords were allowed. A network of state-controlled brothels was developed across Europe. Recent findings suggest that hundreds were established.[1028] The organization of brothels varied from region to region and depended on the location, politics, the degree of collaboration with local authorities and whether or not a similar system had existed prior to the German occupation.[1029] The most beautiful women went to the SS brothels, the less beautiful ones to the soldiers' brothels. The rest ended up in the prisoners' brothels.[1030] The brothel system continued to uphold ideological values in that separate brothels were created for German and non-German customers and prostitutes.[1031] Christa Paul[1032] estimated that approximately 34,140 women were forced to work as prostitutes during the Third Reich.

By the end of 1943, 60 brothels for foreign workers had opened in Reich territory, for the 'protection of German blood' and another 50 were in preparation.[1033] The operational centres were staffed by 600 prostitutes recruited in Paris, Poland and the Reich Protectorate of Bohemia and Moravia. They were strictly monitored for medical, sanitary and safety concerns. The women's takings were large although the lucrativeness of the work has been questioned due to deductions from earnings for living costs.[1034] Some served up to 50 clients a day and one claimed she made as much as RM 200 a day.[1035] She said she owned two tenement houses in Paris and was planning to buy two more with which she intended to retire. The charge per visit ranged from RM 3 to 5 with fees of RM 50 or even 100 being paid in isolated instances.[1036] This was untaxed income and represented a significant payment. Regardless of earnings, it was hard work: In one camp brothel in Oldenburg for example, 6-8 women clocked up 14,161 visits by clients in the course of 1943 – on average at least 5 men per day each for every day of the year.[1037]

Although by no means a central focus of their endeavours, even the brothels were imbued with a 'scientific basis' for their establishment, in keeping with Nazi attempts to situate their ideology within science. For example, one research centre experimented with finding a substitute for plasma in blood transfusions (needed by the military, in particular, to treat wounded soldiers) and brothels were enlisted to assist, as semen suppliers.[1038] Prostitutes at the Klosterstrasse brothel in Stuttgart were instructed to preserve semen-filled sheaths after each act of intercourse and to keep them in a container, which was collected at regular intervals by an authorized representative of the research centre. No details of this research are available, and all those involved had to sign a pledge of secrecy.

The first brothel for concentration camp prisoners – usually accessible only to those holding positions of 'authority' – opened at Gusen, a sub-camp of Mauthausen in 1942.[1039] Thereafter, brothels were opened in Buchenwald, Sachsenhausen, Auschwitz, Flossenbürg, Dachau, Neuengamma, Buna-Monowitz, Majdanek, Stutthof, the Sylt camp at Alderney, and Mittelbau-Dora.[1040] In Auschwitz 1, Block 24 served as a brothel that was known as "the Puff."[1041] Treblinka, a death camp, although not having a formal brothel, did provide 'services' of women for 'deserving' prisoners. Lalko, the camp commander, selected 20 'young, fresh and pretty' girls from a transport from Grodno who were 'married' to deserving kapos and – uncharacteristically – '*Hofjude'* (Head Jews). He conducted both a religious and civil marriage service for them: the civil service consisted of him pointing to the woman and saying 'this is your husband.' The religious aspects were served by providing a nuptial canopy obtained from a nearby village and having the camp orchestra play the wedding march.[1042]

Recruitment for Brothel Work

Women from Ravensbrück served most concentration camps brothels except those in Auschwitz camps that were served by women from Auschwitz.[1043] Nanda Hebermann[1044] served as Block Elder of the 'prostitutes block' in Ravensbrück and confirms that 8-10 prostitutes were regularly recruited and selected from her block to work in camp bordellos. She reports that initially women were not forced to become prostitutes but were asked to 'volunteer' for the work in exchange for more comfortable conditions: they had better food, did not have to perform any other work, had beds rather than cots, nice clothes, and received money which was to be paid out to them in the event of their release. She notes that these women would be sent back every three months and exchanged for others – at least one woman from her block did not survive the violence at Mauthausen. Haas reports that most were promised freedom after six months, (and not three) which promise was not kept, and many, if not most, were returned to Ravensbrück at the end of their six months, suffering from venereal diseases. Wanda Poltawska, one of the girls operated on in Ravensbrück (in the bone, nerve and muscle experiments), confirms that women were recruited for the 'puff' – the soldiers' brothel – with promises of release from the camp.[1045] The women were not given any method of birth control although some were sterilized.[1046] Those who became pregnant were killed or had abortions that sometimes resulted in death.[1047] Inmates of punishment blocks volunteered more readily to escape their situation. Morrison[1048] reports anecdotes that are more irregular regarding volunteering: In a French barrack, some women misunderstood *'bordell'* as Bordeaux and offered to volunteer. In another instance, the call for prostitutes caused some consternation but then several names were given – all of them women over 70. Women who volunteered were sent for a medical check. If turned down, they were scorned by their fellow inmates on their return. In general, however, many women were reluctant to volunteer despite the enticements offered. Stories told by those who returned as well as their obviously sick and frightful appearance were sufficient to discourage volunteers.[1049] As the brothel system expanded and more prostitutes were needed, recruitment methods changed.[1050] SS men would walk down the lines of prisoners during 'roll-call' and pick out women they regarded as suitable. The selected women were then taken to the camp doctor and forced to undress for further inspection.

Many who accepted the invitation had previously been prostitutes but not all. In Ravensbrück, prostitutes who had been arrested as 'asocials' formed the lowest rung of the social ladder.[1051] The category of 'asocials' was very broad and included prostitutes, lesbians, 'gypsies' as well as women who were considered promiscuous or had elected to have abortions. Saidel notes that the majority of 'asocials' were 'poor and dependent on state support. Many did not have fixed residences, or were beggars, charity cases, homeless people, alcoholics, homosexuals, prostitutes, or so-called, 'immoral' priests.[1052] Morrison's suggestion that they were a rather tough type who likely had a jail record and who had learned to survive in the dangerous, underworld of sex-workers is possibly tinged by contemporary, negative prejudices of survivors towards both prostitutes and lesbians.[1053] In contrast, the men who frequented sex workers did not carry a negative connotation.[1054]

The Work in Camp Brothels

Brothels in camps were open for a few hours each evening and for longer on Sundays.[1055] Men would purchase an opportunity to use the brothel with either coupons that had been 'earned' for higher productivity, or money.Most reports indicate the standard rate was anything from half a RM to 2 RM a time of which the girls kept about a half.[1056] The brothels, were, therefore, self supporting. Payment would allow the men 15 minutes with a prostitute[1057] and each woman would serve eight men in an evening.[1058] Men would line up, having paid their way, until a signal – a bell – was given to enter the brothel together with the order 'March.' They would be directed to the first available woman and would wait outside the door for the signal and command 'Begin,' to enter the room. A further bell and command 'Dress and Leave' would indicate there was five minutes left to the end of the 15 minutes period. Women would then have another 15 minutes to clean or disinfect themselves with a potassium permanganate douche and dress, and get ready for the next man.[1059] Intercourse was not always possible: some men were no longer strong enough and others simply wanted the companionship of a woman again. There were peepholes in the doors allowing for supervision by the brothel guards (*Kapo Poufmutter* – German slang for a madame) to ensure only a 'missionary' position was used – and perhaps for the guards' own gratification. Sommer reports that the SS did not miss an opportunity to humiliate prisoners and voyeurism in the brothels was one method used: they would watch what was happening and make dirty comments or kick against the door if the man took too long.[1060] As Roos notes, sex in camp brothels reduced intercourse to a mere animal function. One woman forced to work in the Buchenwald camp brothel reported:

> It was nothing personal, one felt like a robot. They did not take notice of us; we were the lowest of the low. We

> were only good for this. No conversation or small talk, not even the weather was on the agenda. Everything was so mechanical and indifferent...They finished their business and left.[1061]

The brothels did not always follow the rules. Gun reports that in Dachau men could 'arrange' to see particular girls. To do so they would have to subvert the SS kapo and buy the favours and the silence of the girl so she would agree to spend time with him and be more compliant. Food, stolen clothing, jewelry or perfume could be used for the bribe. He reports that one of the kapos was able to maintain one of the 15 girls to himself for a whole year in this manner.[1062] The women did not always keep their earnings to themselves: some had pimps who managed or assisted them by, for example, offering to save a family member, and they in return fared well.[1063] Others dropped food down to '*Musselmen*' who waited below their windows to obtain such scraps.[1064]

Prostitutes, in general, if they could survive the hardships of their work, had a greater chance of survival in the camps as they were better fed and cared for.[1065] Their psychological trauma is, however, unknown and immeasurable although vividly described by Ka-Tzetnik's (pseudonym for Yahiel Feiner De-Nur) noted, but controversial, 1956 fictional novel '*House of Dolls*'.[1066]

Jewish Women as Prostitutes

Jewish women, although persecuted vilely on most other levels, were somewhat protected from this forced indecency – at least on an official if not unofficial level – because of the stringent laws against *Rassenschande*.[1067] The use of Jewish women as prostitutes in German brothels is, however, currently still under debate.

Opposing views exist regarding the use of Jewish women as prostitutes with some scholars arguing that this was rare[1068] and others that it occurred far more often than has been commonly acknowledged.[1069] Sommer reports that there is no evidence that any of the prostitutes were Jewish.[1070] Sommer bases his conclusions on SS documentation regarding women working in brothels such as transport lists, brothel invoice sheets, test tube information slips for blood and cervical smear samples, brothel visitors' lists, and prisoner or personnel cards. He reports that the total number of women serving in Nazi brothels in concentration camps was only 210: 190 in prisoner brothels and 20 in brothels for the Ukrainian guards. Of the 174 names of the women serving in brothels, and judging by names and birthplaces, 114 (66%) were of German nationality, 46 (26%) were Polish, and 3 others (25%) had either German or Polish citizenship (according to different documents). Six women (3%) were classified as Russian but were likely to have been of Belarusian or Ukrainian heritage. One woman was Dutch (1%) In four other cases (2%) no heritage was listed. Of the women, 97 (67%) were 'asocials,' 42 (29%) were political prisoners and 4 (3%) were 'criminals.' According to Sommer the names did not indicate that any of the women were Jewish. Additional lists of women's blood samples sent for syphilis testing indicate that one woman was Jewish but Sommer ascribes her to the role of *Poufmutter* (brothel mother or Madame) based on the ages of the women and their nationalities. Sommer claims that although it is not 100% certain that no Jewish women served in brothels, more than 80% of the women who did serve are known and among them, there is no evidence of Jewish women.

Sommer's qualification that the number of prisoners who could frequent camp brothels was small – probably less than 1% – and were mostly those who occupied higher positions in the camp hierarchy, does not detract from the possibility that Jewish women served in these brothels, or minimize the assault that they experienced.[1071] Sommer does acknowledge that Jewish women who were hiding their identity by using non-Jewish names may have been included.[1072] Jack Eisner's memoirs report such a woman: his love, Halina, a blond Jewish girl from Warsaw who had passed for 'Aryan' before being caught, was recruited and forced into prostitution in Flossenbürg.[1073] Sommer does not consider that Jewish women in mixed marriages (of which there were many) might not have used their 'Jewish' names. In addition, reliance on extant Nazi documentation may not be adequate to reflect the numbers of women serving in the many brothels established by the Nazis (perhaps hundreds[1074]), particularly when these women are reported to have served for only three months (or six) at a time before being changed. Sommer's specific data analysis of such a small sample may not reflect reality accurately.

In contrast, Sinnreich provides arguments that Jewish women were used as prostitutes in ghettos and camps. For example, forced prostitution of Jewish women occurred in ghettos: A. Ruzkensky testified that in 1941, Jewish girls were rounded up by the SS in the Łódź ghetto and put into a brothel.[1075] Mühlhäuser[1076] reports that in some regions the demands for prostitution services exceeded the number of available women: In March 1943, in a brothel in Lvov, Ukraine, the queues for entry to the brothel extended down the street during the peak hours of lunchtimes and evenings. Testimonies report that the *Wehrmacht* commanders would force young local women and girls into service. Sinnriech notes that rounding up women on the streets for forced sexual service in military brothels was a common means of recruitment.[1077] According to these reports, while sexual intercourse with a Jewish woman remained forbidden, exceptions to this were frequent.[1078]

Sinnreich reports that Jewish women were used as prostitutes in all categories of brothels established by the Germans – military, SS, civilian population and foreign workers' brothels. She argues that the fact that regulations forbidding Jewish women to be used in brothels, first published in 1939, were reiterated in 1942, suggests that Jewish women were in fact being used. In addition, she cites numerous testimonies reporting Jewish women's involvement in brothels, and that Jewish ghetto councils were asked to provide lists of young Jewish women to serve in brothels.[1079] She also reports that some Jewish women were used in brothels in France. Ilse B testified that her Jewish aunt and a cousin, who had been interned in a concentration camp, had informed her that Jewish women were forced into bordello service in a military brothel.[1080]

Tory's diary entry for 9 January 1944, reports that in the Kovno ghetto in Lithuania, three Jewish women were brought from the ghetto to serve the sexual needs – and to motivate – those men forced to exhume bodies from mass graves and to eliminate traces of them by burning. The work was repulsive and disheartening: more than once the diggers recognized their own relatives among the bodies while having to extract gold teeth, and to remove any jewelry.[1081]

Sinnreich reports that service in military brothels was devastating and that women's reproductive organs were so damaged they could not have children later. Psychological damage was equally severe.[1082] Dror and Linn confirm that Jewish women were used in military brothels. They report that the Italian journalist and diplomat Curzio Malaparte described a brothel established in 1941 in the city of Soroca, Romania, by the medical services of the 11th German Military Division. This military brothel used about 10 young Jewish women from the city and its environs at a time, as slave labourers. According to Malaparte, a change of girls was provided every twenty days. The girls who were removed were 'shoved into a truck and taken down to the river.' Shenk [the Nazi *Sonderführer*] told Malaparte "that it was not worthwhile to feel sorry for them. They were not fit for anything anymore. They were reduced to rags, and besides, they were Jews."[1083]

Fina Monk, interviewed by David Boder in 1946, reported one young girl serving in an Auschwitz brothel for three months. She also reports that Jewish women thought they might have a better chance of surviving if they served in brothels.[1084] Liana Millu reports that one Jewish girl had volunteered for work in the Auschwitz brothel: her sister refused to speak to her from then on.[1085] Heger confirms the use of Jewish women in Flossenbürg's brothel. He reports that 10 young girls, almost all 'gypsies' and Jews, were brought to the brothel from Ravensbrück, when it was opened in the summer of 1943.[1086]

The various testimonies that do exist regarding the use of Jewish women as prostitutes in concentration camp and other brothels, including military brothels, suggests that this did occur despite Sommer's writings, and the long held view that the *Rassenschande* laws protected Jewish women from this aspect of Nazi abuse. Rosenbaum's report on the importance of obtaining a *Halakhic* ruling from Rabbi Oshry, published in 1949, regarding the ability of Jewish women, who were used as prostitutes in the brothels of the German army, to resume their marital lives with their prewar husbands, is further telling support for the reality of such occurrences.[1087] A particular problem arose with one couple regarding prostitution and marriage. Jewish law prescribes that if a woman voluntarily has intercourse with another man her husband may not live with her once he finds out. If she is forced to have intercourse with another, her husband may continue to live with her. Rosenbaum reports that after the war, a couple was reunited: they had lost all their children in the Holocaust. To his dismay, the husband found, tattooed on her arm the words 'Prostitute for the Armies of Hitler.' The husband was concerned that she might have willingly had intercourse with the Germans. Rabbi Oshry granted permission for them to continue as man and wife, as even if she willingly had had intercourse it was under dire threat of death. He writes, in 1949:

> It is therefore the *din* that this unfortunate, and all her sisters whose bitter fate it was to be seized for such shameful purpose, are permitted to their husbands...and there is not the slightest reason to forbid them to their husbands.[1088]

Rabbi Oshry's choice of words for the direction of this *responsa* to the woman and "all her sisters" is likely careful and has considerable implications for the ongoing debate regarding whether Jewish women had been utilized as prostitutes. Tattooing of Jewish prostitutes as '*Feld-Hure*' is also described in Ka-Tzetnik's 1956 fictional novel '*House of Dolls*.'[1089]

Although contradictory information exists, the weight of available evidence suggests that Jewish women were required to serve within the extensive German brothel system, and were forced to act as prostitutes in ghettos, labour and concentration camps, and by the *Einsatzgruppen*. It is likely that, as preconceptions regarding the protective effect of the *Rassenschande* laws on this aspect of Jewish women's abuse are discounted, and as acknowledging the reality of sexual horrors becomes more common in Holocaust writings, future scholars will confirm that Jewish women were, indeed, utilized as prostitutes.

Purposes for Brothels

Cohen suggests that one of the purposes behind the provision of brothels for prisoners was to divert political prisoners from political activity in the camps. The prisoners in Auschwitz, however, passed on secret instructions not to patronize the brothels, resulting in only the 'green' (criminal) prisoners and not the 'red' (political prisoners) doing so.[1090] Other motives to visit camp brothels included proving their superior positions through their sexuality, desire to feel like a man, to feel human, to experience sex at least once before dying, just to talk to a woman, or to have personal contact with another human being. A further reason for visiting the brothels was through force, for example, among homosexuals.[1091]

In addition to serving the sexual needs of men, prostitutes were used to 'treat' homosexuality. Himmler's idea was that those with pink triangles could be 'cured' of their homosexuality by compulsory regular visits to a brothel. Heinz Heger reports being obliged 'to show up there once a week in order to 'learn' the joys of the other sex.'[1092] As he recalls:

> On three occasions I myself had to visit the brothel on 'Dustnag's' express orders [the camp commandant's nickname], which was already torment enough. What pleasure was I expected to get when the poor girl lifted her legs and said 'Hurry up then, hurry up' so that she could be finished as soon as possible with a situation that was certainly just as painful for her? On top of which I knew that some SS man would be spying on me through the hole. Certainly no 'cure' could be expected from the 'enjoyment of the opposite sex.' Quite the contrary: I was so shattered from this form of sexual intercourse that I never again tried to have sex with a woman, and my homosexual orientation was reinforced.[1093]

Brothels Outside Camps

Brothels established for the German army in occupied countries were also widespread. Salon Kitty in Berlin was, however, special. It was a brainchild of Heydrich and was established in Berlin's *Giesebrechtstrasse* to provide a means of surveillance and supervision of Reich dignitaries.[1094] VIPs, foreign diplomats, and high ranking Nazis, unaware that they were being recorded, visited Salon Kitty, named for its madame, Kitty Schmidt. Kitty managed a group of prostitutes trained in eliciting information whose pillow talk with clients was recorded by 120 'bugs' and preserved on 25,000 wax disks before the war ended. Guests let slip much that was of interest to the SS aided by the additional stimulation of alcohol. However, as the genuinely important embassy staff did not frequent the place, the results in terms of espionage were minimal.[1095]

Prostitution, served by local women voluntarily, also occurred outside concentration camps.[1096] This provided both sexual gratification for the SS and an opportunity to traffic clothes and jewelry stolen from the prisoners arriving at the camps. Prostitutes could afford to buy them.[1097]

Rape by Russians

So called 'Aryan' German women, while protected from the worst horrors of forced prostitution for much of the Nazi era, did suffer the worst of the crime of rape committed primarily by Russian soldiers at the close of the war, although this was indiscriminately directed to all women, including surviving camp inmates and foreigners.

Stories of Russian rape or sexual violence towards the end of World War II are legendary. Numerous accounts of rape[1098] or fear of rape[1099] by Russian soldiers, often fueled by alcohol, exist. As Fixherbert writes, "As the invasion and conquest of Germany was coming to its climax, the Red Army, one of the most disciplined in the world, was given the green light to run riot, rape and pillage."[1100] Hundreds of thousands of German women were raped, ranging from pre-pubescent girls to old women, many if not most of them numerous times.[1101] Gang rape,[1102] sometimes publically while others waited their turn,[1103] and frequently violent sex,[1104] even ending in death,[1105] was a characteristic of the Russian terror that swept Berlin in particular, but also other regions. In some cases, women's bodies were slit open from stomach to anus.[1106] Estimates range from over 100,000[1107] women in Berlin alone to as many as 2 million women altogether[1108] of whom 10,000 died in consequence.[1109] Some suggest that one in three of the women in Berlin were raped. When Russian troops entered Fürstenburg on 30 April 1945, few females in this town of 4-5,000 escaped being raped.[1110] In Dahlem, nuns, young girls, old women, pregnant women and mothers who had just given birth were all raped without pity at a maternity clinic and orphanage.[1111] When gang raped women from Königsburg begged their attackers to put them out of their misery afterwards, the Red Army soldiers appeared to have been insulted: "Russian soldiers do not shoot women," they replied "only German soldiers do that."[1112] Alcohol was a major factor in perpetrating rapes. Sometimes, however, it resulted in the soldier not being able to complete the act. In this situation, they were likely to use a bottle instead with devastating impact.[1113]

In addition to the psychological and physical horrors of the experience, women had to cope with venereal disease[1114] and pregnancy, as not infrequent outcomes.[1115] Doctors, in the face of health, eugenic, racist and humanitarian conflicts, quickly suspended Paragraph 218 prohibiting abortions and for most of the first year after the end of the war, physicians approved medical abortions almost up until the last month of pregnancy if the woman could certify that she had been raped by a Red Army soldier or even a foreigner.[1116] Many of the women who gave birth abandoned the baby in the hospital, partly as they knew their husbands or fiancée's would not accept the child.[1117]

Rapes sometimes occurred with husbands as helpless witnesses.[1118] Other husbands were shot if they tried to intervene.[1119] As Knopp reports "...behind the door I saw a woman lying smeared with blood, her legs splayed. She had literally been raped to death [by Russians] and her husband was lying in the hall, shot through the neck."[1120] Not surprisingly, suicide rates – of individuals as well as families – climbed at the end of the war, probably influenced by these horrific events.[1121] Shame and wounded masculinity drove fathers to kill their wives and children, often with the woman's consent, before killing themselves.[1122] Some men murdered women to spare them from rape or as punishment for having given in, or for fraternizing with Russian soldiers.[1123]

Some Soviet soldiers raped and even killed Jewish women they encountered as these former concentration camp prisoners made their way back to their homes.[1124] When others explained that the woman was Jewish and had been persecuted by the Germans, the soldiers replied 'Frau ist Frau.' As Rose Frochewajg Mellender revealed to Saidel:

> The Russians did come and seek out some girls, you know, and we pretended that we are so very sick, they shouldn't touch us. They were animals, because they didn't see a woman for such a – what did they care if she is [in] a concentration camp, if she's sick, has lice or not? They didn't care. They had the lice, too, you know. And they raped some girls. So we had to hide under the beds and things. It was a struggle all along, all along.[1125]

Despite the horrors of rape, and as described by journalist Martha Hillers, but published anonymously as, 'A Woman of Berlin' many German women entered into relationships with Red Army soldiers.[1126] Some made deliberate decisions to take up with an occupier – preferably an officer with power – to protect themselves from others and to gain commodities or privileges. Some consciously offered themselves in exchange for protection of a loved one such as a daughter while others were forced to have sex alone in a room with a lonely young soldier for whom they occasionally developed ambivalent feelings of hate, pity, and warmth.[1127] The fine lines between consensual sex, prostitution and rape were blurred.[1128]

German propaganda had depicted women's rapes by Russians and had terrorized them in anticipation.[1129] Even if Germans were not aware of actions taken against Jews, they were aware of the German army's atrocities on the eastern front and now expected reprisals: returning German soldiers had reiterated stories of their brutalities towards the Russians, their looting, burning and raping of women and their wholesale murder of innocent people.[1130] The idea of 'Mongol barbarians' raping German women had been used to bolster German fighting spirit on the eastern front. "By the end of the war most German women had already seen graphic newsreel footage of the bodies of violated women, battered old people, and murdered children left behind as the Red Army stormed westward."[1131] As Gilbert writes, "They were afraid of being raped, not just once or twice, but over and over again."[1132] Young women tried to hide or disguise themselves: They covered their heads, blackened their faces, covered their legs, even pretended to have an illness like scarlet fever or insanity. Blondes were especially vulnerable, and families tried to hide young girls.[1133] Sometimes a mother would reveal the hiding places of other girls to protect her own daughter.[1134] The Russians usually came at night, demanding watches or alcohol and then would return drunk seeking women and calling '*Frau Komm*!'[1135] The reality of women's fears was often realized. As Martha Hillers wrote:

> They lined up…each took his turn. She says there were at least twenty, but she doesn't know exactly. She had to bear the brunt of it herself. The other woman wasn't well …I stare at Elvira. Her swollen mouth is sticking out of her pale face like a blue plum…Without a word the redhead opens her blouse and shows us her breasts, all bruised and bitten…[1136]

Some women coped by rationalizing their experiences:

> The old woman said 'try to get away from them [the Russians], by all means, but if they do catch you just shut your eyes and pretend that it is your husband. How often does he fail to ask you if you want his love and force you to it when you do not want it? If you think of it that way you will be able to stand it and it will be over quickly.'[1137]

Similarly, Juliane Hartman, a 19-year-old living in Berlin reported that she had never been told the facts of life and was the first victim on her street. "But looking back at what happened to me, it's as though *I* wasn't really being violated. Instead, I was standing next to myself, alongside my body, a detached observer. That feeling has kept the experience from dominating the rest of my life"[1138] [Italics original]. For others the experience had life-long effects on their ability to have relationships with men.[1139] Grossman, however, suggests that rape of German women after the war was only one of a series of horrific events occurring as a consequence of losing the war including: losing your home, becoming a refugee, having your men folk killed, maimed or taken prisoner, your children sicken or die of disease and malnutrition and the shame of defeat. She concludes, "The story of rape was told as part of the narrative of survival in ruined Germany."[1140] On the other hand, Russian rape of German women served to bolster the latter's own identity as being superior to that of the barbarian conquerors and as victims of abuse.[1141]

Reactions to the rampage of rape that occurred changed as time passed.[1142] As Beevor writes, the late 1940 and 1950s after the men returned from prison camps, were a sexually repressive period in which husbands reasserted their authority. Women were forbidden to mention their experiences of rape as though this had dishonoured the men's ability to protect them: in fact, they had to console their husbands. It remained a taboo subject until the late 1980s when the younger generation encouraged their mothers and grandmothers to speak of these events.[1143] Beevor notes that the subject of the Red Army's rapes in Germany has been repressed in Russia so that even today veterans refuse to talk about it.[1144] Those who do, however, are unrepentant: "They all lifted their skirts for us and lay on the bed," said the leader of one tank company. He even went on to boast that "two million of our children were born" in Germany. Others have stated: "Our fellows were so sex-starved," a Soviet major told a British journalist at the time, "that they often raped old women of sixty, seventy or even eighty – much to these grandmothers' surprise, if not downright delight."[1145]

Reasons for this extreme rampage of Russian sexual assault have been proposed:

> the rapes committed in 1945 – against old women, young women, even barely pubescent girls – were acts of violence, an expression of revenge and hatred. But not all of the soldiers' anger came in response to atrocities committed by the *Wehrmacht* and the SS in the Soviet Union. Many soldiers had been so humiliated by their own officers and commissars during the four years of war that they felt driven to expiate their bitterness, and German women presented the easiest target. Polish women and female slave labourers in Germany also suffered.[1146]

In addition, and perhaps an even more sinister explanation, Russian psychiatrists have written of the brutal 'barracks eroticism' created by Stalinist sexual repression during the 1930s. According to this, Soviet society was depicted as virtually asexual. As Beevor reports:

> Human urges and emotions had to be suppressed. Freud's work was banned, divorce and adultery were matters for strong party disapproval. Criminal sanctions against homosexuality were reintroduced. The new doctrine extended even to the complete suppression of sex education. In graphic art, the clothed outline of a woman's breasts was regarded as dangerously erotic. They had to be disguised under boiler suits. The regime clearly wanted any form of desire to be converted into love for the party and above all for Comrade Stalin.[1147]

This theory proposes that Russians were so totally repressed sexually in the Stalinist age, that they were ignorant and inexperienced with regard to even the most basic elements of sexuality, leading to unrepressed and unmoderated expression when unleashed from these controls. According to this view, the Red Army's rapes were sexual acts rather than motivated by violence. Regardless of the explanation, the sexual horrors occurred and, as with subsequent genocides, have revealed a brutal aspect of humanity that is, as with the Holocaust as a whole, repugnant to acknowledge as a fundamental, if mostly latent, aspect of humanity. As Beevor writes, "there is a dark area of male sexuality which can emerge all too easily, especially in war, when there are no social or disciplinary restraints."[1148]

Recent German discourse on its Nazi past distrusts any narrative that might support German post-war perceptions of themselves as victims of Nazism. As Atina Grossman highlights, such suggestions are feared as they:

> might participate in a dangerous revival of German nationalism, whitewash the Nazi past, and normalize a genocidal war…just announcing apparent 'facts' about the massive incidence of rape perpetrated by soldiers of the Red army which smashed the Nazi war machine is enough to provide enormous anxiety and resistance among many who are not otherwise averse to documenting the widespread existence of male violence against women.[1149]

For example, while facts are difficult to determine, the number of German women raped at the conclusion of the war by the Red Army varies widely up to as many as one to two million, with the actual number of rapes estimated as higher than that as many women were raped repeatedly.[1150] Once the estimates enter the millions, the potential claim by German women that they too were victims of Nazism becomes possible.[1151] Academic debate – and emotions – run high in consequence. Clearly, however, while 'Aryan' German women were largely exempt from violent sexual abuse during the war many were clearly not able to escape this horror at the war's end. In addition, recent accounts of the involvement of at least half a million German women who were conditioned to accept violence, to incite it, or to commit it, in defense of, or as an assertion of Germany's superiority in the eastern territories alone, contrasts sharply with the post-war image of the victimized, overburdened German 'Hausfrau' who was responsible for re-building Germany after the fall of the Nazi regime.[1152]

In their efforts to promote the 'Aryan' Master Race, Nazi ideology imposed exploitative sexual demands on those regarded as 'worthy of life.' Distinctive, however, is that German women could, for the most part, chose whether to respond to these demands or not, unlike the Jewish woman's experience.

Love And Sexuality Among Jews

Despite the increasingly liberal sexuality of the Weimar years, most women in Germany and its neighbouring countries, including Jewish women, were brought up modestly and with considerable sexual naïveté. Magda Herzberger, from Romania (Cluj, Transylvania) reported that she and her friends were ignorant about sex. As a teenager, discussing sex was not allowed. She reports being ignorant about sex even after the end of WWII.[1153] Amos Oz writes fluently of this in his semi-autobiographical novel *A Tale of Love and Darkness*. He describes how young girls had a "terrible sense of modesty…We were buried under a mountain of shame and fear… Dating meant holding hands at most" and "Men would blush if they used words like 'woman', 'suckle' 'skirt' or 'legs'."[1154] He writes:

> Chastity was both a cage and the only railing between you and the abyss. It lay on a girl's chest like a thirty-kilo stone. Even in the dreams she dreamed at night, chastity stayed awake and stood by the bed and watched over her so she could be very ashamed when she woke up in the morning, even if nobody knew.[1155]

For some women, however, the Nazi era changed this. Nechama Tec reports the story of Eva Galer, who came from a small town near Krakow in Poland. Before the war, her father, an orthodox Jew, would not have allowed her to bring a boyfriend into their house. Now after the Nazi takeover, and the humiliation of her father by cutting off his beard in public, his loss of gainful employment, and his subsequent depression, they flirted openly in front of him.[1156] For Jewish women, societal norms regarding love and sexuality changed considerably under Nazi rule. As life generally became more difficult, and as sexuality among Jews became more and more restricted as a result of the Nazi goal to eliminate their reproductive potential, Jews' sexual behaviour was forced to adapt to circumstances.

Love and Sex in the Ghettos

On the one hand, people fell in love in the ghettos, despite everything that was going on around them.[1157] On the other hand, women were forced to resort to using their bodies to survive in the ghettos.[1158] In the Łódź ghetto, a factory manager asked Lucille Eichengreen what she would give him for finding a place for her sister to work. When she said she had no money or valuables he laughed, replying that that was not what he was wanting.[1159] In the Warsaw ghetto, the Ringelblum diaries reveal that some women established sexual relationships to gain male protection. Men established relationships with younger (and sometimes unmarried) women. Sometimes the women's husbands agreed to these extramarital affairs, hoping that they too would be protected. Wives and children were, however, often neglected and left without protection.[1160] Kaplan reports that one survivor today is grateful that her mother had sex with a bureaucrat who then provided their exit papers thereby saving their lives.[1161] The Ringelblum diaries document the actions of the Jewish ghetto police who arrested people in order to send them to the death camps and released them in exchange for sex or money: "For this purpose they had a special room in the hospital."[1162] Kitty Hart's friend Henia was befriended by the commandant of Sosnowiec ghetto and managed to procure a privileged position for herself in Auschwitz-Birkenau. She later talked about the rest of her experiences but remained silent about these, and lived for years with fear of reprisals against her.[1163]

Mary Berg's diary entry of 31 July 1941 reveals another side to this type of relationship in the Warsaw ghetto:

> Everything your heart desires can be had there [Café Hirschfeld] – the most expensive liqueurs, cognac, pickled fish, canned food, duck, chicken, and goose...This café is the meeting place of the most important smugglers and their mistresses; here women sell themselves for a good meal. Sixteen year olds come here with their lovers, the few scoundrels who work for the Gestapo. These girls do not think of what will happen to them later – they are too young for that. They come here to eat well. The next day such girls may be found shot to death together with their lovers. The organized youth of the ghetto deals ruthlessly with traitors.[1164]

Prostitution occurred in ghettos. According to Stiffel, Jewish prostitutes could be seen everywhere in the Warsaw ghetto. As he reports, "On occasion three generations of prostitutes could be seen on a single corner: grandmother, mother and daughter so that they could avoid the final slide down to the level of beggars."[1165] Further, Polish and Jewish smugglers got together in a large bar on Sliska Street to plan the next week's activity with vodka and whores. The Warsaw diaries of Adam Czernaikow record, on 17 January 1942, that "In the Piekielko [street market] before the war, the pimps were openly selling women."[1166] Such Jewish prostitutes were, however, at greater risk of being selected for transports from the ghettos by the *Judenrat*, together with 'gypsies,' those on welfare, criminals and the unemployed.[1167]

Even children became exposed to sexuality, for example, in the Łódź ghetto. Jozef Zelkowicz reported that:

> Children work as coal miners...dump pickers looking for anything that will burn, create heat. In the coal mines girls take off their one dress before stepping into the pit. Boys of 10 or 11 and girls of 13 and 14 get to know the secrets of their mothers and fathers right there in the coal pit. They take care of their physical needs right there and then in full view. No time for amenities.[1168]

Sexuality and Love in Partisan Groups

Sexuality occurred both out of love and as a means of survival in partisan groups that established themselves in forests around Nazi occupied areas. Women's sexual role in the groups was largely determined by the nature of the groups: Jewish or Russian, with sex in Jewish partisan groups being viewed as voluntary more often than in non-Jewish, Russian groups.[1169]

In Jewish groups, women took an active part in partisan missions such as combat or supply gathering missions, sabotage actions or ambushes. Women held command positions and served as 'Liaisons.'[1170] Former members of the Jewish Bielski *otriad* agree that no woman there was ever raped or sent away as all were valued regardless of their 'value' (sexual or otherwise) to the group.[1171] In the forests there were no wedding ceremonies but if a relationship lasted for a while the couple were treated as husband and wife. In the Bielski group many women found stable relationships with one man, some would have sex with many men, and some remained unattached.[1172] Tec reports that Sulia Rubin, for example, agreed to become the partner of a man of much lower social status (a common occurrence in the partisan groups[1173]) and was immediately cared for. She remained married to him for the rest of her life, as was a commonly reported outcome of such partnerings. Lilka – Tuvia Bielski's third wife – fell in love with him when she first met him and also remained married to him. Tec writes further that about 60 percent of the adults were estimated to have lived as couples. Reports suggest that a code of marital ethics existed in this group at least: both Tuvia and Zus Bielski, although they had many lovers, stayed away from married women or women with steady boyfriends.

In contrast, Tec notes that entry into Russian partisan groups was often contingent on a woman's willingness to become an officer's mistress. Not all women were willing to do this, and not all had the looks (or skills in nursing or cooking, for example, that were also valued) required to join. Estimates suggest that only 2-3 percent of all Soviet partisans were women.[1174] Most high-ranking Russian partisans had a mistress. In recognition of this arrangement, such a woman was called a 'transit wife.' If a male partisan helped a woman in any way, he expected to be paid with sexual favours.[1175] All women in these partisan groups were in a dependent position, and were primarily defined as sex objects and excluded from participation in valued activities.[1176] Jewish women, – and most of the women in the Belarusian forests were Jewish – were in an even more dependent and vulnerable position than Christian women in such groups. Whereas many non-Jewish women came to the woods because of a special attachment to a man, Jewish women came to avoid death. Even before they came to the forest they knew that the possibility of rape and murder were real. In contrast, Rina Raviv joined a partisan group in Belorussia and reports not thinking about sex at all in her efforts to survive.[1177] Although male partisans wanted to have sex with women, they also accused them of promiscuity and viewed them with contempt. In conversations, the word 'whore' was often exchanged for the word 'woman.' In 1943, rumours – reported, for example, by Shulman,[1178] a partisan, as fact – that the Germans had infected Jewish women with venereal diseases and sent them to infiltrate and infect the partisan groups, led some units to ostracize their Jewish members and to send them to the Jewish Bielski otriad.

Sexuality in Forced Labour Camps

Sexuality occurred in forced labour camps in exchange for food, as a result of sexual harassment, but also out of genuine love.[1179] Zisha Schwimmer testified after the war that no men were allowed into the three women's barracks of the large Warta labour camp. Nevertheless, some women became pregnant. Punishment for being caught in the women's barracks meant public execution by shooting with the body being left out in the yard overnight to deter others.[1180] In Skarżysko-Kamienna, men and women lived in separate camps but they still managed to become lovers. Couples had sex openly in hallways, without embarrassment. It was a means to getting presents/food, especially if the man was well positioned.[1181]

The testimonies of prisoners from Skarżysko-Kamienna contain several allusions to sexual harassment by overseers of Polish workers. Karay reports that in the HASAG factories Herman Schmitz, the director, treated inmates well but surrounded himself personally with the most beautiful women.[1182] Rina Cypress' testimony reveals that when a factory manager decided to distribute underwear to the female prisoners, Schmitz ordered 'his girls' to lift their skirts to show what was lacking. It was, however, more difficult to approach Jewish women because of the dangers of *Rassenschande.* Nevertheless, there were many rumours of 'forbidden sexual liaisons' and the exploitation of Jewish women. For example, at *Werke B* in the HASAG factories, factory manager Walter Glaue occasionally picked out a young woman in addition to his steady lover. When Bella Sperling was executed on charges of sabotage, rumour had it that Glaue had impregnated her and therefore wished to get rid of her.[1183] August Bandura regularly 'invited' girls to work in his office and was a known rapist.[1184] Paul Kiessling in 1942 had a Jewish 'servant girl' whom he passed on to Johannes Schneider – known for his excesses and murders – who then sent her to the firing squad when she became pregnant.[1185]

Gałlczyński, supervisor of the garden at *Werke B*, was also reported to invite women to 'work' with him in the greenhouses on cold winter days, and several of these women became pregnant.[1186] Karay reports that:

> The most famous tryst in the factory took place in the Werkzeugbau department (for instrument production). Everyone noticed that the foreman, Hugo Ruebesamen, tended to loiter excessively in the vicinity of the most beautiful Jewish woman in the department. The supervisor was informed and he flayed the woman until she bled in an attempt to force her into admitting that she had had sexual relations with Ruebesamen. When she would not she was sent to the SS headquarters in Radom, from which she disappeared without a trace. Although Ruebesamen also refused to confess, he was sentenced to three months imprisonment.[1187]

One (anonymous) participant at the 1983 conference on Women in the Holocaust reported that:

> In Skarżysko there was a German SS man in charge…who used to come in and look for Jewish women… He took out these women and in the morning we found them. I saw them laying dead outside the barbed wire for burial. I later had the occasion…to work there to prepare a house for the Lagerführer S… we started digging – we had to take some land from the little woods where the SS man took care of his victims and as we were digging the foundations, we

> dug up those women. So this was one aspect of sexuality between German and Jewish women.[1188]

Romances between the Jewish prisoners in forced labour camps also occurred[1189] although many remained abstinent throughout.[1190] For others, paper sacks and blankets were arranged around bunks to provide some privacy although neighbours knew full well what was happening.[1191] Initially they condemned this but later became indifferent to it. If a girl came to spend the night with her '*Kuyzen*' (protector) then his pallet mate spent the night on a table. Visitors often shattered the bulb in the women's barracks when they came to visit their girlfriends. Karay explains these occurrences as providing a soul mate for young people, providing material assistance for others, or simply making life easier with a partner. Karay reports that approximately 80% of the camp population was involved in such relationships.[1192] Finding a '*Kuyzen*' was a means to survive. However, she reports, "Several of these relationships turned into true love, leading to marriage after the war."[1193] Such events also led to marriage in the camp, for example between Marilka Monderer and her fiancée Josef Liebermann:

> The parents of Marilka...horrified at what might happen to their young, beautiful daughter in the 'depraved' society of the camp, decided to marry Marilka and her fiancé in a ceremony that met the requirements of Jewish religious law. Rabbi Finkler of Werk A actually produced a *ketuba* (a Jewish marriage certificate). In her subsequent testimony the bride described her 'wedding dress': a skirt, sweater, and a turban of sorts. One of the guests read the *ketuba* and conducted the ceremony. The rings were made of metal, and bottles of drink and some food were found.[1194]

The groom broke a burned out light bulb in place of the traditional glass and the ring was made from a copper shell casing produced in the factory.[1195]

Love and Sexuality in Concentration Camps

Contact across the sexes was not allowed in most concentration camps.[1196] As Lucie Adelsberger reports, in Auschwitz:

> The wire sawed through the closest of family bonds. Siblings, husbands and wives lived in adjoining barracks and were not allowed to talk to each other...Despite the danger, prisoners couldn't stay away from the fences.

> Husbands and wives exchanged things between the wires, as did brothers and sisters, friends and lovers.[1197]

Contact between men and women was highly valued: Alexander Donat reports that in Majdanek, the '*wagonkolonne,*' the working party that took rations from the kitchens to the fields, was difficult work but "The majority of these men would not have exchanged for anything in the world their privilege of visiting the women's field three times a day."[1198]

Kitty Hart in Auschwitz reports that writing letters between men and women was strictly forbidden and if caught was followed by harsh punishments: "Alma Rose conducted the orchestra and gave a solo recital of a famous violin concerto. All those in Block 15 listened to it while kneeling in the snow with arms outstretched out above their heads. Someone in the block had been caught writing a letter to a man."[1199] Similar punishments followed in the men's camp:

> the men behind the fence were made to perform to the lashing whip and order of SS man Wagner 'Los! Auf! Schneller! Nieder! Los! Auf!'...Men, old and young were sitting down, getting up, running fast, laying down on their bellies, all at tremendous speed. If anyone was a second late Wagner was on him beating and kicking him as he shouted his orders. It was a barbarous 'sport.' The men panting and with sweat pouring down their faces, trod over each other and on those who had already collapsed. This would go on for several hours, probably until Wagner was himself exhausted.[1200]

Delbo too reports that in Auschwitz, Lily, her fiancée and the man who had carried a letter between the two, were all shot.[1201]

Despite this, communications between those in love occurred, usually by way of a go-between. Men were as likely as women to write these letters.[1202] In Ravensbrück, a clandestine mail service existed between women and men.[1203] Rudolf Vrba, before his escape from Auschwitz, describes a love affair between his own kapo, Bruno, and Hermione the kapo in charge of the Slovak girls who were sorting clothes. Bruno sent gifts to her that Vrba carried together with the blankets he was required to deliver.[1204] Those who were caught trying to make contact were severely punished. Steiner reports a young man in Treblinka receiving 25 lashes,[1205] and in Ravensbrück, they risked death.[1206]

Rudolph Höss, the SS Commandant of Auschwitz, confirms that valuables brought into the camp could be used to bribe guards for almost anything including visits of male prisoners to the women's camp at night.[1207] Contact between men and women occurred even among the *Sonderkommando* in Birkenau, a group generally rigidly segregated from the remainder of the camp. As he reports:

> the bribery that went on in this connection was quite unbelievable, while the men's inventiveness knew no bounds. ...The presents smuggled into the women's camp, whether bread, margarine, silk stockings, strange commodity in these surroundings – French perfume, had belonged to people who were no longer alive. But to those still living and suffering they gave some solace and comfort in their daily struggle with a very harsh life.[1208]

Despite the rules prohibiting contact between men and women, love, and sexual relationships did develop. Liana Millu reports the romance between her *Kapo,* Mia, and a *Kochany* (lover) which was indulged while her work group was in the fields near Birkenau.[1209] Lili, Liana's friend in this group, treasured a scrap of mirror that she had found and used it to adjust her curls especially when she expected to see the *kochany* whom she also admired. Her eyes would light up and she would smile when she thought of him, even in the *Vernichtungslager* (extermination camp).[1210] In Theresienstadt, there was little or no privacy:[1211] "a couple could lie together under a blanket on a bunk in a crowded, illuminated room, but the sex act, if it happened, had to be quick, quiet, in full clothing, and in unromantic circumstances."[1212] Others had more positive memories of these same conditions. For example as Anna Bergman, a young Czech Jewish woman in Theresienstadt recalls:

> They were 12 girls in a room and sometime 12 men slept there. 'You lose all inhibitions; nobody listens, or looks at anybody – it's unbelievable but it's true. This was the only lovely moment we had: we were all young and healthy; but when I see before me – all those men and girls, twenty-four people doing what we were doing...'[1213]

As Ruth Elias reports regarding Theresienstadt, "The desire for human closeness and touch, for physical love, was especially strong. It was amazing that even in our state of constant malnourishment this longing for love was so powerful. Love meant life."[1214] In support of this, Schiff reports a significant love affair between a woman, Helen, and Paul Epstein, the leader of the Judenrat in Theresienstadt.[1215]

In Birkenau women with fuller figures were regarded as the most beautiful.[1216] Undernourishment and stress, however, weakened the sex drive and couples longed more for close physical contact as an expression of love and comfort.[1217] Müller reports that:

> The main motives for seeking these relationships with women was not so much sexual, but simply the need to have someone to care for; all family ties had been forcibly and abruptly severed, and it was this feeling of desolation,

> of being utterly alone in the world, which awoke in almost everyone the longing to have someone to care for.[1218]

Some report that interest in appearing attractive or caring for one's grooming in order to attract men dissipated in the camps[1219] although at times – such as during selections – improving one's appearance through the use of lipstick or a similar substitute could prove life saving.[1220] In contrast other writers suggest that "women tried to be women...to add some femininity...even asked the seamstresses to add cuffs and collars, to cut clothing to fit" or "to make a comb from wire...and also made two [hair] rollers from wire as well."[1221]

A number of love stories in the camps are reported in the literature. Vrba reports that he fell in love with a girl that he had never spoken to but could see across the fence in Auschwitz-Birkenau: "There in Birkenau, in the depth of death and decay and despair, I began to suffer the sweet agonies of adolescent adoration."[1222] Miriam Litman, captured among the partisans and deported to Auschwitz, was loved by Leon Libak who worked in the *Sonderkommando*. He gave her various items including food that he had managed to obtain as well as a ring that he had made especially for her: it had a red heart in the middle with both their prisoner numbers on it. After the war she received five marriage proposals including one from Leon who had also survived, but she turned them all down as she did not feel ready to marry.[1223]

Perhaps the most famous love story emerging from the camps is that of Mala Zimetbaum, a Polish, Jewish women, and Edek Galinski (or Tadeuz in some versions[1224]) who was not Jewish.[1225] In love, and angry at what was being done in the camps, they both managed to escape from Auschwitz but were recaptured a few days later on the Slovak border, returned to the camps, beaten and led to their executions by hanging in front of the assembled camp inmates. Mala lashed out at her SS captor after cutting an artery in one of her wrists with a concealed blade. Edik too, managed to kill himself before the SS had planned, in a last act of defiance.[1226] Numerous versions of the story have been told, each identifying Mala as a different nationality, but all agree that the love between them was remarkable, flourishing even in Auschwitz-Birkenau, and showing Mala and Edik as defiant of SS punishment even to the tragic end.

Yitzach Arad, reports that love affairs occurred even in Treblinka where men were allowed to enter the women's areas during some evening hours.[1227] Many of these ended tragically, usually when the man was destined for death and his lover chose to accompany him. In the Lower Camp of Treblinka for instance, there were known love affairs between Rakowski, the 'camp elder' during the typhus epidemic, and a young girl, and between the 'barrack elder' Kuba and another young girl. In the extermination area an affair between Heller who was in charge of the kitchen, and an unnamed girl was common knowledge.

A few weddings are also reported in concentration camps: Mr. Brasse, the Nazi appointed photographer at Auschwitz, reports taking photos of a wedding: the couple spent one night together in the camp and the groom was sent away from the camp the next morning.[1228] The wedding of Josepf and Rebecca Bau in February 1944 in Płaszów concentration camp near Krakow was made famous through its inclusion in the award winning film 'Schindler's List.'[1229] A wedding also took place in the extermination area of Treblinka:

> The groom was a mechanic who worked near the motors that provided the gas, and the bride was one of the young girls. They made them a nice wedding according to the Law of Moses and Israel. Even some SS men came to the reception that was in the evening in the kitchen... We played at the wedding and the young people were escorted to the bridal canopy. There was one who knew how to write the *tnaim* [terms of the marriage contract] and to read the prayers. The guests in uniform left. Those invited from the prisoners had a bit of fun. Then they left and the young couple remained alone. A double bed had been prepared for them on a pallet in the kitchen.[1230]

Eli Rozenberg relates that weddings like these, although rare, were performed according to Jewish Law under the direction of prisoner Zalman Lenge, a porter from Warsaw, who at these ceremonies assumed the duties of the cantor and the rabbi.[1231]

Love and sexual contact was also encouraged by the Nazis in the Operation Rinehard extermination camps of Belzec, Sobibor and Treblinka to distract the men from thinking about their ultimate demise or about escape.[1232] As Leon Feldhendler, one of the leaders of the Sobibor revolt, wrote:

> The music, the dancing, and the women all had one purpose – to kill any thought of liberation the prisoners might have; they [the Germans] wanted to turn them into unthinking instruments. Those who looked to them as if they were thinking too much and talking among themselves were taken to Camp III or were whipped. The absence of worry [among the prisoners] was forced; they [the Germans] encouraged love affairs, they allowed meeting with the women, and they allowed card and chess games.[1233]

In contrast Mo Is, reports that no love affairs occurred in Bergen-Belsen.[1234] Others report that sex was very unimportant especially for starving men.[1235] Scherr also contends that no Holocaust memoir exists that centralizes sexuality and eroticism as the focal point of the narrative[1236] although others contend that women discussed sex endlessly in the barracks, possibly as a form of 'compensatory satisfaction.'[1237] Venezia, who worked in the *Sonderkommando* writes:

> I do remember that, one day, among the corpses brought out of the gas chamber, the men found the body of an incredibly beautiful woman. She had the perfect beauty of ancient statues. Those who were supposed to put her in the ovens couldn't bring themselves to destroy such a pure image. They kept her body with them for as long as they could, then they were obliged to burn her as well as the others. I think that was the only time I really 'Looked.' Otherwise everything happened mechanically; there was nothing to see. Even in the room where people got undressed, you didn't pay any attention; you had no right to feel moved.[1238]

There are few reports of masculine sexuality in men's memoirs or testimonies although it is not clear whether this is due to the lesser frequency of their experience of such events or to the lesser frequency of their reporting these events. Feinstein notes men's testimonies might reflect an expectation that interviewers wish to know about their activities and life events rather than about their feelings – a more traditional male image.[1239] Gill, however, reports a loss of penile erection in men in much the same way as women ceased to menstruate.[1240] Des Pres reports that under the horrific conditions of the camps the need for sex disappeared depending on the degree of hunger, exhaustion and distance from danger.[1241]

Even fewer reports are humorous. Vrba, however, reports that in Majdanek, he stood beside Ignatz Geyer, whom he had known in his hometown by the inappropriate nickname of 'Nazi' and with whom he had chased girls. 'Nazi' had been particularly successful in these endeavours. 'Nazi' thought that he was going to die and he was indeed killed soon afterwards but he was determined to die with dignity:

> He looked around at us all and said with a grin, 'What a lousy collection of pricks you lot have!' The crowd stirred. Somebody laughed. The gloom lifted a couple of inches. 'Tell you what,' said the 'Nazi.' 'Let's have a contest. Let's see who has the biggest!' Maybe it was ridiculous. Maybe it was childish. Certainly it was vulgar; but it revived humor, an emotion which was nearly dead at that moment.
>
> 'Nazi,' for the record, won. He gazed down at his prize-winning property, gave a slow grin and said 'A pity you're never going to be used again. But still, you haven't had a bad life!'[1242]

Love Between Jews and Germans

Occasional stories regarding true love affairs between Jews and Germans in camps have also survived. Hanus, one of the few surviving inmates of the extermination camp Maly Trostinec in Belarus, reported on the love affair of Nora Petzelke, a Jewish nurse in charge of the camps' infirmary, and a lower ranking German SS man in this camp.[1243] Together they were responsible for stealing some of the wealth taken from arriving inmates. The SS commander in nearby Minsk eventually detected their double crime, of theft and *Rassenschande*. The SS officer was summoned to Minsk and secretly executed to avoid any embarrassing publicity. Nora was imprisoned, tortured for days and ultimately executed publicly:

> Her face was a distorted mass of dried blood caked onto her skin, her nose broken, and her eyes swollen shut. She had no hair on her scalp; it was ripped out, leaving her skull crusted with dried blood. Her hands were mangled, the nails torn from their beds. Nora no longer seemed human as she drifted in and out of consciousness. As they hauled her suffering body, the fractured bones caused her legs and arms to flap around like a broken lifeless puppet… She could not ascend the gallows, and the hangman had to pull and hold her body up, to place the noose around her neck. Most believed that he hung Nora's corpse. All had to watch in silence and witness how the SS punished a disobedient Jewess.[1244]

Eichengreen also reports, unforgivingly, on the love affair of a cruel Kapo, Maja, who had shared her bed with an SS man to survive and had later married him after the war.[1245]

While Jewish men and women were generally separated in camps, some other categories of prisoners such as Roma and Sinti were not and many lived in 'family camps.' Some individuals in the 'Gypsy' camp reputedly had prolific sexual lives, often benefiting many by sharing their wealth in exchange.[1246] A remarkable report of sexuality as an expression of love is told about the liquidation of the 'Gypsy' family camp in Auschwitz-Birkenau. As Müller, an eyewitness *Sonderkommando* worker reports:

> Towards midnight the changing room was full of people. With every minute that passed the alarm increased… There was another unusual thing, which I had never before witnessed in this ante-room of death. Numerous men were holding their wives in a tight embrace, pressed convulsively against them as if merged into one, passionately but despairingly making love for the last time. It was as if

> this was the way they wanted to say farewell to the most precious thing they had in the world, but also to their own life.[1247]

'Sexual Exchange'

Sex also occurred without love, primarily in exchange for food or other means of survival. Although sex in this context was with the agreement of both partners, it can hardly be termed 'consensual' as currently understood, and is best noted as 'sexual exchange.'[1248] While rape of Jewish women occurred in camps and elsewhere, it was possibly inhibited to some extent by the laws forbidding *Rassenschande,* and because the SS had access to brothels. Nevertheless, other forms of sexual exploitation occurred, primarily between lower levels of the camp hierarchy. Kapos or prison supervisors could and did demand sexual favours from inmates in exchange for bread, medicine, a pair of boots, a better job or to escape selection.[1249] Men of position – for example cooks, butchers or bakers – could always find a lover, and were more capable of sexual activity.[1250] Relatively few SS guarded camps: most of the control was in the hands of prisoners who had accumulated power, and sexual exploitation of other prisoners occurred.[1251] To these men "a female Jewish inmate ceased to be a 'human woman' but became a physical site that possessed the external physical signs of female sexuality but contained no humanity."[1252] As Susan Cernyak-Spatz commented at the 1983 conference on 'Women Survivors of the Holocaust,' sexual relations were only possible [in Auschwitz] if you were not a '*musselman*' (a prisoner suffering from extreme debilitation). These relations occurred between older members of the camp [who had 'seniority'] and the men that came into the camp to do electrical or plumbing work.[1253] Vera Laska, another participant in this conference concurred[1254] although Sybil Milton, reflecting the then current unwillingness to discuss sexual issues in relation to the Holocaust, contradicted these comments saying that sex rarely occurred in the camps, that Jewish women were seldom the victims or initiators of these relationships, that inappropriate public titillation was the reason for stories about sexual relations between SS guards and women in camps, and that this rarely occurred.[1255] Shik explains this reluctance to accept sexual exploitation of women as this had generally occurred with the woman's 'consent' and perhaps on the woman's 'initiative' even if circumstances had made this impossible for women to resist.[1256]

As subsequent testimony has revealed, sexual exploitation of Jewish and other women did occur in camps, and both Jewish men as well as non-Jewish men exploited women. Joan Ringelheim reports on the experiences of 20 year old S. in Theresienstadt:

> ...women survived partly by brains. I worked in the office, in supply, in the education office. I wasn't doing badly... [Up] to a [certain] point you were anonymous...you could lead your own life...people could get married. You also survived by your male connections. It was the males who had the main offices, who ran the kitchens. And did they *use* it. *Did* they use it. That was how you survived as a woman – through the male. I was done in by one. I suppose I didn't sleep high enough, to put it bluntly. Because in that society, that was the only way you could survive.[1257]

Some stories reveal an ironic sense of justice, such as the experiences of Olga Lengyel, written shortly after the war:

> Soon after her arrival in Auschwitz she met Tadek...he was repairing the bunks in her barracks. He became friendly, brought her a shawl, then a potato...He stood close to me. Then as though talking to himself, he said, 'It's a strange thing, even though you have no hair and you are dressed in rags, there is something very desirable about you.' I felt his arm about my waist. His other hand touched me and began to fondle my breast. My world fell to pieces again.[1258]

She refused Tadek, then, and again later, when she was much more in need and starving. Tadek shared his food with another woman who was willing to go with him. Later when Olga worked in the infirmary this woman became a regular visitor. Olga spent her bread ration to buy a rare medicine for her on the black market to combat her syphilis. Unwanted sexual advances are occasionally reported with an element of humorous irony: Hana Müller Bruml, a prisoner from October 1944 to liberation in May 1945 in Kodowa-Sackisch, a subcamp of Gross-Rosen, testified that:

> All we had was a bowl and a spoon. It was so cold at the time that we put them on under our coats and put a string around us ... Mimi was thirty-five and she was the oldest of us. She was also the most flat-chested of all of us. She was going with the bowl, and one of the Mongolian guys stepped out of line to touch her because he thought it was a breast. But instead he touched the dish. It [stepping out of line] was very dangerous for him.[1259]

Others were left degraded and embarrassed by their experiences, whether they had, or had not, indulged in sexual exchange. As Gisella Perl reported:

> one of my acquaintances told me jubilantly that a few old prisoners, Polish men, were working around the latrines,

> and one of them had a piece of string...I snatched up my bread ration for the day and ran. The man with the string, my prospective saviour, was a short, stocky, pock-marked man with wild eyes and a ferocious expression. The Inferno Auschwitz had succeeded in depriving him of his last vestige of human dignity.
>
> I stopped beside him, held out my bread and asked him, begged him to give me a piece of string in exchange for it. He looked me over from head to foot, carefully, then grabbed me by the shoulder and hissed in my ear: 'I don't want your bread...You can keep your bread...I will give you a piece of string but first I want you...you...'
>
> For a second I didn't understand what he meant. I asked him again, smiling, gently, to give me a piece of string... My feet were killing me...The shoes were useless without string...It might save my life....
>
> He wasn't listening to me. 'Hurry up...hurry up...' he said hoarsely. His hand, filthy with the human excrement he was working in, reached out for my womanhood, rudely, insistently.
>
> The next moment I was running, running away from that man, away from the indignity that had been inflicted upon me, forgetting about the string, about the shoes...[1260]

Sexual exchange was sometimes entered into on behalf of others: For instance, Perl reports:

> Kati was just about to break off this relationship when she came across this little girl, but now she decided to continue selling her body to the man in exchange for food which she then took back to the cage and fed to the little girl. Kati was only happy when the child had enough to eat.[1261]

In contrast, some women refused to accept food that had been bartered in exchange for sex or titillation. Tec notes that Renée Hofland had accepted food from a man on the other side of a fence to give to her starving younger sister in exchange for his pleasure in seeing a young and pretty Jewish woman. Her sister refused to accept it, destroying the food as forbidden food.[1262] One further testimony indicates how sex was used to save a life. Miriam Gerchik testified that on arrival in Auschwitz from Hungary in 1944:

> There was one lady among us, a doctor's wife who knew German perfectly, and she had a daughter of about eleven. She wanted the daughter with her and she was young and beautiful, the woman, so she didn't try to cover her private parts with her hands. She went up to the SS who was standing there and asked him what she could do to help, whatever they need to help, she'll do it because she wanted her daughter with her and that's how she brought in her daughter....[1263]

Men and women stole from others or 'organized' articles that they could then trade. Men sometimes traded these articles for sex.[1264] Gisella Perl records her initial and later reactions to these activities – emotions that might well reflect those of many women:

> At first I was deeply shocked at these practices. My pride, my integrity as a woman revolted against the very idea. I begged and preached and, when I had my first case of venereal disease, I even threatened to refuse treatment if they didn't stop prostitution. But later, when I saw that the pieces of bread thus earned saved lives, when I met a young girl whom a pair of shoes, earned in a week of prostitution, saved from being thrown into the crematory, I began to understand – and to forgive.[1265]

In Auschwitz- Birkenau, the main venue for sexual exchange was the washroom and latrine area, which served as a 'love-nest.' As Perl wrote: "It was here that male and female prisoners met for a furtive moment of joyless sexual intercourse in which the body was used as a commodity with which to pay for the badly needed items the men were able to steal from the warehouses."[1266] Lengyel reports that the few men who were allowed to enter the women's camp to effect repairs or ditch digging for example, took their lunch break in these areas, usually surrounded by women "of all ages and shapes, clamouring piteously for crumbs":

> The women stood around them in circles, three or four deep, their hands stretched forth like beggars. Pretty girls sang the latest songs to attract attention. Sometimes the men relented and gave away parts of their lunch. Only then could a woman enjoy a potato, that most luscious of camp luxuries which was ordinarily reserved only for the kitchen workers and the blocovas.[block senior]
>
> Yet it was rarely pity that made the men share their not-too-abundant food. For food was the coin that paid for sexual privileges.[1267]

As Perl notes, "in the latrines, lying in human excrement before the eyes of their fellow prisoners, men and women were writhing in sexual paroxysm."[1268]

The depths to which women had to sink in order to survive cannot be easily fathomed. The modesty and naïveté of young women/girls at that time renders the experience of resorting to sexual exchange even more heartrending. Shoshana Kahn's story, as told to Nechama Tec decades later, reveals the extent of the cognitive dissonance experienced.[1269] She was transferred from a ghetto in Latvia to Kaiserwald camp and was befriended by a 40-year-old 'political guy' who gave her food in exchange for friendship. He was well educated and taught her astronomy, German history, math…she was starved for schooling. He even gave her a book. She did not sleep with him, but on one occasion (only) he asked if he could masturbate while she held him. He did so, but she was terrified. She was scared as she did not know what was going on…she was crying…a penis was for her a scary thing. She was an innocent, 17 year old girl …her relationship with him changed as she never trusted him again. She never told anyone until interviewed decades later. She then regretted not having sex with him as he was so kind to her and life was so different then. He was killed.

On one occasion that has become legend, sexuality was used by a prisoner to try to exact revenge. One version of this story tells that a beautiful woman in the undressing room prior to disinfection in Birkenau noticed that she had attracted the attention of two SS soldiers, Quackernack and Schillinger. Acting seductively she removed her high heeled shoes as they watched, mesmerized by her body. In a second, she hit Quackernack on the forehead with the heel of her shoe, leaped onto him and snatched his pistol. She fired at Schillinger who fell to the floor. She ran and disappeared into the crowd. As an SS guard tried to pull Schillinger out another shot was fired. The SS opened fire and killed all the prisoners, although this did not save Schillinger who died. The story is told in many memoirs and reports although with considerable variation regarding its detail including the mis-identification of Quackernack (who was, however, also possibly present) instead of SS Wilhelm Emmerich,[1270] and the identification of the woman as Franceska Mann, a beautiful dancer at the Melody Palace nightclub in Warsaw.[1271] It does, however reflect an inspirational incident reflecting courage and resistance that was significant for many.[1272] By exposing the use of sexuality or feminism to resist, the story also reverses the customary rape narrative.[1273]

Sexual Survivor Guilt

Societal perspectives following the Holocaust, particularly in Israel, could not readily accept the innocence of those who survived without impugning their moral integrity.[1274] Women were suspected – and condemned – for having survived through sexual exchange and were shunned in consequence, leading to their unwillingness to report such experiences.[1275] Survivor guilt, especially if their survival was associated with the use of sexuality, caused many to keep silent for years.[1276] As Ruth Bondy wrote: "In Israel Jews wanted to know: How did you stay alive? What did you have to do in order to survive? And in their eyes, a glimmer of suspicion: Kapo? Prostitute?"[1277] Some reactions to survivors included censure for women who survived as having – possibly – used their sexuality to save their lives.[1278] Helen Lewis, an Auschwitz survivor who returned to Prague, reports that, in 1946, while travelling on a crowded tram, her sleeves fell back while she was holding on to the overhead straps. A nearby man said loudly and distinctly, "Isn't it funny how only the young and pretty ones have come back?" She reported that the implications were clear and "It hurt as much as anything we had survived. More."[1279] This attitude persisted from the immediate post-war period into the late 1990s in Israel at least: Three Israeli films released between 1987 and 1997 continued to present the image of the whore-survivor: *Tel-Aviv-Berlin* (1987), *Eretz Hadasha* (1994) and *Henrik's Sister* (1997).[1280]

Sexual Abuse of Men

The exact number of women or men who experienced sexual relationships or molestation during the Holocaust cannot be determined.[1281] Most stories of sexual abuse are told by women: few men – like Sam Pivnik[1282] – recount such stories unless these were in the context of (usually coerced) homosexual encounters. Sexual exploitation of men did occur through the limited system of 'pipels' or 'dolly-boys' but sexual abuse appears to have been less widespread for men than for women.[1283] While homosexuality among men (although not between lesbians) was illegal in Germany under paragraph 175 of the Reich Criminal Code[1284] and was prosecuted and severely punished, male-male relationships among camp personnel were widespread. As Heger[1285] reports, the Block seniors and Kapos at Flossenbürg all had a young Pole as a batman or cleaner, although their main function was as a bed partner. Most boys under the age of 16 were sent directly to the gas chambers but some between 12 and 16 were admitted to camps and some were subjected to sexual exploitation in exchange for survival.[1286] Although their relationship brought them some protection as long as the affair lasted, the 'dolly boys' – and other homosexuals – were also constantly abused and called vile names: bum-fuckers, shitty queers and arse-holes.[1287] The name 'pipel,' (sometimes 'piepel') denoting a boy-child prostitute, was derived from the German provincial words for penis and lad.[1288] While homosexuals (distinguished by pink triangles) were always regarded as 'filthy queers,' those who condemned them had no qualms about their relationships with the young 'dolly boys.' Homosexual behaviour in this context was seen as an emergency outlet although loving relationships between two men were viewed as repulsive.[1289] Schiff, in telling the story of Fred, relates the situation of one of these 'pipels' in Schwarsheide, a labour camp associated with Auschwitz:

> He was the much pampered favourite of the pedophile Kapo and had to satisfy every sexual perversity of his sadistic master. In return he did not have to work, was given every luxury he could wish for, and shared the private room of the Kapo. The living quarters of the twosome were quite spacious, furnished, and equipped with a small stove, where the youngster cooked their daily meals. The boy possessed a wide choice of nice clothes, scented with expensive French perfumes. He had soap and towels and scores of toiletries and fragrances, items the rest of the men long ago had forgotten existed.[1290]

Such relationships may well have saved the lives of the 'pipels.'[1291]

Ka-Tzetnik's controversial novels, '*Piepel*' and '*House of Dolls*'[1292] describe paedophilic rape of both boys and girls in the camps, apparently based on the fates of his younger brother and sister before their deaths in the camps, although never verified. The books were written using the pseudonym of Ka-Tzetnik 135633 (meaning one who lives in a *Konzentrationslager*, (concentration camp) or *KZ*) together with his concentration camp number, as the author regarded his prior name and identity to have been burned in the crematoria of Auschwitz. According to Sivan, the fear of dealing with such material is so great, that in Israel, Yehiel Dinur (Ka-Tzetnik) – anonymous for many years – has even been cast in the role of rapist[1293] or as a sleazily unhealthy author.[1294] Sivan reports that 'He has been labelled as mad, outlandish, uncouth, perverse, and unreliable by many eminent scholars.[1295] Sivan, in contradiction, reports that:

> Dinur's inclusion of sexual slavery in the narratives he composed is seen by turns as obscene, pornographic, melodramatic, voyeuristic, vulgar, even as kitsch .....The pervasive animosity toward Ka-Tzetnik in critical writing is a contemporary example of an ancient ritual of repression: when you do not like what you are hearing, stone the messenger.[1296]

As Sivan notes "people want their Holocaust survivors to emerge from hell intact and with a message of hope."[1297] Ka-Tzetnik's insistence on using his 'war name' is seen as proof of his instability – and as a way of dismissing the harsh realities that he reports. It is possible that fear of dealing with sexual, and sexually abusive, issues in general and specifically that relating to men's abuse has concealed yet another aspect of Holocaust history. In the same way as women's sexual and reproductive life experiences in the Holocaust need further exposure to fully understand them, so too do men's.

Lesbian Love

A number of writers report that lesbian love also occurred in the camps, and particularly in Ravensbrück.[1298] By early 1942, Block 11 was referred to as 'the lesbian block.' How many Jewish women were lesbians is not known although Saidel reports that at least two women (Jenny (Henny) Sara Schermann and Mary Pünjer) were killed for being both Jews and lesbians.[1299] While the Nazis outside the camps never criminalized lesbianism, it was a punishable offence in Ravensbrück.[1300] Paragraph 175 had criminalized sexual acts between men but had not addressed female homosexuality,[1301] and Hitler had said, "the emancipation of women was only an invention of the Jewish intellect."[1302]

Conditions in camps and especially in Ravensbrück facilitated lesbianism. Fear and loneliness, friendships, and the absence of men, led to women seeking comfort from other women.[1303] Denise McAdam Clark, a French barrister imprisoned in Block 27 in Ravensbrück, reported that 'Male' partners, who were called 'Jules,' would carve a cross into the foreheads of their 'steadies,' called the '*croix des vaches*' by inmates.[1304] They were often German criminals or asocials with masculine appearance and mannerisms.[1305] According to Morrison, female relationships at Ravensbrück ranged from platonic relationships through intimate and warm friendships to passionate love matches.

Olga Lengyel[1306] also reports on the lesbian nature of 'dance soirees' that occurred in Auschwitz –Birkenau: During the long winter nights of 1944, as the guards became more concerned with the approach of the Russians than with the prisoners, the inmates gave 'parties.' They gathered around to sing and dance accompanied by a harmonica and guitar from the camp orchestra. Couples would pair off during these orgies, some dressed in male attire. Delbo confirms such stories of lesbian orgies in Auschwitz often involving kapos.[1307] Irma Grese is also reported to have had homosexual relationships with inmates after which she would have them killed.[1308] As Susan Cernyk-Spatz reflected at the 1983 Conference on Women and the Holocaust,[1309] lesbian relationships were 'a fact of life' in Auschwitz-Birkenau.

On Liberation

According to Perl, "the liberated thousands [in Bergen-Belsen] completely demoralized after years of Nazi oppression, had no other aims than to satisfy their basic instincts, hunger and sexual desire."[1310] Wanda Poltawska recalls that on their first night of freedom (in Ravensbrück) "Women…their thin cheeks strangely flushed, began gyrating frantically and tearing the clothes off their horribly emaciated bodies; while the men, no less thin and emaciated, flung themselves upon them. Towards morning they fell asleep still entwined in each other's embrace."[1311] Some sought 'love' because it made them feel human again or because they wanted to prove to themselves that they were still men and women; others because they wanted to enjoy their newly won freedom to the fullest. Some also sold their bodies for cigarettes, chocolate and other small comforts.

There is, however, little, if any, evidence of Jewish survivors or Jewish soldiers raping German women after liberation although there was also little sympathy for those who were raped by others, such as by Russian soldiers.[1312] Larry Lotah Orbach[1313] on his return travel from Auschwitz and Buchenwald to his home in Berlin reported:

> As the train chugged on under the night sky, a drunken Russian soldier raped a young German girl in full view of everyone. No one raised a hand to help her; there was no sound but her screams. So much for the Master Race, who in Auschwitz, I had watched slam the head of a Jewish baby into the wall of a shower room. The baby had died instantly, his brain protruding and his blood spurting; they had laughed, full of triumph and swagger. Now they were too weak to protect one of their own children. Nor did I intervene; these were people who had set me apart, told me I could not be one of them.[1314]

Sexualized Humiliation And Emotional Abuse

Systematic dehumanization of the Jews is a central theme in many Holocaust survivors' testimonies.[1315] It is considered one of the most significant factors that enabled ordinary people to implement the most vicious and cruel acts that characterize the *Shoah*. Commencing with social stigmatizing of Jews from the earliest days of the Nazi regime, dehumanization rapidly progressed to emotional and physical humiliation – including abuse of bodily parts that are traditionally associated with femininity, masculinity and sexuality – to a point where the lives of those deemed 'unworthy of life' were regarded with less respect than those of animals. As Bertha described these events:

> For me it was the stripping of entirely everything – of loss, of loss of life, loss of pride, loss of everything. You were really nobody or nothing: you didn't amount to anything. You had no voice, you were not even a number. You were absolutely, absolutely nothing.[1316]

As Ronnie Landau wrote, the extent of the emotional and sexualized humiliation that was imposed was total:

> Then for the first time we became aware that our language lacks words to express this offense, the demolition of a man. ...It is not possible to sink lower than this; no human condition is more miserable than this, nor can it conceivably be so. Nothing belongs to us anymore, they have taken away our clothes, our shoes, even our hair; if we speak they will not listen to us, and if they listen they will not understand. They will even take away our name; and if we want to keep it, we will have to find it in ourselves, the strength to do so, to manage somehow so that behind the name something of us, of us as we are, still remains... It is in this way that one can understand the double meaning of the term 'extermination camp.'[1317]

As Des Pres notes:

> The death of the soul was aimed at. It was to be accomplished by terror and privation, but first of all by relentless assault on the survivors sense of purity and worth. Excremental attack, the physical inducement of disgust and self-loathing, was a principal weapon.[1318]

Gitta Sereny's interview with Frans Stangl, commandant of Treblinka, provides insight into the Nazi logic underlying the extensive humiliation of Jews – what Primo Levi refers to as 'useless violence'- that was implemented in the camps:

> "Why, " I asked Stangl, "if they were going to kill them anyway, what was the point of all the humiliation, why the cruelty?"
>
> "To condition those who actually had to carry out the policies," he said. "To make it possible for them to do what they did."[1319]

Dehumanizing victims provides some explanation for how it was possible for such horrors and indignities to be inflicted. As Levi writes, "it is the sole usefulness of useless violence."[1320] Such actions, however, reflect more on the inhumanity of the perpetrators than the Nazi, ideologically based, accusations of a lack of humanity among the victims.

The segregation of Jews from society through the numerous Nuremberg Laws is a well acknowledged forerunner of events that occurred in camps. So too is the stigmatization that incurred by having a J stamped on the passports of all German Jews. Introduced at the urging of Dr Rothmund, head of the Swiss immigration police, to aid their identification of Jews at Swiss border crossings (in order to refuse them entry to Switzerland), the Nazis adopted the practice enthusiastically.[1321] This external identification was enhanced by the wearing of an identifying Jewish star enforced first in Poland after the start of World War II and later in Germany.[1322] Some forms of abuse and segregation, through their association with intimate bodily parts, functions and appearances, however, had decidedly shameful, embarrassing, and insulting connotations for Jews. Such acts were usually witnessed by onlookers – implicit supporters – encouraged by the Nazis and termed 'paratheatre' by Chalmers.[1323] For example, Kurt Viese and Karl Streblow, accompanied by some men from the Gestapo and the SS, entered Grodno Ghetto 1 and ordered members of the *Judenrat* to clean, with their bare hands, all the toilets in the neighbourhood and then eat what they found there.[1324] Similarly, women in Poland were forced to clean floors and toilets using their hands, coats or their underwear, and when finished to put on these same filthy, wet garments.[1325] Dora Love, in Sauilai ghetto in Lithuania was sent to clean the German barracks. She testified:

> Then, if they got drunk, they played games with us. You know, like dipping your head in their lavatories. Then you went around like that and they had done that to you when the lavatory was full and not when it was washed. And then you walked around with that horrible shit on your head and they walked around saying, '*Die stinkenden Juden.*' ...You weren't treated as human beings...to be treated as a bit of garbage...is much worse.[1326]

In Krakow, Jewish women were banned from curling their hair, walking about in shirtsleeves, or wearing high heels. Their hair was shorn during disinfection operations or when they were picked up for various jobs[1327] ostensibly to eradicate typhus epidemics although possibly as "a means of punishment or symbolic stigmatization, particularly as non-Jewish women's hair was not shaved."[1328] Hodara reports that although men's hair was shorn under similar circumstances the experience was particularly humiliating for women.[1329]

Shaving of Bodily Hair in Camps

In concentration camps, shaving of bodily hair on arrival and sometimes several times in a row at intervals of a few weeks or months was fairly routine for Jewish women.[1330] As De Rochemont, a Dutch political prisoner in Ravensbrück testified:

> In a long line, just as God created us, we waited to be searched for vermin; head lice, clothes lice and body lice, all of us, young and old, handsome and ugly. Whenever a nit was discovered, the hair was shaved off without mercy. A number of heads were shaved, and only those who have experienced this dreadful disgrace can know the depths of shame and humiliation that one reaches then...and yet we laughed, we still could laugh, although it was the laugh that is bred by despair; when the heart bleeds and the pain is too great to cry out, you laugh as we laughed...[1331]

Cecelie Klein described how in Auschwitz, women were required to stand naked on stools while male prisoners cut off the women's hair, shaved their heads and then their intimate parts.[1332] In Bergen-Belsen, Sala Pawlowicz was forced to stand on a raised step, legs apart with arms out at eye level while being shaved. When the guard had finished she was a mass of blood from the nicks and cuts she had been given and her skin was "hot from the razor."[1333] Many experienced this humiliation as dehumanizing: As Livia Bitton-Jackson writes:

> The haircut has a startling effect on every woman's appearance. Individuals become a mass of bodies. Height, stoutness or slimness: There is no distinguishing factor – it is the absence of hair which transformed individual women into like bodies. Age and other personal differences melt away. Instead a blank senseless stare emerges on a thousand faces on one naked, unappealing body. In a matter of minutes even the physical aspect of our numbers seems reduced – there is less of a substance to our dimensions. We become a monolithic mass. Inconsequential.[1334]

Many women endorse this sentiment[1335] including Zwia Rechtman-Schwartz, Olga Weiss Astor, Sara Nomberg-Przytyk, Ibolya S, Ruth Reiser, Lidia Rosenfeld Vago, Isabella Leitner, Lucille Eichengreen, and Sala Pawlowics. In Auschwitz, this dehumanization process was further endorsed by tattooing[1336] while in many other camps, numbers replaced names. Fortunately, the marking of Jews through tattooing a number on the forehead, or through branding the forehead with a Star of David or a swastika, as initially occurred in some ghettos, was abandoned.[1337] As Nomberg-Przytyk records, "It did not bother them that cutting hair close to the skin with dull scissors was excruciatingly painful. It did not bother them that we were women and that without our hair we felt totally humiliated."[1338] Halbmeyr suggests that shaving of women's hair was even more humiliating than nudity. She cites Libusé Nachtmanová, a Czech survivor, who described how the SS men came into the shower rooms. Normally a naked woman would cover her breasts or pubic area with her hands. The shorn women covered their heads with their hands. "They were more ashamed of the loss of hair than of their nudity."[1339] The experiences of head shaving and public nudity were closely tied to their feelings of femininity and sexual identification and were felt as a blow to both.[1340] Lucille Eichengreen wished for something to cover her bald head, not because of the cold or rain, but because of vanity.[1341] Erika Buchmann noted that "one of the main reasons women committed suicide by throwing themselves on the electrically charged barbed wire was because they had just had their heads shaved."[1342] Flaschka remarks that the presence of hair for some women marked them as female in a world of bald women. Looking healthy, having some body weight, looking remotely human or feminine was considered a source of attractiveness, and women who were raped or who witnessed rapes in the camps remarked on this.[1343] Fenalon too, notes that her co-inmate Clara, who was obese, was admired by many who paid court to her with butter and sugar.[1344] Religious women, who, once married, traditionally kept their hair covered in public by either a wig or a scarf, felt both a physical and spiritual nakedness.[1345] Sala Pawlowicz said:

> She wept from humiliation. My hair was part of me: it kept me different from the other girls ...it was degradation for a woman to lose her hair...She saw two other shaved girls: they looked like a new sex, neither masculine nor feminine.[1346]

Ruth Nebel, after being shaved, exclaimed "Kill me! Kill me! I want to be dead!"[1347]

Just as the Nazis attacked women both as women and as Jews, so did they attack Jewish men as both men and as Jews. These included attacks on the secondary sex characteristics of men: beards and earlocks.[1348] Men's beards were cut off in ghettos as reported by Tova Berger in Romania[1349] or even burned as reported by Zelda Moyal in Vilna.[1350] As a final humiliation, "Jews were often made to swallow the hairs of their shorn beards."[1351] Miriam Gerchik from Nyirbator a small town Hungary, testified that it was dangerous for men to go out at night with beards: they would be beaten.[1352] Men's hair was also shaved in concentration camps. Venezia reports:

> He heard someone calling his name...it was his brother calling him, standing right next to him, but they did not recognize each other ...with no hair and wearing ill fitting clothes. It was a really sad moment, perhaps one of the saddest.[1353]

In Dachau concentration camp[1354] as well as in Mauthausen,[1355] a 5 cm wide strip was shorn down the middle of the men's hair, known as the 'camp road.' This measure was used later solely to humiliate Soviet and Italian prisoners-of-war. Men do not mention the regular shaving of their beards in testimonies and few men appearing in photographs of survivors at liberation have facial hair. Few, if any, historical texts or men's memoirs have noted the lack of facial hair growth in concentration camps. Whether this was the (unlikely) result of regular shaving (as few means of shaving were available to men) or was due to hormonal changes following severe malnutrition resulting in decreased facial hair growth (in a similar way to the effects on women's menstruation) is as yet unknown. Shmuel Gronner, a survivor of two and a half years of camp life in Gross Rosen and its satellite labour camps Markstadt and Fünfteichen run by Krupp, confirms that men were not regularly shaved and did not have any personal means of shaving yet did not grow beards.[1356] Lack of hair growth is also reported by Hugo Gryn who was imprisoned in Mauthausen and Günskirchen. Very ill by the end of the war, he eventually recovered and later reported that "...my hair grew again, my teeth became firm in my gums again and I wanted to go home..."[1357] Interestingly, men rarely mention (or were never asked about) feelings of a loss of masculinity resulting from such hormonal changes in camps. On the other hand, the forced shaving of Jewish men's beards or side locks – symbols of both masculinity and religiosity – often accompanied by ridicule and laughter, is readily acknowledged by men as exceptionally humiliating.

Body Searches

Body searches were part and parcel of Nazi raids on Jews in villages, towns and cities. Many report internal examinations of women in ghettos,[1358] No consideration was paid to the sensibilities of women. In Krakow, for example, women were ordered to strip and stand naked in front of all the residents of a house who frequently included neighbours and relatives. Sometimes searches were carried out in the town square.[1359] In Hungary, people were tortured to reveal valuables hidden in their homes or perhaps given to neighbours for safekeeping: "Midwives were brought in to conduct intimate body searches of the women, and both men and women were savagely beaten."[1360] Masters notes that this was done in the presence of police who "often amused themselves by taking a hand in it themselves."[1361] In Hungary, prior to deportation, some women had electric wires inserted into their uterus in front of their family as part of the search for hidden valuables.[1362] Judith Molnar's account of deportation in Szeged, a city in south-eastern Hungary, shows the extent of the examinations and the humiliation involved: The deputy mayor of the town proudly reported to the Ministry of the Interior: "the necessary examination and the body search was carried out by two city doctors, ten midwives and ten office nurses, in the course of ten days, usually working from 5am until late in the evening. An additional city doctor worked for one day."[1363] Zweig notes the complaint of the Bishop of Csanad (Enre Hamvas) to his superior Archbishop Justinian Seredi, that the searches '*per inspectionem vaginae*' were conducted in the presence of men. "What is this if not completely and pervertedly treading on the dignity and modesty of women?"[1364] Thirteen-year-old Maria Ezner and her mother, in Hungary, were both examined by a midwife to see if they had anything hidden in their vaginas.[1365] Perl reports that in the ghetto Maramos in Sziget, Transylvania in 1943: "When they (the Gestapo) had gone through everything without finding any valuables, I had to stand by and watch while they seized one woman after another and with dirty fingers searched the depths of her body for treasures."[1366] Cecilie Klein reported a degrading body search in the Chust ghetto in Hungary: "First we were ordered to strip naked, men and women together. Then the women and the girls were lined up on one side and were ordered to lie on our sides on a wooden table. While an SS officer gawked and jeered, a woman with a stick poked around our private parts."[1367] Even more humiliating and shocking to Cecilie was the behaviour of citizens who had volunteered to witness the degradation of their Jewish neighbours.

Abraham Tory's diary from the Kovno ghetto, on 30 June 1943, reports that Tornbaum, a 'typical German gendarme' forced women to undress, so that he could conduct gynaecological examinations on them (looking for hidden valuables) while at the same time beating them severely.[1368] On 9 July 1943, Tory reports that Mrs Levin was forced to undress completely by German officer Schtitz: "Spread your legs" he commanded before examining all the parts of her body to see if she had hidden anything.[1369] Silvia Gross-Martin also reports on intimate searches conducted in Belgium;

> I don't think anybody truly understood what he [Mayer] was talking about. I certainly did not. Not then and not after I had already seen some of the women completely naked, with their legs spread in a kneebend position, their upper body bent all the way down. They stood motionless like horses in a stall, with everything exposed, their faces to the wall. It was the guards who did the examining.[1370]

In concentration camps, prisoners were ordered to undress, subjected to rapid and brutal removal of all body hair, and often drenched with delousing chemicals. As Kremer notes, "Highlights in women's writings are the shame and terror of facing men who make lewd remarks and obscene suggestions during delousing and shearing procedures as they search women's bodily cavities for hidden valuables."[1371] Lengyel says, "[We] were compelled to undergo a thorough examination in the Nazi manner, oral, rectal, vaginal...We had to lie across a table, stark naked while they probed. All that in the presence of drunken soldiers who sat around the table, chuckling obscenely."[1372] Judith Becker testified also that in Majdanek, every orifice was checked.[1373] Dora Love's testimony is particularly vivid:

> The Germans loved if a mother stood with her children, which happened to my mother, and they loved to then physically molest us and say (in German) 'suchen'(search)...Here we have to look for diamonds in this one. You know they pushed things up your vagina and they'd get you bleeding like a pig on a poke. They were happy. They had mothers crying and screaming more than the actual youngsters to whom they did it...These Germans standing around and laughing and checking their guns and lifting up a breast from a woman and saying 'Maybe she's got diamonds under there.' And putting me on a stretcher and poking around and tearing one to pieces...for the rest

> of one's life, one had various things connected with that, illnesses and so on...[1374]

Women in Ravensbrück[1375] and Auschwitz-Birkenau[1376] were also searched vaginally. Elsa (Frishman) Gleick from Czechoslovakia reported on her examination at the *revier*: the women passing before her "told us that they had been examined in intimate places with rods, and many said this had caused them to bleed. Later rumours reached us that the SS guards took statistics on how many of the Slovakian prisoners were still virgins."[1377] Lucia Bibs reported on the 'gynaecological checks' that the SS performed on Jewish women during the passage through the showers. "After that they cut our hair. Cut our hair all over our bodies. They balded us from head to foot. Then they check what in this hole what in the other hole, everything....We started to cry."[1378]

Ruth Elias reports on her fear regarding discovery of her eighth month pregnancy through the 'gynaecological examination' on admission to Auschwitz:

> Several tables had been set up and the women had to lie on them with their legs spread apart. The SS women, who certainly were not doctors and were not wearing rubber gloves, inserted their hands into the vaginas of the prisoners... When my turn came I lay down on the examination table without saying a word. But after only a few minutes, I was back on my feet again. They had allowed me to rejoin the others. Later I realized that this vaginal examination had nothing to do with the state of our health. It was a search for contraband.[1379]

Body searches were conducted on women admitted to the camps, but also on women who were sent directly to the gas chambers, such as in Treblinka[1380] and Auschwitz.[1381] Leib Langfuss, a member of the *Sonderkommando*, reported that one SS man stood by the doorway feeling the private parts of the young women entering the gas bunker. In other instances, SS men of all ranks pushed their fingers into the sexual organs of pretty young women.[1382] Even after death in the gas chambers, the mouths, vaginas and rectums of the corpses would be pried open to search for valuables.[1383] Prisoner teams known as '*Dentisten*' (Dentists) would be responsible for such searches in Belzec, Sobibor and Treblinka.[1384]

Some reports by men also refer to the intrusiveness of internal body searches. Smith reports that all men as well as women were strip searched, including internally, in the Gyor ghetto in Hungary by the Arrow Cross.[1385] Karay reports that body searches of men (and women) were performed in the HASAG labour camps.[1386] Kogon too, reports that "controls of men which involved them squatting down before the SS, backside forward and legs spread out, was a source of particular glee to the observers."[1387]

Nakedness

Reports of humiliating, forced nakedness in ghettos occur frequently in testimonies. Sala Pawlowicz reports that the Germans staged mass disrobing of men, women and children in the streets of the ghetto. "They forced them to lie in the streets and they walked by laughing and making lewd comment. Then they were beaten on their bare backs and chased through the ghetto."[1388]

The Germans also used or planned to use nakedness to create propaganda against Jews abroad. Iranek-Osmecki reported:

> One day a number of men and women were driven to the public baths where they were ordered to strip and to perform their ablution together, all naked, while the scene was scrupulously filmed... these films were destined for Germany and for abroad. On the eve of the liquidation of the ghetto these films were to give the lie to any disquieting rumours should any news leak out inadvertently. They were to show how well the Jews in Warsaw were doing and also how immoral and despicable we were since both Jewish men and women frequent the same public baths and shamelessly display their naked bodies to one another.[1389]

Forced nudity was common in concentration camps and was shocking, embarrassing and demeaning for prisoners. Women inmates were particularly anguished at their forced nakedness in front of men. They were forced to strip naked in front of soldiers, to stand naked for many hours, even days, in endless parades, to wait, naked, in lines, to be disinfected, or for 'selections,' were whipped naked, and made to dance or run naked. They were simultaneously insulted with comments that often had sexual connotations.[1390] Perl reports that the "laughing SS guards... showed their appreciation for some of the beautiful bodies by slashing them with whips."[1391] Adelsberger, in Birkenau, reports that:

> Twenty-two of us went under the shower, laughing and splashing about, dripping from head to toe and rejoicing in the delightful sensation of being able to indulge our bodies... Herr Schwarzhuber... [the] SS officer inspected us not only in a patronizing, offhanded and condescending way, but as a man in an appraising, smirking, and lascivious manner. He interrogated the naked women one after the other as to their origin, identification number, and their work in the camp, all the while gazing at the contours of our bodies, his eyes measuring our breasts and hips. And we were forced to respond to the quips and queries of this

> cooing man in his SS uniform with our unadorned words and naked bodies...[1392]

Shik reports that Eva Schloss, a 15-year-old, told how SS men came into the shower room, walked around and jeered at the sight of their naked bodies. She reported that it amused them "to pinch the buttocks of the women who were young and pretty" including her own.[1393]

For the younger girls the experience was even more humiliating: Tova Berger, a 16-year-old from a very religious family, where modesty was ingrained from childhood,[1394] found forced nakedness unbearable: "I never was undressed in front of a man and they made all kinds of dirty jokes about our bodies and they looked at us and I was standing there shivering, naked, without hair on my body, and I was exposed. I felt like an animal and I thought "That's the end."[1395] Esther Reichman testified that she had to undress and parade before the Germans while the orchestra played in Auschwitz: "It was like a show, like a theatre, you know. It was horrible."[1396] As Marie-Jose Chombart de Lauwe, of France, testified: "what was humiliating was that we had to undergo an examination for lice. They told us to stand on a stool, but they were *male* deportees who had to look and see if we had lice, even in hidden places."[emphasis in original].[1397] Women had to undress so that they could be inspected for pregnancy.[1398] Olga Lengyel related how once, the clothing of 1,400 women was taken for disinfection but only clothing for 1,200 were returned. Women who did not get clothing and who could not 'organize' clothing or blankets had to go to roll call completely naked. The SS guards knew why this was so, but they beat these 'treacherous females' who were so 'shameless.' These women were liquidated first.[1399] Esther and Sarah[1400] reported the humiliation of being beaten on their buttocks, and nakedness during roll calls and selections. Sala Pawlowicz confirms being given 25 lashes on her naked body. Every time she fainted, she was roused with cold water and the beating would continue until completed.[1401] Charlotte Delbo and others add that mothers were forced to strip in front of their children, a disconcerting experience for both.[1402] According to Menachem K's unpublished diaries cited by Dublon-Knebel:

> ... the mother's enforced nakedness contained an element of sacrilege. During the first moments neither mothers nor sons knew how to cope with the humiliation and embarrassment that had been forced on them. For the sake of the values of the past one of the mothers ordered her son not to look, but the present was stronger, and although he tried not to peep, every now and then he was compelled to look up, if for no other reason than to avoid tripping. Aware of her son's distress, the mother did the only thing that could save him from this terrible embarrassment. She

> managed to overcome her own embarrassment and ordered him to look at her. The ensuing relief was enormous and the shame evaporated.[1403]

Venezia, a *Sonderkommando* worker in Auschwitz, writes about the distress experienced by the elderly when forced to undress in public:

> One time I had to help an old woman get undressed. Like all elderly people she clung to her things. And then, when faced with a man she didn't know, the poor woman was completely distraught. Every time I tried to take her stockings off, she pulled them back up again. I'd roll them down one side and she'd pull them up the other.[1404]

Women had to parade nude before SS doctors in the infirmary before being given permission to stay[1405] or for regular 'selections.'[1406] Mengele himself made the inmates disrobe and march before him, sometimes backwards, with their arms in the air while he whistled Wagner.[1407] Those selected had to climb into the trucks and were taken away, still entirely nude. Vera Laska summarizes the experiences of many who testified:[1408]

> On the rare occasions that the women were marched to the real showers, the grapevine somehow reached the lewdest of the SS, who came to jeer, tease and taunt the defenceless women. Stripping the women naked was also practiced at times of camp selections or on long and boring Sunday afternoons. When the SS had nothing better to do than to order a roll call and expose the powerless women to a cruel parade... They were pushed and shoved into the shower rooms, ordered to strip naked and line up to have all their hair shaved from their heads, underarms and pubic regions. In this pandemonium, as they stood quivering and huddling to hide their nakedness, their modesty was further violated by the SS men ...They made lewd remarks, pointed at them, commented on their shapes, made obscene suggestions, poked into their breasts with their riding crops and sicked their dogs onto them. It was the most shocking of all shocks, a deep blow to their very womanhood...The depravity of the men, indulging themselves in this cheapest, basest and most disgusting of games, as much for the pleasure of seeing naked females as for the sport of frightening them out of their minds, was one of the cruellest tortures to which women were subjected in the concentration camps. Those newly arrived in the jaws of hell were crushed under the deluge of foul language, obscene gestures and the fact that they were

> paraded like cattle on the market in front of men. To many women it meant an unforgivable and never to be forgotten humiliation.[1409]

Both women's and men's reports include comments about forced nakedness. For the most part, however, men were forced to undress in front of men while women were forced to undress in front of men also. While most men found the experience dehumanizing, there is a gender specific dimension of sexual exploitation and abuse in the experiences of women.[1410]

Latrines

Demeaning circumstances regarding toilet facilities in ghettos, on transport trains and in camps have been described. 'Excremental assault' – the title of a chapter in Terrence Des Pres' book '*The Survivor*'[1411]- has been defined as one of the primary means of SS attack on camp inmates.[1412] Des Pres notes:

> The fact is that prisoners were *systematically* subjected to filth. They were the deliberate target of excremental assault. Defilement was a constant threat, a condition of life from day to day, and at any moment it was liable to take an abruptly vicious and sometimes fatal form[1413] [italics original]

And:

> There was no end to this kind of degradation. The stench of excrement mingled with the smoke of the crematoria and the rancid decay of flesh. Prisoners in the Nazi camps were virtually drowning in their own waste, and in fact death by excrement was common.'[1414]

Excerpts from Oskar Rosenfeld's notebooks[1415] from the Łódź ghetto describe further instances:

> 'All out to the latrines.' Everyone races to the toilets: They find one long plank as a kind of bench. Everyone is crowded together: an old man next to a young woman, men mixed with women, children with men etc. And as they sat there answering the call of nature they photographed them, some from below to show them crouching on the bar. What was their purpose? To show how shameless Jews are? Defecating together without distinction as to sex? … This occurred just before getting to Czestochowa again…the

> latrines and the photos…But in the cattle car adults were forced to 'shit as they stood.'[1416]

Anna Lenji testified that when being deported from Hungary to Auschwitz in 1941: "You had to do it the best you had. In your hand, on the soil, in your bag, whatever you had. It stank up to high heaven of course and it was a terrible, terrible, thing. It was hell."[1417] Magda Herzberger, while being deported, recalled an old woman who needed the toilet being told by the Hungarian guards, "You can do it in your pants."[1418] In addition, Isabelle Leitner recalls menstruating while on the transport and having no way to change her napkin.[1419] Amazingly, at least one survivor (Maria Ossowski[1420]) found some ironic humour in a related incident: On the way to Auschwitz-Birkenau, they were not given any toilet facilities. Some were carrying brown paper parcels that they used for this purpose. This became very smelly and when the Germans opened the car doors, she threw the bag from the door. To her amazement, a German soldier with a bayonet ran after it, held his bayonet up and caught it. "I don't have to tell you what happened to his arm and clothes! That was one of those happenings that really brings a grin to your face whenever you think about it."[1421]

Latrines in the camps were deplorable.[1422] Perl describes those at Auschwitz-Birkenau:

> There was one latrine for thirty to thirty-two thousand women and we were permitted to use it only at certain hours of the day. We stood in line to get into this tiny building, knee deep in human excrement. As we all suffered from dysentery, we could rarely wait until our turn came, and soiled our ragged clothes, which never came off our bodies, thus adding to the horror of our existence by the terrible smell which surrounded us like a cloud. The latrine consisted of a deep ditch with planks thrown across it at certain intervals. We squatted on these planks like birds perched on a telegraph wire, so close together that we could not help soiling one another.[1423]

In the camps, Zipora Nir[1424] tells of the humiliation caused to women by having to relieve themselves in front of men at the latrines although De Rochemont acknowledges that as time passed the experience changed: "At one time we nearly died of embarrassment, but now we no longer care, we have risen above shame. The fact that these men stand there watching us, as well as their filthy and obscene remarks, no longer have the power to insult us."[1425] Slava Primozic reports a humiliating order forbidding women to go to the toilet: "When one went to work, outdoors, to cut branches, one was not allowed to leave in order to relieve oneself, everyone did this standing up, and, always the dogs, and with all the guards, all while standing."[1426] Likewise, Miriam Berger testified: "Excuse me, we had constipation and then they wouldn't even let us stay in the toilets. They were chasing [us] out because they didn't have enough toilets. They had to chase people to finishing fast because the next group had to come."[1427] As Primo Levi writes about this "excremental coercion," prisoners also harassed other prisoners to gain access to the latrines:

> It was neither easy nor painless to get used to the collective latrine, at brief and obligatory times, in the presence, right in front of you, of the candidate to the succession; on his feet, impatient, at times pleading, at others bullying, every ten seconds insisting: "Hast du gemacht?" "Aren't you finished yet?"[1428]

Anna Bergman,[1429] in Auschwitz-Birkenau, also testified that the SS "would poke us with long poles on our behinds as we sat, we didn't have time to do what we had to do. It was awful."[1430] Moorhouse[1431] and Perl[1432] note that access to toilet facilities was rigidly controlled or non-existent: "Instead of toilet facilities some women were given bowls which they had to use for drinking water or soup as well as for toilets."[1433] As Lengyel writes "A total lack of paper was another difficulty that made personal hygiene impossible, to say nothing of the cleanliness of the latrines."[1434] As Ellen Loeb reported, in Auschwitz-Birkenau "If you had to go you had to take pieces of your clothing to clean yourself."[1435] Rudolph Vrba reported that he saw twenty dollar bills being used as toilet paper in Birkenau especially by the wealthier kapos.[1436] Leni Yahil reports that at night women were forbidden to go out to the latrines. Instead, four to five hundred people living in a block were provided with two barrels for the purpose of relieving themselves.[1437]

Conditions deteriorated even further as the war drew to a close. Rose Frochewaig Mellender arrived in Ravensbrück after being on the death march from Auschwitz in January 1945:

> They put us… in stalls, where cows used to be…We were there like two days in that mud, without food, without anything, nothing for two days …they said, 'If you have to go there is a big pot, go there. But don't make number two, make number one. What those people did that had to make number two, they were afraid. Don't ask. If they made number two, they beat the hell out of them. So you had to hold for two days.'[1438]

Ignacz Rüb was a Hungarian who survived the death march from Auschwitz to Lanfeshut. He found some half-rotten carrots en route. Before long, they were eaten and the next day everyone got diarrhoea. "It was very cold, freezing, and as we marched along, all this mess was frozen in our trousers and made a noise like cow-bells as we went. The SS laughed their heads off. You can imagine: diarrhoea frozen into ice! It was terrible."[1439]

Clothing

Standard concentration camp uniform was the well known striped shirt, jacket, trousers, cap and clogs for men and dress for women made from thin, cheap material which quickly deteriorated. New clothes were not always re-issued once they were in shreds, but had to be 'organized'. In Auschwitz-Birkenau, clothing was not necessarily cleaned between each use: uniforms removed from dead inmates were simply given to new prisoners.[1440]

Not being able to wash as well as not having appropriate underwear further diminished women's femininity. Hana Muller Bruml in Kodowa-Sackisch, a subcamp of Gross-Rosen, testified that "One day I didn't eat the bread: I exchanged it for some sort of contraption out of which I could make a bra. I wanted a bra so badly. These were the sort of leftovers of civilization."[1441] Fenalon too, notes the importance of bras – a rare commodity in the camps.[1442] Ruth Nebel also spoke of the value of obtaining a bra: she wore the one she obtained unwashed, full of lice, through the years of her imprisonment.[1443] Lina Berensin, a seamstress in Stutthof Camp made herself a bra. Her testimony reveals that she took the lining from the men's jackets that two sisters had received, removed three buttons from the men's shirt she had been given, exchanged a full day's bread ration for a needle that someone had found in her jacket, unravelled thread from around her blanket and used a shard of glass from a broken window to cut the cloth. She wore this bra for seven months before liberation on 23 January 1945.[1444]

Ellen Loeb in Theresienstadt testified that "a lipstick sent to her in the mail was exchanged for half a loaf of bread."[1445] Its value was lifesaving, not only in that it could help a woman look healthier at selections, but also because it restored a sense of femininity to women. As Jim Wheeler, a British private with the 11th Light Field Ambulance, Royal Army Medical Corps reported on the liberation of Bergen-Belsen:

> Shortly after the British Red Cross arrived a very large quantity of lipstick came …Men were screaming for hundreds of other things. Nobody knows who asked for the lipstick, but in the event it was sheer genius on the part of whoever thought of it. It was obvious that nothing did more for these internees than the lipstick. Women lay in beds with no sheets, no nighties but with scarlet lips. You saw them wondering about with nothing but a blanket over

> their shoulders, but with scarlet lips. One saw a woman dead on a post-mortem table, clutched in her hand was a piece of lipstick. It was an attempt and a method to make people feel like individuals.[1446]

Lidia Rosenfeld Vago in Auschwitz-Birkenau reported that:

> Once every several weeks we received clean underpants. To my utter revulsion and pain, I once received a pair of underpants sewn from a *talles* [a prayer shawl]. It was unmistakable, with the dark stripes on the border, and the characteristic fine weave of the cloth. I was not the only one who received such underwear, and I felt sorry for the religious girls. Nevertheless we had to tolerate the degradation.[1447]

Charlotte Delbo in Auschwitz reports, "Except for the privileged few, some ten or twenty girls, and the camp aristocracy – block leaders and their assistants, policewomen and sentenced German felons – no one ever washed."[1448] Not being able to wash was a further humiliation for women.[1449]

Menstruation

Menstruation compounded the women's personal hygiene problems. Gabrielle Herz reported that cardboard playing cards were made from 'Camelia Sanitary Napkins' boxes in the women's prison Moringen suggesting that at this stage of the Nazi era (1936-7) sanitary napkins were available to women prisoners.[1450] As Dora Love, imprisoned in Stutthof, reports:

> In the early stages of the camp I still menstruated, so I used to rip pieces from that skirt and use it like a sanitary towel... we walked around with these wonderful striped dresses with whole chunks torn out and that was the reason why they had been torn out. They were looking for excuses to hit you, so suddenly you were hit for tearing your dress.[1451]

Gitta Sereny reports that in the absence of sanitary napkins or newspaper, the girls used large leaves to protect themselves.[1452] No sanitary napkins or cotton wool were available and folded pieces of linen absorbed poorly, were uncomfortable, and were difficult to wash.[1453] In one ironic situation, a 'sanitary towel' saved a woman from rape: Lucille Eichengreen managed to steal a scarf and hid it between her legs. Before she could remove it an SS man pulled her aside attempting to molest her.

His hands felt the stolen scarf and he pushed her away in disgust shouting "You filthy, useless bitch! Pfui! Menstruating!"[1454]

While the contention of many[1455] that the Nazis put something into their food to prevent menstruation is usually discounted, Jean Jofen's[1456] research suggests that in Auschwitz the use of the drug c*aladium seguinum* to induce sterility may well have been experimentally administered, as attested to by Rudolf Brandt after the war.[1457] Jofen reports that I G Farben was responsible both for the research by Dr Wilhelme Tauboeck into the development of this drug for the induction of infertility as well as for the feeding of inmates at Auschwitz Camp IV and it is likely that the drug was used there. Notwithstanding this, stress and inadequate diet were more likely causes of the loss of menstruation. Schwertfeger reports that as many as 54% of women in Theresienstadt ceased menstruating for between 3 and 17 months.[1458] As Susan Cernyk-Spitz and Gertrude Schneider both testified, it was a blessing they did not menstruate because the sanitary conditions and shortage of rags to stop the blood flow did not allow women to take care of themselves unless they were able to work in privileged jobs.[1459] Having their periods caused embarrassment, and fear of incurring a beating if they soiled themselves[1460] but not having their periods caused psychological distress, and concerns about permanent infertility as Hannah Cukier Horon, Atina Grossmann and others, expressed.[1461] As Fania Fenelon writes, at the thought that their periods might never return, "Catholics crossed themselves, others recited the *Shema* (an important Jewish prayer), everyone tried to exorcise this curse that the Germans were holding over us: sterility."[1462]

Some Reactions to the Inhumane Conditions

It is mindboggling to conceive of the mentality that imposed such degradation as excremental assault, forced nudity and public, intimate, bodily searches, often accompanied by laughter, titillation and derision. These, combined with the horrendous living conditions in most camps, including starvation that could evolve into cannibalism, and work demands that were superhuman, led to understandably inhumane behaviour among some prisoners. Although this aspect of behaviour is not often exposed, many instances confirm its occurrence. For instance, Wanda Poltawska, imprisoned in Ravensbrück reported that "Hunger often drove people to do terrible, mean–spirited things."[1463] Similarly, Gisella Perl writes:

> We counted each other's swallows, jealously, enviously, careful that none of us should get more than her share… Quickly the strongest, most energetic among us jump down from their cages and run to the door, where they catch up with the prisoners carrying the empty pot. Screaming,

> pushing each other aside, fighting, they stick their arms into the pot to get another mouthful of turnips or potato, which stuck to the side of the pot...Like wild animals they attack the carriers, unmindful of the blows and kicks showering down on them.[1464]

Helina Birenbaum similarly reports that women "fought like animals" and trampled each other to obtain scraps of food:

> We had to fight for everything in Majdanek: for a scrap of floor space in the hut on which to stretch out for the night, for a rusty bowl without which we could not obtain the miserable ration of nettle-soup with which they fed us, or yellow stinking water to drink. But I was not capable of fighting. Fear and horror overcame me at the sight of women prisoners struggling over a scrap of free space on the floor, or hitting one another over the head at the soup kettles, snatching bowls – hostile aggressive women, wanting to live at any price. Stunned, aghast, famished, terrified, I watched them from a distance.[1465]

Gisella Perl confirms:

> There was only one law in Auschwitz – the law of the jungle – the law of self preservation. Women who in their former lives were decent self respecting human beings now stole, lied, spied, beat the others and – if necessary – killed them, in order to save their miserable lives. Stealing became an art, a virtue, something to be proud of.[1466]

Schiff confirms Perl's writings:

> Hunger stripped most of the thin veneer of civility, forcing decent people to theft and later to violence ...food was stolen whenever the opportunity lent itself and later, when the death march inmates reached the camp, people even killed for it...In the camp the law of the jungle reigned. Every man for himself. The inmate who did not learn this principle early on had only a brief life expectancy.[1467]

Lengyel provides a somewhat different example of the unwillingness of women to help each other:

> Large buxom women had to wear little dresses that were too short and too tight and did not come to their knees. Slender women were given huge dresses, some with trains. Yet despite the absurdity of the distribution, most of the internees, even those who had the chance, refused to exchange their 'dresses' with their neighbours.[1468]

Venezia, a Sonderkommando worker reports similar reactions among men. He writes, "We slept on a straw mattress, without undressing. If we'd taken anything off any item of clothing whatsoever, even our shoes, they'd have been stolen. And in order to get them back, we'd have had to pay with a ration of bread."[1469]

These and similar extracts lend support to the statements of Gisella Perl, Vera Schiff and Viktor Frankl who said: "Those who died were the best of us…"[1470] Similarly, Primo Levi writes that it was usually "the worst [who] survived, the selfish, the violent, the insensitive, the collaborators of the 'grey zone,' the spies" who survived ["the saved"] …the best all died ["the drowned"].[1471] The 'grey zone' refers, in essence, to the coercive conditions that so demoralized people that they could harm others in order to survive, as illustrated here. Stories of self-centered and often cruel acts perpetrated in the struggle to survive emerge not only from memoires of the camps but also from dairies written while in ghettos.[1472] Adelson and Lapides writing of events in the Łódź ghetto recounts:

> A few hundred people demolished a wooden shed on 67 Brzezinska Street in the Łódź ghetto for firewood. While the wood was being stolen the shed collapsed crushing several people. In spite of their desperate cries no one came to their aid as the robbery continued unabated. 36 year old Frania Szabeck died and two others suffered serious injuries. A lamentable instance of 'moral savagery.'[1473]

In contrast, many scholars have noted that women played a distinctive nurturing role, providing emotional support through creating 'camp families' or 'camp sisters' for each other thereby helping them to survive their inhumane conditions.[1474] Others also report that women were not the only ones to provide emotional support and friendships to each other: men did too.[1475] Notable among these was the friendship between Rudolf Vrba and Fred Wetzler that facilitated their unique escape from Auschwitz.[1476] Richard Glazer who survived Treblinka also recalls:

> My friend Karl Ungar and I were always together. We were like twins. In this camp you could not survive an hour without someone supporting you and vice versa. We knew that we were destined to die…No individual could make it alone… I and my friend Karl survived because we supported each other constantly. We divided everything, even a small piece of bread.[1477]

Gilbert Coquempot, a French resistance fighter imprisoned in Flossenbürg and its sub-camp Ganakur, also reports that companionship contributed to his survival: "I had developed an eye infection, which meant that I could barely see. My companions guided me. I would have been killed without their help."[1478] Alec Ward reports on his close friendship with Chaim Ickowics in Skarżysko-Kamienna labour camp (*Werk C*): "When one of us was down, in spirit or physically, the other would pick him up. We instinctively helped one another. Chaim and I were together for the rest of the war."[1479] and both survived.

While both men and women have reported mutual support experiences, so too did they both report being utterly alone in their struggle to survive.[1480] As Weiss testified, "The Germans turned us into animals. It was every person for himself. I was alone. The only thing was to survive." Margalit Nagel-Gross also testified: "Here there are no brothers, parents or friends, here there is only *me*. Furthermore, the bestiality reached such a level that in many cases a sister was pleased to have got rid of her sister." [Italics original].[1481] As Des Pres notes, in '*Night*', Eli Weisel[1482] provides two pieces of advice for survival in the camps that encapture both these sentiments: In the first, an 'old' inmate speaks to a new admission: "We are all brothers and we are all suffering the same fate. The same smoke floats over our heads. Help one another. It is the only way to survive" and in a later moment in the book, an anonymous inmate remarks: "Listen to me boy. Don't forget that you're in a concentration camp. Here every man has to fight for himself and not think of anyone else. Even of his father. Here there are no fathers, no brothers, no friends. Everyone lives and dies for himself alone." As Des Pres notes, survivors' reports do "include small deeds of courage and resistance, of help and mutual care; but in the larger picture, the image of viciousness and death grows to such enormous intensity that all else – any sign of elementary humanness – pales to insignificance."[1483]

In 1993, Ringelheim retracted her earlier writings about women, writing:

> In the work presented… I seemed to be saying that in spite of rape, abuse and murder of babies; in spite of starvation, separations, losses, terror and violence; in spite of everything ugly and disgusting, women bonded, loved one another. This focus distorted our understanding of a larger situation in which that experience may have played only a small role…Perhaps these friendship stories cover a deeper and more troubled image of intrigue, bitterness, hurt, pain, and brutality. What else happened in the groups? Between the groups? The talk about friendship allowed those of us who heard the stories to admire these women, even to receive some peace and comfort. It helped to lessen the terrible surrounding sounds of the Holocaust. This 'women-centered' perspective and the questions it addressed were misguided… Perhaps it was too frightening to look at women and the Holocaust without having a

way out. It is only human, even for a feminist, to look for something that will make the horror less horrible and even negligible.[1484]

Studying Untoward Behaviour

Studying untoward behaviour of Jews during the Holocaust has been an issue for some decades in relation to all scholarship and not specifically that focussed on women. As early as 1945, Mark Dworzecki, a survivor historian, in an article titled *To Ignore or to Tell the Truth*, called for Holocaust studies to examine the cases of "degeneracy and pollution caused by the insane conditions of a sort never previously known by any people."[1485] Nevertheless, his original article in Yiddish, published in France in June 1945, included a long catalogue of 'immoral behaviours' of Jews in the ghetto which was omitted when the article was published a few weeks later in Hebrew.[1486] Ben-Zion Dinur, an academic, agreed with Dworzecki, calling for 'collecting material about the traitors and degenerates, too' as well as focusing on the human side of the Holocaust, although his later talks no longer mentioned this.[1487] According to Mendel Piekarz,[1488] as time passed historians increasingly presented a sanitized picture of Jewish behaviour during the Holocaust.

In many ways, suppressing the less morally or ethically acceptable aspects of behaviour during the Holocaust does a disservice to its study, particularly if the disastrous experiences of Jews is to be remembered and respected. This applies equally to the study of men's and women's behaviours. The fact that human beings were treated so badly as to force the integrity and humanity of some to be expunged and replaced with vicious, dishonest or disrespectful behaviour towards each other, says more about the perpetrators of such conditions than it does about the most basic human instincts for survival that emerged. Maslow's[1489] hierarchy of needs, which places basic physiological needs at the primary level of functioning of humanity, has been accepted for decades: there is nothing new in the emergence of survival instincts among people when their existence is threatened to the extent imposed by the Nazis on Jews. It is the Nazi's humanity and respect that is at stake, not that of the Jews.

Rape And Sexual Abuse

A specific goal of Nazi ideology was the manipulation and extermination of Jewish reproductive function. Dehumanizing Jews – as beings that were on the lowest rung of the 'Aryan' hierarchy – was an integral step in this process. Rape and sexual violence were not, however, an inherent part of their policy but became part of the violence that appears to be inherent in genocide.[1490] Neither was rape regarded as a 'spoil of war' by the German army: instead, an extensive network of brothels was established to provide sexual release for men although this too might be considered as 'rape.' Sexual violation of Jewish women occurred to provide sexual entertainment, but also as a means of humiliating Jews and confirming their dehumanized status, not worthy, even, of sexual respect. In addition, in times of war, the sexual violation of women is not only an act directed against the woman but is a message from men to men meaning that one group is no longer able to protect their women. Sexual violence then symbolizes the military defeat and humiliation of the male population.[1491] Rape and sexual brutality, especially, but not only, when followed by murder, contributed considerably to the Nazi goal of humiliating all Jews and eliminating their reproductive function. The apparent enjoyment of rape by the perpetrators, frequently associated with excessive sexual brutality, adds an overwhelmingly sadistic edge to these acts.

Rape has been recognized as a universal component of war and genocide: German soldiers raped Belgium women in World War I; Turks raped Armenian women during the Armenian genocide of 1915; Japanese raped Chinese women during the Rape of Nanking 1937-1938 and established brothels where women of 'lower races' from Korea and other Asian countries were kept as 'comfort women;' Russians raped thousands of German women at the end of World War II in 1944-5; Americans raped Vietnamese women in the 1960s and established brothels holding Vietnamese refugees near their military bases; Pakistani soldiers raped Bengali women in 1971; Hutus raped Tutsi women in Rwanda in 1994; Muslim women were raped repeatedly in special camps set up for this purpose in Yugoslavia; and armed militias in Darfur, and the Democratic

Republic of Congo are currently raping thousands of women with atrocious cruelty.[1492] Current news reports indicate that the Islamic State and its followers are continuing this barbarity.[1493]

In World War II, rape victims included Jewish and non-Jewish women, men and children.[1494] Victims were abused in their homes, in hiding, in ghettos, in prisons, in brothels, and in concentration camps. The perpetrators included German soldiers, guards, SS members, non-German allies and collaborators, and civilians as well as fellow prisoners. Victims and perpetrators came from varied countries including Germany, Poland, Czechoslovakia, Belarus, Russia and Hungary, if not others. Sexual abuses were committed in institutionalized structures such as brothels as well as in unsanctioned situations such as when looting homes. Female and male victims of various ages and geographical locations were assaulted both in public as well as in the usual private space that is associated with rape.[1495] Some survived and testified about their own experiences, while others testified about abuses perpetrated against third parties. Yet others remained silent, or were unable to speak out as they were murdered. In addition, Jewish women were abused not only by Germans but also by their collaborators and rescuers, and by Jewish men in positions of power.[1496]

Many Holocaust scholars have been hesitant to consider that sexual violence, in addition to social and physical torment, might have been part of the process of dehumanization and abuse of Jewish as well as other 'undesirable' non-Aryan women.[1497] Plentiful evidence exists documenting sexual contraventions of the racial purity laws particularly relating to non-Aryan groups such as Slavs.[1498] It has sometimes been thought that as 'subhumans,' – emaciated, dirty, and shorn – Jews in particular were unthinkable as sexual objects. They were also believed to have been 'protected' from rape, prostitution or sexual abuse by the *Rassenschande* laws. This view ignores the women who were transferred from 'normal' home conditions to camps, and the women driven directly from their villages and raped or killed by the *Einsatzgruppen* and their accomplices. Such Jews were not much worse off in appearance than their non-Jewish neighbours, were not shaven, wore ordinary clothing and could easily have been – and were – viewed as sexual objects.[1499] As Desbois says:

> the Jewish women selected by the Germans as sex slaves and assassinated at the end of the war are not mentioned in any of the archives. Yet [non-Jewish] witnesses often mention them. They knew them before the occupation and were often present at their assassination. The Holocaust of Jewish women in eastern Europe constitutes a chapter of history that has barely been opened.[1500]

Current interest in rape as a spoil of war in other genocides may be stimulating examination of this issue during the Holocaust.[1501] While rape of Jewish women by German and other non-Jewish men is being recognized more frequently today, rape by Jewish men is less well acknowledged.[1502]

Some historians prefer to use official documentation, such as Nazi documentation, in their consideration of Holocaust history in preference to survivor testimony.[1503] In cases of rape and sexual exploitation, however, such official documentation is understandably rare (such as in court proceedings) or at best, unofficial (such as in *Wehrmacht* soldiers' letters). Sufficient data from survivor and perpetrator testimony exists, however, to validate that Jewish women were used and abused sexually.[1504] Both Hedgepeth and Saidel[1505] and Fogelman[1506] report that approximately 1,000 of the 52,000 interviews conducted at the University of Southern California Shoah Foundation Institute for Visual History and Education mention rape and sexual violence. In the Fortunoff Video Archive at Yale University, created some 10-20 years before the Shoah Foundation interviews were conducted, 10 survivor testimonies out of several thousand recount sexual assault of the interviewee or someone known to them.[1507] These recordings were, however, designed to be shared with family members and school children, which may have inhibited such reports. In these interviews, unlike the Shoah Foundation interviews, the subject was not directly broached. While relatively few of the recorded testimonies recall rape or sexual violence, most of those subjected to these assaults would have been killed. These survivor testimonies, no matter how few, do confirm that rape and sexual violence against Jews did occur.

Many discussions of rape in the literature do not distinguish between rape of Jewish and rape of other non-'Aryan' women during the Nazi era. Nor do they distinguish between rape of Jewish women by Germans or by non-German men including liberators, and rescuers.[1508] Additionally they do not distinguish between the possible motivations behind the rape – for example for sexual pleasure versus sadistic intent – or the severity of violence incurred in addition to the rape itself. As far as is possible, these distinctions are observed here to provide clearer evidence of the occurrence of rape and sexual violation of Jewish women, by Germans in particular, but also by others.

Fear of Rape

Fear of rape was extensive among Jewish and other non-'Aryan' women in Germany and the territories overtaken by the Nazis.[1509] While this fear might be regarded as a 'normal' component of any woman's life, it was, perhaps, more realistically grounded during the war years, simply because rapes did occur and stories of rape were abundant. Judith Isaacson,[1510] a beautiful, vivacious, Jewish teenager, reported that the war meant two physical threats for her: fear of rape and the shortage of food. She was troubled by persistent rumours of Jewish girls being sent to the front as prostitutes, being raped, and then shot and thrown into open ditches. She worried whether she would be able to "convince a German soldier not to rape her." She told her mother that she feared rape more than death and wanted to take poison with her. A few days later, her uncle told her that he had witnessed a mass raping of Jewish girls who were buried alive in mass graves that they had dug.[1511] Thirteen-year-old Eva Heyman in Hungary wrote in her diary on 18 May 1944, of the terrible things being done to women by the gendarmes, "things that it would be better if I didn't write them down in you. Things that I am incapable of putting into words, even though you know, dear diary, that I haven't kept any secrets from you till now."[1512] Fear of rape following liberation is also frequently reported, for example by Anna Lenji and, Eugenia Fefer-Matz,[1513] and by Felicja Karay and her two sisters,[1514] as they made their way home after release from the camps.

Rape of Jewish Women in Ghettos

Rape of Jewish women is reported to have occurred in many ghettos including the Kovno Ghetto[1515] (by Lithuanians), the Riga ghetto (by the Latvian guards),[1516] the Warsaw ghetto (by the SS, Ukrainians and Lithuanians),[1517] Łódź ghetto (by the SS and after liberation by the Russians),[1518] the Siedlce ghetto (by a German watchman),[1519] Kraków ghetto (by Germans),[1520] Theresienstadt (by a German officer),[1521] Lask ghetto in Poland (by German police),[1522] Tacovo ghetto in Czechoslovakia (by Hungarian guards),[1523] in the synagogue of the Satoraljaujhely Ghetto in Hungary (by Hungarian gendarmes),[1524] in the Legionowo Ghetto (by Polish students),[1525] in Tulchin ghetto in Romania (by Romanian gendarmes)[1526] and in the Grodno ghetto (by the Gestapo).[1527]

In many ghettos, rape of Jewish women was perpetrated by German ghetto leaders, by those who enlisted women into forced labour, prior to mass murder, during deportations and on transit trains. The German head of Łódź ghetto, Hans Biebow, is accused of having raped a number of Jewish women in the last years of the war.[1528] He had a violent streak that manifested itself in beating Jews and in raping women. The 'Diary from the Łódź Ghetto' entry for 2 September 1944, includes Jakub Poznanski's report of the attempted rape of a Jewish girl by Biebow who grabbed the 16 year old daughter of Dr Sima Mandels and her engineer husband in the hallway, dragged her into his office and tried to rape her. She started screaming. Biebow shot her in the eye and then ordered her entire family shipped out immediately.[1529] Two other testimonies also report rape by Biebow: Bina W. reports being raped by him.[1530]

Esther H reports that Biebow and another German kept Rita, a beautiful Czech girl, and both raped her. When the prisoners were being evacuated, she was murdered.[1531] Vera Schiff, while confirming the relationship between Biebow and Rita writes that Rita escaped alive at the end of the war but died some years later.[1532]

Survivors testify that Lithuanian collaborators took women away for 'work' during the daytime and raped them at night.[1533] Similarly, Golda Wasserman, in Romania, provided eyewitness accounts of girls being selected to be raped and then returned to the Tulchin ghetto:

> About fifteen kilometers from the ghetto there were Italian and Hungarian reserve divisions. As demanded by the commissariat – officers of these divisions, the Romanian gendarme who was the Commandant of Tulchin selected healthy young girls from the ghetto and sent them away, under the official pretense of working in the kitchen or bakery of those divisions. The girls returned from there having been raped, ill with venereal diseases. Many committed suicide back in the barracks, while some of them were killed when resisting or attempting to flee. The Kommandant selected new girls for 'work.' Selection was carried out every fifteen to twenty days. It is impossible to describe what was happening in the ghetto – the desperate screams of the girls, the pleas of their parents. Some girls tried to run away along the road. The Fascists shot them in the back. Only a few managed to hide in villages, pretending to be locals, or were saved by the partisans after long wonderings in the forest. I belonged to the latter group. Among twenty-five other girls, I was picked to be sent to 'work.'[1534]

The excuse of selection for 'work' was not always employed to disguise sexual exploitation. In 1942, Alexander Kuperman in the Bershad ghetto in Transnistria, saw: "a group of Romanians ... entered the ghetto....They selected three or four young, very beautiful Jewish girls, took them to their barracks, and made them go 'through their ranks.' The girls died."[1535] An unnamed participant at the 1983 conference on 'Women Surviving the Holocaust' reported that in the Czestochowa ghetto, Poland: "I was beaten up, I was raped, not only my body but I was raped mentally, and I survived because I wanted to live. I wanted to do something with my life and I wanted to tell the world what was going on."[1536] Schiff reports being sexually assaulted at the age of about 16 or 17 while standing guard for exits and re-entries during the night at the barracks door, together with a Czech guard, in Theresienstadt. He promised to give her some of his food and when she went to get it, he assaulted her. Her quick thinking saved her:

> For a second he ogled me, and then he lunged at me. I swerved, bending aside, but he caught me by the waist. His revolting paws fondled my breasts and buttocks. He was bending down trying to force a kiss…He was a hefty man, trembling with obscene lust. My only chance was to trick him. Instantly I gripped both his hands and whispered to him urgently: Look, someone just entered the gates, if they catch us both of us will be killed. Is it worth it to die like this? …He let go of me and ran back to the gate at full speed.[1537]

Rape also occurred prior to mass murder. When Kovno was first occupied, Jews were arrested *en masse* and were taken first to jail and then to the nearby Seventh Fort where they were imprisoned and later shot by Lithuanians with German encouragement. Women were raped before being killed.[1538] Mary Berg's Warsaw diary entry of 12 June 1941 records that "There are people from Lublin, Radom, Łódź, and Piotrkow – from all the provinces. All of them tell terrible tales of rape and mass murder."[1539]

Deportations provided another opportunity for rape. Kraków ghetto survivor Jan Rozański described an incident during one of the mass deportations from the ghetto: He and his mother found a young girl at the bottom of the stairs, "She was dead. Her dress lifted and pants torn off her body. She was raped, illegally, and then killed, legally, by the representatives of the 'high race'. She was shot directly in the face."[1540]

The partisan Mikhail Grichanik has provided one report of rape occurring on a transport train moving from the Minsk ghetto to Molodechno in Belarus in November 1941. He reports that at night German guards would come into the boxcars packed with people and select young, beautiful girls, take them away and rape them.[1541]

Rape of Jewish Women by Jewish Men in Ghettos

There are occasional reports of Jewish women being raped by Jewish men, particularly in ghettos. Chaim Rumkowski, the head of the Judenrat in Łódź ghetto, is accused by Lucille Eichengreen of rape of young Jewish girls in the ghetto.[1542] He reportedly proposed that she take a room above her workplace where he could see her: when she refused, he beat her across the shoulders with his cane.[1543] Gina L.[1544] from Łódź also tells that when Rumkowski liked a young girl he wanted to sleep with her. He had the husband of a girl friend of Gina's deported because he wanted to sleep with her. The Łódź Ghetto Chronicle (entry for 24 September 1943) also reports that a Jewish man named 'Ordinanz' had been found guilty of rape by the ghetto court system.[1545] Rita H.[1546] from Pabianice in Poland remembered that Judenrat leader Rubenstein started to molest her when she came to his store to get milk for her mother. Her friends would say this is the only way to get favours from him.

Jewish women were sometimes forced to have sexual relations with Jewish men for the enjoyment of soldiers who looked on. At the beginning of September 1940, Ringelblum wrote in his diary that "In S[osnowiec, Poland] a soldier went into Jewish homes and forced the men to have sexual relations with women in his presence. Shortly after this he was arrested."[1547] Further, in September 1941 the Yiddish newspaper *Proletarisher Gedank* – one of the underground newspapers of the Warsaw ghetto that reported the deportation of the Jews into the fortress of Pomiechowek – stated the following: "the hangmen forced the Jew, noted as 'P.R.,' to choose four girls and to rape them before their eyes."[1548]

Rape in Hiding

Rape of Jewish women also occurred in hiding. The unequal power balance between those hiding and those offering shelter created situations where abuse was possible and exposure was unlikely.[1549] Marion van Binsberger, a rescuer, recalled:

> I found Esther another hiding place because she was being sexually abused by the oldest boy in the family in the house where she was...The person who told me was the boy's sister. Esther had not said a word. He had scared the hell out of her. If she told, he was going to hand her over to the Nazis. That was the threat a lot of them used.[1550]

As Ringelheim reports:

> [A Jewish survivor] told me that she had been molested by male relatives of the people who were hiding her. They threatened to denounce her if she said anything about it. [She] was eleven or twelve when she was first hidden, took the threats seriously. She didn't tell the young Jewish woman who checked on her periodically. She didn't tell her twin sister. After the war, she didn't tell her husband or her daughter... 'This is the first time I ever admitted this' she remarked in 1984.[1551]

Selma Okrnt testified to being hidden by two Polish families in both of which men in the household started to bother her in attempts to sleep with her: she had to move to escape. Similar experiences are also related by Erika G. and her mother in Hungary, Marie P. in France, Ruth P. in Belgium,[1552] Slema Okrnt[1553] and Yehodit Zik Finkel[1554] in Poland, and

Soria Shlomovitsch in Belgium.[1555] Paula Weinstein tells that she was inappropriately touched by a Jewish man who was hiding with her in a Christian household and who attempted to rape her.[1556] Dr Paul Valant, a hidden child and a psychiatrist wrote, in 1995, that about 1 in every 5 hidden children was sexually assaulted. Some, however, recalled their rescuers with ambivalence saying: "regardless what he has done to me, I can't hate him…I wonder if he ever loved me…after all, he saved my life."[1557]

Rescuers beyond Europe's borders were not exempt from charges of rape either. Clara G., a Polish girl, went to England as part of the *Kindertransport.* The man of the house she was sent to raped her repeatedly. He said he would send her, her sister and her brother back to Germany if she said a word. She enlisted the help of a local rabbi who confronted her rapist. His convincing defence, however, led to her being accused of coming on to her assailant. She escaped one night – accompanied by the man's daughter.[1558] Some child survivors were taken in by Jewish families after the war and even then, sexually abused by them. Hanna (pseudonym) who survived the war in hiding in Eastern Europe was taken as an 8 year old to a Satmar Hasidic family in New York. The foster care was arranged by a Jewish organization and the family was paid. She was assaulted by the man of the house who fondled her and tired to enter her manually, although she says he did not succeed. She has had difficulty relating to men, and for a good part of her life was terrified of sex. She has been in therapy for most of her life.[1559]

Rape in the Partisan Groups

Accounts of rape of women, both Jewish and other, in forests or in partisan groups have been reported.[1560] Lidia Brown-Abramson, for example, was raped as a virgin teenager by a partisan. She never enjoyed sex after that even though she later married and had children. She always saw the sexual act as exploitation following this experience.[1561] As Tec notes, no one knows how common forest rapes were.[1562]

Rape in Prison

Few, if any, have survived to report being raped while held in custody by the Gestapo. British Major Edgar Hargreaves, however, himself captured and tortured mercilessly by the Gestapo for a year, watched, in prison, as girls were being tortured: stripped naked they were raped and one that he observed had her nipples cut off.[1563] Blyuma Isaakovna Bronfin, from Khmelnik in the Vinnitsa region of Ukraine, was arrested and jailed. She reported that in the evenings the Germans and the local police would come, select young women and then take them away, only to throw them back in the cell after torturing and abusing them.[1564] Anna Morgulis testified to being arrested in Odessa and thrown into jail where she was badly beaten. That night Romanian soldiers burst into their cell and raped all the women, young and old. Every night the officers would take girls to spend the night with them.[1565]

Rape by German Soldiers and the *Einsatzgruppen*

Numerous testimonies reveal that Jewish women were raped throughout Nazi occupied Europe usually where individuals could carry out such abuse without their superiors knowing.[1566] Sometimes the rapes took place in homes, at other times women were taken to nearby places and raped, sometimes publicly, yet others were raped and then killed. Women were raped during pogroms, and prior to the mass murders of Jews implemented by the *Einsatzgruppen.* On some occasions, rape was accompanied by brutal torture. Resistance was futile and usually resulted in additional cruelties and death. While Germans are frequently reported as perpetrators of these rapes, non-German collaborators were also implicated.

Many report rape in women's homes: A Jewish doctor testified; "One continually hears of the raping of Jewish girls in Warsaw. The Germans suddenly enter a house and rape 15- or 16-year old girls in the presence of their parents and relatives."[1567] Fanya Gottesfeld Heller waited 50 years before writing about the rape of her aunt in front of her husband, after a Gestapo raid.[1568] In Poland, Jacob Apenszlak recalled that the Jews of Wloclawek were driven out of their homes, robbed, tortured and forced to do hard labour. Women were raped.[1569] In Mazowiecki, Poland, Jezechiel F.[1570] testified, "At night the Germans would force their way into Jewish homes and rape women and girls. The other members of the household would be locked up in another room."

Women were also taken from their homes and raped elsewhere. The attractive wife of a Jew at the Iron Gate Place in the Warsaw ghetto was abducted and permitted to return home after she had been raped.[1571] On 18 February 1940, two German sergeants seized two Jewish girls in the Polish town of Piotrkow, eighteen-year-old Miss Nachmanowics and seventeen-year-old Miss Satanowska, forced them at gunpoint to the cemetery, and raped them.[1572] In one incident in Nasielek, Poland, some 1,600 Jews were whipped all night in what was called a 'whipping orgy.' During this, two Jewish sisters were dragged from their beds in the night and taken to a cemetery, one was raped and the other given five zlotys and told to wait until next time.[1573] Nina Rusman (Kaplan) testified in 1988 at a trial against the German officer who had raped her. She was 13 or 14 at the time, became pregnant, had an abortion which was botched, leaving her bleeding, in need of medical care and ultimately sterile.[1574] Jezechiel F in Poland, reports further "some of the girls, those of the more educated type, would be taken by the Germans to their barracks where they would be raped and killed."[1575] Similar rapes are reported in Belarussia[1576] and in Russia: [1577] For example, B M Sorina reported that in the Shtetl of Khislavichi, Smolensk, Germans raped girls before killing them. Similar reports of German rapes of Jewish women were reported in Lithuania and Latvia by Dr Viktor Kutorga, Nesya Miselevich, Sheyna Gram, and Khaim and Yakov Izraelit.[1578]

Some rapes or attempted rapes were accompanied by extreme brutality. In Lvov, Jewish women were dragged out of their apartments with the help of Ukrainians: some had their breasts cut off in the middle of the street, and/or were raped, as reported in the Jewish underground newspaper *Junge Stimme* in October 1941.[1579] Another report on the Lvov attack suggests that "The *pièce de resistance* of this macabre show was the corpse of a woman whose baby was pinned to her breast with a German bayonet."[1580] Sala Pawlowics reported that as a young teenager she was stripped and beaten by a Polish-German in Lask ghetto in Poland. He declared that he could not have her because she was 'Jewish and filthy.' Instead, he whipped her repeatedly across her breasts and flung her out into the street naked.[1581] In the Shtetl of Cherikov in Belorussia a group of German soldiers raped two girls in broad daylight on the main square.[1582]

Rapes were sometimes perpetrated by multiple men. In 1942, all 600 villagers from the largely Polish town of Adampol were shot and killed. The Germans then brought Jewish girls from nearby Wlodawa, to one of the village houses, which they used as a brothel for the German army officers stationed close to nearby Sobibor.[1583] Desbois reports many atrocities committed by the *Einsatzgruppen* in eastern Europe including multiple rapes of Jewish women.[1584] For instance, in the Ukrainian village of Busk, the Germans kept 30 or so pretty Jewish women to work in the Gestapo offices to serve as sex objects for them. When they left the town, all the women had been pregnant. The Germans did not kill the women themselves but called on a nearby commando from Sokol to assassinate them.

Klavdia L recounted that in Novosokolniki, Russia, 11 Jewish women were put into a house, humiliated and abused and then the house set on fire. All the women perished.[1585] A German woman, Frau Charlotte (Lotte) Müller worked in the resistance against Hitler's regime and was ultimately imprisoned in Ravensbrück. She later reported that when Jewish women were arrested they were first '*versault*' [meaning spoil or destroy, in this case rape]. One was shot to death because of antimilitary work…" She was pretty as a picture," added her old friend, "And the SS all had their way with her until she almost died."[1586]

Pogroms, which led to mass murders of Jews, were associated with rape. In the Romanian pogrom in Iassi of 28-29 June 1940, in which between 13-15,000 were killed, Jewish women were raped, attacked or killed on the spot. Further 'actions' followed which included rapes of Jewish women.[1587] Rakhil Fradis-Milner of the Shtetl Yedintsy, Khotin District. Ukraine, reported that on 5 June 1941 the Germans occupied the shtetl and between then and the end of July, 28 800 people were shot and numerous young girls, practically children, were raped.[1588] In Transnistria, the Nazis and their Romanian allies accompanied mass murder with rape.[1589] Naum Epelfeld of Berdychev testified that:

> two soldiers entered the basement where we stayed... they stopped near a girl and a woman, and ordered them to follow. They took them to an empty office and raped them. The girl's name was Gusta: she was our neighbour's daughter. Gusta Glozman was fourteen or fifteen years old. Soon she would be killed, together with her parents.[1590]

Podolsky reports further that Nazis and their allies rounded up men, women and children in the Ukraine region, made them undress, sometimes raped the women, and then shot them at the edges of mass graves. Dina Pronichva provided an eyewitness account of the Babi Yar massacre of 29-30 September 1941:

> She was taken to Babi Yar with her parents and saw groups of women getting undressed, one after another and led to the execution site, an open pit, and shot by submachine gunners... She was ordered to disrobe and was pushed to the edge of the pit where another group of women was waiting to be murdered. Before the shooting started she fell into the pit. She kept still and pretended to be dead. When it became completely dark and quiet she opened her eyes and saw that the killers had left. She also witnessed rape: 'At the opposite side of the ravine, seven or so Germans brought two young Jewish women. They went down lower to the ravine, chose an even place and began to rape these women by turns. When they became satisfied, they stabbed the women with daggers, so that they even did not cry out. And they left the bodies like this, naked, with their legs open.'[1591]

The teacher, Emelia Borisova Kotlova, also reported that before killing women at Babi Yar they were raped.[1592] As recalled by Lev Rozhetsky, a schoolboy at the time, rape, robbery and murder again occurred when Romanian and German troops took Odessa on 16 October 1944.[1593]

Resistance to rape usually led to worse consequences than sexual assault. In Ukraine, a teacher Kruglyak, in the city of Shpola near Kiev, reported that two Germans visited 35-year-old Manya Glayzer, intending to rape her. She resisted. Instead, they stabbed her to death, murdered her mother and cut off the head of her 14-year-old brother.[1594] In addition, F Krasotkin recalled that on 15 October 1941, the Jews of Mstislavl, Belarus, were ordered into the town square where the Germans selected young women, forced them into a shop, stripped them naked, and raped and tortured them. Those who resisted were shot on the square. The remaining Jews were taken by force to the Kagalny ditch. Men were killed first followed by women and older children. Small children were thrown into the ditch alive. The schoolteacher Minkina-Orlovskaya pleaded with them to spare her 6-year-old son whose father was Russian. In reply, they raised the infant on their bayonets and flung him into the ditch. [1595] Perla Aginskaya reported that during a pogrom in Minsk, a girl of about 18 was raped. She was lying naked on a table, with deep blackish wounds in her chest. There were gunshot wounds around her genitals. She had been raped and murdered.[1596]

Na'ama Shik[1597] lists a number of testimonies reporting rapes of Jewish women by non-German, military collaborators: Meir Rubinstein tells how his wife was raped and murdered by Poles, Edith Wolf reports that a Yugoslav Nazi collaborator tried to rape her, Brina Levin Freidman and Sonia Perminger both tell about Jewish girls who were raped and then murdered by Lithuanians; Naomi Donat was raped by a Hungarian policeman, Vera Varesh reports being a virgin when she was raped by a Hungarian soldier, Ita Shmulevski was sexually harassed by a Hungarian guard, Yulan Petrover tells how a Hungarian soldier raped and then murdered her sister. In Poland, Czeslaw Mierzejewski raped Jewish Judes Ibram before killing her in the Jedwabne massacre of 10 July 1941.[1598] Rapes occurred in Italy too, as the SS took over control of that territory.[1599]

Rape in Labour Camps

Rape of Jewish women was often reported in labour camps. Sometimes this was perpetrated by the camp commander and his staff for their personal sexual entertainment, either in the camp setting or in their own quarters, and sometimes women were abused as sexual slaves by one individual. On occasion, women were forced to indulge in sexual activity as a public exhibition and in other situations rape in public was imposed as a 'punishment' for the woman. On one reported occasion, women were raped by other prisoners at the instigation of the camp staff.

Sexual abuse of Jewish women for the entertainment of the camp staff is reported a number of times. In Croatia, at the Loborgrad labour camp, Jewish women were subjected to repeated rape by the commander and his staff,[1600] and on 24 August 1943, 24 Jewish girls were raped in an all night orgy at the Janowska labour camp.[1601] Karay[1602] reports numerous rapes of Jewish women in the forced labour camp Skarżysko-Kamienna, particularly well known for its sexual abuse: The leadership of this camp regularly raped the prisoner population and survivors have identified numerous German officers as having taken part including: Kurt Krause and Otto Eisenschmidt, and mentioned by nearly all the witnesses, Fritz Bartenschlager. Bartenschlager, would attend selections to choose 'escort girls.' In October 1942, for example, five women were taken to a party in his apartment, together with Franz Schippers, Willi Seidel and Iwan Romanko, where they were ordered to serve the guests in the nude and were ultimately raped by them and then murdered the following day. In January 1943, Bartenschlager's visitors included SS district commander Herbert Boettcher and Frans Shippers, the SS commander of Radom. Three women, including nineteen-year-old Gucia Milchman, who was renowned throughout the camp for her extraordinary beauty, Ruchama Eisenberg, and Mania Silberman, were brutally raped then murdered. Felicja Karay describes the camp as a place where the 'rites of manhood' were expressed in the orgies of drunkenness and gang rapes of Jewish girls.

Sinnreich reports that the sexual abuse in Skarżysko-Kamienna was so pervasive that it went on openly as part of the camp culture.[1603] Milla D. testified that a girl was taken away from her machine and raped by five or six Germans in the office in the centre of the factory. She noted that there were many such incidents. Also, Luba M. testified that one night a few Germans came and took about 20 girls under the age of 15, including her cousin. Bronia S. reported that a *Volksdeutche* (ethnic German) at the factory told her the girls who were disappearing were being raped.

In the Glowen forced labour camp near Sachsenhausen in Germany, German guards dragged Jewish women from their beds at night for sex. Rose S.'s testimony regarding Tschenstochau-Pelzery camp in Poland is similar:

> A *Wehrmacht* soldier came to the barracks and started talking to her and some of her female family members. Four or five weeks later when they were all asleep he returned drunk and started to pull her blanket off. One of her family members stood between her and the soldier and told her to run. The soldier then grabbed another girl. He dragged her off and raped her. The girl came back at 4 am bleeding, screaming and crying. She was taken to the hospital. [1604]

Other commanders chose the most beautiful women arriving in transports to serve as 'housemaids' who were later killed. Selection of women as room cleaners followed by rape was also reported in Haidari concentration camp in Greece. Lya C. in that camp, was selected by a German one morning and sent to clean the bathroom, where he raped her.[1605]

Voyeuristic and exhibitionist rapes and sexual exploitation also occurred. Sala Pawlowicz provides first-hand experience of such sexual abuse. She reports that in the HASAG labour camp at Pelcery, Poland, the Nazis would file in and then methodically work their way through as many girls as they could before tiring. They would then leave after beating the girls they had not violated. Women would be pounced on and violated "in food lines, at the bathroom, everywhere."[1606] Sometimes the Nazis would pick out one girl, rape her and beat her, for five or six days in a row, and then change to another. She reports one occasion when a man and woman were forced to strip naked and embrace each other in front of a barrack full of girls. Stieglitz "ran around them, laughing and rolling his eyes. "That's right...that's right...more!...more! Embrace! Kiss! And he pounded them with his stick. ...Then he paraded them up and down beating the watching girls across the breasts."[1607] Survivor Paula N. related another incident of public rape that took place in Bruss-Sophienwalde camp (Poland):[1608] A woman in the camp became pregnant. She confided in the camp commandant about her pregnancy, believing that he was kind-hearted. Rather than the sympathetic treatment she anticipated he put her on a deportation list to Stutthof. The girl hid to avoid deportation but was eventually found by four German guards. She was gang-raped in front of everyone at the camp and then thrown onto the truck going to Stutthof.

Ringelheim reports a more unusual incident of prisoners being enticed into raping other prisoners as revealed to her in an interview with one survivor, 'G,' in a camp near Lublin and Majdanek:

> the commandant decided to open the gates of the men's camp and allow them to go over to the women's. 'The men came. I was pretty young then. Strangest thing – so many of these men tried right away to screw...[They were] like a horde of animals...I had this vision for a long time – this horde of sick men jumping'...It was one of her worst memories from the Holocaust.[1609]

Rape in Concentration Camps

Rape of Jewish women has been reported in the major concentration camps including Auschwitz, Treblinka, Sobibor, Bergen-Belsen, and

Ravensbrück.[1610] Rape of young Jewish women by Ukrainian assistants occurred on the way to the gas in Treblinka.[1611] Rape also occurred in the barracks after admission to camps. In Sobibor, two Austrian women, Ruth and Gisela, who were actresses, were kept in the kitchen of the house where some SS men lived. After being used by the SS men, they were shot.[1612] The SS and their associates raped women as did Kapos. Sometimes rape was associated with luridly, cruel acts.

Selection of women from the camp barracks for rape is frequently reported. Sara M. who was raped at Ravensbrück as a young girl testified that she was taken from her barracks by a woman, given candy and led to a small room. She recalled:

> There were two men there and there were some other people in the room I think. I was put on a table...I was very violently sexually abused... And I remember being hit, I remember crying and I wanted to get out of there. And I was calling people and screaming and I remember one thing that stands out in my mind that one of them told me that they would stand me up on my head and cut me right in half. And they wanted me to stop screaming and I've had nightmares about that most of my life.[1613]

A number of reports of rape by the SS or their associates in Auschwitz-Birkenau can be found. Ruth Elias, for example, wrote that:

> Drunken SS men sometimes made unexpected appearances in our block: the door would suddenly be flung open, and they would roar in on their motorcycles ...Young Jewish women would be pulled from their bunks, taken away somewhere, and raped...Any women who refused to go with the SS men were savagely beaten, so no one offered any resistance. I cannot describe the pitiable state of these poor women when they came back to the barracks.[1614]

Her reports are confirmed by other survivor testimonies including that of Laura Varon[1615] who was raped by drunken Nazis in Auschwitz-Birkenau together with about ten other girls, and Pearl Grossmann,[1616] who witnessed the rape of a fellow camp inmate by a Ukrainian soldier. Zofia Minc also reports a blatant attempt at rape by the shift commander in Auschwitz:

> I went into Richter's office...He...began explaining to me what an honor it was for me to be found attractive by a German, an SS man, a member of the supreme race... He jumped on me brutally and began tearing my clothes. I defended myself with all my might...suddenly the door

> creaked. Richter jumped behind the desk and I moved in the direction of the exit.[1617]

Similarly, Cecilie Klein's testimony reveals that:

> While they waited for their clothes to be disinfected, all the women were nude and subjected to the soldiers' 'lewd and cruel threats,' but one young girl was singled out and taken to the officers' barracks to be returned two days later, scarcely recognizable, incoherent, face and body swollen and bruised.[1618]

In Bergen-Belsen, Mo Is recalls that kapos had the right to rape women. Similarly, Roman Halter, a Polish Jewish youth in Auschwitz recalls that:

> The women were not put in the women's block, but in this big block next to us. The Kapos and their deputies came to rape the women at night and there were terrible screams and groans coming from that block, and the husbands in our block wept because they could understand the shouts.[1619]

Some rapes were associated with extreme cruelty. Herman S, a crematoria worker reported that:

> A blond haired, blue-eyed woman was naked and Mengele was yelling at her asking if she was Jewish. She replied yes, and Mengele wrapped his cane around her neck. She pushed Mengele and knocked him back. The SS men pushed her down and then Mengele took his cane and sodomized her with it. He saw the blood running out. Mengele left her lying there for two hours. She was bleeding to death. Mengele then pulled out his cane and told him [the SS man] to take her to the crematorium. She was still faintly alive.[1620]

Emil G. reported that while he was in Auschwitz, the Germans arranged a 'show' in which they took twenty Jewish women prisoners and raped them in front of one of the labor groups. He knew one of the raped women from his hometown. She survived the war but committed suicide soon afterward.[1621]

Judith Berger Becker arrived in Ravensbrück from Auschwitz in February 1945 as the war was drawing to a close. She reported that:

> One day she and some others were forced to carry an urn of coffee to a barrack where there were some women who were making horrible noises – 'animal sounds, and they opened their mouths, and they kept pointing, pointing,

> pointing, it was…I didn't understand what was going on. I didn't see. Until they just wouldn't let go, and they kept holding on to me, and this, and this, and this, and then they made gestures on their pubis, and it turned out that all of the women in that barrack had had their tongues cut out.
>
> They were all of the same age, approximately, they were all of the same stature, they were all petite, pretty women, young, I would say, it's hard to estimate, but I would say no more than the early twenties, and they had hair, they were not shaven, they had hair, which is significant…And they were gesticulating sexual overtones, 'and here,' and making horrible, horrible, noises. By the time I understood, or thought I understood, the German guard was already whipping me, and I had to go out…But I've never found out who those women were…I mean the brutality, to cut out their tongues, so that they couldn't report, in other words, they were using every opportunity to tell somebody, they probably were killed, I don't know…I may well be the only one who can report about it…We were never taken there again.[1622]

It is not known whether these atrocities were committed in Ravensbrück or if the women were transported to Ravensbrück from elsewhere.

Although sexual contact with Jewish women was forbidden, it did occur in camps though most who were raped would not have survived to tell of their experience. As Saidel reports, several of the survivors of Ravensbrück that she interviewed gave testimonies regarding other women being raped, although none reported this experience themselves.[1623]

Rape of Women in Occupied Europe

German soldiers also raped Jewish as well as non-Jewish women, sometimes most violently. Rape of a woman could end with her murder and was occasionally followed by sexual abuse of her dead body.[1624] The religious affiliation of the victim is not always identified.

The SS-Sonderkommando Dirlewanger – named after its violently sadistic commander Oskar Dirlewanger – fought partisans, raped and tortured young women and slaughtered Jews in Belorussia from the beginning of 1942. Dirlewanger had a doctorate in Economics, but was a drunkard with a penchant for young girls. In 1934, he was sent to prison for driving while drunk, causing several accidents with injuries and repeatedly having sex in an official car with a girl under the age of consent which in Germany at that time was 14.[1625]

Kuper reports witnessing a scene of rape by German soldiers:

> Then from the hut came sudden shouting, laughter, a scream, more shouting, again a woman's voice screaming as if calling to the heavens to help. The door opened and a man came stumbling out of the hut, walking in my direction.
>
> When he came closer I realized he was crying. His arms outstretched towards the sky, begging God for help...He laughed hysterically...and said 'They're raping my wife. She's five months pregnant and they're raping her.' He turned and continued to walk without direction. 'Oh Holy Mother, how can you allow this? The whole German army is raping my Jadwiga!' Sometime later a single shot rang out...from the hut came the persistent cry of a young child screaming, 'Mummy is dead!'[1626]

Rape and sexual slavery also occurred. Mühlhäuser reports the rape of a Russian teacher, Genia Demianova, following her capture by Germans on 5 August 1941 in the Russian city of Pskov. After she failed to escape, the commanding officer tortured her with a whip and brutally raped her. He then boasted of his sexual success afterwards:

> There is a roar of cheering, the clinking of many glasses. The sergeant is standing by the open doorway:'The wildcat is tamed.' He is saying. 'Boys, she was a virgin. What do you say to that?'
>
> Another burst of cheering, then he closes the door. But I am not left alone for long. The others come in. Ten, a hundred, a thousand, one after another. They fling themselves upon me, digging into my wounds while they defiled me...Then everything passed. The Germans kept coming, spitting obscene words towards me, guffawing as they tortured me.[1627]

Genia was kept in a school building and sexually enslaved for several days.

Germans also turned a blind eye to their allies, for example, Ukrainians or Lithuanians, committing rape and looting. As Fremont reports: "They [the Ukrainians] were beating people with clubs and pushing us down the street. They sealed all of us in a big courtyard. They grabbed women and raped them, right there in the streets, in the courtyard, in front of everyone. Like a pack of wild animals with the smell of blood."[1628]

Some of the cruelest acts of rape accompanied by sexual violence were reported on 7 January 1942 by Vyacheslav M Molotov, the People's Commissioner of Foreign Affairs of the Soviet Union. He published an extensive account of eyewitness testimonies to German soldiers' sexual assaults which, during the Nuremberg trails, became known as the Molotov Note.[1629] This document reports that rape, gang rape and sexual torture were forms of violance that accompanied the war in eastern Europe. The document does not distinguish between crimes committed against Jewish women versus non-Jewish women although it does clarify that Jewish families were some of those targeted by German soldiers. According to the Molotov Note, in the City of Lvov [Ukraine], 32 women working in a garment factory were violated and then murdered by German storm troopers. Also, near the town of Borisov in Belorussia, 75 women and girls were captured by German troops while attempting to flee. The Germans raped and then savagely murdered 36 of them. By order of a German named Hummer, the soldiers marched L. I. Melchokova, a 16 year old girl, into the forest, where they raped her. Some other women who had also been dragged into the forest saw some boards near the trees and the dying Melchokova nailed to the boards. The Germans cut off her breast in the presence of these women, among whom were V. I. Alperenko and V. H. Bereznikova.

Wehrmacht Soldiers' Stories of Rape

Sexual assault of Jewish women was perpetrated by German soldiers, and not only SS personnel, despite the laws forbidding this. Such assault had no limits but did frequently result in the woman being shot afterwards to prevent her from incriminating the soldiers.

According to Jan Fleischauer's reports of *Wehrmacht* soldiers' stories,[1630] army generals had trouble keeping emlisted men's sexual desires under control with brothels. Sexual diseases were so widespread that whole companies were routinely required to undergo treatment. The importance of womanizing among the men is revealed in a secretly recorded conversation:

> Wallus: In Warsaw, our troops had to wait in line in front of the building's door. In Radom, the first room was full while the truck people stood outside. Each woman had 14 to 15 men per hour. They replaced the women every two days.
>
> Niwiem: "I have to say that we weren't nearly as respectable in France sometimes. When I was in Paris, I saw our soldiers grabbing girls in the middle of a bar,

> throwing them across a table and — end of story! Married women, too![1631]

Wehrmacht soldiers frequently went abroad for the first time as a result of the war: less than 4% of Germans had passports when the Nazis came to power. Further, romanticized memories, including sexual exploits, were common such as:

> Müller: When I was in Kharkov (in present-day Ukraine), everything was destroyed except the center of the city. A wonderful city, a wonderful memory. All the people there spoke a little German, which they had learned in school. And in Taganrog (in Russia) there were wonderful cinemas and wonderful beach cafés. I went everywhere in a truck. And all you saw were women doing compulsory labor.
> Fausst: Oh, my God!
> Müller: They were building roads, drop-dead gorgeous girls. So we drove by, pulled them into the truck, screwed them and then threw them out again. Boy, they sure cursed at us.[1632]

Some soldier's stories include scenes of sexual violence:

> Reimbold: In the first officers' prison camp where I was being kept here, there was a really stupid guy from Frankfurt, a young lieutenant, a young upstart. There were eight of us sitting around a table and talking about Russia. And he said: 'Oh, we caught this female spy who had been running around in the neighborhood. First we hit her in the tits with a stick and then we beat her rear end with a bare bayonet. Then we fucked her, and then we threw her outside and shot at her. When she was lying there on her back, we threw grenades at her. Every time one of them landed near her body, she screamed.[1633]

Germans did not only rape in the combat zone: it became a way of life in the military rear as well, where German men raped women younger than 10 and older than 80.[1634] Both 'Slavic' or 'ethnic German' as well as Jews were chosen as victims with the knowledge of the Nazi authorities who did not regard sexual violence as a primary crime in the situation of war and occupation. The Barbarossa Decree of 13 May 1941, which regulated the activities of German courts martial 'in the east' established that no criminal offences commited by German soldiers against Soviet civilians were to be punished unless they were serious. Sexual violence was seldom regarded as serious and there were very few prosecutions for offences against the civilian populations for looting, rape or murder especially in the early stages of Operation Barbarossa[1635] (The German invasion of the Soviet Union). Of the

1.5 million members of the German armed forces condemned by court-martial for offences of all kinds, only 5,349 were for sexual offences.[1636] The courts dealt with these offences leniently. The army ignored misbehaviour by the troops as long as it did not affect morale. Theft and rape accompanied wilful acts of destruction. The Reich Criminal Code established the minimum punishment for rape as one year imprisonment and the maximum as fifteen years imprisonment although the courts could exceed these parameters.[1637] The death sentence for rape of Russian, Polish and Ukrainian women by German soldiers was likely given in less than 1% of cases that came to court – in Snyder's case reviews this sentence was passed only once. Few completed rapes received the maximum sentence. Most attempted rapes that resulted in charges being laid led to 6 months imprisonment.

Post-War Distancing from *Wehrmacht* Crimes

A recent exhibition of nearly 1,000 photographs and documents taken by *Wehrmacht* soldiers themselves entitled '*War of Extermination: Crimes of the Wehrmacht 1941-1944*' was created by the *Hamburger Institut für Sozialforschung* (Hamburg Institute for Social Research) and toured Germany and Austria from 1995-1999. Following complaints, a revised exhibition entitled *Vernichtungskrieg: Verbrechen der Wehrmacht 1941 bis 1944* (Crimes of the German *Wehrmacht*: Dimensions of a War of Annihilation 1941-1944) travelled from 2001 to 2004 and has since been displayed at the Deutsches Historisches Museum (German History Museum) in Berlin. Sexual acts depicted in this include violent rape, contact with sexual slaves, voluntary brothel workers, and prostitutes on the streets, as well as prostitutional relationships – stable relationships in which the man supplied the woman with food or protection.[1638] The exhibition was controversial, as Germans were not prepared to accept that the army (and not just the SS or Nazi party) was involved in such atrocities: early objections were clarified in the revised exhibition although the message of the first exhibition remained constant in the second.[1639] The German wish to distance themselves from the crimes of the Holocaust – for example, by separating the roles of the SS and Nazis from that of the *Wehrmacht* – is understandable if not excusable. Combined with the strong sense of victimhood that prevailed for many years after the war – 'we too were victims of Hitler' – reconciliation of conflicting perceptions and reality remains challenging.

Male Rape

While most accounts of rape refer to women, a few report male rapes. A Jewish survivor from Germany reported two SS men had raped him at age 16 when he and his family had been deported from Germany to the Riga ghetto.[1640] Harry B. in Magdeburg camp in Germany remembers a Hungarian Jew whose son was abused by camp officials. In the morning, they brought the boy back crying. His father begged to be taken in his place. The German forced the son to be his father's hangman, to kick the box out from under his father as he was being hanged.[1641] In addition, Nathan O. experienced physical beatings and sexual abuse at Gusen. One of the Block elders took him to the bathroom and sodomized him.[1642]

After Effects

Many women who were raped experienced long lasting effects. For most, sex became a conflicted area of their lives, with most not enjoying their sexuality.[1643] As, Lidia Brown-Abramson who was raped by a partisan as a teenager reported in an interview with Nechama Tec many years later:

> I never experience pleasure from sex, never. I waited for my husband not to want it, not to be able to perform. I am always in control during the sexual act. I never relax, I never let myself go. I also don't know how to love.[1644]

Similarly, Barbara Stimler, a Polish Jewish woman who was interned in the Łódź ghetto and later transferred to Auschwitz-Birkenau, testified in 1992 that she had been hidden by a Pole on a farm where two German soldiers had entered and raped her and her friend Irma Weiss.[1645] In consequence, she had difficulties with sexual contact throughout her life: Her husband could not touch her and only when Martin Gilbert asked for her life story in the late 1980s did her husband find out she had been raped. She reported that "her sex life was not a sex life." Likewise, Inge F. recalled in 1966, at the age of 70, being raped by a German officer decades earlier in Theresienstadt. She was so ashamed she never told anyone and never married – she could not stand the thought of going to bed with a man.[1646] As Nutkiewicz notes, survivors – and particularly women who were raped – go to great lengths to silence themselves. It is not uncommon for their children to be ignorant or nearly ignorant of their parent's stories.[1647] Others, such as Nina Rusman (Kaplan) were left sterile.[1648]

Clearly, rape occurred, and Jewish women were not exempt despite the laws against *Rassenschande.* While sexual indulgence may have been the apparent motivation in many cases, such as when women were used for entertainment, the deeper intentions of humiliation, dehumanization, disrespect, and fear of the 'Jewish enemy', probably paid a considerable role in facilitating these events, and particularly those involving public sexual abuse and brutal sexual violence. While a number of instances have been recorded here, the incidence of rape is likely to have been far higher. Many, if not most, victims were murdered following their assault to prevent them from incriminating the perpetrators with the crime of *Rassenschande.* Oral and written testimonies may mention such events but rarely describe them: such memories may be too painful to recall, or women may be socialized not to expose such details, or interviewers are hesitant to explore these matters deeply.[1649] As rape becomes an increasingly acknowledged component of – if not a weapon of – war in modern genocides, it is likely that hesitancy regarding examining this experience will dissipate. As few survivors remain to tell their stories, let alone those who experienced rape, this body of knowledge regarding this aspect of the Holocaust will probably remain lost forever.

Sexualized Physical Brutality

Rape, however, was not the only form of sexualized violence that took place during the Nazi era. While Nazi ideology depicted the Jews as licentious and sexually abusive, in fact, the Nazis were the perpetrators of the most heinous acts of sexual depravity and violence of these times. Worse still, they were reported as apparently laughing or enjoying their actions, which far exceeded the conventions of wartime cruelty. Such acts were pervasive, occurring in ghettos, labour camps, prisons, concentration camps, and in the killing fields of the *Einsatzgruppen*. While rape may have been an act of arousal, if not passion, as well as violence, sexual brutality reflects darker motivations such as fear, hatred, disrespect, and dehumanization of the victim, or sadism, misogyny, a need for power and aggrandizement, or the establishment superiority of the perpetrator. Sexual brutality towards pregnant women and newborns or young children, found its place in the culture of cruelty that emerged under Nazi rule, and that was harnessed to achieve their goal of destroying the reproductive lives of Jews.

In Ghettos

Ghettos provided little escape from Nazi sexual brutality. Dr Edith Kramer reports that women in the Łódź ghetto were offered a chance to go to work in Poland. Before going they were required to bath: "This provided a good chance for the SS men to beat the naked girls with whips."[1650] Sexual perversion is further described by Mary Berg in her diary of the Łódź ghetto (December 1939):

> The cruelty of the Germans is increasing from day to day, and they are beginning to kidnap young boys and girls to use in their nightmarish 'entertainments.' They gather five to ten couples together in a room, order them to strip, and make them dance to the accompaniment of a phonograph record. Two of my schoolmates experienced this in their own home.[1651]

Martin Gray,[1652] reports having seen the Germans "set fire to 6 Gesia, which was serving as a hospital for the [Warsaw] ghetto, he'd seen them dash out the brains of newborn babies against the walls, rip open the bellies of pregnant women, and throw casualties into the flames." Numerous reports[1653] include descriptions of Nazi cruelty to newborns or young children including throwing them on the floor and trampling their heads with boots, smashing their heads against rocks, tree trunks, a wall, the side of a truck, or the wheels of the train; shooting babies in their cribs, using them as target practice after throwing them into the air, tearing their legs apart from their bodies, killing children in front of their mothers and enjoying their despair, throwing them into the mass graves and burying them alive, or dropping newborns out of windows onto the bayonets of their comrades below. In the Koritz Memorial Book Dr Jakob Wallah testifies that on the liquidation of the Koritz ghetto (in the occupied Russian territories):

> I would like to bear everlasting witness to a horror that I witnessed in the first days of the occupation of the town by the Nazi beasts; there sat the Kommandant [*sic*] of the town, on the porch of the Ohmonovitch home, he and his wife and children. At some distance a Jewish girl aged three was wondering about. The Kommandant called one of the murderers, ordered him to seize the child and throw him in the air like a ball. The murderer shot the child as a hunter shoots down a bird. The infant fell to the ground covered in blood. The Kommandant's family laughed and applauded. The younger daughter clung to him and pleaded,' Daddy, do it again.'[1654]

Sexually Related Cruelty Implemented by the *Einsatzgruppen*

The Aba Gefen diaries note that what happened in Lithuania happened everywhere the Nazis invaded:[1655] In Slonim, Belorussia, Liza Chapnik reported that 19,000 Jews were taken to pits to be murdered: Lithuanians in Gestapo uniforms were walking along the streets with children's heads on swords: "They wanted to frighten people. It was absolutely unbelievable."[1656] The Nazis and their allies assaulted Jewish women before murdering them. On Thursday 30 October 1941 Gefen's diary reports:

> Mrs Matulevitch related that in one village the men were assembled in the synagogue and murdered; the women

> and children were given a day's grace. When they were brought next day to the death-pit, the girls were raped, then killed. The women were forced to undress, pushed into the pit, then shot. Only the little children were left. Even the most hardened killers shirked the task of the murder of infants. But one volunteer, the Lithuanian chief of police, covered his nice uniform with a white smock and methodically smashed the heads of Jewish babies against the stone wall of the Christian cemetery, adjacent to the killing site. Then calmly he returned home to his wife and four little children. On Sunday he attended chapel in the friendly company of the parish priest.[1657]

Faye Shulman, a partisan, also reports horrific sexual brutality against women and children in villages. She records two Nazis laughing while taking six-month-old twins into the backyard of their home, tearing their arms and legs from their bodies and throwing them into the air for target shooting.[1658] On entering a village she and her group saw that:

> A young woman in her twenties lay half-naked under a tree in front of the house. Her tongue had been cut out and her breasts cut off. Beside her was a dead baby. Pools of blood lay all around. The woman was still alive and she made feeble gestures for help. She wanted to live.[1659]

On a cold night in Czestochowa the police surrounded a densely populated Jewish area shouting '*Juden Raus*!' They forced thousands of half-naked men and women to assemble in a large square where they were beaten until bleeding. Young girls were taken into the synagogue, forced to undress, sexually assaulted and tortured.[1660]

The *Einsatzgruppen* were particularly distinguished by their brutality[1661] including ripping open the bellies of pregnant women and cutting off the breasts of nursing mothers, shooting pregnant women in the belly before throwing them into the burial pits, and conducting body searches of sex organs and anuses looking for valuables. Others might hurl a fist into the belly of a pregnant woman and throw her alive into the grave. Michael Kutz remembered watching *Einsatzgruppen* members tearing babies from their mother's arms, tossing them into the air and firing revolvers at them, killing them, in an *Aktion* in Nieśwież, Belarussia.[1662] The brutality of the *Einsatzgruppen* has yet to be fully documented: the initial findings of Patrick Desbois[1663] in Ukraine reveal such horrors as bludgeoning children to death for crying, burying children alive together with their parents as the latter were shot, taking Jewish children from the lines going to their deaths and using them overnight before murdering them the following day, and shooting children while in the arms of their mothers or fathers. P Zozulya from the Shtetl of Chudnov, Zhitomir region of Ukraine testified that on 15-16 February 1944 Liza Gnip went into labour before she reached the pit:

> With his own dirty hands, a German butcher tore the baby out of the womb of its mother along with her innards, and then took the newborn by its little leg and smashed its head against the trunk of an old pine tree – that was how he awakened its life – and then tossed the infant to its bullet-riddled mother in the common grave.[1664]

Such reports are confirmed even in testimonies given by former SS members after the war: SS Mann Ernst Göbel testified that:

> The victims were shot by the firing squad with carbines, mostly by shots in the back of the head, from a distance of one metre on my command........Meanwhile Rottenführer Abraham shot the children with a pistol. There were about five of them. These were children whom I would think were aged between two and six years. The way Abraham killed the children was brutal. He got hold of some of the children by the hair, lifted them up from the ground, shot them through the back of their heads and then threw them into the grave. After a while I just could not watch this anymore and I told him to stop. What I meant was that he should not lift the children up by the hair, he should kill them in a more decent way.[1665]

Cruelty Perpetrated by Soldiers

The massacre in the Greek town of Distomo also reflects the sexually directed aspects of Nazi cruelty. Just outside the village, SS troops were attacked by partisans shortly after D Day on 11 June 1944. They returned to the village and spent the next few hours killing the population viciously. As Nicholas reports:

> Pregnant women were eviscerated with bayonets and their intestines wrapped around their necks. People were decapitated and children's heads crushed. Houses were burned with all the occupants inside. Women and little girls were raped and then executed. All the beasts of burden were killed too. It was estimated that between 50 to 60 percent of the dead were children.[1666]

Hermand Jost[1667] reports specific cruelty directed towards a pregnant woman. As a member of the Hitler Youth, he watched as an SS man ordered his dog to knock down a very pregnant woman. He then 'stomped on her belly" until she died from internal injuries. Daniel Rose tells of a similar atrocity regarding a newly delivered woman in a French village. Crying as the SS, "howling with glee," kicked her newborn baby through her doorway, like a soccer ball, ultimately bashing its head with their rifles, the SS turned on her, slitting open her belly and dancing on her until her bowels exploded.[1668]

Children too, did not escape sexual brutality. In the same French village, the SS tied the smallest children, boys and girls, to the chairs in the schoolroom. Rose reports that they:

> tell them to suck the soldiers' organs like their mothers' breasts. Then when the soldiers have had their way, the children are told to imagine it as milk and swallow happily, and their teachers are to make sure they do not cry as they swallow.[1669]

Sexualized Brutality in Prisons

Those in prison were perhaps even more readily exposed to sexual brutality:

> Käthe Baronowitz was an active communist who led a cell of ten people. Her landlord who was in the SA spied on her and she and 83 other communists were arrested. The cruelties and perversities of the interrogation can hardly be described. [She] had to undress completely. A howling pack goaded on by alcohol surrounded her. They stuck pens in her vagina and paper flags which they burned so that they could gloat over the tortured woman's screams of pain. They called her a 'Jew whore' as they tormented her. Ultimately she was sentenced to twelve years of hard labour.[1670]

Witness Jadwiga Dzido at the Nuremberg Doctors Trial reported being beaten while naked by the Gestapo in Lublin.[1671] Klaus Barbie is perhaps best known among sexually brutal prison commanders. Erna Paris, in her account of Barbie's crimes wrote:

> Women were always tortured naked, to the deep enjoyment of the torturers. Barbie kept two German shepherd dogs. One was trained to lunge and bite. The other was trained to mount naked women who had first been ordered on their hands and knees. A humiliation that cut deeper than the whip, than having one's fingernails pulled out, or one's

> nipples burned with cigarettes. He threatened the lives of his victim's families, sometimes presenting them in person, or pretending that they were just downstairs about to be tortured.[1672]

Barbie humiliated and degraded women in addition to torturing them. He cared nothing for them, and probably gained some sexual satisfaction himself: he is reported to have fondled his French secretary while he conducted torture sessions. "He kicked heads, injected acid into human bladders and hung almost lifeless people upside down from ceiling hooks while he took a break from business to play a little love song on the piano."[1673] Father Bonaventura Boudet, a member of a French mission who was arrested on 9 July 1943 and cruelly interrogated by the Gestapo at the *Ecole de Sainte Militaire* where Barbie was based, watched as others were tortured. He later reported that fingers and toes were cut off with kitchen knives, women's breasts were severed and their nipples torn off, limbs were burned and severed from the body. He reported one victim being scalped and his eyes torn out.[1674] On 18 September 1943, Klaus Barbie was personally cited by Himmler and on 9 November 1943, he was awarded the Iron Cross, First Class, with sword.[1675]

Sexual Cruelty in Labour and Concentration Camps

Sexual brutality in labour camps could be equally vicious: For example, Felicja Karay, writing about Skarżysko-Kamienna, reported that "although the work was not arduous, anyone who earned the displeasure of the German women managers faced a bitter fate. Marianne Tietge was notorious for her blows and kicks to the genitals of men and women alike, and Dora Pawlowska was no better."[1676] Jewish women were treated the worst in many camps: for example, in some they were not allowed to use toilets in facilities but had to go out in the open, and were beaten with metal truncheons at the slightest provocation or simply for sport. As the allies grew closer women were treated with more brutality: one camp commander's speciality was putting out the eyes of women with his whip, lashing other parts of women's bodies or flaying them to death.[1677]

While humiliation, nudity and voyeurism were common in the concentration camps, more extreme forms of sexual brutality also occurred including 10-25 lashes with a cane or whip that could be repeated up to four times at 14 day intervals often on the naked buttocks.[1678] The lash as an instrument of punishment was administered on a special wooden rack, to which the prisoner was strapped on his or her stomach, head down and legs drawn forward, exposing the buttocks. As reported by Cohen,[1679] on 4 April 1942, the following order was issued: "The Reich Führer SS and Chief of the German Police has decreed that when he has decided on corporal punishment (both of male and female prisoners in protective or preventive custody), if the word 'intensified' has been added, the punishment is to be administered to the *naked buttocks*"[Italics original].[1680] Prisoners were forced to count the number of lashings: if they miscounted, the lashings started again. Hebermann, in Ravensbrück, reports that following the 25th blow to one (silent) prostitute, the commandant shouted: "start screaming you pig:" he enjoyed hearing the prisoner whimpering or screaming.[1681] Theoretically, camp headquarters had to apply for confirmation from Berlin when corporal punishment had to be meted out, and the camp physician had to certify that the prisoner was in good health. Down to the end, however, the procedure widely practiced in most camps was that the prisoner went to the whipping rack immediately, while on receipt of confirmation from Berlin the punishment was repeated, this time 'officially.' After receiving the whipping the delinquent usually had to execute from 50 -150 knee bends – to 'strengthen the muscles'.[1682] In Buchenwald, Kogon reports further that when a prisoner received his 25 lashes he had to bend over and immerse his head into the excrement filled toilet bowl….he was not permitted to wipe the excrement from his face.

Notable Individuals

In many cases that have been reported by survivors, these incidents of cruelty can be traced back to particular individuals or groups. Distinctive among these are Josef Mengele, Ivan Demaniuk, Adolf Tauber, Werner Grahn and the Ustashi (Croatian collaborators). Women also indulged in sexual brutality including, particularly, Hermine Braunsteiner and Irma Grese.

Josef Mengele, in Auschwitz, better known for other crimes, was also reported to have indulged in sexual brutality. For instance there are many stories of Dr Mengele striking people with his long riding crop, in one case running it over tattoos on the bosoms of Russian women, as a Polish woman survivor described "then striking them there, while not at all excited but….casual…just playing around a little as though it were a little funny."[1683] Judith Becker testified that when she was sent from Birkenau to Płaszów she and over a thousand women had to wait for Mengele for 12 hours as he was doing an experiment on fertility:

> He had been collecting from different transports what he used to call '*Gnaedige Juedische Maedchen*' which means girls who were young and who had a very aristocratic look, Jewish aristocratic look and obviously good breeding….

> really well taken care of and when he had enough of them collected he invited soldiers who came from the front to rape them. And he sat and clocked it – how many of them submitted, and how many of them went out of their minds and how many of them fought back and were killed – and that experiment took him a whole night and that's what we had to wait for so when he came to do the selection he was in a terrific mood because he had had a whole night's entertainment. And the 'Sonderkommando' told me he would do this quite regularly. He would enjoy the sight of Jewish pride and Jewish aristocracy broken. That gave him a real jolt because it confirmed all his crazy notions about, that Jews cannot be aristocratic, they cannot be noble, they cannot be moral. And so that's why we had to wait for him.[1684]

On one occasion, Mengele was clearly attracted to a tall blonde and statuesque Jewish woman. When she undressed as required for a selection he was transfixed by her. Mengele could not concede to feeling any attraction to her and dispatched her to Block 10, the infamous experimental block. A few weeks later, she was observed by other inmates wandering about in a daze, hardly recognizable. She looked like a shrivelled old woman with swollen disfigured limbs, and a stomach bloated by the numerous surgeries that had been performed on her.[1685]

The Ukrainian Ivan Demaniuk in Treblinka took particular pleasure in hurting others, and especially women. Eli Rozenberg[1686] testified that he:

> stabbed the women's naked thighs and genitals with a sword before they entered the gas chambers and also raped young women and girls. The ears and noses of old Jews which weren't to his liking he used to cut off. When someone's work wasn't to his satisfaction, he used to beat the poor man with a metal pipe and break his skull. Or he would stab him with his knife. He especially enjoyed entwining people's heads between two strands of barbed wire and then beating the head while it was caught between the wires. As the prisoner squirmed and jumped from the blows, he became strangled between the wires.[1687]

In Treblinka, Steiner reports that the camp commander had a dog trained to attack a man's private parts. The dog was called 'Man' and the Jews 'Dogs:' He would attack when given the order "Look, Man, that dog isn't working" (*"Sieh mal, Mensch, dieser Hund arbeitet nicht!"*)[1688] Delbo reports observing the SS training their dogs to attacks humans: "The SS at the head of the line is carrying a dummy. It is a large stuffed doll dressed just like us. A discoloured striped suit, filthy, too long in the sleeves. The SS holds her by one arm. He lets the feet drag, raking the gravel. They even tied canvas boots on to her feet."[1689] The dogs were trained to attack the dummy. Denise McAdam Clark, a French barrister imprisoned in Ravensbrück reported after the war that boxer dogs were trained to be vicious. She saw them tear people apart. In winter, the SS 'dressed' them in little dog coats embroidered with swastikas.[1690] Olga Lengyel, in confirmation, reports:

> I shall never forget the agony of one mother who told me that she was forced to undress her daughter and to look on while the girl was violated by dogs whom the Nazis had specially trained for this sport. That happened to other young girls. They were compelled to labor in the quarries for twelve to fourteen hours day. When they dropped from exhaustion their guards' favourite form of amusement was to urge the dogs to attack them.[1691]

Dr Edith Kramer, while imprisoned in Berlin, watched the Gestapo training police dogs to jump at fluttering skirts fastened to wooden rods.[1692]

As Fania Fenelon wrote shortly after the war, SS Rapportführer Adolf Tauber, in Auschwitz-Birkenau, was known for his sadistic acts towards women. He took pleasure in hunting out weaker women and at roll calls enjoyed making women kneel in the icy mud with their hands above their heads.[1693]

Fenelon reports that he had:

> brought a thousand women out into the snow, lined them up, entirely naked, in the freezing air, then, moving along the ranks, lifted their breasts with the tip of his whip. Those whose breasts sagged went to the left, those whose breasts remained firm went to the right and were spared a little longer, except of course, for those who perished in the cold.[1694]

Dachau war Crimes Court proceedings also note the actions of SS officer Werner Grahn who would "disappear into the bunker" early in the morning and leave again in the evening. His work – 'a translation office' – was always accompanied by the screaming of women. Hans Karl von Posern, a German lawyer from Dresden, testified that a friend of his:

> who worked in the crematorium showed me bodies of women whose breasts and thighs had been whipped and their eyebrows beaten open. 'These are translations,' he said. We estimated the number of Grahn's victims at approximately seven hundred.[1695]

Overall, the Ustashi are credited with the worst of the sadistic crimes directed towards women and men of the time, both in general and in camps such as the notorious Jasenovac. Irwin Black reports:

> In the annals of wartime savagery against the Jews there was no group as sadistic as the Croatian Ustashi. Using chainsaws, axes, knives and rocks, frenzied Swastika-bedecked Ustashi brutally murdered thousands of Jews at a time. Ustashi leaders openly paraded around Zagreb with necklaces comprised of Jewish tongues and eyeballs cut and gouged from women and children, many of them raped and then dismembered or decapitated. Pavelich (the Ustashi leader) himself was fond of offering wicker baskets of Jewish eyeballs as gifts to his diplomatic visitors.[1696]

Saul Friedlander also documents some of the atrocities committed by the Ustashi in Croatia: "Butchers knives, hooks and axes were used to chop up victims. There are photos of Serb women with their breasts hacked off with pocket knives, men with eyes gouged out, emasculated and mutilated."[1697] Steiner's reports of treatment of the Warsaw ghetto uprising prisoners in Treblinka, however, rivals some of these stories. There, bellies of women were slit open vertically with swords and "...after collecting the disembowelled women at the exits to the gas chambers, some prisoners were forced to mount them in a simulated act of lovemaking."[1698]

Notorious Women

Men were not the only perpetrators of sexual brutality. Some women achieved notoriety in this respect as well. Susan Cernyak-Spatz, stated that in her experience in Auschwitz-Birkenau, women were crueler and more sadistically vicious than any SS man. She noted that it was rare for men to play games with their dogs in which the point was for the dog to attack a woman's *derriere,* but the women guards did. Margot Drechsler set her Alsatian dog on the women prisoners in Birkenau for every minor infringement of the rules. She also trained her dog near the barracks, urging it on to bite and tear stuffed dolls in striped clothes.[1699]

Hermine Braunsteiner was an overseer at Ravensbrück concentration camp and later a guard at Majdanek where she was responsible for selecting inmates for the gas chambers. Survivors describe her as tough and extremely cruel. She is said to have brandished a whip whose straps were filled with lead bullets. She hated children and would tear small children away from their mothers. Women would scream and faint when she flogged them with her whip. She is reported as one of the most vicious.[1700] Olga Lengyel in Auschwitz-Birkenau reported the sadistic cruelty of Irma Grese, a notorious camp guard. She relates one story as follows:

> Irma Griese had selected a handsome Georgian man to become her lover. When he refused she beat his true love, a slim, Polish woman, brutally in front of him while she was naked. The door opened. First the man came out. I shall never forget his blazing dark eyes and his face filled with inexpressible hate. Then the Polish girl came out. She was in a dreadful state. Red welts extended across her face and across her chest. The sadistic SS had spared not even her face....I never saw the handsome Georgian again. The beautiful beast had him shot. The girl? From Irma's maid we found out about her, too. Griese had had her sent to the Auschwitz brothel.[1701]

On occasion, female kapos were also sadistically cruel to other women. Nechama Tec provides an explanation for at least one of these – Erika – who told another prisoner that:

> She had seen her parents, her brother and sister and family murdered in front of her eyes. Because she was beautiful she was kept out and made to have sex with the Germans... she reports being turned into an animal and took it out on new healthy prisoners coming into the camps.[1702]

Sexual Brutality Directed Towards Homosexuals

Some of the most grievous tortures of a sexually sadistic nature were imposed on homosexual prisoners in concentration camps. Heger describes the torture to death of a homosexual man:

> He was stripped naked and his hands tied to a hook in a wall so that he could not touch the ground with his feet. First he was tickled with goose feathers on the soles of his feet, the armpits, between the legs and other parts of his naked body. Then the SS brought two metal bowls, one filled with cold water one with hot. These bowls were placed between his legs alternatively so that his testicles hung in the hot, then cold water. This continued until the victim lost consciousness screaming in agony. A bucket of cold water was thrown over him to bring him around

> and then the torture stared again, 'this time with bits of skin now hanging visibly down from the victim's scalded scrotum.' Then they shoved a broom handle deep into his anus – his body jerked and tore at the chains. Eventually they cut him down. One of the SS brought a wooden chair down on the victims head with all his force, killing him.[1703]

Confirmation of aspects of this method of torture for men is provided by Haas, who, was tortured by the Gestapo after escaping from Dachau and being caught:

> The guards pulled down my pants and underwear, then slung me over a wooden horse and tied my dangling hands and legs together underneath it ...Rubber gloved hands separated my buttocks and something hard and cold was pushed up my anus. I didn't know that it was an electrode. A searing shock tore through my innards and tied my intestines into previously unknown knots of agony. I screamed. The odour of feces and burning flesh reached my nose.[1704]

Heger also reports the cruel torture served on a gay priest who was caught praying: The SS beat him indiscriminately on his stomach, belly and sexual organs until his unconscious states could no longer be revived. When they finally stopped and left the man they said, "Okay you randy old rat-bag, you can piss with your asshole in future.' He died shortly after."[1705] Men with pink triangles were given the hardest jobs and were constantly harshly abused for their sexual preferences[1706] to the extent that it is estimated that the death rate of homosexuals throughout the Third Reich was 50% compared to 40% for political prisoners and 35% for Jehovah's witnesses.[1707]

Sexual Satisfaction Through Cruelty

Fairly often, mention is made of sexual arousal and satisfaction being gained through acts of torture or horror. Irma Grese, in Auschwitz-Birkenau, is noted by Gisela Perl as falling into this category:

> One day she happened to visit the hospital while I was performing an operation on a young woman's breast, cut open by whipping and subsequently infected. I had no instruments whatsoever, except a knife which I had to sharpen on a stone. Breast operations are particularly painful, and as there was not a drop of anesthetic in this

> mock hospital, my patient screamed with pain all through the operation.
>
> Irma Greze [Grese] put down her whip…sat down on the corner of the bench which served as an operating table and watched me plunge my knife into the infected breast which spurted blood and pus in every direction.
>
> I happened to look up and encountered the most horrible sight I have ever seen, the memory of which will haunt me the rest of my life. Irma Greze was enjoying the sight of this human suffering. Her tense body swung back and forth in a revealing rhythmical motion. Her cheeks were flushed and her wide open eyes had the rigid, staring look of complete sexual paroxysm.
>
> From that day on she went around in camp, her bejewelled whip poised, picked out the most beautiful young women and slashed their breasts open with the braided wire end of her whip. Subsequently those breasts got infected by the lice and dirt which invaded every nook and corner of the camp. They had to be cut open if the patient was to be saved. Irma Greze invariably arrives to watch the operation, kicking the victim if her screams interfered with her pleasure and giving herself completely to the orgiastic spasms which shook her entire body and made saliva run down from the corner of her mouth.[1708]

Fenelon confirms Grese's penchant for breast abuse: "The women had learned to dread the penalty of her attentions, the least of which meant a whiplash on the nipple."[1709]

In Ravensbrück, 19-year-old Chief SS supervisor Dorothea Binz, with a whip and a dog constantly with her, would come to watch the floggings accompanied by Captain Edmund Bräuning. They would stand arm in arm enjoying the show and "were often seen in a passionate embrace during or after this kind of 'ceremony."[1710] Maria Karczmarz-Lysakowskaalso reports that Maria Mandel, a dreaded overseer in Ravensbrück, was notorious for her enjoyment of human suffering particularly when whippings were being conducted.[1711] Laska also reports that some of the meanest SS guards would taunt women whose husbands/loved ones were far away or murdered, by parading in front of the women with their boyfriends, encouraging them to fondle and embrace them.[1712]

Sexual satisfaction from cruelty was also evident in Majdanek. Alexander Donat who survived slave labour in this notorious camp, reported that:

> Some [of the executioners] derived their greatest pleasure from refined torture and were delighted by the professional approval of their colleagues. Some were motivated by sadistic curiosity: they wanted to see how a man suffers and dies. Still others achieved a sexual enjoyment from the last fatal spasms of their victims.[1713]

Janusz's method of killing was different. A kapo in Majdanek, he would throw himself on his victim and lie on top of him, almost caressingly wrapping his fingers around the victim's throat. To the uninitiated, it might seem that the two bodies were throbbing in erotic ecstasy, and in fact, the kapo did have an orgasm at such moments, while his companions looked on in snickering admiration. This might happen once, or even twice a day.[1714]

Daniel Goldhagen reports on the sexual gratification Karl Wagner derived from the sadistic beatings that he administered to naked women in the clothing work camp in Lublin. According to Goldhagen, "Wagner was 'absolutely abnormal' not because he was brutal to the women, not because he beat them, but because of the unusual, clear sadistic sexual component of his brutality."[1715] Similarly, Klauss Scheurenberg reports that in Eichmann's headquarters in Wulkow, the commandant also gained sexual pleasure from watching beatings of men. As he reports, "He sent some of us to Sachsenhausen to be gassed; he shot some; and he beat some to death with a chain. At some point in the beatings, he always reached a climax and his pants got wet."[1716]

Sexual gratification was also obtained from cruelty to homosexuals. As Heger reports, the camp commander in Flossenbürg, "of small stature, smooth shaven and about forty-five year of age… a repulsive beast," stood by and watched as homosexuals were beaten:

> At each stroke his eyes lit up and after a few strokes his whole face was red with excitement. He buried his hands in his trouser pockets and could clearly be seen to masturbate, quite unperturbed by our presence. After satisfying himself in this way, the perverted swine suddenly disappeared, being no longer interested in the further execution of the punishment. …I myself witnessed on more than thirty occasions how this camp commander got sexual satisfaction from watching the lashings inflicted on the 'horse' and the perverted lust with which he followed each stroke and the screams of the victim.[1717]

Less well known are reports associating Hitler with sexual satisfaction derived from witnessing sadistic cruelty. Marianne Hoppe reports viewing the film '*The Rebel*' with Hitler and his response as the French came through a narrow pass and rocks fell on them. "Hitler became terribly excited and began rubbing his knee. He started to moan as the rocks began to roll. I don't know if he was crazy or what, but he had a kind of orgasm."[1718] Others too have reported on Hitler's sexual perversions.[1719]

Two other incidents regarding Hitler in this context are reported by Evans.[1720] German propaganda always showed the latest (flattering) news of war events in cinemas. Generally, horrific pictures were banned from these – they showed only optimistic images. Hitler did, however, make a personal request to the Ministry on 10 July 1942 for shots of Russian atrocities to be included. He specifically asked that such atrocities should include genitals being cut off and the placing of hand grenades in the trousers of prisoners. His request does not seem to have been followed. In addition, following the failed [Stauffenberg] assassination attempt on him, Hitler ordered the hangings of the first five men to be executed to be filmed. They were suspended from crude hooks and especially thin rope was used so that they would die slowly by strangulation. As they died, their trousers were pulled down in a last act of humiliation. He watched this film at night in his headquarters.

It is perhaps, not surprising that acts of extreme sexual brutality were, at the least, tolerated by the Nazis in their efforts to suppress sexuality and reproduction of Jews.

Epilogue

The integral place of Nazi policies towards reproductive aspects of life and sexuality in their linked goals of creating a Master Race (geno-coercion) and eliminating those deemed as not meeting their idealized racial purity standards, and particularly Jewish women, (genocide or gendercide), as exposed in this text, is an under-emphasised area of Holocaust research. Some reasons for this might include the sensitivity of the issue of gender- and sex- related violence in the Holocaust, and hesitation to examine this topic as it might desecrate the memory of the victims. This book is not intended to desecrate the memory of the Holocaust or its victims, but rather to honour their memory by recognising the realities that they faced. While Nazi policy determined to create the 'Master Race,' its implementation, particularly with regard to reproduction and sexuality, was implemented by a multitude of players, in varying ways. The medical profession, among others, played their role.

How Could This Happen?

Questions are repeatedly asked as to how Germans, and particularly Nazis, could lead 'normal' lives while simultaneously committing acts of cruelty. The numerous acts of oppression directed to all aspects of Jewish lives and particularly to their sexual and reproductive life, as described in this book, might lead to speculation that the perpetrators were evil, hardhearted men and women, likely to behave with similar cruelty in most aspects of their lives. Even a cursory examination of this concept reveals that this is not so. For example, Alec, from Poland, imprisoned in Auschwitz, recalls watching the SS help little children down from the lorries that were carrying them to the gas chambers, 'almost lovingly,' while knowing that some of them had three or four of their own children at home.[1721] As Leon Greenman, a British, Jewish inmate of Buna-Monowitz revealed, the Nazis could cuddle a rabbit one minute and kill him the next.[1722] Reinhard Heydrich's nephew, decades after the war, revealed that his uncle could "...perfunctorily dash... off his signature...

to have fifty thousand Jews murdered and that same evening play… the violin in a quartet."[1723] Dublon-Knebel writing about Ravensbrück, in like vein, commented that one of the SS overseers, a young woman of about 20, would amuse herself with one of the babies every morning by bathing and pampering it. She could totally discount the atrocities she had recently committed.[1724] Fania Fenelon also reported on Frau Maria Mandel's (one of the most notorious SS Overseers of the Women's Camp in Auschwitz-Birkenau) adoption of a small child from a transport: the boy was pampered for a time and then sent to his death.[1725] Similarly, Frau Charlotte Müller reports that a brutal SS guard, Frau Lehman, in Ravensbrück, after beating a group of women prisoners with a club turned around and went to nurse her baby.[1726] The women prisoners who worked in the home of SS Camp Commandant Hoppe in Gdansk reported that at home he acted completely normally, even in his dealings with them.[1727] Franz Stangl, the commander of Treblinka would go home every now and then, but never told his wife about his job.[1728] Charlotte Delbo reports that SS officer Adolf Taube, who sent thousands of women to the gas chambers, set his dog on many, and could shoot women because they were not entering a block fast enough, one day knelt down in front of a prisoner – Carmen – and with his penknife sharpened the ends of her laces so they would slip through the eyelet holes of her shoes. After helping her, he stood up and said "*Gut.*"[1729]

Grief[1730] also reports on the remarkable co-existence of the ability to annihilate and to be normal among the SS. Gabai, a stoker who was ordered to burn corpses in the ovens recalls:

> Once they brought a girl from Hungary who had a two day old baby. She knew she was about to be murdered. We had nothing to do that night. We sat around idly and offered her a chair to sit down, some food, and cigarettes. She told us that she was a singer and talked for about half an hour. We sat in front of the furnaces. Next to us sat a Dutch SS man…a rather nice, likable guy. He also listened in. When the story was over, he stood up and said, 'Very well, we can't sit here like this forever, now it's death's turn.' She was asked what she preferred, that we kill the baby first or her. She said, 'Me first. I don't want to see my child dead.' Then the Dutchman stood up, brought over the rifle, shot her, and threw her into the furnace. The he picked up the baby, bang-bang, and that was that.[1731]

Dehumanizing 'the enemy' was standard practice in Nazi times, and still is so in the training of combat soldiers. What is remarkable about the incident reported by Grief is that in this instance the woman to be murdered was allowed to 'become human' and was still murdered 'in cold blood.'

The Nazi imbalance between normality and abnormality extended even to sexual activities. One well known writer on sex in the late 1930s, Dr Johannes Schultz epitomizes this juxtaposition: he espoused uncommonly liberal, anti-guilt, views regarding sexuality: he defended child and adolescent masturbation, and decried that the vast majority of women of all social levels received almost no sexual education at all, and hence were vulnerable to frigidity. He stressed that sexual desire in women was normal and desirable. Yet he simultaneously endorsed exterminating the handicapped and was personally involved in decisions regarding whether homosexuals should be sent to concentration camps or set free. At the German Institute for Psychological Research he and his co-workers forced accused homosexuals to perform coitus with a female prostitute while the commission watched. Whoever performed heterosexually to their satisfaction was set free: those who could not were sent to concentration camps as incurable.[1732]

Sexuality has, in fact, been suggested as one possible explanation for how some Germans were able to juxtapose their aberrant cruelty with normality. Both Claudia Koonz and Gudren Schwarz, suggest that German women's maintenance of a comfortable domestic life enabled men to commit the atrocities.[1733] Men could relax from their horrific roles and reassure themselves that they were good, decent men. Having sexual access to their wives in camps apparently cured men of their inability to function and "a wife's death could limit a man's effectiveness by triggering undisciplined sexual relationships with non-Aryan women."[1734] Because of the importance of sexual relief (and to maximise the opportunities for the SS to procreate) the SS planned opportunities for non-resident wives to visit at the camps for extended periods. Höss's and Wirth's families lived with them in Auschwitz for much of their time there, as did the wives or families of other commandants and doctors.[1735] Arrangements were also made for the wife of Dr Delmotte to stay with him in Auschwitz when he became disturbed by having to participate in selections and on learning what was happening in Auschwitz. His regular access to her apparently made him more "quiet."[1736]

Lifton proposes a psychological concept that he called 'doubling' – the separation of the personality into two distinct selves – to explain how physicians could separate their murderous camp duties from their normal lives and their honourable self-concept.[1737] On the other hand, Dr Ernst B, who was particularly helpful to other prisoner doctors, found that his life in Auschwitz and at home conflicted – his wife had not relished his appointment to Auschwitz – and he needed to keep them separate.[1738] Allowing wives to live with their SS partners in Auschwitz was not, apparently, always a successful measure: one young, newly married man committed suicide as a result of the jobs he was required to do despite his wife's presence.[1739]

Explaining how Nazis (and Germans) living normal lives could have committed, or tolerated, such atrocities has challenged researchers for decades and numerous theories have been proposed to explain this. The early understanding that such acts were committed by a few pathological persons proved untenable in the light of available evidence of both mass involvement in implementing Nazi policies and the apparent normality of senior members of the Nazi party. Other theories have been proposed to explain this phenomenon. These range from delusional mass psychosis proposed by Lucy Dawidowicz,[1740] through persuasion and pressure to conform (for example the Asch conformity studies[1741]), authoritarianism (Adorno et al's Authoritarian Personality[1742]) obedience to authority (the Milgram experiments[1743]), following role assignments (the Zimbardo prison study[1744]), as well as competition and conflict over scarce resources (Sherif's Realistic Group Conflict theory[1745]). Further explanations have invoked cultural explanations such as prevalent antisemitism. James Waller[1746] proposes that a combination of individual and collective factors contribute to the ability to perpetrate 'extraordinary evil.' These include forces that shape our response to authority such as: the characteristics of the perpetrator or actor (e.g. ethnocentrism, xenophobia, or the desire for social dominance, cultural belief systems, moral disengagement, and rational self interest); the context of the actions (including a culture in which cruelty becomes acceptable) and the definition of the target (incorporating an 'us-them' dichotomy, dehumanizing and blaming the victims).

Most of these explanations arise from a perspective that judges the perpetrators' actions as being evil or cruel requiring explanation or justification within a 'normal' world. The concept of 'doubling' for example, suggests that the normal self had to be psychologically separated from the perpetrator's cruel self to allow the perpetrator to maintain his or her psychological integrity. Ideas of mass psychosis suggest that all those involved were 'abnormal:' an unlikely reality. What is less often recognized is that Nazis, SS and other German perpetrators of acts of extraordinary cruelty viewed such acts as normal, and, in fact, desirable. Killing Jews and others deemed 'undesirable' was in keeping with pervasive and persuasive Nazi ideology, and was regarded by those who accepted this as a beneficial and desirable contribution to creating a superior Master Race and eliminating any threats – like Jews – to this. As Dr Arthur Gütt, in 1935, published in *The Structure of Public Health in the Third Reich:*

> ...love of one's fellow men had to disappear, especially in regard to inferior and a-social elements, and that it was the supreme duty of a state to allow life and sustenance only to that part of the nation which was sound and free from hereditary taint, in order to secure the continuance of a racially pure people free from hereditary taint for all eternity.[1747]

Their actions were, in their eyes, not cruel and evil as we now judge them, but heroic, admired and praiseworthy. Their behaviour was not incongruent with their normal selves: it was, in fact, totally in keeping with their personal sense of integrity.[1748] Given this understanding, it is not surprising that many, if not most, of the doctors charged with conducting the disreputable medical experiments of the time expressed little remorse or regret but rather remained convinced of their value and normality. As Spitz writes:

> "There was not one scintilla of remorse shown by any of these defendants. [at the Nuremberg Doctors Trial]. I was stunned by the evil, expressionless, hard faces of these doctors and assistants during the trial. They often expressed resentment when testifying, spewing defensive justifications and denying responsibility."[1749]

Dr Schilling's appeal to the Dachau court to be able to finish his report on his experiments in which he had infected over 1,000 prisoners with malaria supports this view. The doctors on trial believed they should be honoured for their achievements rather than criminalized.[1750] Höss, Commandant of Auschwitz, also showed no sign of guilt, as he believed that everything that he had done was right.[1751]

If one is convinced that Jews and others deemed undesirable were closer to vermin, lice and sources of infectious disease, for example, as integrated into Nazi ideology and so ably, and pervasively, portrayed in Nazi propaganda, then killing them is viewed as heroic rather than heinous. The perpetrators' acceptance of Nazi ideology as glorious makes it possible to understand the vast numbers of Germans (and others) who became enmeshed in perpetrating, or complying with, Nazi inspired crimes. It also explains how the Nazi dignitaries tried in the Nuremberg courts were found to be generally normal people. As SS Major-General Globocnik commented during a visit to Majdanik/Lublin on 15 August 1942:

> But gentlemen, if after us such a cowardly and rotten generation should arise that it does not understand our work which is so good and so necessary, then gentlemen, all National Socialism will have been for nothing. On the contrary, bronze plaques should be put up with the inscription that it was we, we who had the courage to achieve this gigantic task. And Hitler said " Yes, my good Globocnik, that is the word, that is my opinion too."[1752]

Similarly, the failure of the medical profession to accept responsibility for its considerable role in implementing the Holocaust and to redeem itself in the post-war years can be best understood within this conceptualization. So too can the inability of many Germans and their accomplices to accept responsibility for their actions, for many decades, be understood.

Most theories of perpetrator behaviour do not take a gendered view. Adding an analysis of the ability of men and women to perpetrate acts of extreme cruelty on both men and women – particularly in the highly respected German society of the time – might add a further dimension of value. Such culturally admired societies traditionally respected the value of saving women's and children's lives as a priority in times of danger – rather than targeting them as priorities for extermination. While rape and violence against women are becoming increasingly public topics of discourse, particularly in current genocidal settings, such acts of atrocity were not expected, or a focus of, post-Holocaust analysis. Exposure – and particularly visual images – of the atrocities revealed on liberation of the concentration camps stunned the world: a gendered focus on the events of the Holocaust only emerged some decades later. What role gender plays in explaining how such behaviours could have occurred, and who perpetrated them, is yet to be explored.

To compound the puzzle, rape and sexual exploitation of Jewish women in particular, were not condoned as part of Nazi ideology, precluding these actions from being considered as a simple distortion of evil into ideological good. Explanation of these aspects of the horrors perpetrated against women needs to incorporate additional variables including rape as a spoil of war, rape as an act of cruelty against those deemed vastly inferior and not worthy of recognition as human and sentient beings, and rape as the satisfaction of sexual urges outside of the normal constraints of peace-time life. Added to this is the frequently reported, apparent enjoyment of the many lurid acts of sexual cruelty, female (and male) reproductive organ torture and vicious murder of pregnant women, infants and their mothers among others. As illustrated in this text, these actions were not limited to a few, rare, pathological sadists, although these did exist as well.[1753] There is, as yet, no simple explanation as to how and why German society descended to such depths of depravity, particularly in their treatment of women and children, but also with regard to men. Given our increasing respect for both genders in the modern western world, the horrors inflicted on women during the Nazi era, at a time when male death in war was expected, but not necessarily that of women or children, take on an even greater dimension of evil than if these actions occurred today. Although by no means excusing this behaviour, it is worth noting that it is not exceptional: other situations in our recent history reveal similar acts of despicable atrocity. These include ideologically motivated acts of the Ku Klux Klan, murder of doctors staffing abortion clinics in the United States, physical abuse of aboriginal children forced into residential schools in Canada, persecutory actions of the Apartheid era in South Africa, and the increasingly frequent terrorist crimes being perpetrated against civilian Jews, Muslims, Blacks and other marginalized groups globally. Additional atrocities against women have recently been implemented on a more widespread scale in Bosnia, Rwanda, Darfur and the Democratic Republic of Congo. It is clear that we still have much to understand about human nature's ability to commit unspeakable crimes, particularly when driven by ideologically inspired fear, hatred, or greed.

"Sweetening the Holocaust"

"Sweetening the Holocaust"[1754] remains a current danger in Holocaust historiography. While there are a few positive memories of events in the Holocaust as well as many negative, it must be noted that we only have access to the testimonies of the survivors: the millions who died, and whose testimonies if available would likely be predominantly ones of loss and death, cannot be written. Few such stories survive although one of the most widely read of all memoirs is that of Anna Frank who did, indeed, perish.[1755] In addition, most memoirs tell the stories of the writer: few, like that of Schiff, deliberately set out to record the lives and deaths of others who were killed.[1756] The need to individualize and focus on the lives of those in the Holocaust rather than their deaths, in order to make them accessible to the younger generation (as is Yad Vashem's teaching philosophy[1757]), may well soften the events of the Holocaust and carry with it the risk of minimizing its devastation and impact. Most pregnant women or women with young children were the first to be gassed in extermination and concentration camps: the stories of triumphant motherhood are particularly few and far between making a glowing version of their survival difficult. As Friedman writes:

> One of the ever present dangers of Holocaust research and writing is the affixing of uplift and hope where there is none to be found. Lawrence Langer's warning is apt: The need to make the Holocaust more harmless than it was has many roots, and hence many branches, leaves, and blossoms. Its efforts to sweeten the bitter fruits of mass murder will have to be monitored for decades, and perhaps generations, if we are to prevent what happened from slipping into a vague limbo of forgetfulness, a footnote to contemporary history instead of the central historical moment of our time.[1758]

Langer's writings on this issue are strikingly confrontational. He posits that Western man has a need for mental self-preservation and that it is "almost impossible for him to admit disturbing evidence."[1759] He notes that our language helps us deal with atrocities that we do not want to face.

Referring to victims as survivors and martyrs rather than as the murdered is less devastating: the words help build "verbal fences between the atrocities of the camps and ghettos and what we are mentally willing – or able – to face." He reflects that the existence of many thousands of hours of recorded testimonies bear witness to the naivety of conceptions of heroism, choice and resistance among those who died as well as those who lived to record their stories. Such conceptualizations reflect the discomfort of the chroniclers rather than the facts. He exhorts us to be honest about the devastation wrought by the Holocaust and the apparently ready ability of those in power to wreak cruel havoc in the lives of others including abuse and killing. He notes further that we are reluctant to acknowledge that even though we might consider Nazi actions as evil, at the time they themselves viewed their practices as good, strongly supported by a political and moral value system that is, today, totally foreign to our way of thinking.

Langer further suggests that we distort our morality in recounting tales of the Holocaust. As he notes, Adina Blady Szwajger, a Jewish doctor, poisoned the sick children in the children's hospital in Warsaw as the Germans were rounding them up for deportation to Treblinka: she is sometimes recalled as a hero for saving the children from the horrors of the gas chamber. Yet the use of the word 'hero' to describe the killing of children is 'bizarre' and reflects our 'poverty of language' in describing moral integrity. Even more poignant in this case, is Hilberg's suggestion that Swajger's act of poisoning the children was performed to keep her promise to the children not to abandon them when she knew she, as a ward chief, had a 'ticket' allowing her to be saved. By murdering the children, she could leave the hospital and not break her promise.[1760] Swajger's own account of this incident reflects the horrors of the moment and her lifelong distress regarding her actions.[1761] While Swajger does not portray herself as heroic, memory has sometimes painted her with this brush.[1762] Further, Langer recounts that an SS man involved in the horrific murder of children at Bullenhauser Damm was acquitted by a court in Hamburg in 1964 on the grounds that he did not cause the children to suffer more than the destruction of their lives: he killed them painlessly while they were unconscious. Our moral integrity is again brought into question: Given his circumstances, did he indeed murder them 'humanely'? Is such a contradictory concept a viable one? As Levi[1763] notes, however, it is impossible, and inappropriate, to judge the perpetrators of questionable actions undertaken in the upside-down world of the Nazi era. Notwithstanding the considerable moral dilemmas that such actions raise, Langer cites them as examples of our need to distort the horrors of the time into more palatable events. He asks, "How much darkness must we acknowledge before we will be able to confess that the Holocaust story cannot be told in terms of heroic dignity, moral courage, and the triumph of the human spirit in adversity?"[1764] Even Yad Vashem, with its official title of the Israeli 'Holocaust Martyrs' and Heroes' Remembrance Authority' falls under this rubric.

The actions of prisoner doctors who murdered newborns, or who terminated apparently healthy pregnancies, have tempted scholars to judge their actions, either with reluctant admiration or with condemnation, despite Levi's warning that judgement is not possible. This review emphasises even further our need to look squarely in the face of such actions and to recognize that it is not the actions of the doctors that should be condemned but those of the Nazis who imposed such horrendous conditions on them that they were forced into despicable moral dilemmas and consequent murderous behaviours. No amount of praise for the bravery of health caregivers or that of the mothers who lived and testified to their experiences, can, or should, minimize the appropriate placement of blame. Nazi ideology, pervasively and effectively propagandized, promoted both genocide of Jews, as well as geno-coercion, of 'Aryan' women. Those who implemented these principles should be judged as wanting, and not those who were forced into compromising situations and decisions to confront, avoid or escape it.

Yael Danieli,[1765] a psychiatrist specializing in caring for Holocaust survivors, contextualizes the phenomenon of our need to sweeten the Holocaust. She reports that at heart human beings wish to believe that we are good. We want to feel optimistic and proud about ourselves. She reports, however, four 'blows' to humanity's self love. According to this construct, Copernicus gave the first blow – 'the Cosmological blow' – when humankind realized it was not the centre of the universe. The second blow – 'the Biological blow' – was dealt by Darwin's questioning of humankind's supremacy over the animal kingdom. Freud gave the third blow – 'the Psychological blow' – by showing that the ego is not even the master of the psyche. Danieli believes that the Nazis gave the fourth blow – 'the Ethical blow' – by 'shattering our 'naïve belief that the world we live in is a just place, and that human life is of value.' It is now time that we recognize a fifth blow – 'the Ideological blow.' Ideology, including some formalized religions (as opposed to spirituality), and acts perpetrated within such – often extremist – frameworks, have throughout the ages, frequently led to our moral, ethical and spiritual impoverishment. We clearly need to acknowledge, as Father Patrick Desbois writes:

> I am convinced that there is only one race: a human race that shoots two-year-old children. For better or for worse I belong to that human race and this allows me to acknowledge that an ideology can deceive minds to the point of annihilating all ethical reflexes and all recognition of the human in the other.[1766]

The dangers of ideological fanaticism are globally evident today, as they were in the Nazi era, and are clearly to be feared.

Appendix

CHRONOLOGY OF EVENTS RELATING TO MEDICINE, WOMEN'S ISSUES, CHILDBEARING AND SEXUALITY IN THE NAZI ERA			
DATE	**NAZI ERA MILESTONES**	**MEDICAL ISSUES**	**CHILDBEARING, SEXUALITY AND WOMEN'S ISSUES**
Prior to 1933			
			Magnus Hirschfeld establishes *Institute for Sexual Science* in Berlin.[1767]
1927		US Supreme Court upholds State of Virginia's law sanctioning sterilization of the institutionalized hereditarily 'unfit'.[1768]	
1928		Sterilization laws passed by Switzerland[1769]	
1929		Denmark introduces first national sterilization law largely applied to mentally ill in institutions.[1770]	
30 Dec. 1930			Denunciation of birth control by the Papal encyclical *'Casti Connubii'* (*On Christian Marriage*).[1771]
Prior to 1933		Finland, Sweden and Iceland pass sterilization laws.[1772]	
1933			
30 Jan.	Hitler becomes Chancellor of Germany.[1773]		

CHRONOLOGY OF EVENTS RELATING TO MEDICINE, WOMEN'S ISSUES, CHILDBEARING AND SEXUALITY IN THE NAZI ERA			
DATE	**NAZI ERA MILESTONES**	**MEDICAL ISSUES**	**CHILDBEARING, SEXUALITY AND WOMEN'S ISSUES**
28 Feb.			Decree for the protection of the Volk and State: rounding up thousands of prostitutes who were sent to workhouses and camps[1774]
22 March	Dachau established[1775]		First women's prison Gotteszell, opened.[1776]
7 April		Law for Reconstitution of German Civil Service expels Jewish medical professionals from Universities.[1777]	
20 April		Non-Aryan doctors excluded from practice.[1778]	
May			Helen Stöcker 's *League for the Protection of Motherhood* banned.[1779] All marriage and sex counselling centres closed.[1780]
6 May			*Institute for Sexual Science* raided and destroyed by students from the Berlin School for Physical Education and members of the National Socialist German Students' League.[1781]
10 May	*Bücherverbrennung* (Public book burnings).[1782]		
26 May			Legislation restricts abortion and prohibits voluntary sterilization[1783]
1 June			Marriage Loans for couples to encourage births following public health examination.[1784]

CHRONOLOGY OF EVENTS RELATING TO MEDICINE, WOMEN'S ISSUES, CHILDBEARING AND SEXUALITY IN THE NAZI ERA			
DATE	**NAZI ERA MILESTONES**	**MEDICAL ISSUES**	**CHILDBEARING, SEXUALITY AND WOMEN'S ISSUES**
14 July			Law for the Prevention of Hereditarily Diseased Offspring passed taking effect 1 January 1934.[1785]
20 July	Vatican signs Concordat with Germany		
4 Oct.		Editor's Law: German Jewish medical scholars forbidden from publishing in German books or journals.[1786]	
Oct.			First women's concentration camp opens at Moringen.[1787]
Nov.			Law against Dangerous Habitual Criminals enacted, providing castration for male sexual offenders.[1788]
24 Nov.		Ethical guidelines protecting animals from research involving freezing, drowning, burning and poisoning passed in Germany.[1789]	
1933			German Mother's Honour Cross instituted.[1790]
1934			
26 Jan.	Germany and Poland sign 10 year non-aggression pact.[1791]	Norway passes sterilization laws.[1792]	
24 Feb.			Gertrud Scholtz-Klink becomes the leader of the *National Socialist Women's Union and the German Women's Agency*.[1793]

CHRONOLOGY OF EVENTS RELATING TO MEDICINE, WOMEN'S ISSUES, CHILDBEARING AND SEXUALITY IN THE NAZI ERA			
DATE	**NAZI ERA MILESTONES**	**MEDICAL ISSUES**	**CHILDBEARING, SEXUALITY AND WOMEN'S ISSUES**
3 July		A centralized system of State Health Offices with departments for Hygiene and Health law is created.[1794]	Laws prohibiting marriage with 'alien races and the 'defective' among the 'German-blooded' passed.[1795]
2 Aug.	President Paul von Hindenberg dies. Hitler declares himself Führer of the Third Reich.[1796]		
1935			
1935		*Was du Erbst'* (*What you inherit)* and *Erb Krank* (*The Hereditarily Ill*) (1935): silent movies showing images of severely mentally handicapped patients.[1797]	
1 Jan.		National Law on sterilization introduced in Sweden.[1798]	
11 March			Sterilization of 'Rhineland bastards' planned.[1799]
26 June			Nazi sterilization Law amended to allow for sterilization on 'eugenic' grounds and for compulsory sterilization.[1800]
28 June			Paragraph 175 of the German criminal code is amended to broaden the grounds for punishing homosexuality.[1801]
15 Sept.	Reich Citizenship Law defines who is a Jew and who is a '*Mischlinge*'.[1802]		

CHRONOLOGY OF EVENTS RELATING TO MEDICINE, WOMEN'S ISSUES, CHILDBEARING AND SEXUALITY IN THE NAZI ERA			
DATE	**NAZI ERA MILESTONES**	**MEDICAL ISSUES**	**CHILDBEARING, SEXUALITY AND WOMEN'S ISSUES**
18 Oct.			Marital Health Law prohibits marriage if either partner has mental ill health, hereditary ill health, severe contagious disease, tuberculosis, or venereal disease.[1803] All prospective spouses to produce a 'certificate of fitness to marry'.[1804] Marital Health Law allows castration of male homosexuals with their consent, if a public health doctor judges castration to be useful in 'liberating him, from a degenerate sex drive.'[1805]
14 Nov.			Law for the Protection of German Blood and German Honour prohibits marriage or sexual relations between German Jews and persons of 'German or related blood'.[1806]
12 Dec.			Himmler establishes the *Lebensborn* program.[1807]
Dec.		Wagner pronounces Reich Physicians' Ordinance with compulsory membership for physicians: incorporates sterilization and race science into practice.[1808]	

CHRONOLOGY OF EVENTS RELATING TO MEDICINE, WOMEN'S ISSUES, CHILDBEARING AND SEXUALITY IN THE NAZI ERA			
DATE	**NAZI ERA MILESTONES**	**MEDICAL ISSUES**	**CHILDBEARING, SEXUALITY AND WOMEN'S ISSUES**
1935			'Ten Commandments for Choosing a Mate' created by the Reich Committee for Public Health[1809] Doctors and midwives required to notify regional state health office of induced abortions and miscarriages before 32nd week of pregnancy and all preterm births.[1810] Jewish baby Hessy Levinsohn Taft, six months old, chosen (without knowledge of her origins) as the archetype of Aryan babyhood by Nazi family magazine *Sun in the House*.[1811] Goebbels increases publicity campaign against alleged sexual scandals involving Catholic priests.[1812]
1936			
		By 1936, 35 American states had passed forced sterilization laws.[1813]	
Feb.		Ministry of Interior establishes information system on patients in mental hospitals.[1814]	Child allowances introduced from the fifth child under age 16.[1815] State sponsored brothel system in military settings solidified.[1816]
20 Feb.		Nazi Racial Policy Office releases film *Hereditarily Ill (Erbkrank)*	

CHRONOLOGY OF EVENTS RELATING TO MEDICINE, WOMEN'S ISSUES, CHILDBEARING AND SEXUALITY IN THE NAZI ERA			
DATE	**NAZI ERA MILESTONES**	**MEDICAL ISSUES**	**CHILDBEARING, SEXUALITY AND WOMEN'S ISSUES**
1 – 16 Aug.	Olympic games held in Berlin[1817]		
23 Sept.	Sachsenhausen camp established.[1818]		
10 Oct.			Himmler creates Reich Central Office for Combating Homosexuality and Abortion.[1819]
1937			
1937		*Opfer der Vergangenheit* (*Victims of the Past*): film promoting euthanasia shown by law in 5,300 movie theatres.[1820]	
April-June			Rhineland bastards are forcibly sterilized.[1821]
12 June	Secret orders from Heydrich concerning protective custody of 'sacral violators' (*Rassenschände*) after they have served their prison sentence[1822]		
15 July	Buchenwald camp established[1823]		
1938			
12 March	*Anschluss*: the Third Reich annexes Austria.[1824]		
21 March			Moringen camp for women closes. Prisoners are transferred to newly opened Lichtenburg camp.[1825]
3 May	Flossenbürg camp established.[1826]		

CHRONOLOGY OF EVENTS RELATING TO MEDICINE, WOMEN'S ISSUES, CHILDBEARING AND SEXUALITY IN THE NAZI ERA			
DATE	**NAZI ERA MILESTONES**	**MEDICAL ISSUES**	**CHILDBEARING, SEXUALITY AND WOMEN'S ISSUES**
6-15 July	Evian Conference attended by 32 nations does not help refugees.[1827]		
8 Aug.	First Austrian concentration camp established at Mauthausen.[1828]		
17 Aug.			Jewish women in Germany required to add 'Sarah' to their names: men must add 'Israel'.[1829]
28 Sept.		Jewish doctor's medical licences are revoked: they may only treat other Jews.[1830]	
29-30 Sept.	Munich Conference agreement to annex part of Czechoslovakia.[1831]		
5 Oct.	German Jews' passports marked with red 'J'.[1832]		
9-10 Nov.	*Kristallnacht* pogrom.[1833]		
1938			New marriage law makes it possible for men and women to divorce on grounds of 'premature infertility or refusal of partner to procreate.'[1834] Child allowances extended to include children under 21.[1835]

CHRONOLOGY OF EVENTS RELATING TO MEDICINE, WOMEN'S ISSUES, CHILDBEARING AND SEXUALITY IN THE NAZI ERA			
DATE	**NAZI ERA MILESTONES**	**MEDICAL ISSUES**	**CHILDBEARING, SEXUALITY AND WOMEN'S ISSUES**
1939			
1939		Films *Das Erbe* (*The Inheritance*); *Dasein ohne Leben* (Existence *Without Life*) and *Geisterkrank* (*The Mentally Ill*) suggest euthanasia is humane.[1836]	*Lebensborn* program extended to kidnapping of biologically valuable children in occupied countries.[1837]
30 Jan.	Hitler speech to Reichstag: World War will mean 'the annihilation of the Jewish race in Europe'.[1838] Hitler later dates this speech as occurring on 1 September.[1839]		
15 March	Germany takes over the rest of Czechoslovakia.[1840]		
May		The Reich Committee for the Scientific Registering of Serious Hereditary and Congenital Illnesses established: formerly the Reich Committee for Hereditary Health Matters.[1841]	
15 May			Ravensbrück camp for women established.[1842]
25 July		First child killed setting precedent for the Euthanasia program.[1843]	

CHRONOLOGY OF EVENTS RELATING TO MEDICINE, WOMEN'S ISSUES, CHILDBEARING AND SEXUALITY IN THE NAZI ERA			
DATE	**NAZI ERA MILESTONES**	**MEDICAL ISSUES**	**CHILDBEARING, SEXUALITY AND WOMEN'S ISSUES**
18 Aug.		All infants and children up to three, with serious mental or physical disabilities, to be reported to Reich Ministry of Interior.[1844]	
23 Aug.	Nazi-Soviet non-aggression pact signed.[1845]		
31 Aug.		Decree officially brought the program of sterilization of mentally ill and handicapped children to an end to be replaced by the Euthanasia program.[1846]	
1 Sept.	Germany invades Poland: start of WWII[1847]	Hitler charges Brandt and Bouhler to 'grant merciful deaths' to incurably sick patients: order signed in October and backdated to 1 September.[1848]	
3 Sept.	France and Great Britain declare war on Germany.[1849]		
9 Sept.			Brothels officially created in military zone of Poland. Brothels created for foreign labourers in Germany.[1850]
17 Sept.	Soviet troops invade Poland.[1851]		
21 Sept.		The Reich Ministry of the Interior orders that all institutions caring for mental patients, epileptics and the feebleminded report to it.[1852]	
29 Sept.- 1 Nov.		SS killing squads murder 2342 hospitalized psychiatric patients in Kocborowo, Poland.[1853]	

CHRONOLOGY OF EVENTS RELATING TO MEDICINE, WOMEN'S ISSUES, CHILDBEARING AND SEXUALITY IN THE NAZI ERA			
DATE	**NAZI ERA MILESTONES**	**MEDICAL ISSUES**	**CHILDBEARING, SEXUALITY AND WOMEN'S ISSUES**
28 Oct.			Himmler calls upon racially 'valuable' Germans to produce children, even illegitimate ones, to fill the nation's need for soldiers.[1854]
Oct. back-dated to 1 Sept.		Hitler signs order authorizing Euthanasia program.[1855]	
1 Oct.		Questionnaires sent to mental hospitals to assess patients for Euthanasia[1856].	
8 Oct.	First ghetto established (Piotrkow Trybunalski) in Poland.[1857]		
Oct.-Dec.		SS shoot or gas in sealed vans, 4,400 'incurable' patients in Polish mental hospitals near Posen and Chelm-Lubelski[1858]	
Dec.-Jan.		Patients from the Tiegenhof hospitals in Prussia are murdered in sealed vans.[1859]	
1940			
Early Jan.		First experimental gassing of mental patients in German hospitals initiated at Brandenburg.[1860]	
8 Feb.	Łódź ghetto established and sealed on 30 April.[1861]		

CHRONOLOGY OF EVENTS RELATING TO MEDICINE, WOMEN'S ISSUES, CHILDBEARING AND SEXUALITY IN THE NAZI ERA			
DATE	**NAZI ERA MILESTONES**	**MEDICAL ISSUES**	**CHILDBEARING, SEXUALITY AND WOMEN'S ISSUES**
9 April–22 June	Germany conquers Denmark, Norway, Holland, Belgium and France.[1862]	A proclamation from the Reich Interior Ministry determines that all Jews in institutions are to be killed regardless of illness.[1863]	
27 April	Auschwitz established.[1864]		
24 Sept.		*Jud Süß* [1865] released. *Der Ewige Jude* in production[1866]	
Oct.	Warsaw ghetto established and sealed by mid-Nov.[1867]		
28 Nov.		*Der Ewige Jude* premiers in Berlin.[1868]	
1941			
Jan.		Gassing of patients begins at Hadamar.[1869]	
21 Jan.			Himmler criminalizes all forms of contraception except condoms.[1870]
1 March	Himmler orders construction of Birkenau camp.[1871]		Sterilization experiments commence and continue until January 1945.[1872]
Spring		Operation 14f13 begins.[1873]	
6 April	German army invades Yugoslavia and Greece.[1874]		
13 May			Barbarossa Decree establishes that no criminal offences commited by German soldiers against Soviet civilians were to be punished unless they were serious, including sexual offences.[1875]

CHRONOLOGY OF EVENTS RELATING TO MEDICINE, WOMEN'S ISSUES, CHILDBEARING AND SEXUALITY IN THE NAZI ERA			
DATE	**NAZI ERA MILESTONES**	**MEDICAL ISSUES**	**CHILDBEARING, SEXUALITY AND WOMEN'S ISSUES**
22 June	Operation Barbarossa – the invasion of the Soviet Union – begins.[1876]		
8 July	Jews in Baltic States forced to wear Star of David.[1877]		
31 July	Göring signs orders authorizing Heydrich to prepare the 'final solution of the Jewish question.'[1878]		
6,13,20 July and 3 Aug.		Bishop Clemens August von Galen denounces 'euthanasia' killings.[1879]	
24 Aug.		Centralized euthanasia program is formally stopped.[1880]	
29 Aug.		*Ich Klage An* (*I Accuse*) film promotes euthanasia.[1881]	
3 Sept.		600 Soviet POWs experimentally gassed with Zyklon B in Auschwitz.[1882]	
15 Sept.	Jews in Germany forced to wear Star of David.[1883]		
29-30 Sept.	33,000 Jews from Kiev murdered by *Einsatzgruppen C* at Babi Yar.[1884]		

CHRONOLOGY OF EVENTS RELATING TO MEDICINE, WOMEN'S ISSUES, CHILDBEARING AND SEXUALITY IN THE NAZI ERA			
DATE	**NAZI ERA MILESTONES**	**MEDICAL ISSUES**	**CHILDBEARING, SEXUALITY AND WOMEN'S ISSUES**
15 Oct.	Deportation of Jews from Germany, Austria, Luxembourg, and Czechoslovakia eastwards to ghettos in Poland, Lithuania and Latvia begins.[1885]		
Late Nov.	First Jews arrive at Theresienstadt.[1886]		
7 Dec.	Japan attacks Pearl Harbour: USA declares war on Japan.[1887]		
8 Dec.		Gassing of Jews in sealed vans begins at Chelmno.[1888]	
11 Dec.	USA declares war on Germany and Italy.[1889]		
1941			Jewish women alleged to serve in military brothel in Soroca, Romania, opened by the 11th German military Division.[1890]
1942			
20 Jan.	Wannsee Conference to coordinate the 'Final Solution.'[1891]		
Jan./ Feb.	First experiments (low pressure) on prisoners in Dachau.[1892]		
5 Feb.			Births forbidden in Vilna ghetto.[1893]
26 March			Separate women's camp established in Auschwitz.[1894]

CHRONOLOGY OF EVENTS RELATING TO MEDICINE, WOMEN'S ISSUES, CHILDBEARING AND SEXUALITY IN THE NAZI ERA			
DATE	**NAZI ERA MILESTONES**	**MEDICAL ISSUES**	**CHILDBEARING, SEXUALITY AND WOMEN'S ISSUES**
16 March	Belzec death camp becomes operational.[1895]		Orders given to establish brothels in concentration camps.[1896]
4 April			Himmler visits Auschwitz, approves flogging of female prisoners on the naked buttocks.[1897]
1 May	Sobibor death camp becomes operational.[1898]		
7 May			Rabbi Oshry in Kovno ghetto agrees to the use of a diaphragm to prevent pregnancy (and therefore to save the mother's life).[1899]
30 May			Carl Clauberg requests permission for sterilization experiments in Auschwitz.[1900]
1 June	Treblinka death camp opens. French and Dutch Jews must wear Star of David.[1901]		
23 June			Viktor Brack submits proposal to Himmler for the sterilization of 2-3 million Jewish workers.[1902] Himmler approves on 30 June.[1903]
July			First brothel opened in Gusen camp in Mauthausen.[1904]
7 July			Himmler approves Clauberg's request.[1905]

CHRONOLOGY OF EVENTS RELATING TO MEDICINE, WOMEN'S ISSUES, CHILDBEARING AND SEXUALITY IN THE NAZI ERA			
DATE	**NAZI ERA MILESTONES**	**MEDICAL ISSUES**	**CHILDBEARING, SEXUALITY AND WOMEN'S ISSUES**
10 July			Himmler orders Clauberg to carry out sterilization procedures on Jewish women in Ravensbrück.[1906]
13 July			Births in Shavli ghetto banned as from 15 August 1942.[1907]
24 July			Gestapo forbids pregnancy in Kovno ghetto.[1908]
22 July–12 Sept.	Mass deportation of Jews from Warsaw ghetto sent mostly to Treblinka.[1909]		
Summer		Adult euthanasia begins again on a large scale in institutions throughout Germany and Austria. Lethal overdoses of medications and starvation are now methods of killing rather than gassing.[1910]	
9 Aug.			Rabbi Oshry in Kovno agrees to abortion to save a mother's life.[1911]
15 Aug.			Hitler orders last surviving son in every family where more than one son had been killed, to return home.[1912]
8 Sept.			Pregnant women to be killed by Gestapo in Kovno ghetto.[1913]
8 Oct.			Female orchestra organized in Birkenau.[1914]

CHRONOLOGY OF EVENTS RELATING TO MEDICINE, WOMEN'S ISSUES, CHILDBEARING AND SEXUALITY IN THE NAZI ERA			
DATE	**NAZI ERA MILESTONES**	**MEDICAL ISSUES**	**CHILDBEARING, SEXUALITY AND WOMEN'S ISSUES**
28 Dec.			Clauberg begins sterilization experiments in Birkenau.[1915]
1942			Conti orders doctors to help childless couples have offspring. Research into optimal time in menstrual cycle for conception instigated.[1916]
1943			
18 Jan.	Warsaw ghetto uprising begins[1917]		
2 Feb.	Soviets defeat German army at Stalingrad.[1918]		
9 March			New Law imposed death penalty for anyone carrying out abortions that would 'impair the vitality of the German people.'[1919]
19-30 April	Bermuda Conference[1920]		
19 April–30 May	Warsaw ghetto is destroyed.[1921]		
6 May			Decree forbidding the admission of pregnant women into Ravensbrück or the women's section of the concentration camps Auschwitz and Lublin (Majdanek).[1922]
Spring	Anti-Jewish/typhus exhibition opens in Warsaw		
30 May		Josef Mengele arrives in Auschwitz.[1923]	

CHRONOLOGY OF EVENTS RELATING TO MEDICINE, WOMEN'S ISSUES, CHILDBEARING AND SEXUALITY IN THE NAZI ERA			
DATE	**NAZI ERA MILESTONES**	**MEDICAL ISSUES**	**CHILDBEARING, SEXUALITY AND WOMEN'S ISSUES**
Mid June	Himmler orders liquidation of remaining ghettos.[1924]		
19 June		Vatican protests euthanasia in encyclical *Mystici Corporis* (*On the Mystical Body of Christ*).[1925]	
July			Compulsory abortion order issued in Theresienstadt.[1926] Brothels established in Flossenbürg and Buchenwald.[1927]
2 Aug.	Treblinka prisoners revolt.[1928]		
1 Oct.			German Medical Council of Berlin approves abortions for foreign workers.[1929]
Oct.			Brothels established in Auschwitz-Stammlager[1930]
1-2 Oct.	Danes rescue 7,200 Danish Jews[1931]		
14 Oct.	Sobibor prisoners revolt.[1932]		
23 Oct.			1800 Polish Jews arrive in Auschwitz from Bergen-Belsen. A dancer, Franceska Mann acts seductively, grabs an SS revolver and shoots Staff Sergeant Schillinger twice, killing him and wounding SS Sergeant Emerick. All the women are gassed but their legend lives on.[1933]
Nov.			Brothel established in Auschwitz- Monowitz[1934]

CHRONOLOGY OF EVENTS RELATING TO MEDICINE, WOMEN'S ISSUES, CHILDBEARING AND SEXUALITY IN THE NAZI ERA			
DATE	**NAZI ERA MILESTONES**	**MEDICAL ISSUES**	**CHILDBEARING, SEXUALITY AND WOMEN'S ISSUES**
1944			
April			Brothel established in Dachau.[1935]
May			Brothel established in Neuengamma.[1936]
15 May– 9 July	430,000 Hungarian Jews deported to Auschwitz.[1937]		
6 June	D- Day.[1938]		
Aug.			Brothel established in Sachsenhausen.[1939]
7 Oct.	Revolt by Jewish Sonderkommando in Auschwitz-Birkenau.[1940]		
26 Nov.	Himmler orders destruction of crematoria in Auschwitz-Birkenau[1941]		
1945			
17-18 Jan.	Forced evacuation of Auschwitz prisoners[1942]		
27 Jan.	Soviet troops enter Auschwitz and find 31,894 prisoners of whom 16,577 are women.[1943]		
Feb.			Brothel opened in Mittelbau-Dora.[1944]
March-April		Euthanasia continues in institutions not yet liberated by Allies.[1945]	
11 April	Buchenwald camp liberated by American forces.[1946]		
15 April	Bergen-Belsen camp liberated by British forces.[1947]		

CHRONOLOGY OF EVENTS RELATING TO MEDICINE, WOMEN'S ISSUES, CHILDBEARING AND SEXUALITY IN THE NAZI ERA			
DATE	**NAZI ERA MILESTONES**	**MEDICAL ISSUES**	**CHILDBEARING, SEXUALITY AND WOMEN'S ISSUES**
29-30 April	Ravensbrück camp liberated by Soviet forces: 3500 female prisoners found.[1948]		
Spring			Multiple rapes of German and other women by Red Army.[1949]
30 April	Adolf Hitler and Eva Braun commit suicide.[1950]		
7-8 May	Germany surrenders.[1951]		
17 Sept. -17 Nov.		Bergen-Belsen war crimes trials: Irma Grese sentenced to death.[1952]	
1946-1947			
9 Dec. 1946 -20 Aug. 1947		Nazi Doctors war crimes trial. 23 Germans prosecuted: 16 found guilty. 7 sentenced to death.[1953]	Over 1000 marriages in Belsen DP camp between 1945-1947.[1954]
Late Aug.		The Nuremberg Code designed to protect the rights of research subjects is issued following the Doctor's Trial.[1955]	
1948			
2 June			Karl Brandt, Karl Gebhardt, Rudolf Brandt, Joachim Murgowsky, Viktor Brack, executed for participation in sterilization crimes.[1956]

Notes

[1] Adam Jones, *Genocide: A Comprehensive Introduction*, 2nd ed. (Routledge/Taylor & Francis Publishers, 2010), 13.

[2] Claudia Koonz, *Mothers in the Fatherland: Women, the Family and Nazi Politics* (New York: St Martin's Press, 1987), 3.

[3] Victoria Harris, *Selling Sex in the Reich: Prostitutes in German Society, 1914-1945* (Oxford: Oxford University Press, 2010), 30,194.

[4] Wendy Lower, *Hitler's Furies: German Women in the Nazi Killing Fields* (New York: Houghton Mifflin, 2013), 12.

[5] Na'ama Shik, "Infinite Loneliness: Some Aspects of the Lives of Jewish Women in the Auschwitz Camps According to Testimonies and Autobiographies Written Between 1945 and 1948.," in *Lessons and Legacies VIII: From Generation to Generation*, ed. Doris L. Bergen (Evanston, Illinois: Northwestern University Press, 2008), 131-33.

[6] ———, ed. *Sexual Abuse of Jewish Women in Auschwitz-Birkenau*, Brutality and Desire: War and Sexuality in Europe's Twentieth Century (Hounddsmills, Basingstoke, Hampshire: Palgrave Macmillan, 2009), 237.

[7] Judith Baumel, "Gender and Family Studies of the Holocaust: the Development of a Historical Discipline," in *Life, Death and Sacrifice; Women and Family in the Holocaust*, ed. Esther Hertzog (Jeruslaem: Geffen, 2008), 26.

[8] Atina Grossmann, *Jews, Germans, and the Allies: Close Encounters in Occupied Germany* (Princeton: Princeton University Press, 2007), 196.

[9] "Holocaust," (Titus Productions, 1978).

[10] Agata Tuszynska, *Vera Gran: The Accused* (New York Alfred A Knopf, 2013), 205.

[11] Helga Amesberger, "Reproduction Under the Swastika: The Other Side of the Nazi Glorification of Motherhood," in *Sexual Violence Against Jewish Women During the Holocaust*, ed. Sonja M Hedgepeth and Rochelle G Saidel (Waltham, Massachusetts: Brandeis University Press, 2010), 140-41; "*Erlass zum Verbot der Einweisung schwangerer Häftlinge in die Frauenkonzentrationslager Ravensbrück bzw. in die Frauenabteilungen der Konzentrationslager Auschwitz und Lublin* [Decree forbidding the admission of pregnant inmates into the women's concentration camp Ravensbrück or the women's section of the concentration camps Auschwitz and Lublin].". (Ravensbrück Memorial in Sammlungen, May 6 1943).

[12] Grossmann, *Jews, Germans, and the Allies: Close Encounters in Occupied Germany*: 227.

[13] Jeffrey Herf, *Nazi Propaganda for the Arab World* (New Haven: Yale University Press, 2009), 23; Leni Yahil, *The Holocaust: The Fate of European Jewry* (Oxford: Oxford University Press, 1990), 71.

[14] Sarah Gordon, *Hitler, Germans, and the "Jewish Question"* (Princeton: Princeton University Press, 1984), 92.

[15] Dana Lori Chalmers, "The Influence of Theatre and Paratheatre on the Holocaust" (Masters Thesis, Concordia University, 2008), 17.

[16] Ibid., 16; ibid.

[17] Fritz Hippler. "Der Ewige Jude," (Germany: Deutsche Film Gesellschaft, 1940).
[18] Veit Harlan, "Jud Süβ," (Germany: Terra-Filmkunst GmbH, 1934).
[19] Chalmers, "The Influence of Theatre and Paratheatre on the Holocaust," 17.
[20] Saul Friedländer, *The Years of Persecution: Nazi Germany and the Jews 1933-1939* (London: Phoenix, 1997), 185.
[21] Gordon, *Hitler, Germans, and the "Jewish Question"*: 92.
[22] Yitzhak Arad, *Belzec, Sobibor, Treblinka: The Operation Reinhard Death Camps* (Bloomington: Indiana University Press, 1987), 1.
[23] Chalmers, "The Influence of Theatre and Paratheatre on the Holocaust," 11.
[24] Ibid.
[25] Ibid., 13.
[26] Mark Mazower, *Dark Continent: Europe's Twentieth Century* (New York: Vintage Books, 1998), 102.
[27] James M Glass, *Life Unworthy of Life: Racial Phobia and Mass Murder in Hitler's Germany* (New York: Basic Books, 1997), 8.
[28] Raul Hilberg, *The Destruction of the European Jews* (New York: Holmes and Meier, 1985), 18.
[29] Glass, *Life Unworthy of Life: Racial Phobia and Mass Murder in Hitler's Germany*: 8.
[30] Arad, *Belzec, Sobibor, Treblinka: The Operation Reinhard Death Camps*: 1.
[31] Michael Kater, *Doctors Under Hitler* (Chapel Hill: The University of North Carolina Press, 1989), 179.
[32] Glass, *Life Unworthy of Life: Racial Phobia and Mass Murder in Hitler's Germany*: 9.
[33] Ibid.
[34] Robert Jay Lifton, *The Nazi Doctors: Medical Killing and the Psychology of Genocide* (New York: Basic Books, Inc, 1986), 31.
[35] Glass, *Life Unworthy of Life: Racial Phobia and Mass Murder in Hitler's Germany*: 9; ibid.
[36] Kater, *Doctors Under Hitler*: 162, 79-81.
[37] Adolf Hitler, *Mein Kampf* (London: Hurst and Blackett, 1939), 160-2; ibid.
[38] Kater, *Doctors Under Hitler*: 179-81; Michael Burleigh and Wolfgang Wipperman, *The Racial State: Germany 1933-1945* (Cambridge: Cambridge University Press, 1991), 37.
[39] ———, *The Racial State: Germany 1933-1945*: 37; Richard Steigman-Gall, *The Holy Reich: Nazi Conceptions of Christianity, 1919-1945* (Cambridge: Cambridge University Press, 2003), 30-31.
[40] Lord Russell of Liverpool, *The Scourge of the Swastika* (London: The Military Book Club, 1954), 228.
[41] Patricia Szobar, "Telling Sexual Stories in the Nazi Courts of Law: Race Defilement in Germany, 1933-1945," *Journal of the History of Sexuality* 11, no. 1/2 (2002): 147.
[42] Hitler, *Mein Kampf*: 43.
[43] Julia Roos, "Backlash Against Prostitutes' Rights: Origins and Dynamics of Nazi Prostitution Policies.," *Journal of the History of Sexuality* 11, no. 1/2 (2002): 79.
[44] Hilberg, *The Destruction of the European Jews*: 53; Saul Friedländer, *Nazi Germany and the Jews 1939-1945: The Years of Extermination* (New York: Harper Perennial, 2007), 48.
[45] Szobar, "Telling Sexual Stories in the Nazi Courts of Law: Race Defilement in Germany, 1933-1945," 147.
[46] Hitler, *Mein Kampf*: 160-2.
[47] Kater, *Doctors Under Hitler*: 179-81.
[48] Burleigh and Wipperman, *The Racial State: Germany 1933-1945*: 41, 201.
[49] Glass, *Life Unworthy of Life: Racial Phobia and Mass Murder in Hitler's Germany*: xix.
[50] Kater, *Doctors Under Hitler*: 179-81.
[51] Harlan, "Jud Süβ."
[52] Richard J Evans, *The Third Reich at War* (New York: The Penguin Press, 2009), 571-2.

[53] Hippler, "Der Ewige Jude."
[54] Evans, *The Third Reich at War*: 571-2.
[55] Ibid., 541.
[56] Helga Amesberger and Brigitte Halbmayr, "Nazi Differentiations Mattered: Ideological Intersections of Sexualized Violence During National Socialist Persecution," in *Life, Death, and Sacrifice: Women and Family in the Holocaust*, ed. Esther Herzog (Jerusalem: Gefen Publishing House, 2008), 181; ibid.
[57] Robert N Proctor, "Racial Hygiene: The Collaboration of Medicine and Nazism," in *Medicine, Ethics and the Third Reich: Historical and Contemporary Issues*, ed. John J Michalczyk (Kansas City: Sheed and Ward, 1944), 36.
[58] Kater, *Doctors Under Hitler*: 161.
[59] Burleigh and Wipperman, *The Racial State: Germany 1933-1945*: 78.
[60] Roger A. Ritvo and Diane M Plotkin, *Sisters in Sorrow: Voices of Care in the Holocaust* (College Station: Texas A & M University Press, 1998), 129.
[61] Kater, *Doctors Under Hitler*: 192.
[62] Ernst Hiemer, *Der Giftpilz (The Poisonous Mushroom)* (Germany: Julies Streicher, 1938).
[63] Kater, *Doctors Under Hitler*: 192-6.
[64] Eric A Johnson and Karl-Heinz Reuband, *What We Knew: Terror, Mass Murder, and Everyday Life in Nazi Germany* (Basic Books, 2005), 16.
[65] Glass, *Life Unworthy of Life: Racial Phobia and Mass Murder in Hitler's Germany*: xix.
[66] Kater, *Doctors Under Hitler*: 236-37.
[67] Nadav, *Medicine Ethics and the Third Reich*; 42.
[68] Glass, *Life Unworthy of Life: Racial Phobia and Mass Murder in Hitler's Germany*: 40.
[69] Israel Gutman, ed. *Encyclopedia of the Holocaust* (New York: Macmillan Publishing Company, 1990), 1076.
[70] Burleigh and Wipperman, *The Racial State: Germany 1933-1945*: 49.
[71] Rita Steinhardt Botwinick, ed. *A Holocaust Reader* (New Jersey: Prentice Hall, 1998), 122-3; Stephen C Feinstein, "Jewish Women in Time: The Challenge of Feminist Artistic Installations About the Holocaust," in *Experience and Expression: Women, the Nazis, and the Holocaust*, ed. Elizabeth R Baer and Myrna Goldenberg (Detroit: Wayne State University Press, 2003), 244.
[72] Hilberg, *The Destruction of the European Jews*: 42-3.
[73] Botwinick, *A Holocaust Reader*, 122-3; Feinstein, "Jewish Women in Time: The Challenge of Feminist Artistic Installations About the Holocaust," 244; Victor Klemperer, *I Shall Bear Witness: The Diaries of Victor Klemperer 1933-1941.* (London: Weidenfeld and Nicolson, 1998), 128.
[74] Feinstein, "Jewish Women in Time: The Challenge of Feminist Artistic Installations About the Holocaust," 258.
[75] Hippler, "Der Ewige Jude."
[76] Shlomo Venezia, *Inside the Gas Chambers: Eight Months in the Sonderkommando of Auschwitz* (Malden, Massachusetts: Polity, 2009), 161.
[77] Gordon, *Hitler, Germans, and the "Jewish Question"*: 16-7.
[78] Marion A Kaplan, *Between Dignity and Despair: Jewish Life in Nazi Germany* (New York: Oxford University Press, 1998), 79.
[79] Rudolf Höss, *Death Dealer: The Memoirs of the SS Kommandant of Auschwitz*, ed. Steven Paskuly (New York: Da Capo Press, 1996), 269-70.
[80] Kaplan, *Between Dignity and Despair: Jewish Life in Nazi Germany*: 77.
[81] Richard J Evans, *The Third Reich in Power* (USA: Penguin Books, 2006), 551; Glass, *Life Unworthy of Life: Racial Phobia and Mass Murder in Hitler's Germany*: 51-2.
[82] Deborah Dwork and Robert Jan van Pelt, *Holocaust: A History* (New York: W.W. Norton and Company, 2003), 42-3; Hilberg, *The Destruction of the European Jews*: 47.
[83] Edwin Black, *IBM and the Holocaust* (New York: Three Rivers Press, 2001), 155.
[84] Evans, *The Third Reich in Power*: 551; Gordon, *Hitler, Germans, and the "Jewish Question"*: 179.

[85] Amesberger and Halbmayr, "Nazi Differentiations Mattered: Ideological Intersections of Sexualized Violence During National Socialist Persecution," 192.

[86] Glass, *Life Unworthy of Life: Racial Phobia and Mass Murder in Hitler's Germany*: 51-2.

[87] Szobar, "Telling Sexual Stories in the Nazi Courts of Law: Race Defilement in Germany, 1933-1945," 155-62.

[88] Ibid., 158.

[89] Hilberg, *The Destruction of the European Jews*: 45.

[90] Gordon, *Hitler, Germans, and the "Jewish Question"*: 172.

[91] Hilberg, *The Destruction of the European Jews*: 42-3; Glass, *Life Unworthy of Life: Racial Phobia and Mass Murder in Hitler's Germany*: 51-2; Kaplan, *Between Dignity and Despair: Jewish Life in Nazi Germany*: 80.

[92] Hilberg, *The Destruction of the European Jews*: 42-3; Kaplan, *Between Dignity and Despair: Jewish Life in Nazi Germany*: 80.

[93] Gabriele Herz, *The Women's Camp in Moringen: A Memoir of Imprisonment in Germany, 1936-1937* (New York: Berghahn Books, 2006), 160, footnote 25

[94] Ibid., 120.

[95] Lynn H. Nicholas, *Cruel World: The Children of Europe in the Nazi Web* (New York: Vintage Books, 2006), 56.

[96] Gerald L Posner and John Ware, *Mengele: The Complete Story* (New York: Cooper Square Press, 2000), 15.

[97] Gordon, *Hitler, Germans, and the "Jewish Question"*: 102-4.

[98] Ibid., 122.

[99] Kaplan, *Between Dignity and Despair: Jewish Life in Nazi Germany*: 61.

[100] Balys Sruoga, *Forest of the Gods* (Lithuania: Versus Aureus, 2005), 258-9.

[101] Arad, *Belzec, Sobibor, Treblinka: The Operation Reinhard Death Camps*: 117.

[102] Höss, *Death Dealer: The Memoirs of the SS Kommandant of Auschwitz*: 119,310.

[103] Gisella Perl, *I was a Doctor in Auschwitz*, Reprint edition 2007 ed. (North Stratford, NH: Ayer Company Publishers, 1948), 74.

[104] Lore Shelly, *Twenty Women Prisoner's Accounts* (San Francisco: Mellen Research University Press, 1991), 88.

[105] Tova Berger, " " in *Massuah Institute for the Study of the Holocaust, Tel Aviv, VT-2007* 7.

[106] Joshua Rubenstein and Ilya Altman, eds., *The Unknown Black Book: The holocaust in the German-Occupied Soviet Territories* (Bloomington: Indiana University Press, 2010), 70.

[107] Glass, *Life Unworthy of Life: Racial Phobia and Mass Murder in Hitler's Germany*: 60,156.

[108] Ibid.

[109] John Cornwell, *Hitler's Scientists: Science, War and the Devil's Pact* (New York: Viking, 2003), 350.

[110] Evans, *The Third Reich in Power*: 510.

[111] Hartmut M Hanauske-Abel, "Not a Slippery Slope or Sudden Subversion: German Medicine and National Socialism in 1933," *BMJ: British Medical Journal* 313, no. 7070 (1996): 1461.

[112] Richard J Evans, *The Coming of the Third Reich* (USA: Penguin Books, 2005), 37-8.

[113] Burleigh and Wipperman, *The Racial State: Germany 1933-1945*: 39-40.

[114] Glass, *Life Unworthy of Life: Racial Phobia and Mass Murder in Hitler's Germany*: 41.

[115] Burleigh and Wipperman, *The Racial State: Germany 1933-1945*: 99; Cornwell, *Hitler's Scientists: Science, War and the Devil's Pact*: 3448.

[116] Lisa Pine, *Nazi Family Policy 1933-1945* (Oxford: Berg, 1997), 69.

[117] Elie Cohen, *Human Behaviour in the Concentration Camp* (London: Free Association Books, 1988), 244.

[118] Sheila Faith Weiss, "German Eugenics, 1890-1933," in *Deadly Medicine: Creating the Master Race*, ed. Dieter Kuntz (Washington: United States Holocaust Memorial Museum, 2008), 24.

[119] Richard Grunberger, *A Social History of the Third Reich* (Harmondsworth, UK: Penguin Books, 1974), 303-4; ibid; Anna Maria Sigmund, *Women of the Third Reich* (Richmond Hill, Ontario, Canada: NDE Publishing, 2000), 13.

[120] Dagmar Hájková and Hana Housková, "The Stations of the Cross," in *Medicine, Ethics and the Third Reich* ed. John J Michalczyk (Kansas City: Sheed and Wade, 1984), 130-31.

[121] Burleigh and Wipperman, *The Racial State: Germany 1933-1945*: 136-7.

[122] Gisela Bock, "Nazi Sterilization and Reproductive Policies," in *Deadly Medicine: Creating the Master Race*, ed. Dieter Kuntz (Washington: United States Holocaust Memorial Museum, 2008), 62; Burleigh and Wipperman, *The Racial State: Germany 1933-1945*: 136-7; Evans, *The Third Reich in Power*: 507-9.

[123] Ian Kershaw, *Hitler: Profiles in Power*, ed. Keith Robbins (London: Longman, 1991), 103.

[124] Proctor, "Racial Hygiene: The Collaboration of Medicine and Nazism," 37.

[125] Ibid.

[126] Mazower, *Dark Continent: Europe's Twentieth Century*: 97.

[127] Burleigh and Wipperman, *The Racial State: Germany 1933-1945*: 136; Evans, *The Third Reich in Power*: 507-9; Grunberger, *A Social History of the Third Reich*: 305.

[128] Burleigh and Wipperman, *The Racial State: Germany 1933-1945*: 252-4; Gisela Bock, "Racism and Sexism in Nazi Society: Motherhood, Compulsory Sterilization, and the State.," in *Different Voices: Women and the Holocaust*, ed. Carol Rittner and John K. Roth (New York: Paragon House, 1993), 170-75; ———, "Racism and Sexism in Nazi Germany" in *When Biology Becomes Destiny* ed. Renate Bridenthal, Atina Grossman, and Marion Kaplan (New York: 1984), 280.

[129] ———, "Nazi Sterilization and Reproductive Policies," 68.

[130] Cornwell, *Hitler's Scientists: Science, War and the Devil's Pact*: 348.

[131] Burleigh and Wipperman, *The Racial State: Germany 1933-1945*: 49, 168.

[132] Michael Burleigh, "Nazi "Euthanasia" Programs," in *Deadly Medicine: Creating the Master Race*, ed. Dieter Kuntz (Washington: United States Holocaust Memorial Museum, 2008), 131.

[133] Bock, "Nazi Sterilization and Reproductive Policies," 78.

[134] ———, "Racism and Sexism in Nazi Germany" 275.

[135] Grunberger, *A Social History of the Third Reich*: 305.

[136] Bock, "Racism and Sexism in Nazi Society: Motherhood, Compulsory Sterilization, and the State.," 170-5.

[137] Nicholas, *Cruel World: The Children of Europe in the Nazi Web*: 16-17.

[138] Benjamin Sax and Dieter Kuntz, *Inside Hitler's Germany: A Documentary History of Life in the Third Reich* (Lexington, Massachusetts: D. C. Heath and Co., 1992), 212-4.

[139] Ibid.

[140] Bock, "Racism and Sexism in Nazi Society: Motherhood, Compulsory Sterilization, and the State.," 170-5.

[141] Tessa Chelouche, "Doctors, Pregnancy, Childbirth and Abortion during the Third Reich," *IMAJ* 9(2007): 203.

[142] Evans, *The Third Reich in Power*: 509.

[143] ———, *The Coming of the Third Reich*: 145; Kater, *Doctors Under Hitler*: 36.

[144] Bock, "Racism and Sexism in Nazi Society: Motherhood, Compulsory Sterilization, and the State.," 170; ———, "Racism and Sexism in Nazi Germany" 280.

[145] ———, "Nazi Sterilization and Reproductive Policies," 69-70.

[146] ———, "Racism and Sexism in Nazi Society: Motherhood, Compulsory Sterilization, and the State.," 170-5.

[147] Evans, *The Third Reich in Power*: 508.

[148] Henry David, Jochen Fleischhacker, and Charlotte Hohn, "Abortion and Eugenics in Nazi Germany" *Population and Development Review* 14 no. 1 (March 1998): 91.

[149] Hanauske-Abel, "Not a Slippery Slope or Sudden Subversion: German Medicine and National Socialism in 1933," 1457.

[150] Bock, "Nazi Sterilization and Reproductive Policies," 69-70.

[151] Hanauske-Abel, "Not a Slippery Slope or Sudden Subversion: German Medicine and National Socialism in 1933," 1457.

[152] Ibid., 1455-57.

[153] Proctor, "Racial Hygiene: The Collaboration of Medicine and Nazism," 37; Bock, "Racism and Sexism in Nazi Society: Motherhood, Compulsory Sterilization, and the State.," 62; Friedländer, *The Years of Persecution: Nazi Germany and the Jews 1933-1939*: 40.

[154] Evans, *The Third Reich in Power*: 508.

[155] Ibid.

[156] Bock, "Nazi Sterilization and Reproductive Policies," 79.

[157] Koonz, *Mothers in the Fatherland: Women, the Family and Nazi Politics*: 257-86.

[158] Leo Alexander, "Public Mental Health Practices in Germany: Sterilization and execution of patients suffering from nervous and mental disease. Combined Intelligence Objectives Sub-Committee, Item no 24, File no XXVIII-50, Copy 41," (London: IWM, 19 August 1945), 6.

[159] Koonz, *Mothers in the Fatherland: Women, the Family and Nazi Politics*: 257-86.

[160] Kater, *Doctors Under Hitler*: 146.

[161] Evans, *The Third Reich at War*: 82.

[162] Ibid.

[163] Ibid; Donald Dietrich, "Nazi Eugenics: Adaptation and Resistance Among German Catholic Intellectual Leaders," in *Medicine, Ethics and the Third Reich: Historical and Contemporary Issues* ed. John J Michalczyk (Kansas City: Sheed and Ward, 1994), 50; Friedländer, *The Years of Persecution: Nazi Germany and the Jews 1933-1939*: 39.

[164] Proctor, "Racial Hygiene: The Collaboration of Medicine and Nazism," 38.

[165] Glass, *Life Unworthy of Life: Racial Phobia and Mass Murder in Hitler's Germany*: 34.

[166] Dan Bar-On, *Legacy of Silence: Encounters with Children of the Third Reich* (Cambridge Massachusetts: Harvard University Press, 1989), 80.

[167] Cornwell, *Hitler's Scientists: Science, War and the Devil's Pact*: 88; Evans, *The Coming of the Third Reich*: 145; Daniel Nadav, "Sterilization, "Euthanasia", and the Holocaust - The Brutal Chain," in *Medicine, Ethics and the Third Reich: Historical and Contemporary Issues*, ed. John J Michalczyk (Kansas City: Sheed and Ward, 1994), 45; K Binding and A E Hoche, "Die Freigabe der Vernichtung lebensunwerten lebens. Ihr Maß und ihre Form.," (Leipzig1920).

[168] Cornwell, *Hitler's Scientists: Science, War and the Devil's Pact*: 88; Evans, *The Coming of the Third Reich*: 145.

[169] Hilberg, *The Destruction of the European Jews*: 225.

[170] Frank Chalk and Kurt Jonassohn, *The History and Sociology of Genocide* (New Haven: Yale University Press, 1990), 355.

[171] Susan Benedict, "Caring While Killing: Nursing in the "Euthanasia" Centers," in *Experience and Expression: Women, the Nazis, and the Holocaust*, ed. Elizabeth R Baer and Myrna Goldenberg (Detroit: Wayne State University Press, 2001), 96; John J Michalczyk, *Medicine, Ethics, and the Third Reich: Historical and Contemporary Issues* (Kansas City: Sheed and Ward, 1994), 64.

[172] ———, *Medicine, Ethics, and the Third Reich: Historical and Contemporary Issues*: 64; ibid.

[173] Chalk and Jonassohn, *The History and Sociology of Genocide* 355.

[174] Friedländer, *The Years of Persecution: Nazi Germany and the Jews 1933-1939*: 209.

[175] Evans, *The Third Reich at War*: 78; Lifton, *The Nazi Doctors: Medical Killing and the Psychology of Genocide*: 51-.

[176] Alexander Mitscherlich and Fred Mielke, *Doctors of Infamy: The Story of the Nazi Medical Crimes* (New York: Henry Schuman Inc, 1949), 91; Cornwell,

Hitler's Scientists: Science, War and the Devil's Pact: 348; Evans, *The Third Reich at War*: 78.

[177] Burleigh, "Nazi "Euthanasia" Programs," 133.

[178] Sax and Kuntz, *Inside Hitler's Germany: A Documentary History of Life in the Third Reich*: 214-7.

[179] Burleigh, "Nazi "Euthanasia" Programs," 133.

[180] Gerhard L Weinberg, "Two Separate Issues? Historiography of World War II and the Holocaust," in *Holocaust Historiography in Context: Emergence, Challenges, Polemics and Achievements.*, ed. David Bankier and Dan Michman (Jerusalem: Yad Vashem-Berghahn Books, 2008), 383.

[181] Henry Freidlander, "From "Euthanasia" to the "Final Solution"," in *Deadly Medicine*, ed. Dieter Kuntz (Washington: United States Holocaust Memorial Museum, 2008), 163.

[182] Burleigh, "Nazi "Euthanasia" Programs," 133-34; Lifton, *The Nazi Doctors: Medical Killing and the Psychology of Genocide*: 52.

[183] Alexander, "Public Mental Health Practices in Germany: Sterilization and execution of patients suffering from nervous and mental disease. Combined Intelligence Objectives Sub-Committee, Item no 24, File no XXVIII-50, Copy 41," 15, Appendix 3, No 1, page 83.

[184] Hilberg, *The Destruction of the European Jews*: 226; Nicholas, *Cruel World: The Children of Europe in the Nazi Web*: 52.

[185] Hilberg, *The Destruction of the European Jews*: 226; Alexander, "Public Mental Health Practices in Germany: Sterilization and execution of patients suffering from nervous and mental disease. Combined Intelligence Objectives Sub-Committee, Item no 24, File no XXVIII-50, Copy 41," 10.

[186] Lifton, *The Nazi Doctors: Medical Killing and the Psychology of Genocide*: 51.

[187] Evans, *The Third Reich at War*.

[188] Nicholas, *Cruel World: The Children of Europe in the Nazi Web*: 52.

[189] Lifton, *The Nazi Doctors: Medical Killing and the Psychology of Genocide*: 51.

[190] Freidlander, "From "Euthanasia" to the "Final Solution"," 163.

[191] Cornwell, *Hitler's Scientists: Science, War and the Devil's Pact*: 349; Lifton, *The Nazi Doctors: Medical Killing and the Psychology of Genocide*: 51.

[192] Posner and Ware, *Mengele: The Complete Story*: xv.

[193] Vivien Spitz, *Doctors From Hell: The Horrific Accounts of Nazi Experiments on Humans* (Boulder: Sentient Publications, 2005), 236; Nadav, "Sterilization, "Euthanasia", and the Holocaust - The Brutal Chain," 42-43; Yahil, *The Holocaust: The Fate of European Jewry*: 308; Bar-On, *Legacy of Silence: Encounters with Children of the Third Reich*: 80.

[194] Freidlander, "From "Euthanasia" to the "Final Solution"," 164.

[195] Lucy Dawidowicz, *The War Against the Jews 1933-1945* (New York: Bantam Books, 1975), 178.

[196] Mitscherlich and Mielke, *Doctors of Infamy: The Story of the Nazi Medical Crimes*: 92.

[197] Cohen, *Human Behaviour in the Concentration Camp*: 107; ibid.

[198] Dawidowicz, *The War Against the Jews 1933-1945*: 178.

[199] Hilberg, *The Destruction of the European Jews*: 226.

[200] Evans, *The Third Reich at War*: 524-50.

[201] Lifton, *The Nazi Doctors: Medical Killing and the Psychology of Genocide*: 77.

[202] Evans, *The Third Reich at War*: 84-5; Nicholas, *Cruel World: The Children of Europe in the Nazi Web*: 52.

[203] Michalczyk, *Medicine, Ethics, and the Third Reich: Historical and Contemporary Issues*.

[204] Chalk and Jonassohn, *The History and Sociology of Genocide* 534.

[205] Lifton, *The Nazi Doctors: Medical Killing and the Psychology of Genocide*: 51.

[206] Chalk and Jonassohn, *The History and Sociology of Genocide* 534.

[207] Benedict, "Caring While Killing: Nursing in the "Euthanasia" Centers," 97.

[208] Evans, *The Third Reich at War*: 80; Lifton, *The Nazi Doctors: Medical Killing and the Psychology of Genocide*: 51.

[209] Mitscherlich and Mielke, *Doctors of Infamy: The Story of the Nazi Medical Crimes*: 100; USA Government, *Nuremberg Medical Case, vol 1, pp 695.* (Washington.: U S Government Printing Office,), 800.

[210] Evans, *The Third Reich at War*: 84-5.

[211] Burleigh, "Nazi "Euthanasia" Programs," 139.

[212] Evans, *The Third Reich at War.*

[213] Glass, *Life Unworthy of Life: Racial Phobia and Mass Murder in Hitler's Germany*: 9.

[214] Burleigh, "Nazi "Euthanasia" Programs," 136-39.

[215] Nicholas, *Cruel World: The Children of Europe in the Nazi Web*: 43.

[216] Benedict, "Caring While Killing: Nursing in the "Euthanasia" Centers," 97.

[217] Arad, *Belzec, Sobibor, Treblinka: The Operation Reinhard Death Camps*: 9; ibid; ibid; Glass, *Life Unworthy of Life: Racial Phobia and Mass Murder in Hitler's Germany*: 61; ibid; ibid; ibid; ibid; Lifton, *The Nazi Doctors: Medical Killing and the Psychology of Genocide*: 100.

[218] Glass, *Life Unworthy of Life: Racial Phobia and Mass Murder in Hitler's Germany*: 61.

[219] Alexander, "Public Mental Health Practices in Germany: Sterilization and execution of patients suffering from nervous and mental disease. Combined Intelligence Objectives Sub-Committee, Item no 24, File no XXVIII-50. Copy 41," 15.

[220] Benedict, "Caring While Killing: Nursing in the "Euthanasia" Centers," 97.

[221] Gordon J Horowitz, *In the Shadow of Death: Living Outside the Gates of Mauthausen* (New York: The Free Press, 1990), 69.

[222] Mitscherlich and Mielke, *Doctors of Infamy: The Story of the Nazi Medical Crimes*: 104; Klemperer, *I Shall Bear Witness: The Diaries of Victor Klemperer 1933-1941.*: 369.

[223] Burleigh, "Nazi "Euthanasia" Programs," 148.

[224] Weinberg, "Two Separate Issues? Historiography of World War II and the Holocaust," 392.

[225] Alan Adelson and Robert Lapides, eds., *Łódź Ghetto: Inside a Community Under Siege* (New York: Viking, 1989), 156.

[226] Cohen, *Human Behaviour in the Concentration Camp*: 15.

[227] Evans, *The Third Reich at War*: 528; Freidlander, "From "Euthanasia" to the "Final Solution"," 177.

[228] Glass, *Life Unworthy of Life: Racial Phobia and Mass Murder in Hitler's Germany*: 158-60; Nicholas, *Cruel World: The Children of Europe in the Nazi Web*: 52.

[229] Chalk and Jonassohn, *The History and Sociology of Genocide* 534-.

[230] Glass, *Life Unworthy of Life: Racial Phobia and Mass Murder in Hitler's Germany*: 62.

[231] Chalk and Jonassohn, *The History and Sociology of Genocide* 534-; Evans, *The Third Reich at War*: 95-98.

[232] ———, *The Third Reich at War*: 95-98.

[233] Ibid.

[234] Lifton, *The Nazi Doctors: Medical Killing and the Psychology of Genocide*: 95-97; Chalk and Jonassohn, *The History and Sociology of Genocide* 534-; Burleigh, "Nazi "Euthanasia" Programs," 150; Grunberger, *A Social History of the Third Reich*: 568.

[235] Yahil, *The Holocaust: The Fate of European Jewry*: 309; ibid; Chalk and Jonassohn, *The History and Sociology of Genocide* 534; Lifton, *The Nazi Doctors: Medical Killing and the Psychology of Genocide*: 95-97; Proctor, "Racial Hygiene: The Collaboration of Medicine and Nazism," 38.

[236] Lifton, *The Nazi Doctors: Medical Killing and the Psychology of Genocide*: 95-97.

[237] Alexander, "Public Mental Health Practices in Germany: Sterilization and execution of patients suffering from nervous and mental disease. Combined Intelligence Objectives Sub-Committee, Item no 24, File no XXVIII-50. Copy 41," 33-34.

[238] Lifton, *The Nazi Doctors: Medical Killing and the Psychology of Genocide*: 95-97.

[239] Arad, *Belzec, Sobibor, Treblinka: The Operation Reinhard Death Camps*: 9; Glass, *Life Unworthy of Life: Racial Phobia and Mass Murder in Hitler's Germany*: 62.

[240] Lifton, *The Nazi Doctors: Medical Killing and the Psychology of Genocide*: 95-97; Benedict, "Caring While Killing: Nursing in the "Euthanasia" Centers," 97.
[241] Alexander, "Public Mental Health Practices in Germany: Sterilization and execution of patients suffering from nervous and mental disease. Combined Intelligence Objectives Sub-Committee, Item no 24, File no XXVIII-50. Copy 41," 33-34.
[242] Evans, *The Third Reich at War*.
[243] Hilberg, *The Destruction of the European Jews*: 226.
[244] Evans, *The Third Reich at War*: 524-50.
[245] Cornwell, *Hitler's Scientists: Science, War and the Devil's Pact*: 350.
[246] Burleigh, "Nazi "Euthanasia" Programs," 150.
[247] Ibid; Lifton, *The Nazi Doctors: Medical Killing and the Psychology of Genocide*: 142.
[248] David Hogan and David Aretha, eds., *The Holocaust Chronicle* (Illinois: Publications International, 2001), 692.
[249] Sax and Kuntz, *Inside Hitler's Germany: A Documentary History of Life in the Third Reich*: 214-17.
[250] Posner and Ware, *Mengele: The Complete Story*: xv; Vashem Yad, "The Implementation of the Final Solution: Auschwitz-Birkenau Extermination Camp," http://www1.yadvashem.org/yv/en/holocaust/about/05/auschwitz_birkenau.asp.
[251] Burleigh, "Nazi "Euthanasia" Programs," 151.
[252] Freidlander, "From "Euthanasia" to the "Final Solution"," 184.
[253] Nadav, "Sterilization, "Euthanasia", and the Holocaust - The Brutal Chain," 49.
[254] Burleigh, "Nazi "Euthanasia" Programs," 151.
[255] Chalk and Jonassohn, *The History and Sociology of Genocide* 356.
[256] David Bankier and Dan Michman, *Holocaust Historiography in Context: Emergence, Challenges, Polemics and Achievements* (Jerusalem: Yad Vashem and Berghahn Books, 2008), 330-1.
[257] Ibid., 337.
[258] Raul Hilberg, *The Politics of Memory: The Journey of a Holocaust Historian* (Chicago: Ivan R Dee, 1996), 63-80.
[259] Glass, *Life Unworthy of Life: Racial Phobia and Mass Murder in Hitler's Germany*: 33.
[260] Marc Hillel and Clarissa Henry, *Of Pure Blood* (New York: Pocket Books, 1975), 27.
[261] Ibid., 28.
[262] Evans, *The Third Reich in Power*: 516-17; Paul Weindling, "The 'Sonderweg' of German Eugenics: Nationalism and Scientific Internationalism," *The British Journal for the History of Science* 22, no. 3 (1989): 327.
[263] Evans, *The Third Reich in Power*: 516-17.
[264] Grunberger, *A Social History of the Third Reich*: 322.
[265] Weindling, "The 'Sonderweg' of German Eugenics: Nationalism and Scientific Internationalism," 328.
[266] Evans, *The Third Reich in Power*: 516-17.
[267] Charu Gupta, "Politics of Gender: Women in Nazi Germany," *Economic and Political Weekly* 26, no. 17 (April 27 1991): WS-40.
[268] Leila J Rupp, "Mother of the 'Volk': The Image of Women in the Nazi Ideology" *Signs* 3, no. 2 (1977): 363-4.
[269] Bock, "Racism and Sexism in Nazi Germany" 285.
[270] Gupta, "Politics of Gender: Women in Nazi Germany," WS-42; Rupp, "Mother of the 'Volk': The Image of Women in the Nazi Ideology" 371.
[271] Gupta, "Politics of Gender: Women in Nazi Germany," Ws-44; Myrna Goldenberg, "Lessons Learned from Gentle Heroism: Women's Holocaust Narratives," *Annals of the American Academy of Political and Social Sciences* 548(1996): 80.
[272] Rupp, "Mother of the 'Volk': The Image of Women in the Nazi Ideology" 377.
[273] Pine, *Nazi Family Policy 1933-1945*: 64.
[274] Ibid., 69.

[275] Evans, *The Third Reich in Power*: 332; George Mosse, *Nazi Culture: Intellectual, Cultural and Social Life in the Third Reich* (London1966), 41; Sigmund, *Women of the Third Reich*: 12.

[276] John H. Waller, *The Devil's Doctor: Felix Kersten and the Secret Plot to Turn Himmler Against Hitler* (New York: John Wiley and Sons, 2002), 124.

[277] Grunberger, *A Social History of the Third Reich*: 333.

[278] Waller, *The Devil's Doctor: Felix Kersten and the Secret Plot to Turn Himmler Against Hitler*: 124.

[279] Stephen H Norwood, *the Third Reich in the Ivory Tower: Complicity and Conflict on American Campuses* (Cambridge: Cambridge University Press, 2009), 115.

[280] Ibid.

[281] Rupp, "Mother of the 'Volk': The Image of Women in the Nazi Ideology" 371.

[282] Evans, *The Third Reich in Power*: 516-17; Gupta, "Politics of Gender: Women in Nazi Germany," WS-41; Claudia Koonz, "The Competition for a Women's Lebensraum 1928-1934," in *When Biology Becomes Destiny: Women in Weimar and Nazi Germany*, ed. Renate Bridenthal, Atina Grossmann, and Marion Kaplan (New York: Monthly Review Press, 1984), 199.

[283] Hitler, *Mein Kampf*: 144.

[284] Grunberger, *A Social History of the Third Reich*: 322.

[285] Ibid; Sigmund, *Women of the Third Reich*: 9.

[286] Burleigh and Wipperman, *The Racial State: Germany 1933-1945*: 249; Koonz, "The Competition for a Women's Lebensraum 1928-1934," 199.

[287] ———, *Mothers in the Fatherland: Women, the Family and Nazi Politics*: 140-43, 66-67.

[288] Sigmund, *Women of the Third Reich*: 115.

[289] Koonz, *Mothers in the Fatherland: Women, the Family and Nazi Politics*: 140-43, 66-67; Burleigh and Wipperman, *The Racial State: Germany 1933-1945*: 249; Sigmund, *Women of the Third Reich*: 120.

[290] Pine, *Nazi Family Policy 1933-1945*: 56,78.

[291] Grunberger, *A Social History of the Third Reich*: 334.

[292] Koonz, *Mothers in the Fatherland: Women, the Family and Nazi Politics*: 189; Mazower, *Dark Continent: Europe's Twentieth Century*: 76; Bock, "Nazi Sterilization and Reproductive Policies," 72.

[293] Grunberger, *A Social History of the Third Reich*: 367.

[294] Burleigh and Wipperman, *The Racial State: Germany 1933-1945*: 249.

[295] Paul Roland, *Nazi Women: the Attraction of Evil* (London: Arcturus, 2014), 94-7.

[296] Mazower, *Dark Continent: Europe's Twentieth Century*: 83.

[297] Grunberger, *A Social History of the Third Reich*: 334.

[298] Hillel and Henry, *Of Pure Blood*: 30; Burleigh and Wipperman, *The Racial State: Germany 1933-1945*: 249.

[299] Sigmund, *Women of the Third Reich*: 84.

[300] Hans Peter Bleuel, *Sex and Society in Nazi Germany* (Philadelphia: J.B.Lipincott Company, 1971), 153.

[301] Koonz, *Mothers in the Fatherland: Women, the Family and Nazi Politics*: 185-86; Burleigh and Wipperman, *The Racial State: Germany 1933-1945*: 249.

[302] Koonz, *Mothers in the Fatherland: Women, the Family and Nazi Politics*: 185-86.

[303] Evans, *The Third Reich in Power*: 516-17; Rupp, "Mother of the 'Volk': The Image of Women in the Nazi Ideology" 370.

[304] Koonz, *Mothers in the Fatherland: Women, the Family and Nazi Politics*: 149, 77.

[305] Sigmund, *Women of the Third Reich*: 15.

[306] Ibid., 17.

[307] H Trevor-Roper, ed. *The Bormann Letters. The Private correspondence between Martin Bormann and his wife from January 1943 to April 1945* (London: 1954), 42ff.

[308] Koonz, *Mothers in the Fatherland: Women, the Family and Nazi Politics*: 177; Conrad Taeuber and Irene B Taeuber, "German Fertility Trends," *The American Journal of Sociology* 46, no. 2 (1940): 153.
[309] Bock, "Nazi Sterilization and Reproductive Policies," 82-85; Burleigh and Wipperman, *The Racial State: Germany 1933-1945*: 249; Nicholas, *Cruel World: The Children of Europe in the Nazi Web*: 57.
[310] Burleigh and Wipperman, *The Racial State: Germany 1933-1945*: 25-252; Renate Bridenthal, Atina Grossmann, and Marion Kaplan, eds., *When Biology Became Destiny: Women in Weimar and Nazi Germany* (New York: Monthly Review Press, 1984), 25.
[311] Burleigh and Wipperman, *The Racial State: Germany 1933-1945*: 150-252.
[312] Koonz, *Mothers in the Fatherland: Women, the Family and Nazi Politics*: 185-86; Burleigh and Wipperman, *The Racial State: Germany 1933-1945*: 249; Nicholas, *Cruel World: The Children of Europe in the Nazi Web*: 57.
[313] Koonz, *Mothers in the Fatherland: Women, the Family and Nazi Politics*: 149.
[314] Ibid., 185-86.
[315] Burleigh and Wipperman, *The Racial State: Germany 1933-1945*: 250-52.
[316] Grunberger, *A Social History of the Third Reich*: 324.
[317] Sax and Kuntz, *Inside Hitler's Germany: A Documentary History of Life in the Third Reich*: 381-82; Höss, *Death Dealer: The Memoirs of the SS Kommandant of Auschwitz*: 327-29.
[318] Evans, *The Third Reich in Power*: 518.
[319] Bock, "Racism and Sexism in Nazi Germany" 284-85.
[320] ———, "Racism and Sexism in Nazi Society: Motherhood, Compulsory Sterilization, and the State.," 405-06.
[321] Evans, *The Third Reich in Power*: 518.
[322] Nicholas, *Cruel World: The Children of Europe in the Nazi Web*: 58-61.
[323] Bock, "Nazi Sterilization and Reproductive Policies," 82-85; Mazower, *Dark Continent: Europe's Twentieth Century*: 86; Bock, "Racism and Sexism in Nazi Germany" 278.
[324] Pine, *Nazi Family Policy 1933-1945*: 105.
[325] Bock, "Racism and Sexism in Nazi Society: Motherhood, Compulsory Sterilization, and the State.," 410; ———, "Racism and Sexism in Nazi Germany" 278.
[326] Evans, *The Third Reich in Power*: 518; Mazower, *Dark Continent: Europe's Twentieth Century*: 86; Taeuber and Taeuber, "German Fertility Trends," 163.
[327] ———, "German Fertility Trends," 160-63.
[328] Chelouche, "Doctors, Pregnancy, Childbirth and Abortion during the Third Reich," 203.
[329] Grunberger, *A Social History of the Third Reich*: 305.
[330] Gupta, "Politics of Gender: Women in Nazi Germany," WS-41; Chelouche, "Doctors, Pregnancy, Childbirth and Abortion during the Third Reich," 203.
[331] Bock, "Racism and Sexism in Nazi Germany" 276; David, Fleischhacker, and Hohn, "Abortion and Eugenics in Nazi Germany" 93-94; Nicholas, *Cruel World: The Children of Europe in the Nazi Web*: 57.
[332] David, Fleischhacker, and Hohn, "Abortion and Eugenics in Nazi Germany" 93-94.
[333] Ibid.
[334] Grunberger, *A Social History of the Third Reich*: 305 Footnote.
[335] Koonz, *Mothers in the Fatherland: Women, the Family and Nazi Politics*: 185-86.
[336] David, Fleischhacker, and Hohn, "Abortion and Eugenics in Nazi Germany" 95.
[337] Bock, "Racism and Sexism in Nazi Germany " 276.
[338] ———, "Racism and Sexism in Nazi Society: Motherhood, Compulsory Sterilization, and the State.."; David, Fleischhacker, and Hohn, "Abortion and Eugenics in Nazi Germany" 95.
[339] Chelouche, "Doctors, Pregnancy, Childbirth and Abortion during the Third Reich," 203; L Poliakov, *Harvest of Hate.* (Syracuse, New York1954), 272-4.
[340] Bock, "Racism and Sexism in Nazi Germany" 283.
[341] Ibid., 277; Grunberger, *A Social History of the Third Reich*: 420.

[342] Bock, "Racism and Sexism in Nazi Germany" 277.
[343] David, Fleischhacker, and Hohn, "Abortion and Eugenics in Nazi Germany" 97-98.
[344] Grunberger, *A Social History of the Third Reich*: 464.
[345] Ibid., 312.
[346] Koonz, *Mothers in the Fatherland: Women, the Family and Nazi Politics*: 192.
[347] Ibid., 189; Burleigh and Wipperman, *The Racial State: Germany 1933-1945*: 252-54.
[348] Grunberger, *A Social History of the Third Reich*: 312.
[349] Hillel and Henry, *Of Pure Blood*: 33.
[350] Grunberger, *A Social History of the Third Reich*: 309.
[351] Evans, *The Third Reich in Power*: 518.
[352] Mazower, *Dark Continent: Europe's Twentieth Century*: 86.
[353] Evans, *The Third Reich at War*: 543; Jeremy Noakes, *Nazism 1919-1945, IV: The German Home Front in World War II: A Documentary Reader* (Exeter1998), 374.
[354] Evans, *The Third Reich at War*: 543; Noakes, *Nazism 1919-1945, IV: The German Home Front in World War II: A Documentary Reader* 374-84.
[355] Grunberger, *A Social History of the Third Reich*: 306.
[356] Bleuel, *Sex and Society in Nazi Germany*: 157.
[357] Ibid.
[358] Lifton, *The Nazi Doctors: Medical Killing and the Psychology of Genocide*: 43; Bock, "Nazi Sterilization and Reproductive Policies," 86.
[359] Larry V Thompson, "Lebensborn and the Eugenics Policy of the Reichsführer - SS," *Central European History* 4, no. 1 (1971): 56-57.
[360] Steigman-Gall, *The Holy Reich: Nazi Conceptions of Christianity, 1919-1945*: 233; Grunberger, *A Social History of the Third Reich*: 446.
[361] Thompson, "Lebensborn and the Eugenics Policy of the Reichsführer - SS," 57.
[362] Sax and Kuntz, *Inside Hitler's Germany: A Documentary History of Life in the Third Reich*: 381-82.
[363] Thompson, "Lebensborn and the Eugenics Policy of the Reichsführer - SS," 61.
[364] Sax and Kuntz, *Inside Hitler's Germany: A Documentary History of Life in the Third Reich*: 381-82; Grunberger, *A Social History of the Third Reich*: 314.
[365] Bock, "Racism and Sexism in Nazi Society: Motherhood, Compulsory Sterilization, and the State.," 86; Carol Rittner and John Roth, eds., *Different Voices: Women and the Holocaust* (New York: Paragon House, 1993), 8-9; Nicholas, *Cruel World: The Children of Europe in the Nazi Web*: 60-65; Evans, *The Third Reich in Power*: 521.
[366] Grunberger, *A Social History of the Third Reich*: 314.
[367] Thompson, "Lebensborn and the Eugenics Policy of the Reichsführer - SS," 54.
[368] Bernt Engelmann, *In Hitler's Germany: Everyday Life in the Third Reich* (New York: Pantheon Books, 1986), 195-97.
[369] Hillel and Henry, *Of Pure Blood*: 34, 88.
[370] Nicholas, *Cruel World: The Children of Europe in the Nazi Web*: 60-65.
[371] Engelmann, *In Hitler's Germany: Everyday Life in the Third Reich*: 195-97.
[372] Ibid.
[373] Burleigh and Wipperman, *The Racial State: Germany 1933-1945*: 65-66.
[374] Höss, *Death Dealer: The Memoirs of the SS Kommandant of Auschwitz*: 327-29.
[375] Nicholas, *Cruel World: The Children of Europe in the Nazi Web*: 60-65.
[376] Bar-On, *Legacy of Silence: Encounters with Children of the Third Reich*: 285.
[377] Pine, *Nazi Family Policy 1933-1945*: 39-42.
[378] Bleuel, *Sex and Society in Nazi Germany*: 162.
[379] Engelmann, *In Hitler's Germany: Everyday Life in the Third Reich*: 196; Nicholas, *Cruel World: The Children of Europe in the Nazi Web*: 60-65.
[380] Engelmann, *In Hitler's Germany: Everyday Life in the Third Reich*: 197-99.
[381] Höss, *Death Dealer: The Memoirs of the SS Kommandant of Auschwitz*: 327-29.
[382] Engelmann, *In Hitler's Germany: Everyday Life in the Third Reich*: 201.
[383] Thompson, "Lebensborn and the Eugenics Policy of the Reichsführer - SS," 59-60.

[384] Engelmann, *In Hitler's Germany: Everyday Life in the Third Reich*: 200-01.
[385] Bleuel, *Sex and Society in Nazi Germany*: 162.
[386] Thompson, "Lebensborn and the Eugenics Policy of the Reichsführer - SS," 73.
[387] Engelmann, *In Hitler's Germany: Everyday Life in the Third Reich*: 195-97.
[388] Alfons Heck, *A Child of Hitler* (New York: Bantam Books 1986), 153.
[389] Hillel and Henry, *Of Pure Blood*: 34.
[390] Bleuel, *Sex and Society in Nazi Germany*: 154-5, 67-72.
[391] Ibid., 172.
[392] Waller, *The Devil's Doctor: Felix Kersten and the Secret Plot to Turn Himmler Against Hitler*: 124-25.
[393] Hillel and Henry, *Of Pure Blood*: 74-84; Gupta, "Politics of Gender: Women in Nazi Germany," WS-41; Guido Knopp, *Hitler's Children* (Phoenix Mill, Gloucestershire: Sutton Publishing Limited, 2002), 111.
[394] Grunberger, *A Social History of the Third Reich*: 315-17; Sigmund, *Women of the Third Reich*: 18.
[395] Heck, *A Child of Hitler*: 75,97.
[396] Sigmund, *Women of the Third Reich*: 19.
[397] Grunberger, *A Social History of the Third Reich*: 315-17.
[398] Ibid., 315.
[399] Ibid., 315-17.
[400] Höss, *Death Dealer: The Memoirs of the SS Kommandant of Auschwitz*: 327-29.
[401] Ibid.
[402] Chalk and Jonassohn, *The History and Sociology of Genocide* 356.
[403] Grunberger, *A Social History of the Third Reich*: 318.
[404] Bleuel, *Sex and Society in Nazi Germany*: 166.
[405] Sigmund, *Women of the Third Reich*: 19.
[406] Frank Capra, "Prelude to War," in *Why We Fight Series* (USA: Platinum, 1942).
[407] Burleigh and Wipperman, *The Racial State: Germany 1933-1945*: 65-66.
[408] Johannes Steinhoff, Peter Pechel, and Dennis Showalter, *Voices From the Third Reich: An Oral History* (Washington: Da Capo Press, 1989), 465.
[409] Engelmann, *In Hitler's Germany: Everyday Life in the Third Reich*: 193.
[410] Bleuel, *Sex and Society in Nazi Germany*: 161.
[411] Thompson, "Lebensborn and the Eugenics Policy of the Reichsführer - SS," 68-69; Richard Breitman, *The Architect of Genocide: Himmler and the Final Solution* (New York: Alfred A Knopf, 1991), 108-09.
[412] Thompson, "Lebensborn and the Eugenics Policy of the Reichsführer - SS," 76.
[413] Ibid., 61.
[414] Höss, *Death Dealer: The Memoirs of the SS Kommandant of Auschwitz*: 327-29.
[415] Hillel and Henry, *Of Pure Blood*: 88.
[416] Thompson, "Lebensborn and the Eugenics Policy of the Reichsführer - SS," 75.
[417] Ibid., 66; Bleuel, *Sex and Society in Nazi Germany*: 162.
[418] Koonz, *Mothers in the Fatherland: Women, the Family and Nazi Politics*: 470 Note 22.
[419] Bock, "Nazi Sterilization and Reproductive Policies," 86; ———, "Racism and Sexism in Nazi Society: Motherhood, Compulsory Sterilization, and the State.," 86.
[420] Thompson, "Lebensborn and the Eugenics Policy of the Reichsführer - SS," 66; Bleuel, *Sex and Society in Nazi Germany*: 162.
[421] Evans, *The Third Reich at War*: 546.
[422] Thompson, "Lebensborn and the Eugenics Policy of the Reichsführer - SS," 66; Bleuel, *Sex and Society in Nazi Germany*: 162.
[423] Grunberger, *A Social History of the Third Reich*: 310.
[424] Thompson, "Lebensborn and the Eugenics Policy of the Reichsführer - SS," 71-72.
[425] Nicholas, *Cruel World: The Children of Europe in the Nazi Web*: 274-75.

[426] Hillel and Henry, *Of Pure Blood*: 124; Bock, "Nazi Sterilization and Reproductive Policies," 86; Engelmann, *In Hitler's Germany: Everyday Life in the Third Reich*: 200; Bleuel, *Sex and Society in Nazi Germany*: 165.

[427] Hillel and Henry, *Of Pure Blood*: 146.

[428] Roland, *Nazi Women: the Attraction of Evil*: 111.

[429] Bock, "Nazi Sterilization and Reproductive Policies," 86; Thompson, "Lebensborn and the Eugenics Policy of the Reichsführer - SS," 73; Pine, *Nazi Family Policy 1933-1945*: 39-42; Burleigh and Wipperman, *The Racial State: Germany 1933-1945*: 65-66; Nicholas, *Cruel World: The Children of Europe in the Nazi Web*: 242.

[430] Hillel and Henry, *Of Pure Blood*: 152.

[431] Evans, *The Third Reich at War*: 31-32; Burleigh and Wipperman, *The Racial State: Germany 1933-1945*: 65-66, 71-73.

[432] Thompson, "Lebensborn and the Eugenics Policy of the Reichsführer - SS," 73; Burleigh and Wipperman, *The Racial State: Germany 1933-1945*: 65-66, 71-73.

[433] Thompson, "Lebensborn and the Eugenics Policy of the Reichsführer - SS," 73.

[434] Engelmann, *In Hitler's Germany: Everyday Life in the Third Reich*: 200; Nicholas, *Cruel World: The Children of Europe in the Nazi Web*: 242.

[435] Hillel and Henry, *Of Pure Blood*: 160; Mark Mazower, *Hitler's Empire: How the Nazis ruled Europe* (New York: Penguin Books, 2008), 216.

[436] Anton Gill, *The Journey Back From Hell: Conversations with Concentration Camp Survivors* (London: Grafton Books, 1988), 337.

[437] Evans, *The Third Reich at War*: 31-32; Burleigh and Wipperman, *The Racial State: Germany 1933-1945*: 65-66, 71-73.

[438] Bleuel, *Sex and Society in Nazi Germany*: 165-66.

[439] Edith Hahn Beer and Susan Dworkin, *The Nazi Officer's Wife: How One Jewish Woman Survived the Holocaust* (New York: Rob Weisbach Books, 1999), 271.

[440] Elizabeth Heineman, "Gender, Sexuality, and Coming to Terms with the Nazi Past," *Central European History* 38, no. 1 (2–5): 56-59.

[441] Atina Grossmann, "Feminist Debates about Women and National Socialism," *Gender and History* 3, no. 3 (1991): 253.

[442] Annemarie Troger, "Die Dolchstosslegende der Linken:" Frauen haben Hitler en die Macht gebracht", "in *Frau und Wissenschaft: Beitrage zur Berliner Sommeruniversitat fur Frauen*, ed. Gruppe Berliner Dozentinnen (Berlin: Courage Verlag, 1976); Grossmann, "Feminist Debates about Women and National Socialism," 353.

[443] ———, "Feminist Debates about Women and National Socialism," 352.

[444] Ibid., 355.

[445] Koonz, *Mothers in the Fatherland: Women, the Family and Nazi Politics*: 323-7.

[446] Ibid.

[447] Ibid.

[448] Kaplan, *Between Dignity and Despair: Jewish Life in Nazi Germany*: 76.

[449] Miriam Gillis-Carlebach, *Each Child is my Only One: Lotte Carlebach-Preuss, The Portrait of a Mother and Rabbi's wife* (New York: Peter Lang, 2014), 108.

[450] Kaplan, *Between Dignity and Despair: Jewish Life in Nazi Germany*: 141.

[451] Yahil, *The Holocaust: The Fate of European Jewry*: 198.

[452] Kaplan, *Between Dignity and Despair: Jewish Life in Nazi Germany*: 84-91.

[453] Ilse Koehn, *Mischling, Second Degree: My Childhood in Nazi Germany* (New York: Bantam Books, 1978), viiiff.

[454] Klemperer, *I Shall Bear Witness: The Diaries of Victor Klemperer 1933-1941*; ibid.

[455] Kaplan, *Between Dignity and Despair: Jewish Life in Nazi Germany*: 232.

[456] Michael Smith, *Foley: the Spy Who Saved 10,000 Jews* (London: Hodder and Stoughton, 1999), 147.

[457] Dawidowicz, *The War Against the Jews 1933-1945*: 280-1.

[458] Friedländer, *Nazi Germany and the Jews 1939-1945: The Years of Extermination*: 38.

[459] Dawidowicz, *The War Against the Jews 1933-1945*: 281.

[460] Ibid., 288.
[461] Raul Hilberg, Stanislaw Staron, and Josef Kermisz, *The Warsaw Diary of Adam Czerniakow: Prelude to Doom* (New York: Stein and Day, 1982), 300.
[462] Kazimierz Iranek-Osmecki, *He Who Saves One Life* (New York: Crown Publishers, 1971), 43-4.
[463] Mary Berg, *The Diary of Mary Berg* (Oxford: Oneworld, 1945, 2007), 109.
[464] Adibna Blady Szwajger, *I Remember Nothing More: The Warsaw Children's Hospital and Jewish Resistance* (New York: Simon and Schuster, 1988), 30.
[465] Roger Moorhouse, *Killing Hitler: The Plots, the Assassins, and the Dictator Who Cheated Death* (New York: Bantam Books, 2006), 122.
[466] Berg, *The Diary of Mary Berg*: xxiii.
[467] Yehudit Inbar, *Spots of Light: To Be a Woman in the Holocaust* (Jerusalem: Yad Vashem, 2007), 11.
[468] Lawrence Langer, "Gendered Suffering? Women in Holocaust Testimonies," in *Women in the Holocaust*, ed. Dalia Ofer and Lenore Weitzman (New Haven: Yale University Press, 1998), 354.
[469] Berg, *The Diary of Mary Berg*: 11.
[470] Kaplan, *Between Dignity and Despair: Jewish Life in Nazi Germany*: 164.
[471] Jonathan Friedman, "Togetherness and Isolation: Holocaust Survivor Memories of Intimacy and Sexuality in the Ghettos," *The Oral History Review* 28, no. 1 (2001): 4-5.
[472] Berg, *The Diary of Mary Berg*: 103.
[473] Ibid., 175.
[474] Ibid., 133.
[475] Dawidowicz, *The War Against the Jews 1933-1945*: 297.
[476] Berg, *The Diary of Mary Berg*: 185.
[477] Adelson and Lapides, *Łódź Ghetto: Inside a Community Under Siege*, 383.
[478] Berg, *The Diary of Mary Berg*: 185.
[479] Ibid., 190.
[480] Esther Katz and Joan Miriam Ringelheim, eds., *Proceedings of the Conference Women Surviving the Holocaust*, Occasional Papers (The Institute for Research in History, 1983), 54.
[481] Adelson and Lapides, *Łódź Ghetto: Inside a Community Under Siege*, 377.
[482] Ibid., 383.
[483] Vera Schiff, *Theresienstadt: The Town The Nazis Gave to The Jews* (Toronto: Lugus Publications, 1996), 81.
[484] Byron Dobell, "Had She Lived," *The Nation* October 8(2007): 19.
[485] Schiff, *Theresienstadt: The Town The Nazis Gave to The Jews*: 126.
[486] Ibid., 50.
[487] Ruth Bondy, "Women in Theresienstadt and the Family Camp in Birkenau," in *Women in the Holocaust*, ed. Dalia Ofer and Lenore J Weitzman (New Haven: Yale University Press, 1998), 320-21.
[488] Dawidowicz, *The War Against the Jews 1933-1945*: 297.
[489] Adelson and Lapides, *Łódź Ghetto: Inside a Community Under Siege*, 295.
[490] Ibid., 380.
[491] Dawidowicz, *The War Against the Jews 1933-1945*: 339.
[492] Kaplan, *Between Dignity and Despair: Jewish Life in Nazi Germany*: 165.
[493] Lucille Eichengreen and Harriet Hyman Chamberlain, *From Ashes to Life: My Memories of the Holocaust* (San Francisco: Mercury House, 1994), 66.
[494] Michal Unger, "The Status and Plight of Women in the Lodz Ghetto," in *Women in the Holocaust*, ed. Dalia Ofer and Lenore J Weitzman (New Haven: Yale University Press, 1998), 158.
[495] Ellen Ben-Sefer, "Forced Sterilization and Abortion as Sexual Abuse," in *Sexual Violence Against Jewish Women During the Holocaust*, ed. Sonja M Hedgepeth and Rochelle G Saidel (Waltham, Massachusetts: Brandeis University Press, 2010), 168.

[496] Galia Peled, "Pregnancy as Resistance in the Holocaust," (Jerusalem: Yad Vashem, 2005), 51.

[497] Filip Müller, *Eyewitness Auschwitz: Three Years in the Gas Chambers* (Chicago: Ivan R Dee, 1979), 143.

[498] Hilberg, Staron, and Kermisz, *The Warsaw Diary of Adam Czerniakow: Prelude to Doom*: 330.

[499] Leah Preiss, "Women's Health in the Ghettos of Eastern Europe. Jewish Women: A Comprehensive Historical Encyclopedia" *Jewish Women's Archive*(1 March 2009), http://jwa.org/encyclopedia/article/womens-health-in-ghettos-of-eastern-europe.

[500] Hogan and Aretha, *The Holocaust Chronicle*, 274.

[501] Ritvo and Plotkin, *Sisters in Sorrow: Voices of Care in the Holocaust*: 11.

[502] Hannah Arendt, *Eichmann in Jerusalem* (New York: The Viking Press, 1963), 244.

[503] Preiss, "Women's Health in the Ghettos of Eastern Europe. Jewish Women: A Comprehensive Historical Encyclopedia". 5/10.

[504] Yitzakh Arad, Israel Gutman, and Abraham Margoliot, *Documents on the Holocaust*, ed. Yitzakh Arad, Israel Gutman, and Abraham Margoliot (Lincoln, Nebraska, : University of Nebraska Press, 1999), 450-53.

[505] Lawrence Langer, *Versions of Survival: The Holocaust and the Human Spirit* (New York: State University of New York Press, 1982), 97.

[506] Arad, Gutman, and Margoliot, *Documents on the Holocaust*: 450-53; E Yerushalmi, *Pinkas Shavli (Records of Shavli)* (Jerusalem1958), 88.

[507] Raul Hilberg, "Two Thousand Years of Jewish Appeasement," in *The Holocaust: Problems in European Civilization*, ed. Donald L Niewyk (Boston, New York: Houghton, Mifflin Company, 1997), 112.

[508] John Bartlow Martin and S L Sheiderman, "The Mother Who Lived a Miracle," *McCall's* November 1957; Peled, "Pregnancy as Resistance in the Holocaust," 22-24.

[509] Avraham Tory, *Surviving the Holocaust: The Kovno Ghetto Diary* (Cambridge Massachusetts: Harvard University Press, 1990), 114.

[510] Ibid., 123.

[511] Aharon Peretz, "The Trial of Adolf Eichmann," The Nizkor Project, http://www.nizkor.org/hweb/people/e/eichmann-adolf/transcripts/Sessions/Session-028-04.html.

[512] Irving J. Rosenbaum, *The Holocaust and Halakhah* (USA: KTAV Publishing House, 1976), 40-41.

[513] Ibid., 41-42; Rachel Biale, *Women and Jewish Law: The Essential Texts, Their History, and Their Relevance for Today.* (New York: Schocken Books, 1984), 235.

[514] Rosenbaum, *The Holocaust and Halakhah*: 43-44.

[515] Peretz, "The Trial of Adolf Eichmann".

[516] Tory, *Surviving the Holocaust: The Kovno Ghetto Diary*: 132.

[517] Ibid., 372.

[518] Ibid., 395-9.

[519] Ibid., 229.

[520] Friedman, "Togetherness and Isolation: Holocaust Survivor Memories of Intimacy and Sexuality in the Ghettos," 8.

[521] Ibid., 9.

[522] Ritvo and Plotkin, *Sisters in Sorrow: Voices of Care in the Holocaust*: 12.

[523] Hermann Rauschning, "Testimony of Abrams Gerzovich Suzkever. Trail of the major war criminals before the International Military Tribunal.Nuremberg, November 14, 1945) October 1946. Vol 8. Proceedings February 20, 1946 - March 7 1946.," (Nuremberg1947), 312.

[524] Rubenstein and Altman, *The Unknown Black Book: The holocaust in the German-Occupied Soviet Territories*, 369.

[525] Jonathan Friedman, *Speaking the Unspeakable: Essays on Sexuality, Gender, and Holocaust Survivor Memory* (Lanham: University Press of America, 2002), 44.

[526] Nechama Tec, *Resilience and Courage: Women, Men and the Holocaust* (New Haven: Yale University Press, 2003), 68-9.

[527] Ibid.

[528] Laurel Holliday, *Children in the Holocaust and World War II: Their Secret Diaries* (New York: Pocket Books, 1995), 187-8.

[529] Ruth Schwertfeger, *Women of Theresienstadt: Voices from a Concentration Camp* (Oxford: Berg Publishers, 1989), 61.

[530] Schiff, *Theresienstadt: The Town The Nazis Gave to The Jews*: 48.

[531] Lyn Smith, *Remembering: Voices of the Holocaust* (New York: Carroll and Graf Publishers, 2005), 142; Amesberger and Halbmayr, "Nazi Differentiations Mattered: Ideological Intersections of Sexualized Violence During National Socialist Persecution," 142-2.

[532] Anna Bergman, in *Imperial War Museum Sound Archive, London, 26752*; Smith, *Remembering: Voices of the Holocaust*: 150.

[533] Ruth Reiser, "The Only Medicine was Charcoal," in *Sisters in Sorrow: Voices of Care in the Holocaust*, ed. Roger A Ritvo and Diane M Plotkin (College Station: Texas A&M University Press, 1998), 68.

[534] Bondy, "Women in Theresienstadt and the Family Camp in Birkenau," 315.

[535] Dina Gottliebova-Babbitt, in *USC Shoah Foundation Institute for Visual History and Education On-Line Archive, 46122 (Accessed 14 February 2012).*

[536] Hana Muller Bruml, "I was a Nurse in Theresienstadt," in *Sisters in Sorrow: Voices of Care in the Holocaust*, ed. Roger A Ritvo and Diane M Plotkin (College Station: Texas A&M University Press, 1998), 34.

[537] Ruth Elias, *Triumph of Hope: From Theresienstadt and Auschwitz to Israel*, trans. Margot Bettauer Dembo (New York: John Wiley and Sons, 1988), 102.

[538] Schiff, *Theresienstadt: The Town The Nazis Gave to The Jews*: 126.

[539] Schwertfeger, *Women of Theresienstadt: Voices from a Concentration Camp*: 61.

[540] Nicholas, *Cruel World: The Children of Europe in the Nazi Web*: 236.

[541] Dwork and Pelt, *Holocaust: A History*: 297.

[542] Bondy, "Women in Theresienstadt and the Family Camp in Birkenau," 316.

[543] Anna Lenji, in *Massuah Institute for the Study of the Holocaust, Tel Aviv, 033c/4312.*

[544] Schiff, *Theresienstadt: The Town The Nazis Gave to The Jews*: 53.

[545] Szwajger, *I Remember Nothing More: The Warsaw Children's Hospital and Jewish Resistance*: 7.

[546] Friedman, "Togetherness and Isolation: Holocaust Survivor Memories of Intimacy and Sexuality in the Ghettos," 8.

[547] Adelson and Lapides, *Łódź Ghetto: Inside a Community Under Siege*, 127.

[548] Friedman, "Togetherness and Isolation: Holocaust Survivor Memories of Intimacy and Sexuality in the Ghettos," 8.

[549] Adelson and Lapides, *Łódź Ghetto: Inside a Community Under Siege*, 342-4.

[550] Katz and Ringelheim, *Proceedings of the Conference Women Surviving the Holocaust*, 141.

[551] Ibid., 41.

[552] Ibid.

[553] Smith, *Remembering: Voices of the Holocaust*: 112.

[554] Friedman, *Speaking the Unspeakable: Essays on Sexuality, Gender, and Holocaust Survivor Memory*: 44.

[555] Kaplan, *Between Dignity and Despair: Jewish Life in Nazi Germany*: 82-83.

[556] Ibid., 224.

[557] Preiss, "Women's Health in the Ghettos of Eastern Europe. Jewish Women: A Comprehensive Historical Encyclopedia". 4/10.

[558] R Shadowsky, "Organization of First Aid and Medical Help in the Vilna Ghetto (Yiddish)," *Bletter vegen Vilna* (1947).

[559] Carol Ann Lee, *The Hidden Life of Otto Frank* (New York: Harper Collins, 2002), 92.

[560] Ritvo and Plotkin. *Sisters in Sorrow: Voices of Care in the Holocaust*: 95-96.
[561] Glass. *Life Unworthy of Life: Racial Phobia and Mass Murder in Hitler's Germany*: 184.
[562] Smith. *Remembering: Voices of the Holocaust*.
[563] Hogan and Aretha. *The Holocaust Chronicle*. 387.
[564] Hilberg. *The Destruction of the European Jews*: 199.
[565] Adelson and Lapides. *Łódź Ghetto: Inside a Community Under Siege*. 227; Malcolm C MacPherson. *The Blood of His Servants: The True Story of One Man's Search for his Family's Friend and Executioner* (New York: Times Books. 1984). 114; Irene Eber. *The Choice: Poland 1939-1945* (New York: Schocken Books. 2004). 34; Daniel Mendelsohn. *The Lost: A Search for Six of the Six Million* (New York: Harper Perennial. 2006). 227; Hogan and Aretha. *The Holocaust Chronicle*. 361; Martin Gilbert. *The Boys: The Story of 732 Young Concentration Camp Survivors* (New York: Henry Holt and Company. 1997). 127.
[566] Anthony Masters. *The Summer That Bled: The Biography of Hannah Senesh* (London: Michael Joseph. 1972). 206.
[567] Gideon Hausner. *Justice in Jerusalem*. (New York: Schoken Books. 1968); Masters. *The Summer That Bled: The Biography of Hannah Senesh*: 297.
[568] Donat. *Holocaust Kingdom*: 317.
[569] Smith. *Remembering: Voices of the Holocaust*: 121.
[570] Eichengreen and Chamberlain. *From Ashes to Life: My Memories of the Holocaust*: 53; ibid.
[571] Mendelsohn. *The Lost: A Search for Six of the Six Million*: 128.
[572] Dalia Ofer. "Motherhood Under Siege." in *Life, Death, and Sacrifice: Women and Family in the Holocaust* (Jerusalem: Gefen Publishing House. 2008). 58.
[573] Michelle Donet. in *Massuah Institute for the Study of the Holocaust,Tel Aviv, 033c/3681*.
[574] Bankier and Michman. *Holocaust Historiography in Context: Emergence, Challenges, Polemics and Achievements*: 508; David P Boder. "The Tale of Anna Kovitzka; A Logico-Systematic Analysis or an Essay in Experimental Reading." in *Collection 1238* (Los Angeles: Charles E Young Research Library. UCLA Undated).
[575] Kaplan. *Between Dignity and Despair: Jewish Life in Nazi Germany*: 188.
[576] Ofer. "Motherhood Under Siege." 58.
[577] Kaplan. *Between Dignity and Despair: Jewish Life in Nazi Germany*: 188.
[578] Nicholas. *Cruel World: The Children of Europe in the Nazi Web*: 393.
[579] Gilbert. *The Boys: The Story of 732 Young Concentration Camp Survivors*: 331.
[580] Hilberg. *The Destruction of the European Jews*: 145.
[581] Ofer. "Motherhood Under Siege." 58; Nicholas. *Cruel World: The Children of Europe in the Nazi Web*: 392.
[582] Olga Kovacz. in *USC Shoah Foundation Institute for Visual History and Education On-Line Archive, 3012 (Accessed 14 February 2012)*; Irene Weiss. in *USC Shoah Foundation Institute for Visual History and Education On-Line Archive, 393 (Accessed 14 February 2012)*.
[583] Nicholas. *Cruel World: The Children of Europe in the Nazi Web*: 342.
[584] Rudolf Vrba. *I Escaped from Auschwitz* (New Jersey: Barricade Books. 2002). 43.
[585] Shelly. *Twenty Women Prisoner's Accounts*: 137.
[586] Tec. *Resilience and Courage: Women, Men and the Holocaust*: 249-50.
[587] Szwajger. *I Remember Nothing More: The Warsaw Children's Hospital and Jewish Resistance*: 148.
[588] Ibid., 149.
[589] Frank Stiffel. *The Tale of the Ring: A Kaddish* (New York: Bantam Books. 1984). 126.
[590] Kaplan. *Between Dignity and Despair: Jewish Life in Nazi Germany*: 207-20.
[591] Tec. *Resilience and Courage: Women, Men and the Holocaust*: 249-50.
[592] Rhodea Shandler. *A Long Labour: A Dutch Mother's Holocaust Memoir* (Vancouver, Canada: Ronsdale Press. 2007). 97-109.
[593] Tec. *Resilience and Courage: Women, Men and the Holocaust*: 254-5.

[594] Rubenstein and Altman, *The Unknown Black Book: The holocaust in the German-Occupied Soviet Territories*, 107.
[595] Martin Gilbert, *The Righteous: The Unsung Heroes of the Holocaust* (London: Black Swan, 2002), 117.
[596] Leo Marcus, "Notes of Leo Marcus written in March 1943, during the third year of World War II in Holland, on the occasion of the birth of his fourth daughter, Leonie, while the family was in hiding.," (Tel Aviv, IsraelMarch 1943).
[597] Margarete Myers Feinstein, "Absent Fathers, Present Mothers: Images of Parenthood in Holocaust Survivor Narratives," *Nashim: A Journal of Jewish Women's Studies* Spring, no. 13 (2007): 156-57.
[598] Ernest Weiss, 24 November 2009
[599] Dwork and Pelt, *Holocaust: A History*: 351.
[600] Saul Rubinek, *So Many Miracles* (Markham, Ontario: Viking, 1988), 121-22.
[601] Gilbert, *The Righteous: The Unsung Heroes of the Holocaust*: 84.
[602] Gill, *The Journey Back From Hell: Conversations with Concentration Camp Survivors*: 14.
[603] William G. Niederland, *Folgen der Vervolgung: das überlebenden-Syndrom, Seelenmord,* (Suhrkamp, 1980), 229ff, 35.
[604] Nicholas, *Cruel World: The Children of Europe in the Nazi Web*: 373; Eber, *The Choice: Poland 1939-1945*: 42; Adelson and Lapides, *Łódź Ghetto: Inside a Community Under Siege*, 453; Safira Rapoport, ed. *Yesterdays and Then Tomorrows: Holocaust Anthology of Testimonies and Readings* (Jerusalem: The International School of Holocaust Studies Yad Vashem, 2002), 93; Yahil, *The Holocaust: The Fate of European Jewry*: 443; Katz and Ringelheim, *Proceedings of the Conference Women Surviving the Holocaust*, 88.
[605] Smith, *Remembering: Voices of the Holocaust*: 191.
[606] Michael Nevins, "Moral Dilemmas Faced by Jewish Doctors During the Holocaust," www.jewishvirtuallibrary.org/jsource/Judaism/dilemma.html.
[607] Götz Aly, *Hitler's Beneficiaries: Plunder, Racial War, and the Nazi Welfare State* (New York: Metropolitan Books, 2006), 156; Anna Rosmus, "Involuntary Abortions for Polish Forced Labourers," in *Experience and Expression: Women, the Nazis, and the Holocaust*, ed. Elizabeth R Baer and Myrna Goldberg (Detroit: Wayne State University, 2003), 77.
[608] Gill, *The Journey Back From Hell: Conversations with Concentration Camp Survivors*: 272.
[609] Tec, *Resilience and Courage: Women, Men and the Holocaust*: 135.
[610] Felicja Karay, *Death comes in Yellow: Skarżysko-Kamienna Slave Labor Camp.* (London: Routledge, 1996), 80-81, 116.
[611] Ibid., 215-16.
[612] Katz and Ringelheim, *Proceedings of the Conference Women Surviving the Holocaust*, 35.
[613] Phyllis Young, in *USC Shoah Foundation Institute for Visual History and Education On-Line Archive, 8359 (Accessed 14 February 2012).*
[614] John Sack, *An Eye For An Eye: The Untold Story of Jewish Revenge Against Germans in 1945* (New York: Basic Books, 1993), 19.
[615] Bergman; Smith, *Remembering: Voices of the Holocaust*: 233.
[616] Katz and Ringelheim, *Proceedings of the Conference Women Surviving the Holocaust*, 51.
[617] Tec, *Resilience and Courage: Women, Men and the Holocaust*: 322.
[618] Ibid.
[619] Szwajger, *I Remember Nothing More: The Warsaw Children's Hospital and Jewish Resistance*: 146.
[620] Tec, *Resilience and Courage: Women, Men and the Holocaust*: 325.
[621] Friedman, *Speaking the Unspeakable: Essays on Sexuality, Gender, and Holocaust Survivor Memory*: 48.

[622] Tec, *Resilience and Courage: Women, Men and the Holocaust*: 321-22.
[623] Ibid., 337-39.
[624] Gill, *The Journey Back From Hell: Conversations with Concentration Camp Survivors*: 3.
[625] Ritvo and Plotkin, *Sisters in Sorrow: Voices of Care in the Holocaust*: 141.
[626] Gill, *The Journey Back From Hell: Conversations with Concentration Camp Survivors*: 261.
[627] Rochelle G. Saidel, *The Jewish Women of Ravensbrück Concentration Camp* (Madison, Wisconsin: The University of Wisconsin Press, 2004), 51,212.
[628] Katherina von Kellenbach, " Reproduction and Resistance During the Holocaust," in *Women and the Holocaust: Studies in the Shoah*, ed. Esther Fuchs (Lanham, Maryland: 1999), 20; Peled, "Pregnancy as Resistance in the Holocaust," 12.
[629] ———, "Pregnancy as Resistance in the Holocaust," 1.
[630] Lucy Dawidowicz, *The Holocaust and the Historians* (Cambridge, Massachusetts: Harvard University Press, 1981), 133.
[631] Peled, "Pregnancy as Resistance in the Holocaust," 5.
[632] Inbar, *Spots of Light: To Be a Woman in the Holocaust.*
[633] Sara R Horowitz, "Women in Holocaust Literature: Engendering Trauma Memory," in *Women in the Holocaust* ed. Dalia Ofer and Lenore Weitzman (New Haven: Yale University Press, 1998), 371.
[634] Peled, "Pregnancy as Resistance in the Holocaust," 25.
[635] Horowitz, "Women in Holocaust Literature: Engendering Trauma Memory," 372.
[636] Primo Levi, *The Drowned and the Saved* (New York: Vintage International, 1989), 120.
[637] United States Holocaust Memorial Museum, http://www.ushmm.org/research/center/encyclopedia/.
[638] Eric Lichtblau, "The Holocaust Just Got More Shocking," http://www.nytimes.com/2013/03/03/sunday-review/the-holocaust-just-got-more-shocking.html?pagewanted=all&_r=0.
[639] Evans, *The Third Reich at War*: 367.
[640] Saidel, *The Jewish Women of Ravensbrück Concentration Camp*: 1.
[641] Jewish Virtual Library., "Auschwitz-Birkenau Concentration Camp," http://www.jewishvirtuallibrary.org/jsource/Holocaust/auschbirk.html.
[642] Ronald Paul Hill and Elizabeth C Hirschman, "Human Rights Abuses by the Third Reich: New Evidence form the Nazi Concentration Camp Buchenwald," *Human Rights Quarterly* 18, no. 4 (1996): 860.
[643] Liverpool, *The Scourge of the Swastika*: 178; Sam Pivnik, *Survivor: Auschwitz, the Death March and My Flight for Freedom* (London: Hodder and Stoughton, 2012), 185; Sala Pawlowicz, *I Will Survive* (New York: W W Norton and Company, Inc, 1962), 82; Father Patrick Desbois, *The Holocaust by Bullets:A Priest's Journey to Uncover the Truth Behind the Murder of 1.5 Million Jews* (New York: Palgrave, Macmillan, 2008), 223, Chapter5, Note 2; Robert M Edsel and Bret Witter, *The Monuments Men* (New York: Center Street, 2009), 295; Evans, *The Third Reich at War*: 698; Hájková and Housková, "The Stations of the Cross."; Mo Is, *U.B.B.: Unforgettable Bergen-Belsen* (Montreal: A Emeth Publisher, 1993); Jack G. Morrison, *Ravensbrück: Everyday Life in a Women's Concentration Camp 1939-1945* (Princeton: Markus Weiner Publishers, 2000); Michael Nutkiewicz, "Shame, Guilt, and Anguish in Holocaust Survivor Testimony," *The Oral History Review* 30, no. 1 (2003); Perl, *I was a Doctor in Auschwitz*; Smith, *Remembering: Voices of the Holocaust*; Eichengreen and Chamberlain, *From Ashes to Life: My Memories of the Holocaust*: 125; Grossmann, *Jews, Germans, and the Allies: Close Encounters in Occupied Germany*: 137; Gill, *The Journey Back From Hell: Conversations with Concentration Camp Survivors*: 466.
[644] ———, *The Journey Back From Hell: Conversations with Concentration Camp Survivors*: 446.
[645] Cohen, *Human Behaviour in the Concentration Camp*: 53; ibid.

[646] Amesberger, "Reproduction Under the Swastika: The Other Side of the Nazi Glorification of Motherhood," 140-41; "*Erlass zum Verbot der Einweisung schwangerer Häftlinge in die Frauenkonzentrationslager Ravensbrück bzw. in die Frauenabteilungen der Konzentrationslager Auschwitz und Lublin* [Decree forbidding the admission of pregnant inmates into the women's concentration camp Ravensbrück or the women's section of the concentration camps Auschwitz and Lublin].".

[647] Deborah Lipstadt, "Introduction," in *Auschwitz: A Doctor's Story*, ed. Lucie Adelsberger (Boston: Northeastern University Press, 1995), xxiii; Joan Ringelheim, "Women and the Holocaust: A Reconsideration of Research.," in *Different Voices: Women and the Holocaust*, ed. Carol Rittner and John K Roth (New York: 1993), 392.

[648] Lipstadt, "Introduction."; Bradley E Smith and Agnes F Peterson, *Heinrich Himmler: Geheimreden 1933 bis 1945* (Frankfort1974).

[649] Na'ama Shik, "Mother-Daughter Relationships in Auschwitz-Birkenau, 1942-1945," in *Mutterliche macht und väterliche Autorität: Elternbilder im deutschen Diskurs*, ed. Josë Brunner (2008), 108; Koonz, *Mothers in the Fatherland: Women, the Family and Nazi Politics*: 425; Olga Lengyel, in *USC Shoah Foundation Institute for Visual History and Education On-Line Archive, 46138 (Accessed 14 February 2012)*, 36.

[650] Liana Millu, *Smoke Over Birkenau* (Evanston, Illinois: Northwestern University Press, 1986), 53.

[651] Perl, *I was a Doctor in Auschwitz*: 28; Lucie Adelsberger, *Auschwitz: A Doctor's Story* (Boston: Northeastern University Press, 1995), 85, 100-01; Elie Wiesel, *Memoirs: All Rivers Run to the Sea* (Toronto: Alfred A Knopf, 1995), 78.

[652] Gilbert, *The Boys: The Story of 732 Young Concentration Camp Survivors*: 184.

[653] Wanda Symonowicz, ed. *Beyond Human Endurance: The Ravensbrück Women tell Their Stories* (Warsaw, Poland: Interpress Publishers, 1970), 37,60,71,115.

[654] Hogan and Aretha, *The Holocaust Chronicle*, 361.

[655] Ibid., 355.

[656] Sara Nomberg-Przytyk, *Auschwitz: True Tales from a Grotesque Land* (Chapel Hill: University of North Carolina Press, 1985), 69.

[657] Vera Benedek, in *Massuah Institute for the Study of the Holocaust, Tel Aviv, 033c/3450*; Miriam Rosenthal, in *Yad Vashem Archives, Jeruslem, Tape 209A and 209, 069 209 209a, 3543503* (February 18, 1981); Laura Varon, in *Massuah Institute for the Study of the Holocaust, Tel Aviv, VD-1390* (14 November 1996); Gail Ivy Berlin, "The 'Canada' Commando as a Force for Resistance in Auschwitz: Redefining Heroism," http://www.theverylongview.com/WATH/essays/canada.htm.

[658] Tec, *Resilience and Courage: Women, Men and the Holocaust*: 161-62.

[659] Ibid., 80-81.

[660] Hadassah Becker, in *Massuah Institute for the Study of the Holocaust, Tel Aviv, 033c/618* (29 November 1987), 53-54.

[661] Olga Lengyel, *Five Chimneys: A Woman Survivor's True Story of Auschwitz*, First Academy Chicago edition, 1995 ed. (Chicago: Ziff-Davis Publishing Company, 1947), 91-92; Lidia Rosenfeld Vago, "One Year in the Black Hole of Our Planet Earth: A Personal Narrative," in *Women in the Holocaust*, ed. Dalia Ofer and Lenore J Weitzman (New Haven: Yale University Press, 1998), 277; Danuta Czech, *The Auschwitz Chronicle 1939-1945*, trans. Barbara Harshav, Martha Humphreys, and Stephen Shearier (New York: Henry Holt, 1990); Vrba, *I Escaped from Auschwitz*: 131; Lifton, *The Nazi Doctors: Medical Killing and the Psychology of Genocide*: 216; Rittner and Roth, *Different Voices: Women and the Holocaust*, 424; Giuliana Tedeschi, *There is a Place on Earth: A Woman in Birkenau* (England: Random House, 1992), 95.

[662] Czech, *The Auschwitz Chronicle 1939-1945*: 652; John K Roth, "Equality, Neutrality, Particularity: Perspectives on Women and the Holocaust," in *Experience and Expression*, ed. Elizabeth R Baer and Myrna Goldenberg (Detroit: Wayne State University Press, 2003), 15.

[663] Friedländer, *Nazi Germany and the Jews 1939-1945: The Years of Extermination*: 639.

[664] Höss, *Death Dealer: The Memoirs of the SS Kommandant of Auschwitz*: 158; Rapoport, *Yesterdays and Then Tomorrows: Holocaust Anthology of Testimonies and Readings*, 133.

[665] Sima Vaisman, *A Jewish Doctor in Auschwitz: The Testimony of Sima Vaisman* (New Jersey: Melville House Publishing, 2005), 53.

[666] Vrba, *I Escaped from Auschwitz*: 10.

[667] Müller, *Eyewitness Auschwitz: Three Years in the Gas Chambers*: 117; Miklos Nyiszli, *Auschwitz: A Doctor's Eyewitness Account* (New York: Arcade Publishing 1960), 52; Spitz, *Doctors From Hell: The Horrific Accounts of Nazi Experiments on Humans*: 243.

[668] Müller, *Eyewitness Auschwitz: Three Years in the Gas Chambers*: 117.

[669] Kitty Hart, *I Am Alive* (London: Abelard-Schuman, 1961), 106.

[670] Venezia, *Inside the Gas Chambers: Eight Months in the Sonderkommando of Auschwitz*: 108.

[671] Rapoport, *Yesterdays and Then Tomorrows: Holocaust Anthology of Testimonies and Readings*, 133.

[672] Koonz, *Mothers in the Fatherland: Women, the Family and Nazi Politics*: 425.

[673] Bruml, "I was a Nurse in Theresienstadt," 41.

[674] Vaisman, *A Jewish Doctor in Auschwitz: The Testimony of Sima Vaisman*: 44.

[675] Lucette Matalon Lagnado and Sheila Cohn Dekel, *Children of the Flames: Dr Josef Mengele and The Untold Story of the Twins of Auschwitz* (New York: William Morrow and Company, Inc, 1991), 81.

[676] Perl, *I was a Doctor in Auschwitz*: 80-82; Ernie Weiss, *Out of Vienna: Eight Years of Flight from the Nazis* (USA: Xlibris Corporation, 2008), 226-27; Vaisman, *A Jewish Doctor in Auschwitz: The Testimony of Sima Vaisman*: 57; Ruth Nebel, "The Story of Ruth," in *When Biology Became Destiny: Women in Weimar and Nazi Germany*, ed. Renate Bridenthal, Atina Grossmann, and Marion Kaplan (New York: Monthly Review Press, 1984), 339.

[677] Perl, *I was a Doctor in Auschwitz*: 80-82.

[678] Ibid., 81-2.

[679] Ibid., 63-65.

[680] Lengyel, *Five Chimneys: A Woman Survivor's True Story of Auschwitz*: 161.

[681] Adelsberger, *Auschwitz: A Doctor's Story*: 100-01.

[682] Lipstadt, "Introduction," xxii.

[683] Amesberger, "Reproduction Under the Swastika: The Other Side of the Nazi Glorification of Motherhood," 144.

[684] Ben-Sefer, "Forced Sterilization and Abortion as Sexual Abuse," 163.

[685] Spitz, *Doctors From Hell: The Horrific Accounts of Nazi Experiments on Humans*: xix.

[686] Tracy Rich, "Judaism 101: Life, Death and Mourning," http://www.jewfaq.org/death.htm; Biale, *Women and Jewish Law: The Essential Texts, Their History, and Their Relevance for Today.*: 219,20,35.

[687] Ben-Sefer, "Forced Sterilization and Abortion as Sexual Abuse," 164.

[688] Perl, *I was a Doctor in Auschwitz*: 81; Szwajger, *I Remember Nothing More: The Warsaw Children's Hospital and Jewish Resistance*: 166.

[689] Lengyel, *Five Chimneys: A Woman Survivor's True Story of Auschwitz*: 113-16.

[690] Lifton, *The Nazi Doctors: Medical Killing and the Psychology of Genocide*: 183.

[691] Edith Polgar, in *USC Shoah Foundation Institute for Visual History and Education On-Line Archive, 3994 (Accessed 14 February 2012)*.

[692] Tec, *Resilience and Courage: Women, Men and the Holocaust*: 164.

[693] Varon, 15-16.

[694] Perl, *I was a Doctor in Auschwitz*: 119.

[695] Lagnado and Dekel, *Children of the Flames: Dr Josef Mengele and The Untold Story of the Twins of Auschwitz*: 80; Lengyel, *Five Chimneys: A Woman Survivor's True Story of Auschwitz*: 113-16.

[696] ———, *Five Chimneys: A Woman Survivor's True Story of Auschwitz*: 113-16.
[697] Lagnado and Dekel, *Children of the Flames: Dr Josef Mengele and The Untold Story of the Twins of Auschwitz*: 80.
[698] Ibid., 81.
[699] Perl, *I was a Doctor in Auschwitz*: 84; Lagnado and Dekel, *Children of the Flames: Dr Josef Mengele and The Untold Story of the Twins of Auschwitz*: 80.
[700] Perl, *I was a Doctor in Auschwitz*: 125.
[701] Posner and Ware, *Mengele: The Complete Story*: 49, xvi.
[702] Becker, 74.
[703] Elias, *Triumph of Hope: From Theresienstadt and Auschwitz to Israel*: 126.
[704] Ibid., 115-19.
[705] Ibid., 143-53.
[706] Ibid.
[707] Brian Moser, "The Search for Mengele," (USA: First Run Features, 1985).
[708] Peled, "Pregnancy as Resistance in the Holocaust," 16-17.
[709] Adelsberger, *Auschwitz: A Doctor's Story*: 100-01.
[710] Margarita Schwalbova, "They Were Murdered in the Infirmary," in *Sisters in Sorrow: Voices of Care in the Holocaust*, ed. Roger A Ritvo and Diane M Plotkin (College Station, USA: Texas A & M University Press, 1998), 162-63.
[711] Peled, "Pregnancy as Resistance in the Holocaust," 16-17; Hogan and Aretha, *The Holocaust Chronicle*, 274.
[712] Peled, "Pregnancy as Resistance in the Holocaust," 15-16; Stanislawa-Leszczynska, "Report of a Midwife from Auschwitz," in *Auschwitz-Birkenau Report #41335* (1965), 188-89.
[713] Lillian Steinberg, in *USC Shoah Foundation Institute for Visual History and Education On-Line Archive, 49918 (Accessed 14 February 2012).*
[714] Peled, "Pregnancy as Resistance in the Holocaust," 16-18,; Stanislawa-Leszczynska, "Report of a Midwife from Auschwitz," 188-89.
[715] Walter Winter, *Winter Time: Memoirs of a German Sinto Who Survived Auschwitz* (Hertfrodshire: University of Hertfordshire Press, 2004), 127-8.
[716] Hogan and Aretha, *The Holocaust Chronicle*, 350.
[717] Schwalbova, "They Were Murdered in the Infirmary," 162-63.
[718] Nomberg-Przytyk, *Auschwitz: True Tales from a Grotesque Land*: 68-71.
[719] Peled, "Pregnancy as Resistance in the Holocaust," 15-16; Stanislawa-Leszczynska, "Report of a Midwife from Auschwitz," 188-89.
[720] Adelsberger, *Auschwitz: A Doctor's Story*: 100-01; Lengyel, *Five Chimneys: A Woman Survivor's True Story of Auschwitz*: 113.
[721] ———, *Five Chimneys: A Woman Survivor's True Story of Auschwitz*: 113.
[722] Judith Rubenstein, in *USC Shoah Foundation Institute for Visual History and Education On-Line Archive, 747 (Accessed 14 February 2012).*
[723] Perl, *I was a Doctor in Auschwitz*: 85-86, 124.
[724] Inbar, *Spots of Light: To Be a Woman in the Holocaust*: 32.
[725] Nomberg-Przytyk, *Auschwitz: True Tales from a Grotesque Land*: 69.
[726] Janos Szasz, "A Holocaust Szemei (Eyes of the Holocaust)," ed. Steven Spielberg and the Survivors of the Shoah Visual History Foundation (USA2002).
[727] Silvia Gross-Martin, *Silvia* (New York: Welcome Rain Publishers, 2000), 241.
[728] Langer, "Gendered Suffering? Women in Holocaust Testimonies," 356-57.
[729] Lengyel, *Five Chimneys: A Woman Survivor's True Story of Auschwitz*: 113-16.
[730] Millu, *Smoke Over Birkenau*: 55-56, 87-91.
[731] Matilda Klein, in *USC Shoah Foundation Institute for Visual History and Education On-Line Archive, 6525 (Accessed 14 February 2012)*; Masza Rosenroth, in *USC Shoah Foundation Institute for Visual History and Education On-Line Archive, 198 (Accessed 14 February 2012)*; Susan Rubin, in *USC Shoah Foundation Institute for Visual History and Education On-Line Archive, 51522 (Accessed 14 February 2012)*; Mollie Stauber,

in *USC Shoah Foundation Institute for Visual History and Education On-Line Archive, 512 (Accessed 14 February 2102).*

[732] Perl, *I was a Doctor in Auschwitz*: 83-84.

[733] Friedman, *Speaking the Unspeakable: Essays on Sexuality, Gender, and Holocaust Survivor Memory*: 43-49.

[734] Saidel, *The Jewish Women of Ravensbrück Concentration Camp*: 211.

[735] Eva Galt, in *Yad Vashem Archives,Jerusalem,O.3/10275.1.12.1996.9.*

[736] Marion Gottesman, in *USC Shoah Foundation Institute for Visual History and Education On-Line Archive,16163, (Accessed 14 February 2012).*

[737] Maria Scheffer, in *USC Shoah Foundation Institute for Visual History and Education On-Line Archive, 4187 (Accessed 14 February 2012).*

[738] Zsoka Prochazka, in *USC Shoah Foundation Institute for Visual History and Education On-Line Archive, 39069, Accessed 14 February 2012.*

[739] Yehudit Harris, in *Massuah Institute for the Study of the Holocaust, Tel Aviv, 033c/5515* (26 August 1997), 28.

[740] Amesberger and Halbmayr, "Nazi Differentiations Mattered: Ideological Intersections of Sexualized Violence During National Socialist Persecution," 189; ibid; Morrison, *Ravensbrück: Everyday Life in a Women's Concentration Camp 1939-1945*: 270.

[741] ———, *Ravensbrück: Everyday Life in a Women's Concentration Camp 1939-1945*: 270.

[742] Saidel, *The Jewish Women of Ravensbrück Concentration Camp*: 33.

[743] Hester Baer and Elizabeth Baer, "Introduction," in *The Blessed Abyss: Inmate #6582 in Ravensbrück Concentration Camp for Women*, ed. Hester Baer and Elizabeth Baer (Detroit: Wayne State University Press, 2000), 30-1; Nanda Hebermann, *The Blessed Abyss: Inmate #6582 in Ravensbrück Concentration Camp for Women* (Detroit: Wayne State University press, 2000), 170.

[744] Germaine Tillion, *Ravensbrück - An Eyewitness Account of a Woman's Concentration Camp* (New York: Anchor Press, 1975), 77; Ben-Sefer, "Forced Sterilization and Abortion as Sexual Abuse," 164.

[745] Saidel, *The Jewish Women of Ravensbrück Concentration Camp*: 31.

[746] Charlotte Müller, *Die Klempnerkolonne in Ravensbrück: Erinnerungen des Häftlings Nr. 10787 (The plumber column of Ravensbrück: recollections of prisoner Nr 10787)* (Berlin: Dietz Verlag, 1981), 184; Saidel, *The Jewish Women of Ravensbrück Concentration Camp*: 19.

[747] Morrison, *Ravensbrück: Everyday Life in a Women's Concentration Camp 1939-1945*: 270.

[748] Tec, *Resilience and Courage: Women, Men and the Holocaust*: 376.

[749] Symonowicz, *Beyond Human Endurance: The Ravensbrück Women tell Their Stories* 11.

[750] Morrison, *Ravensbrück: Everyday Life in a Women's Concentration Camp 1939-1945*: 270.

[751] Amesberger, "Reproduction Under the Swastika: The Other Side of the Nazi Glorification of Motherhood," 142.

[752] Eugen Kogon, *The Theory and Practice of Hell: The German Concentration Camps and the System Behind Them* (New York: Berkeley Books, 1950), 230.

[753] Harris, 29.

[754] Eichengreen and Chamberlain, *From Ashes to Life: My Memories of the Holocaust*: 121-2.

[755] Perl, *I was a Doctor in Auschwitz*: 170-71.

[756] Friedman, *Speaking the Unspeakable: Essays on Sexuality, Gender, and Holocaust Survivor Memory*: 43-9.

[757] Fania Fenelon, *Playing for Time* (New York: Berkley Books, 1977), 276-77.

[758] Perl, *I was a Doctor in Auschwitz*: 175-6.

[759] Langer, "Gendered Suffering? Women in Holocaust Testimonies," 355-56.

[760] Ester Lebenswold, in *USC Shoah Foundation Institute for Visual History and Education On-Line Archive, 9230 (Accessed 14 February 2012).*
[761] Young.
[762] Wladyslawa Tracz, in *USC Shoah Foundation Institute for Visual History and Education On-Line Archive, 46621 (Accessed 14 February 2012).*
[763] Estelole Laughlin, in *USC Shoah Foundation Institute for Visual History and Education On-Line Archive, 21582 (Accessed 14 February 2012).*
[764] Edith Reifer, in *USC Shoah Foundation Institute for Visual History and Education On-Line Archive, 36331 (Accessed 14 February 2012).*
[765] Friedman, *Speaking the Unspeakable: Essays on Sexuality, Gender, and Holocaust Survivor Memory*: 43-9.
[766] Handa Stark, in *USC Shoah Foundation Institute for Visual History and Education On-Line Archive, 182 (Accessed 14 February 2012).*
[767] Horowitz, "Women in Holocaust Literature: Engendering Trauma Memory," 372.
[768] Amesberger, "Reproduction Under the Swastika: The Other Side of the Nazi Glorification of Motherhood," 141-42.
[769] Smith, *Remembering: Voices of the Holocaust*: 287; Bergman.
[770] Anonymous, "Woman born in Nazi concentration camp tells remarkable tale of Holocaust survival to Linton pupils," *Haverhill Echo*, 24 March 2012.
[771] Rachela Schlufman, in *USC Shoah Foundation Institute for Visual History and Education On-Line Archive, 6076 (Accessed 14 February 2012).*
[772] Halina Strnad, in *USC Shoah Foundation Institute for Visual History and Education On-Line Archive, 31815 (Accessed 14 February 2012).*
[773] Rosenthal, 33.
[774] Amesberger, "Reproduction Under the Swastika: The Other Side of the Nazi Glorification of Motherhood," 143; Edith Serras, in *David P Boder Archive, Voices of the Holocaust, Spool 34,* (August 7 1946).
[775] Elliot Berlin and Joe Fab, "Paper Clips," (Canada: Motion Picture Distribution, 2006).
[776] Nomberg-Przytyk, *Auschwitz: True Tales from a Grotesque Land*: 69.
[777] H O Bluhm, "How did they survive?," *American Journal of Psychotherapy* 11, no. 1 (1948): 3; Cohen, *Human Behaviour in the Concentration Camp*: 158.
[778] Stanislawa-Leszczynska, "Report of a Midwife from Auschwitz," 187; Peled, "Pregnancy as Resistance in the Holocaust," 17.
[779] Schwalbova, "They Were Murdered in the Infirmary," 162-63.
[780] Morrison, *Ravensbrück: Everyday Life in a Women's Concentration Camp 1939-1945*: 270.
[781] Winter, *Winter Time: Memoirs of a German Sinto Who Survived Auschwitz*: 88-89.
[782] Amesberger, "Reproduction Under the Swastika: The Other Side of the Nazi Glorification of Motherhood," 144; Britta Pawelka, "A Women in Concentration camps Bergen-Belsen, Ravensbrück.," in *Als Häftlinge geboren - Kinder in ravensbrück [Born as a prisoner - Children in Ravensbrück.] in Frauen in Konzentrationslagern. Bergen-Belsen, Ravensbrück.*, ed. Klaus Füllberg-Stollberg et al (Bremen Edition Temmem, 1944), 158.
[783] Helen Epstein, *Conversations With Sons and Daughters of the Holocaust* (New York: Penguin Books, 1988), 90.
[784] Grossmann, *Jews, Germans, and the Allies: Close Encounters in Occupied Germany*: 76.
[785] Ibid., 184.
[786] Eva Fogelman, "Sexual Abuse of Jewish Women During and After the Holocaust: A Psychological Perspective," in *Sexual Violence Against Jewish Women During the Holocaust*, ed. Sonja M Hedgepeth and Rochelle G Saidel (Waltham, Massachusetts: Brandeis University Press, 2010), 270.
[787] Jutta T Bendremer, *Women Surviving the Holocaust: In Spite of the Horror*, Symposium Series 43 (Lewiston: The Edwin Mellen Press, 1997), 41.
[788] Eichengreen and Chamberlain, *From Ashes to Life: My Memories of the Holocaust*: 136.

789 Rosenbaum, *The Holocaust and Halakhah*: 143.

790 Elias, *Triumph of Hope: From Theresienstadt and Auschwitz to Israel*: 230.

791 Michael Brenner, *After The Holocaust: Rebuilding Jewish Lives in Postwar Germany* (Princeton: Princeton University Press, 1997), 26.

792 Schiff, *Theresienstadt: The Town The Nazis Gave to The Jews*: 157.

793 Grossmann, *Jews, Germans, and the Allies: Close Encounters in Occupied Germany*: 188.

794 Gill, *The Journey Back From Hell: Conversations with Concentration Camp Survivors*: 57.

795 Brenner, *After The Holocaust: Rebuilding Jewish Lives in Postwar Germany*: 23.

796 Grossmann, *Jews, Germans, and the Allies: Close Encounters in Occupied Germany*: 42.

797 Brenner, *After The Holocaust: Rebuilding Jewish Lives in Postwar Germany*: 23.

798 Grossmann, *Jews, Germans, and the Allies: Close Encounters in Occupied Germany*: 188.

799 Ibid., 196.

800 Ibid., 3,186,93; Rubenstein.

801 Amesberger, "Reproduction Under the Swastika: The Other Side of the Nazi Glorification of Motherhood," 150.

802 Saidel, *The Jewish Women of Ravensbrück Concentration Camp*: 197-98.

803 Epstein, *Conversations With Sons and Daughters of the Holocaust*: 213-14.

804 Ibid., 90.

805 Katz and Ringelheim, *Proceedings of the Conference Women Surviving the Holocaust*, 136.

806 Lagnado and Dekel, *Children of the Flames: Dr Josef Mengele and The Untold Story of the Twins of Auschwitz*: 188, 202.

807 Margarete Myers Feinstein, "Hear the Voices: The Need for Personal Narratives in Holocaust Studies.," *CSW Update Newsletter* (2010): 28; Grossmann, *Jews, Germans, and the Allies: Close Encounters in Occupied Germany*: 208-10.

808 Gina Roitman and Jane Hawtin, "My Mother, the Nazi Midwife, and Me," (Canada: JHL Productions, 2013).

809 Grossmann, *Jews, Germans, and the Allies: Close Encounters in Occupied Germany*: 215.

810 Elias, *Triumph of Hope: From Theresienstadt and Auschwitz to Israel*: 260-62.

811 Bendremer, *Women Surviving the Holocaust: In Spite of the Horror*: 88.

812 Feinstein, "Absent Fathers, Present Mothers: Images of Parenthood in Holocaust Survivor Narratives," 173.

813 Katz and Ringelheim, *Proceedings of the Conference Women Surviving the Holocaust*, 137.

814 Charlotte Delbo, *Auschwitz and After* (New Haven: Yale University Press, 1995), 270.

815 Epstein, *Conversations With Sons and Daughters of the Holocaust*: 198.

816 Schiff, *Theresienstadt: The Town The Nazis Gave to The Jews*: 164.

817 Gill, *The Journey Back From Hell: Conversations with Concentration Camp Survivors*: 364.

818 Langer, "Gendered Suffering? Women in Holocaust Testimonies," 356-57.

819 Amesberger, "Reproduction Under the Swastika: The Other Side of the Nazi Glorification of Motherhood," 150.

820 Grossmann, *Jews, Germans, and the Allies: Close Encounters in Occupied Germany*: 191.

821 Ibid.

822 Tec, *Resilience and Courage: Women, Men and the Holocaust*: 253.

823 Shelly, *Twenty Women Prisoner's Accounts*: 140.

824 Lagnado and Dekel, *Children of the Flames: Dr Josef Mengele and The Untold Story of the Twins of Auschwitz*: 225-26.

[825] Dan Bar-On and Julia Chaitin, *Parenthood and the Holocaust*, ed. Search and Research Lectures and Papers 1 (Jerusalem: Yad Vashem, 2001), 58.
[826] Katz and Ringelheim, *Proceedings of the Conference Women Surviving the Holocaust*, 55.
[827] Amesberger, "Reproduction Under the Swastika: The Other Side of the Nazi Glorification of Motherhood," 150.
[828] Ibid., 149.
[829] Feinstein, "Absent Fathers, Present Mothers: Images of Parenthood in Holocaust Survivor Narratives," 173.
[830] Vera Schiff, *Hitler's Inferno: Eight Intimate and Personal Histories from the Holocaust* (Jacksonville, Florida: Raj Publishing Inc, 2002), 14.
[831] Horowitz, "Women in Holocaust Literature: Engendering Trauma Memory," 364-65.
[832] Bar-On and Chaitin, *Parenthood and the Holocaust*: 41-42.
[833] Weiss.
[834] Gill, *The Journey Back From Hell: Conversations with Concentration Camp Survivors*: 65.
[835] Rubinek, *So Many Miracles*: 183.
[836] Szwajger, *I Remember Nothing More: The Warsaw Children's Hospital and Jewish Resistance*: 166.
[837] Feinstein, "Jewish Women in Time: The Challenge of Feminist Artistic Installations About the Holocaust," 32.
[838] Hogan and Aretha, *The Holocaust Chronicle*, 643-47.
[839] Schiff, *Theresienstadt: The Town The Nazis Gave to The Jews*: 163.
[840] Höss, *Death Dealer: The Memoirs of the SS Kommandant of Auschwitz*: 223-24.
[841] Lifton, *The Nazi Doctors: Medical Killing and the Psychology of Genocide*: 191.
[842] Ibid., 303-36.
[843] Ibid., 229-32.
[844] Symonowicz, *Beyond Human Endurance: The Ravensbrück Women tell Their Stories*
[845] Lengyel, *Five Chimneys: A Woman Survivor's True Story of Auschwitz*: 70.
[846] Lifton, *The Nazi Doctors: Medical Killing and the Psychology of Genocide*: 223-24.
[847] Gill, *The Journey Back From Hell: Conversations with Concentration Camp Survivors*: 374.
[848] Caroline Moorehead, *A Train in Winter: A Story of Resistance, Friendship and Survival in Auschwitz* (London: Vintage Books, 2012), 237.
[849] Glass, *Life Unworthy of Life: Racial Phobia and Mass Murder in Hitler's Germany*: 63; ibid; ibid; ibid; ibid.
[850] Cornwell, *Hitler's Scientists: Science, War and the Devil's Pact*: 357,62; Evans, *The Third Reich at War*: 605-6; Freidlander, "From "Euthanasia" to the "Final Solution"," 655-6; Glass, *Life Unworthy of Life: Racial Phobia and Mass Murder in Hitler's Germany*: 63; Lagnado and Dekel, *Children of the Flames: Dr Josef Mengele and The Untold Story of the Twins of Auschwitz*: 127; Spitz, *Doctors From Hell: The Horrific Accounts of Nazi Experiments on Humans*: 65,85,115-7,03,35,57,87,99,209,19; Symonowicz, *Beyond Human Endurance: The Ravensbrück Women tell Their Stories* 7-27.
[851] Spitz, *Doctors From Hell: The Horrific Accounts of Nazi Experiments on Humans*: 231.
[852] Cornwell, *Hitler's Scientists: Science, War and the Devil's Pact*: 350.
[853] Cohen, *Human Behaviour in the Concentration Camp*: 109.
[854] Glass, *Life Unworthy of Life: Racial Phobia and Mass Murder in Hitler's Germany*: 63,96; Spitz, *Doctors From Hell: The Horrific Accounts of Nazi Experiments on Humans*: 6.
[855] Glass, *Life Unworthy of Life: Racial Phobia and Mass Murder in Hitler's Germany*: 65; Nyiszli, *Auschwitz: A Doctor's Eyewitness Account*: 221.
[856] Ben-Sefer, "Forced Sterilization and Abortion as Sexual Abuse," 160.
[857] Spitz, *Doctors From Hell: The Horrific Accounts of Nazi Experiments on Humans*: 191; Baer and Baer, "Introduction," 30-1.

[858] ———, "Introduction," 30-1; Wanda Poltawska, *And I Am Afraid Of My Dreams* (London: Hodder and Stroughton, 1964), 80.

[859] Lifton, *The Nazi Doctors: Medical Killing and the Psychology of Genocide*: 270-78.

[860] Roitman and Hawtin, "My Mother, the Nazi Midwife, and Me."; Lifton, *The Nazi Doctors: Medical Killing and the Psychology of Genocide*: 270-78.

[861] USA Government, *Nuremberg Medical Case, vol 1, pp 695.* ; ibid., Vol 1, p 721; Arad, Gutman, and Margoliot, *Documents on the Holocaust*: 272-73; Cohen, *Human Behaviour in the Concentration Camp*: 98.

[862] ———, *Human Behaviour in the Concentration Camp*: 97; ibid; USA Government, *Nuremberg Medical Case, vol 1, pp 695.* : Vol1, p 695; ibid.

[863] Shane Blackman, *Chilling Out: The cultural politics of substance consumption, youth and drug policy.* (Berkshire, England: Open University Press, McGraw Hill, 2004), 32.

[864] British Intelligence Objectives Sub-Committee, "Interrogation report no 518. Ref No AIU/PIR/137. Target no: C24/744, BWCE/N/INT/"T"/1 162" (London: Imperial War Museum, 12 June 1947).

[865] Government USA, "Case 1 Medical June 21-26. Official transcript of the American Military Tribunal in the matter of the USA against Karl Brandt yet al, defendants sitting at Nurnberg, Germany," (London: Imperial War Museum, 21 June 1947).

[866] Mitscherlich and Mielke, *Doctors of Infamy: The Story of the Nazi Medical Crimes*: 131-35.

[867] British Intelligence Objectives Sub-Committee, "Interrogation report no 518. Ref No AIU/PIR/137. Target no: C24/744, BWCE/N/INT/"T"/1 162".

[868] Lifton, *The Nazi Doctors: Medical Killing and the Psychology of Genocide*: 278.

[869] Ibid., 282; Cohen, *Human Behaviour in the Concentration Camp*: 97; Lengyel, *Five Chimneys: A Woman Survivor's True Story of Auschwitz*: 190.

[870] Lifton, *The Nazi Doctors: Medical Killing and the Psychology of Genocide*: 283.

[871] Mitscherlich and Mielke, *Doctors of Infamy: The Story of the Nazi Medical Crimes*: 139.

[872] Hanauske-Abel, "Not a Slippery Slope or Sudden Subversion: German Medicine and National Socialism in 1933," 137, Footnote 11.

[873] Posner and Ware, *Mengele: The Complete Story*: 31-32.

[874] Lifton, *The Nazi Doctors: Medical Killing and the Psychology of Genocide*: 281.

[875] Ibid., 247; Hermann Langbein, *Menschen in Auschwitz* (Vienna: Europe Verlag, 1972), 256.

[876] Mitscherlich and Mielke, *Doctors of Infamy: The Story of the Nazi Medical Crimes*: 136.

[877] Czech, *The Auschwitz Chronicle 1939-1945*: 172; Ritvo and Plotkin, *Sisters in Sorrow: Voices of Care in the Holocaust*: 15-16.

[878] Shelly, *Twenty Women Prisoner's Accounts*: 80,84.

[879] Ibid., 139.

[880] Ibid., 80,84.

[881] Cohen, *Human Behaviour in the Concentration Camp*: 97.

[882] Höss, *Death Dealer: The Memoirs of the SS Kommandant of Auschwitz*: 360.

[883] Leon Uris, *Exodus: A Novel of Israel* (London: William Kimber, 1959).

[884] Lifton, *The Nazi Doctors: Medical Killing and the Psychology of Genocide*: 248.

[885] Ibid., 284.

[886] Yahil, *The Holocaust: The Fate of European Jewry*: 369; Hanauske-Abel, "Not a Slippery Slope or Sudden Subversion: German Medicine and National Socialism in 1933," 137; Lengyel, *Five Chimneys: A Woman Survivor's True Story of Auschwitz*: 190.

[887] Höss, *Death Dealer: The Memoirs of the SS Kommandant of Auschwitz*: 350.

[888] Guenter Lewy, *The Nazi Persecution of the Gypsies* (Oxford: Oxford University Press, 2000), 161-62.

[889] Lifton, *The Nazi Doctors: Medical Killing and the Psychology of Genocide*: 270-78.

[890] Ibid.

[891] Ibid; Blackman, *Chilling Out: The cultural politics of substance consumption, youth and drug policy.*

[892] Cohen, *Human Behaviour in the Concentration Camp*: 97.
[893] Mitscherlich and Mielke, *Doctors of Infamy: The Story of the Nazi Medical Crimes*: 143.
[894] Winter, *Winter Time: Memoirs of a German Sinto Who Survived Auschwitz*: 98.
[895] Lewy, *The Nazi Persecution of the Gypsies*: 199.
[896] Hanauske-Abel, "Not a Slippery Slope or Sudden Subversion: German Medicine and National Socialism in 1933," 136, Footnote 7.
[897] Lifton, *The Nazi Doctors: Medical Killing and the Psychology of Genocide*: 283.
[898] Ibid., 277-78.
[899] Olga Lengyel, "Scientific Experiments," in *Women and the Holocaust: Different Voices*, ed. Carol Rittner and John K Roth (New York: Paragon House, 1993), 121.
[900] William E Seidelman, "Medicine and Murder in the Third Reich," *Dimensions: A Journal of Holocaust Studies* 13, no. 1 (1999): 2.
[901] Lengyel, *Five Chimneys: A Woman Survivor's True Story of Auschwitz*: 190.
[902] Moorehead, *A Train in Winter: A Story of Resistance, Friendship and Survival in Auschwitz*: 301.
[903] Hanauske-Abel, "Not a Slippery Slope or Sudden Subversion: German Medicine and National Socialism in 1933," 138.
[904] United States Holocaust Memorial Museum, "Homosexuals: Victims of the Nazi Era, 1933-1945," fcit.usf.edu/holocaust/people/USHMMHOM.HTM
[905] Heinz Heger, *The Men with the Pink Triangle* (New York: Alyson Books, 1980), 12-13; Kogon, *The Theory and Practice of Hell: The German Concentration Camps and the System Behind Them*: 172.
[906] Joshua M. Greene, *Justice at Dachau: The Trials of an American Prosecutor* (New York: Broadway Books, 2003), 49; Tom Bower, *The Paperclip Conspiracy: The Hunt for Nazi Scientists* (Boston: Little, Brown and Company, 1987), 223-24; Cornwell, *Hitler's Scientists: Science, War and the Devil's Pact*: 358,60; Morrison, *Ravensbrück: Everyday Life in a Women's Concentration Camp 1939-1945*: 247; Mitscherlich and Mielke, *Doctors of Infamy: The Story of the Nazi Medical Crimes*: 28-9.
[907] Spitz, *Doctors From Hell: The Horrific Accounts of Nazi Experiments on Humans*: 96-100; Cohen, *Human Behaviour in the Concentration Camp*: 87; USA Government, *Nuremberg Medical Case, vol 1, pp 695.* : Vol1 p 251.
[908] Liverpool, *The Scourge of the Swastika*: 186-87.
[909] Kogon, *The Theory and Practice of Hell: The German Concentration Camps and the System Behind Them*: 166.
[910] Hogan and Aretha, *The Holocaust Chronicle*, 624.
[911] Lifton, *The Nazi Doctors: Medical Killing and the Psychology of Genocide*: 294.
[912] Edwin Black, *Nazi Nexus: America's Corporate Connections to Hitler's Holocaust* (Washington D C: Dialog Press, 2009), 66-74.
[913] Posner and Ware, *Mengele: The Complete Story*: 31-32.
[914] Evans, *The Third Reich at War*: 611; Posner and Ware, *Mengele: The Complete Story*: 34.
[915] Lagnado and Dekel, *Children of the Flames: Dr Josef Mengele and The Untold Story of the Twins of Auschwitz*: 70-1.
[916] Lifton, *The Nazi Doctors: Medical Killing and the Psychology of Genocide*: 357-59.
[917] Black, *Nazi Nexus: America's Corporate Connections to Hitler's Holocaust*: 79.
[918] Lagnado and Dekel, *Children of the Flames: Dr Josef Mengele and The Untold Story of the Twins of Auschwitz*: 140.
[919] Lifton, *The Nazi Doctors: Medical Killing and the Psychology of Genocide*.
[920] Glass, *Life Unworthy of Life: Racial Phobia and Mass Murder in Hitler's Germany*: 65.
[921] Gilbert: *Holocaust Journey:* (Vancouver: Douglas and McIntyre, 1997), 159-60; Lifton, *The Nazi Doctors: Medical Killing and the Psychology of Genocide*: 297-98.
[922] Evans, *The Third Reich at War*: 612.
[923] Glass, *Life Unworthy of Life: Racial Phobia and Mass Murder in Hitler's Germany*: 65.
[924] Lifton, *The Nazi Doctors: Medical Killing and the Psychology of Genocide*: 291.

[925] Spitz, *Doctors From Hell: The Horrific Accounts of Nazi Experiments on Humans*: 266.

[926] Martin Gilbert, *The Holocaust: A Record of the Destruction of Jewish Life in Europe During the Dark Years of Nazi Rule* (London: Board of Deputies of British Jews, 1978), 53.

[927] Hogan and Aretha, *The Holocaust Chronicle*, 637.

[928] Spitz, *Doctors From Hell: The Horrific Accounts of Nazi Experiments on Humans*: 266.

[929] Hogan and Aretha, *The Holocaust Chronicle*, 637.

[930] Lagnado and Dekel, *Children of the Flames: Dr Josef Mengele and The Untold Story of the Twins of Auschwitz*: 127; Cornwell, *Hitler's Scientists: Science, War and the Devil's Pact*: 357.

[931] Spitz, *Doctors From Hell: The Horrific Accounts of Nazi Experiments on Humans*: 62.

[932] Horowitz, *In the Shadow of Death: Living Outside the Gates of Mauthausen*: 133-4.

[933] Mitscherlich and Mielke, *Doctors of Infamy: The Story of the Nazi Medical Crimes*: 4.

[934] Cohen, *Human Behaviour in the Concentration Camp*: 268.

[935] Mitscherlich and Mielke, *Doctors of Infamy: The Story of the Nazi Medical Crimes*: 27; Cohen, *Human Behaviour in the Concentration Camp*: 82-3; USA Government, *Nuremberg Medical Case, vol 1, pp 695.* : 245.

[936] Arthus Caplan, "The Relevance of the Holocaust in Bioethics Today," in *Medicine, Ethics, and the Third Reich: Historical and Contemporary Issues*, ed. John J Michalczyk (Kansas City: Sheed and Ward, 1994), 6.

[937] Michael Grodin, "Historical Origins of the Nuremberg Code," in *Medicine, Ethics and the Third Reich: Historical and Contemporary Issues*, ed. John J Michalczyk (Kansas City: Sheed and Wade, 1994); Michael A Grodin, George J Annas, and Leonard H Glantz, "Medicine and Human Reich: A Proposal for International Action," in *Medicine, Ethics and the Third Reich:Historical and Contemporary Issues*, ed. John J Michalczyk (Kansas City: Sheed and Wade, 1994); Michael Kater, "An Historical and Contemporary View of Jewish Doctors in Germany," in *Medicine, Ethics and the Third Reich*, ed. John J Michalczyk (Kansas City: Sheed and Ward, 1944); Seidelman, "Medicine and Murder in the Third Reich."

[938] Mitscherlich and Mielke, *Doctors of Infamy: The Story of the Nazi Medical Crimes*.

[939] David, Fleischhacker, and Hohn, "Abortion and Eugenics in Nazi Germany" 82.

[940] Jay Katz, "The Concentration Camp Experiments: Their Relevance for Contemporary Research with Human Beings," in *Medicine, Ethics and the Third Reich* ed. John J Michalczyk (Kansas City: Sheed and Ward, 1944), 73.

[941] Caplan, "The Relevance of the Holocaust in Bioethics Today," 7.

[942] Katz, "The Concentration Camp Experiments: Their Relevance for Contemporary Research with Human Beings," 74-78.

[943] Ibid., 82-83; USA Government, *Nuremberg Medical Case, vol 1, pp 695.* : Vol 11, p 181.

[944] Katz, "The Concentration Camp Experiments: Their Relevance for Contemporary Research with Human Beings," 82-83.

[945] George Annas, "The Changing Landscape of Human Experimentation: Nuremberg, Helsinki and Beyond," in *Medicine, Ethics and the Third Reich: Historical and Contemporary Issues*, ed. John J Michalczyk (Kansas City: Sheed and Wade, 1994), 107.

[946] Katz, "The Concentration Camp Experiments: Their Relevance for Contemporary Research with Human Beings," 82-83.

[947] Annas, "The Changing Landscape of Human Experimentation: Nuremberg, Helsinki and Beyond," 111.

[948] Ibid., 1221.

[949] Grodin, Annas, and Glantz, "Medicine and Human Reich: A Proposal for International Action," 198.

[950] Katz, "The Concentration Camp Experiments: Their Relevance for Contemporary Research with Human Beings," 74-78.

[951] Dónai P O'Mathúna, "Human Dignity in the Nazi Era: implications for contemporary bioethics," *MBC Medical Ethics* 7, no. 2 (2006), www.biomedcentral.com/1472-6939/7/2.
[952] Ibid.
[953] Beverley Chalmers, "Informed Choice for Women," in *ANDRIA Congress: 'The respected birth to choose for gaining health'* (Cesena, Italy 2007).
[954] Gupta, "Politics of Gender: Women in Nazi Germany," WS-42.
[955] C Sathayamals, "Is Medicine Inherently Sexist?," *Socialist Health Review* 1, no. 2 (September 1984): 53-7.
[956] Evans, *The Coming of the Third Reich*: 128-9, 375-6.
[957] Ibid., 375-6.
[958] David, Fleischhacker, and Hohn, "Abortion and Eugenics in Nazi Germany" 87.
[959] Evans, *The Coming of the Third Reich*: 128.
[960] Ibid., 233.
[961] Ibid., 375-6.
[962] Burleigh and Wipperman, *The Racial State: Germany 1933-1945*: 187.
[963] Ibid.
[964] Evans, *The Coming of the Third Reich*: 375-6; Burleigh and Wipperman, *The Racial State: Germany 1933-1945*: 189-90.
[965] Evans, *The Coming of the Third Reich*: 375-6; Burleigh and Wipperman, *The Racial State: Germany 1933-1945*: 189.
[966] Evans, *The Coming of the Third Reich*: 430.
[967] Koonz, *Mothers in the Fatherland: Women, the Family and Nazi Politics*: 140-43, 66-67.
[968] M Hodann, *International Group for the Investigation of Contraception* (London 1934). Cited byDavid, Fleischhacker, and Hohn, "Abortion and Eugenics in Nazi Germany" 89.
[969] Morrison, *Ravensbrück: Everyday Life in a Women's Concentration Camp 1939-1945*: 40.
[970] Dagmar Herzog, "Hubris and Hypocrisy, Incitement and Disavowal: Sexuality and German Fascism.," *Journal of the History of Sexuality* 11, no. 1/2 (2002): 11.
[971] Evans, *The Third Reich in Power*: 244-6.
[972] Grunberger, *A Social History of the Third Reich*: 557-8.
[973] Ibid.
[974] Evans, *The Third Reich in Power*: 288.
[975] Ibid., 280.
[976] Ibid., 246.
[977] Koonz, *Mothers in the Fatherland: Women, the Family and Nazi Politics*: 287.
[978] Ibid.
[979] Annette F Timm, "Sex with a Purpose: Venereal Disease, and Militarized Masculinity in the Third Reich," *Journal of the History of Sexuality* 11, no. 1/2 (2002): 223-24.
[980] Erna Paris, *Unhealed Wounds: France and the Klaus Barbie Affair* (Toronto: Methuen, 1985), 38.
[981] Timm, "Sex with a Purpose: Venereal Disease, and Militarized Masculinity in the Third Reich," 46-7.
[982] Marione Ingram, *The Hands of War* (New York: Skyhorse Publishing, 2013), 57.
[983] Timm, "Sex with a Purpose: Venereal Disease, and Militarized Masculinity in the Third Reich," 223-4.
[984] Hitler, *Mein Kampf*: 145.
[985] George Mosse, *The Image of Man: The Creation of Modern Masculinity* (New York1996), 175-76.
[986] Herzog, "Hubris and Hypocrisy, Incitement and Disavowal: Sexuality and German Fascism.," 5.
[987] Timm, "Sex with a Purpose: Venereal Disease, and Militarized Masculinity in the Third Reich," 234.

[988] Elizabeth Heineman, "Sexuality and Nazism: The Doubly Unspeakable?," *Journal of the History of Sexuality* 11, no. 1/2 (Jan-Apr 2002): 44.

[989] Klemperer, *I Shall Bear Witness: The Diaries of Victor Klemperer 1933-1941.*: 131.

[990] Herzog, "Hubris and Hypocrisy, Incitement and Disavowal: Sexuality and German Fascism.," 9.

[991] Grunberger, *A Social History of the Third Reich*: 310.

[992] Ibid., 356.

[993] Heineman, "Sexuality and Nazism: The Doubly Unspeakable?," 30.

[994] Bleuel, *Sex and Society in Nazi Germany*: 241-4.

[995] Knopp, *Hitler's Children*: x.

[996] Ibid., 111.

[997] Grunberger, *A Social History of the Third Reich*: 424.

[998] Bleuel, *Sex and Society in Nazi Germany*: 241-4.

[999] Grunberger, *A Social History of the Third Reich*: 318.

[1000] Herzog, "Hubris and Hypocrisy, Incitement and Disavowal: Sexuality and German Fascism.," 7.

[1001] Ibid., 7, 9 Note 13.

[1002] Timm, "Sex with a Purpose: Venereal Disease, and Militarized Masculinity in the Third Reich," 228-9.

[1003] Ibid., 234.

[1004] Herzog, "Hubris and Hypocrisy, Incitement and Disavowal: Sexuality and German Fascism.," 8-9.

[1005] Ibid., 10-12.

[1006] Ibid., 12.

[1007] Udo Pini, *Leibeskult und Liebeskitsch. Erotik im Dritten Reich* (Munich1992), 219,326,53.

[1008] Heineman, "Sexuality and Nazism: The Doubly Unspeakable?," 29.

[1009] Heck, *A Child of Hitler*: 147.

[1010] Grunberger, *A Social History of the Third Reich*: 424.

[1011] Evans, *The Third Reich in Power*: 472.

[1012] Timm, "Sex with a Purpose: Venereal Disease, and Militarized Masculinity in the Third Reich," 247.

[1013] Regina Mühlhäuser, "Between 'Racial Awareness' and Fantasies of Potencies: Nazi Sexual Politics in the Occupied Territories of the Soviet Union, 1942-1945.," in *Brutality and Desire: War and Sexuality in Europe's Twentieth Century*, ed. Dagmar Herzog (Houndmills, Basingstoke, Hampshire: Pelgrave Macmillan, 2009), 208, 13.

[1014] Ibid.

[1015] Bleuel, *Sex and Society in Nazi Germany*: 213.

[1016] Birthe Kundrus and Patricia Szobar, "Forbidden Company: Romantic Relationships between Germans and Foreigners 1933-1945," *Journal of the History of Sexuality* 11, no. 1/2 (2002): 206.

[1017] Bleuel, *Sex and Society in Nazi Germany*: 213.

[1018] Evans, *The Third Reich at War*: 544.

[1019] Kundrus and Szobar, "Forbidden Company: Romantic Relationships between Germans and Foreigners 1933-1945," 206.

[1020] Ibid., 209.

[1021] Ibid.

[1022] Bleuel, *Sex and Society in Nazi Germany*: 225; Lifton, *The Nazi Doctors: Medical Killing and the Psychology of Genocide*: 270-1.

[1023] Lengyel, *Five Chimneys: A Woman Survivor's True Story of Auschwitz*: 195.

[1024] Höss, *Death Dealer: The Memoirs of the SS Kommandant of Auschwitz*: 278; Lifton, *The Nazi Doctors: Medical Killing and the Psychology of Genocide*: 270-1; Morrison, *Ravensbrück: Everyday Life in a Women's Concentration Camp 1939-1945*: 201-4.

[1025] Lengyel, *Five Chimneys: A Woman Survivor's True Story of Auschwitz*: 201-03.

[1026] Bleuel, *Sex and Society in Nazi Germany*: 138-9.
[1027] Ibid., 226.
[1028] Lichtblau, "The Holocaust Just Got More Shocking".
[1029] Mühlhäuser, "Between 'Racial Awareness' and Fantasies of Potencies: Nazi Sexual Politics in the Occupied Territories of the Soviet Union, 1942-1945.," 202-07.
[1030] Robert Sommer, *Das KZ-Bordell (The Concentration Camp Bordello; Sexual Forced Labor in National Socialist Concentration Camps).* (Paderborn Schoeningh Verlag, 2009); ibid.
[1031] Roos, «Backlash Against Prostitutes' Rights: Origins and Dynamics of Nazi Prostitution Policies.,» 92.
[1032] Baer and Baer, «Introduction,» 32-34.
[1033] Bleuel, *Sex and Society in Nazi Germany*: 228.
[1034] Evans, *The Third Reich at War*: 351-3.
[1035] Bleuel, *Sex and Society in Nazi Germany*: 228.
[1036] Ibid.
[1037] Evans, *The Third Reich at War*: 351-3.
[1038] Bleuel, *Sex and Society in Nazi Germany*: 227.
[1039] Morrison, *Ravensbrück: Everyday Life in a Women's Concentration Camp 1939-1945*: 201-4; Saidel, *The Jewish Women of Ravensbrück Concentration Camp*: 213; Sybil Milton, "Women and the Holocaust: The Case of German and German-Jewish Women," in *Different Voices: Women and the Holocaust*, ed. Carol Rittner and John K Roth (New York: Paragon House, 1993), 226; Albert Haas, *The Doctor and the Damned* (New York: St Martin's Press, 1984), 234-6.
[1040] Jack Eisner, *The Survivor of The Holocaust* (New York: Kensington Books, 1980), 231; Morrison, *Ravensbrück: Everyday Life in a Women's Concentration Camp 1939-1945*: 201-4; Saidel, *The Jewish Women of Ravensbrück Concentration Camp*: 213; Smith, *Remembering: Voices of the Holocaust*: 231; Sruoga, *Forest of the Gods*: 299; Solomon H Stecknoll, *The Alderney Death Camp* (London: Grenada Publishing, 1982), 85.
[1041] Venezia, *Inside the Gas Chambers: Eight Months in the Sonderkommando of Auschwitz*: 37; Posner and Ware, *Mengele: The Complete Story*: 24; Lee, *The Hidden Life of Otto Frank*: 141-2.
[1042] Jean-Francois Steiner, *Treblinka* (New York: Simon and Schuster, 1967), 333, 60.
[1043] Baer and Baer, "Introduction," 32-4.
[1044] Hebermann, *The Blessed Abyss: Inmate #6582 in Ravensbrück Concentration Camp for Women*: 32-4, 131.
[1045] Poltawska, *And I Am Afraid Of My Dreams*: 104.
[1046] Hebermann, *The Blessed Abyss: Inmate #6582 in Ravensbrück Concentration Camp for Women*: 32-4.
[1047] Haas, *The Doctor and the Damned*: 234-6; Baer and Baer, "Introduction," 32-4.
[1048] Morrison, *Ravensbrück: Everyday Life in a Women's Concentration Camp 1939-1945*: 201-4.
[1049] Gross-Martin, *Silvia*: 286-7.
[1050] Sommer, *Das KZ-Bordell (The Concentration Camp Bordello; Sexual Forced Labor in National Socialist Concentration Camps).* : 172; ———, "Sexual Exploitation of Women in Nazi Concentration Camp Brothels," in *Sexual Violence Against Jewish Women During the Holocaust*, ed. Sonja M Hedgepeth and Rochelle G Saidel (Waltham, Massachusetts: Brandeis University Press, 2010), 438-49.
[1051] Morrison, *Ravensbrück: Everyday Life in a Women's Concentration Camp 1939-1945*: 45.
[1052] Saidel, *The Jewish Women of Ravensbrück Concentration Camp*: 37.
[1053] Morrison, *Ravensbrück: Everyday Life in a Women's Concentration Camp 1939-1945*: 45.
[1054] Saidel, *The Jewish Women of Ravensbrück Concentration Camp*: 213.
[1055] Haas, *The Doctor and the Damned*: 234-6.

[1056] Nerin E Gun, "Dachau, 1945," in *A Taste of War: Eyewitness Accounts of World War II*, ed. Harld Elk Straubing (New York: Sterling Publishing Co, Inc., 1992), 246-7.
[1057] Haas, *The Doctor and the Damned*: 234-6.
[1058] Baer and Baer, "Introduction," 32-4.
[1059] Haas, *The Doctor and the Damned*: 234-6.
[1060] Sommer, *Das KZ-Bordell (The Concentration Camp Bordello; Sexual Forced Labor in National Socialist Concentration Camps).* : 178.
[1061] Roos, "Backlash Against Prostitutes' Rights: Origins and Dynamics of Nazi Prostitution Policies.," 94.
[1062] Gun, "Dachau, 1945," 246-7.
[1063] Ibid.
[1064] Haas, *The Doctor and the Damned*: 234-6.
[1065] Sommer, "Sexual Exploitation of Women in Nazi Concentration Camp Brothels," 54.
[1066] 135633 Ka-Tzetnik, *House of Dolls* (London: Granada, 1973).
[1067] Kitty Hart, *Return To Auschwitz* (London: Grafton Books, 1983), 163; Eisner, *The Survivor of The Holocaust*: 236; Haas, *The Doctor and the Damned*: 234-6.
[1068] Sommer, "Sexual Exploitation of Women in Nazi Concentration Camp Brothels," 174.
[1069] Helene J Sinnreich, "The Rape of Jewish Women During the Holocaust," in *Sexual Violence Against Jewish Women During the Holocaust*, ed. Sonja M Hedgepeth and Rochelle G Saidel (Waltham, Massachusetts: Brandeis University Press, 2010), 116.
[1070] Sommer, "Sexual Exploitation of Women in Nazi Concentration Camp Brothels," 174.
[1071] ———, *Das KZ-Bordell (The Concentration Camp Bordello; Sexual Forced Labor in National Socialist Concentration Camps).* : 183.
[1072] ———, "Sexual Exploitation of Women in Nazi Concentration Camp Brothels," 53.
[1073] Eisner, *The Survivor of The Holocaust*: 238-39.
[1074] Lichtblau, "The Holocaust Just Got More Shocking".
[1075] Sinnreich, "The Rape of Jewish Women During the Holocaust," 116.
[1076] Mühlhäuser, "Between 'Racial Awareness' and Fantasies of Potencies: Nazi Sexual Politics in the Occupied Territories of the Soviet Union, 1942-1945.," 202-07.
[1077] Sinnreich, "The Rape of Jewish Women During the Holocaust," 116.
[1078] Mühlhäuser, "Between 'Racial Awareness' and Fantasies of Potencies: Nazi Sexual Politics in the Occupied Territories of the Soviet Union, 1942-1945.," 202-07.
[1079] Sinnreich, "The Rape of Jewish Women During the Holocaust," 116.
[1080] Ibid.
[1081] Tory, *Surviving the Holocaust: The Kovno Ghetto Diary*: 509.
[1082] Sinnreich, "The Rape of Jewish Women During the Holocaust," 116.
[1083] Esther Dror and Ruth Linn, "The Shame is Always There," in *Sexual Violence Against Jewish Women During the Holocaust*, ed. Sonja M Hedgepeth and Rochelle G Saidel (Waltham, Massachusetts: Brandeis University Press, 2010), 276, 90 (Notes).
[1084] Mühlhäuser, "Between 'Racial Awareness' and Fantasies of Potencies: Nazi Sexual Politics in the Occupied Territories of the Soviet Union, 1942-1945.," 202-07.
[1085] Millu, *Smoke Over Birkenau*: 153.
[1086] Heger, *The Men with the Pink Triangle*: 99.
[1087] Rosenbaum, *The Holocaust and Halakhah*: 145-46.
[1088] Ibid., 147.
[1089] Ka-Tzetnik, *House of Dolls*.
[1090] Cohen, *Human Behaviour in the Concentration Camp*: 142.
[1091] Sommer, *Das KZ-Bordell (The Concentration Camp Bordello; Sexual Forced Labor in National Socialist Concentration Camps).* : 183.
[1092] Heger, *The Men with the Pink Triangle*: 89.
[1093] Ibid., 100.
[1094] Bleuel, *Sex and Society in Nazi Germany*: 225; Waller, *The Devil's Doctor: Felix Kersten and the Secret Plot to Turn Himmler Against Hitler*: 38.
[1095] Bleuel, *Sex and Society in Nazi Germany*: 225.

[1096] Ernst Klee, Willi Dressen, and Volker Reiss, eds., *The Good Old Days: The Holocaust As Seen By Its Perpetrators and Bystanders* (Old Saybrook, Connecticut: Konecky and Konecky, 1991), 234; Evans, *The Third Reich at War*: 291.

[1097] Klee, Dressen, and Reiss, *The Good Old Days: The Holocaust As Seen By Its Perpetrators and Bystanders*, 234; Evans, *The Third Reich at War*: 291; Venezia, *Inside the Gas Chambers: Eight Months in the Sonderkommando of Auschwitz*: 18; Donald L. Niewyk, *The Holocaust: Problems and Perspectives of Interpretation* (Boston: Houghton Mifflin, 1997), 75.

[1098] Alison Owings, *Frauen: German Women Recall the Third Reich* (London: Penguin Books, 1993), 147,68,76,405,34,47,65; Antony Beevor, "Introduction," in *A Woman in Berlin*, ed. Anonymous (New York: Picador, 2000), xxi; Sack, *An Eye For An Eye: The Untold Story of Jewish Revenge Against Germans in 1945*: 48-9,54; Lalli Horstman, *Nothing For Tears* (London: Weidenfeld and Nicolson, 1953), 40, 84, 88-9, 104-6, 19, 30,40, 47,53, 68, 76 ; Steinhoff, Pechel, and Showalter, *Voices From the Third Reich: An Oral History*: 429,37,46,48,54-5,58-9,69; Anonymous, *A Woman in Berlin: Eight Weeks in the Conquered City* (New York: Picador, 2000), 95,136,204.

[1099] Agate Nesaulle, *A Woman in Amber: Healing the Trauma of War and Exile* (New York: Penguin Books, 1995), 54; Rubinek, *So Many Miracles*: 153; Gross-Martin, *Silvia*: 279; Gilbert, *The Boys: The Story of 732 Young Concentration Camp Survivors*: 53; Saidel, *The Jewish Women of Ravensbrück Concentration Camp*: 155,75; ibid; ibid.

[1100] Katrin Fitzherbert, *True to Both My Selves: A Family Memoir of Germany and England in Two World Wars* (London: Virago Press, 1997), 172.

[1101] Owings, *Frauen: German Women Recall the Third Reich*: 405; Ana Porter, *Kasztner's Train: The True Story of Rezsö Kasztner, Unknown Hero of the Holocaust* (Vancouver: Douglas & McIntyre, 2007), 326; Sack, *An Eye For An Eye: The Untold Story of Jewish Revenge Against Germans in 1945*: 48-9.

[1102] Mazower, *Dark Continent: Europe's Twentieth Century*: 217; Owings, *Frauen: German Women Recall the Third Reich*: 164; Anonymous, *A Woman in Berlin: Eight Weeks in the Conquered City*: 136; Steinhoff, Pechel, and Showalter, *Voices From the Third Reich: An Oral History*: 437; Porter, *Kasztner's Train: The True Story of Rezsö Kasztner, Unknown Hero of the Holocaust*: 326; Gilbert, *The Boys: The Story of 732 Young Concentration Camp Survivors*: 53; Fitzherbert, *True to Both My Selves: A Family Memoir of Germany and England in Two World Wars*: 135; Antony Beevor, *The Fall of Berlin 1945.* (New York: Penguin Books, 2002), 29, 31, 67, 312, .

[1103] Grossmann, *Jews, Germans, and the Allies: Close Encounters in Occupied Germany*: 53.

[1104] Evans, *The Third Reich at War*: 710; Owings, *Frauen: German Women Recall the Third Reich*: 164.

[1105] Beevor, *The Fall of Berlin 1945.* : 326; ibid; Evans, *The Third Reich at War*: 710.

[1106] Grossmann, *Jews, Germans, and the Allies: Close Encounters in Occupied Germany*: 53.

[1107] Hans Magnus Enzenberger, "introduction," in *A Woman in Berlin: Eight weeks in the conquered city: A Diary*, ed. Anonymous (New York: Picador, 2000), xi; Moorhouse, *Killing Hitler: The Plots, the Assassins, and the Dictator Who Cheated Death*: 311.

[1108] Owings, *Frauen: German Women Recall the Third Reich*: 146.

[1109] Grossmann, *Jews, Germans, and the Allies: Close Encounters in Occupied Germany*: 49.

[1110] Morrison, *Ravensbrück: Everyday Life in a Women's Concentration Camp 1939-1945*: 305.

[1111] Antony Beevor, The Guardian, http://zhopa007.livejournal.com/ ; ———, *The Fall of Berlin 1945.* : 326.

[1112] ———, *The Fall of Berlin 1945.* : 31.

[1113] Ibid.

[1114] Steinhoff, Pechel, and Showalter, *Voices From the Third Reich: An Oral History*: 446.

[1115] Horstman, *Nothing For Tears*: 106; Evans, *The Third Reich at War*: 710; Beevor, *The Fall of Berlin 1945.* : 412.

[1116] Atina Grossmann, "A Question of Silence: The rape of German Women by Occupation Soldiers," *October* 72, no. Berlin 1945: War and Rape "Liberators take Liberties" (1995): 55; ———, *Jews, Germans, and the Allies: Close Encounters in Occupied Germany*: 38.

[1117] Beevor, *The Fall of Berlin 1945.* : 412.

[1118] Evans, *The Third Reich at War*: 710; Porter, *Kasztner's Train: The True Story of Rezsö Kasztner, Unknown Hero of the Holocaust*: 326; Steinhoff, Pechel, and Showalter, *Voices From the Third Reich: An Oral History*: 458-9.

[1119] Beevor, *The Fall of Berlin 1945.* : 412.

[1120] Knopp, *Hitler's Children*: 247.

[1121] Evans, *The Third Reich at War*: 733.

[1122] Ibid; Beevor, *The Fall of Berlin 1945.* : 312.

[1123] Grossmann, *Jews, Germans, and the Allies: Close Encounters in Occupied Germany*: 77.

[1124] Porter, *Kasztner's Train: The True Story of Rezsö Kasztner, Unknown Hero of the Holocaust*: 343; Beevor, *The Fall of Berlin 1945.* : 294, 345-46.

[1125] Saidel, *The Jewish Women of Ravensbrück Concentration Camp*: 171.

[1126] Anonymous, *A Woman in Berlin: Eight Weeks in the Conquered City.*

[1127] Grossmann, "A Question of Silence: The rape of German Women by Occupation Soldiers," 54; Beevor, *The Fall of Berlin 1945.* : 345; Grossmann, *Jews, Germans, and the Allies: Close Encounters in Occupied Germany*: 53.

[1128] Beevor, *The Fall of Berlin 1945.* : 414.

[1129] Grossmann, *Jews, Germans, and the Allies: Close Encounters in Occupied Germany*: 50.

[1130] Gross-Martin, *Silvia*: 279.

[1131] Grossmann, "A Question of Silence: The rape of German Women by Occupation Soldiers," 50; Beevor, *The Fall of Berlin 1945.* : 28.

[1132] Gilbert, *The Boys: The Story of 732 Young Concentration Camp Survivors*: 53.

[1133] Moorhouse, *Killing Hitler: The Plots, the Assassins, and the Dictator Who Cheated Death*: 311.

[1134] Beevor, *The Fall of Berlin 1945.* : 410.

[1135] Moorhouse, *Killing Hitler: The Plots, the Assassins, and the Dictator Who Cheated Death*: 311.

[1136] Anonymous, *A Woman in Berlin: Eight Weeks in the Conquered City*: 136.

[1137] Horstman, *Nothing For Tears*: 88.

[1138] Steinhoff, Pechel, and Showalter, *Voices From the Third Reich: An Oral History*: 454-5.

[1139] Beevor, *The Fall of Berlin 1945.* : 410.

[1140] Grossmann, "A Question of Silence: The rape of German Women by Occupation Soldiers," 53; ———, *Jews, Germans, and the Allies: Close Encounters in Occupied Germany*: 52.

[1141] ———, *Jews, Germans, and the Allies: Close Encounters in Occupied Germany*: 51.

[1142] Beevor, *The Fall of Berlin 1945.* : 410.

[1143] Anonymous, *A Woman in Berlin: Eight Weeks in the Conquered City*: xxi.

[1144] Beevor, *The Fall of Berlin 1945.* : 31.

[1145] Ibid.

[1146] ———, "Introduction," xix.

[1147] ———, *The Fall of Berlin*: 32

[1148] ———, *The Fall of Berlin 1945.* : 326-27.

[1149] Grossmann, "A Question of Silence: The rape of German Women by Occupation Soldiers," 45.

[1150] Ibid., 46.

[1151] Ibid., 49.

[1152] Lower, *Hitler's Furies: German Women in the Nazi Killing Fields*: 166-68.
[1153] Ritvo and Plotkin, *Sisters in Sorrow: Voices of Care in the Holocaust*: 197.
[1154] Amos Oz, *A Tale of Love and Darkness* (London: Vintage Books, 2005), 188.
[1155] Ibid., 175.
[1156] Tec, *Resilience and Courage: Women, Men and the Holocaust*: 28.
[1157] Eisner, *The Survivor of The Holocaust*: 72-3; Szwajger, *I Remember Nothing More: The Warsaw Children's Hospital and Jewish Resistance*: 146; Eichengreen and Chamberlain, *From Ashes to Life: My Memories of the Holocaust*: 65.
[1158] Eber, *The Choice: Poland 1939-1945*: 98-9; Johnson and Reuband, *What We Knew: Terror, Mass Murder, and Everyday Life in Nazi Germany*: 202; Kaplan, *Between Dignity and Despair: Jewish Life in Nazi Germany*: 208.
[1159] Eichengreen and Chamberlain, *From Ashes to Life: My Memories of the Holocaust*: 49.
[1160] Dalia Ofer, "Gender Issues in Diaries and Testimonies of the Ghetto: The Case of Warsaw," in *Women in the Holocaust*, ed. Dalia Ofer and Lenore J Weitzman (New Haven: Yale University Press, 1998), 163.
[1161] Kaplan, *Between Dignity and Despair: Jewish Life in Nazi Germany*: 72.
[1162] Emanuel Ringelblum, *RingelblumYoman ve-Reshimot Mitkufat, ha-Milhama [Diary and Notes from the Warsaw Ghetto: Sept 1939-December 1942]* (Jerusalem: Yad Vashem, September 1939-December 1942), 432.
[1163] Gill, *The Journey Back From Hell: Conversations with Concentration Camp Survivors*: 150.
[1164] Berg, *The Diary of Mary Berg*: 81-2.
[1165] Stiffel, *The Tale of the Ring: A Kaddish*: 53.
[1166] Hilberg, Staron, and Kermisz, *The Warsaw Diary of Adam Czerniakow: Prelude to Doom*: 317.
[1167] Evans, *The Third Reich at War*: 313.
[1168] Adelson and Lapides, *Łódź Ghetto: Inside a Community Under Siege*, 135-6.
[1169] Tec, *Resilience and Courage: Women, Men and the Holocaust*: 313.
[1170] Aviva Kempner, "Comment" (paper presented at the Women Surviving the Holocaust, 1983), 93.
[1171] Nechama Tec, "Women Among the Forest Partisans," in *Women in the Holocaust*, ed. Dalia Ofer and Lenore J Weitzman (New Haven: Yale University Press, 1998), 230.
[1172] ———, *Resilience and Courage: Women, Men and the Holocaust*: 313.
[1173] ———, "Women Among the Forest Partisans," 225-9.
[1174] ———, *Resilience and Courage: Women, Men and the Holocaust*: 4.
[1175] ———, "Women Among the Forest Partisans," 225-6.
[1176] Inbar, *Spots of Light: To Be a Woman in the Holocaust*: 56,87; Tec, *Resilience and Courage: Women, Men and the Holocaust*: 305.
[1177] ———, *Resilience and Courage: Women, Men and the Holocaust*: 328.
[1178] Faye Schulman, *A Partisan's Memoir: Woman of the Holocaust* (Toronto: Second Story Press, 1995), 146.
[1179] Tec, *Resilience and Courage: Women, Men and the Holocaust*: 135.
[1180] Gilbert, *The Boys: The Story of 732 Young Concentration Camp Survivors*: 151.
[1181] Tec, *Resilience and Courage: Women, Men and the Holocaust*: 135; Karay, *Death comes in Yellow: Skarżysko-Kamienna Slave Labor Camp.* : 116,209.
[1182] ———, "Women in the Forced-Labor Camps," in *Women in the Holocaust*, ed. Dalia Ofer and Lenore J Weitzman (New Haven: Yale University Press, 1998), 288-90.
[1183] Ibid., 289-90; ———, *Death comes in Yellow: Skarżysko-Kamienna Slave Labor Camp.* : 153.
[1184] ———, *Death comes in Yellow: Skarżysko-Kamienna Slave Labor Camp.* : 147.
[1185] Ibid., 186.
[1186] ———, "Women in the Forced-Labor Camps," 290; ———, *Death comes in Yellow: Skarżysko-Kamienna Slave Labor Camp.* : 152.
[1187] ———, "Women in the Forced-Labor Camps," 290.

[1188] Katz and Ringelheim, *Proceedings of the Conference Women Surviving the Holocaust*, 165.
[1189] Karay, "Women in the Forced-Labor Camps," 296; ———, *Death comes in Yellow: Skarżysko-Kamienna Slave Labor Camp.* : 116.
[1190] ———, "Women in the Forced-Labor Camps," 296.
[1191] ———, *Death comes in Yellow: Skarżysko-Kamienna Slave Labor Camp.* : 116, 209.
[1192] Ibid., 158, 209, 45.
[1193] ———, "Women in the Forced-Labor Camps," 297.
[1194] Ibid.
[1195] ———, *Death comes in Yellow: Skarżysko-Kamienna Slave Labor Camp.* : 158.
[1196] Ritvo and Plotkin, *Sisters in Sorrow: Voices of Care in the Holocaust*: 131; Adelsberger, *Auschwitz: A Doctor's Story*: 111; Sruoga, *Forest of the Gods*: 273-5; Morrison, *Ravensbrück: Everyday Life in a Women's Concentration Camp 1939-1945*: 256-7; Elias, *Triumph of Hope: From Theresienstadt and Auschwitz to Israel*: 114.
[1197] Adelsberger, *Auschwitz: A Doctor's Story*: 111.
[1198] Niewyk, *The Holocaust: Problems and Perspectives of Interpretation*: 86-7.
[1199] Hart, *I Am Alive*: 75.
[1200] Ibid., 99.
[1201] Delbo, *Auschwitz and After*: 160-61.
[1202] Sruoga, *Forest of the Gods*: 273-5.
[1203] Morrison, *Ravensbrück: Everyday Life in a Women's Concentration Camp 1939-1945*: 256-7.
[1204] Vrba, *I Escaped from Auschwitz*: 137-9.
[1205] Steiner, *Treblinka*: 365.
[1206] Morrison, *Ravensbrück: Everyday Life in a Women's Concentration Camp 1939-1945*: 256-7.
[1207] Höss, *Death Dealer: The Memoirs of the SS Kommandant of Auschwitz*: 42.
[1208] Müller, *Eyewitness Auschwitz: Three Years in the Gas Chambers*: 62-3.
[1209] Millu, *Smoke Over Birkenau*: 23.
[1210] Ibid., 25,33.
[1211] Bondy, "Women in Theresienstadt and the Family Camp in Birkenau," 320; Bruml, "I was a Nurse in Theresienstadt," 29.
[1212] Bondy, "Women in Theresienstadt and the Family Camp in Birkenau," 320.
[1213] Smith, *Remembering: Voices of the Holocaust*: 142.
[1214] Elias, *Triumph of Hope: From Theresienstadt and Auschwitz to Israel*: 99.
[1215] Schiff, *Hitler's Inferno: Eight Intimate and Personal Histories from the Holocaust*: 24.
[1216] Lengyel, *Five Chimneys: A Woman Survivor's True Story of Auschwitz*: 197.
[1217] Bondy, "Women in Theresienstadt and the Family Camp in Birkenau," 320.
[1218] Müller, *Eyewitness Auschwitz: Three Years in the Gas Chambers*: 62-3.
[1219] Schwertfeger, *Women of Theresienstadt: Voices from a Concentration Camp*: 58.
[1220] Inbar, *Spots of Light: To Be a Woman in the Holocaust*: 67,82.
[1221] Ibid., 70-2.
[1222] Vrba, *I Escaped from Auschwitz*: 190-1.
[1223] Inbar, *Spots of Light: To Be a Woman in the Holocaust*: 21-2.
[1224] Nomberg-Przytyk, *Auschwitz: True Tales from a Grotesque Land*: 178.
[1225] Fenelon, *Playing for Time*: 178-84; Hart, *Return To Auschwitz*: 165-6; Nomberg-Przytyk, *Auschwitz: True Tales from a Grotesque Land*: 100-04; Tedeschi, *There is a Place on Earth: A Woman in Birkenau*: 128; Levi, *The Drowned and the Saved*: 155-6.
[1226] Fenelon, *Playing for Time*: 178-84.
[1227] Arad, *Belzec, Sobibor, Treblinka: The Operation Reinhard Death Camps*: 229.36.
[1228] Irek Dobrowolski, "The Portraitist," (Poland: Auschwitz Museum, 2005).
[1229] Carla Hinton, "Israeli sisters visit Oklahoma City to tell their parents' Holocaust story," Newsok.com/article/3557742; Steven Spielberg, "Schindler's List," (1993).
[1230] Arad, *Belzec, Sobibor, Treblinka: The Operation Reinhard Death Camps*: 236.

[1231] Ibid., 217; Eli Rozenberg, in *Yad Vashem Archives, Jerusalem, 0-3/4039*, 7-8.
[1232] Arad, *Belzec, Sobibor, Treblinka: The Operation Reinhard Death Camps*: 226.
[1233] Ibid.
[1234] Is, *U.B.B.: Unforgettable Bergen-Belsen*: 109.
[1235] Robert Clary, *From the Holocaust to Hogan's Heroes: The Autobiography of Robert Clary* (Lanham, Maryland: Madison Books, 2001), 79-80; Venezia, *Inside the Gas Chambers: Eight Months in the Sonderkommando of Auschwitz*: 97; Vera Laska, "Women in the Resistance and in the Holocaust," in *Different Voices: Women and the Holocaust*, ed. Carol Rittner and John Roth (New York: Paragon House, 1993), 263-4; Gill, *The Journey Back From Hell: Conversations with Concentration Camp Survivors*: 194.
[1236] Rebecca Scherr, "The Uses of Memory and Abuses of Fiction: Sexuality in Holocaust Film, Fiction and memoir.," in *Experience and Expression: Women, the Nazis, and the Holocaust*, ed. Elizabeth R Baer and Myrna Goldenberg (Detroit: Wayne State University Press, 2003), 289.
[1237] Ibid., 296.
[1238] Venezia, *Inside the Gas Chambers: Eight Months in the Sonderkommando of Auschwitz*: 97.
[1239] Feinstein, "Absent Fathers, Present Mothers: Images of Parenthood in Holocaust Survivor Narratives," 175.
[1240] Gill, *The Journey Back From Hell: Conversations with Concentration Camp Survivors*: 105.
[1241] Terrence Des Pres, *The Survivor: An Anatomy of Life in the Death Camps* (New York: Oxford University Press, 1976), 190.
[1242] Vrba, *I Escaped from Auschwitz*: 60-1.
[1243] Schiff, *Hitler's Inferno: Eight Intimate and Personal Histories from the Holocaust*: 274.
[1244] Ibid.
[1245] Eichengreen and Chamberlain, *From Ashes to Life: My Memories of the Holocaust*: 190.
[1246] Adelsberger, *Auschwitz: A Doctor's Story*: 34,61.
[1247] Müller, *Eyewitness Auschwitz: Three Years in the Gas Chambers*: 151.
[1248] Shik, *Sexual Abuse of Jewish Women in Auschwitz-Birkenau*, 235.
[1249] Feinstein, "Jewish Women in Time: The Challenge of Feminist Artistic Installations About the Holocaust," 263.
[1250] Bondy, "Women in Theresienstadt and the Family Camp in Birkenau," 320.
[1251] Shik, *Sexual Abuse of Jewish Women in Auschwitz-Birkenau*, 233.
[1252] Ibid., 239.
[1253] Katz and Ringelheim, *Proceedings of the Conference Women Surviving the Holocaust*, 141.
[1254] Vera Laska, *Women in the Resistance and in the Holocaust* (Westport Connecticut: Greenwood Press, 1983), 25.
[1255] Katz and Ringelheim, *Proceedings of the Conference Women Surviving the Holocaust*, 19-20.
[1256] Shik, *Sexual Abuse of Jewish Women in Auschwitz-Birkenau*, 239.
[1257] Ringelheim, "Women and the Holocaust: A Reconsideration of Research.," 376.
[1258] Lengyel, *Five Chimneys: A Woman Survivor's True Story of Auschwitz*: 60-3.
[1259] Ritvo and Plotkin, *Sisters in Sorrow: Voices of Care in the Holocaust*: 45.
[1260] Perl, *I was a Doctor in Auschwitz*: 57-8.
[1261] Ibid., 90.
[1262] Tec, *Resilience and Courage: Women, Men and the Holocaust*: 144.
[1263] Miriam Gerchik, "Massuah, Tel Aviv, 033c/3600," 8.
[1264] Perl, *I was a Doctor in Auschwitz*: 76.
[1265] Ibid., 78-9.
[1266] Ibid., 78.
[1267] Lengyel, *Five Chimneys: A Woman Survivor's True Story of Auschwitz*: 196.

1268 Perl, *I was a Doctor in Auschwitz*: 78-9.

1269 Tec, *Resilience and Courage: Women, Men and the Holocaust*: 144-6.

1270 Kirsty Chatwood, "Schillinger and the Dancer: Representing Agency and Sexual Violence in Holocaust Testimonies," in *Sexual Violence Against Jewish Women During the Holocaust*, ed. Sonja M Hedgepeth and Rochelle G Saidel (Waltham, Massachusetts: Brandeis University Press, 2010), 61; Winter, *Winter Time: Memoirs of a German Sinto Who Survived Auschwitz*: 81.

1271 ———, *Winter Time: Memoirs of a German Sinto Who Survived Auschwitz*: 135, note 67.

1272 Scherr, "The Uses of Memory and Abuses of Fiction: Sexuality in Holocaust Film, Fiction and memoir.," 293.

1273 Chatwood, "Schillinger and the Dancer: Representing Agency and Sexual Violence in Holocaust Testimonies," 61.

1274 Nomi Levenkron, "Death and the Maidens: "Prostitution," Rape, and Sexual Slavery during World War II," in *Sexual Violence Against Jewish Women During the Holocaust*, ed. Sonja M Hedgepeth and Rochelle G Saidel (Waltham, Massachusetts: Brandeis University Press, 2010).

1275 Shik, "Infinite Loneliness: Some Aspects of the Lives of Jewish Women in the Auschwitz Camps According to Testimonies and Autobiographies Written Between 1945 and 1948.," 148.

1276 Levenkron, "Death and the Maidens: "Prostitution," Rape, and Sexual Slavery during World War II," 16.

1277 Shik, *Sexual Abuse of Jewish Women in Auschwitz-Birkenau*, 237.

1278 Horowitz, "Women in Holocaust Literature: Engendering Trauma Memory," 369-70.

1279 Gill, *The Journey Back From Hell: Conversations with Concentration Camp Survivors*: 419.

1280 Yvonne Kozlovsky-Golan, """Public Property": Sexual Abuse of Women and Girls in Cinematic Memory," in *Sexual Violence Against Jewish Women During the Holocaust*, ed. Sonja M Hedgepeth and Rochelle G Saidel (Waltham, Massachusetts: Brandeis University Press, 2010), 244-45.

1281 Levenkron, "Death and the Maidens: "Prostitution," Rape, and Sexual Slavery during World War II," 16.

1282 Pivnik, *Survivor: Auschwitz, the Death March and My Flight for Freedom*: 92.

1283 Shik, "Infinite Loneliness: Some Aspects of the Lives of Jewish Women in the Auschwitz Camps According to Testimonies and Autobiographies Written Between 1945 and 1948.," 145-6.

1284 Evans, *The Third Reich in Power*: 529-30.

1285 Heger, *The Men with the Pink Triangle*: 59.

1286 Shik, "Infinite Loneliness: Some Aspects of the Lives of Jewish Women in the Auschwitz Camps According to Testimonies and Autobiographies Written Between 1945 and 1948.," 145-6.

1287 Laska, "Women in the Resistance and in the Holocaust," 261.

1288 Miryam Sivan, "Stoning the Messenger: Yehiel Dinur's House of Dolls and Piepel," in *Sexual Violence Against Jewish Women During the Holocaust*, ed. Sonja M Hedgepeth and Rochelle G Saidel (Waltham, Massachusetts: Brandeis University Press, 2010), 213.

1289 Gill, *The Journey Back From Hell: Conversations with Concentration Camp Survivors*: 33-4.

1290 Schiff, *Hitler's Inferno: Eight Intimate and Personal Histories from the Holocaust*: 145-6.

1291 Ibid., 337.

1292 135633 Ka-Tzetnik, *Piepel* (London: The New English Library, 1961); ———, *House of Dolls*.

1293 Sivan, "Stoning the Messenger: Yehiel Dinur's House of Dolls and Piepel," 210-11.

[1294] Art Spiegelman, "Drawing the Holocaust," www.nybooks.com/blogs/nyrblog/2011/oct/21/drawing-holocaust/?utm_m...
[1295] Sivan, "Stoning the Messenger: Yehiel Dinur's House of Dolls and Piepel," 210-11.
[1296] Ibid., 203.
[1297] Ibid., 210-1.
[1298] Hebermann, *The Blessed Abyss: Inmate #6582 in Ravensbrück Concentration Camp for Women*: 136; Morrison, *Ravensbrück: Everyday Life in a Women's Concentration Camp 1939-1945*: 42,130; Elias, *Triumph of Hope: From Theresienstadt and Auschwitz to Israel*: 168; Höss, *Death Dealer: The Memoirs of the SS Kommandant of Auschwitz*: 149; Poltawska, *And I Am Afraid Of My Dreams*: 57.
[1299] Saidel, *The Jewish Women of Ravensbrück Concentration Camp*: 37.
[1300] Morrison, *Ravensbrück: Everyday Life in a Women's Concentration Camp 1939-1945*: 130.
[1301] Heger, *The Men with the Pink Triangle*: 11; Morrison, *Ravensbrück: Everyday Life in a Women's Concentration Camp 1939-1945*: 130.
[1302] Laska, "Women in the Resistance and in the Holocaust," 263.
[1303] Morrison, *Ravensbrück: Everyday Life in a Women's Concentration Camp 1939-1945*: 130.
[1304] Ibid; Gill, *The Journey Back From Hell: Conversations with Concentration Camp Survivors*: 327.
[1305] Morrison, *Ravensbrück: Everyday Life in a Women's Concentration Camp 1939-1945*: 130.
[1306] Lengyel, *Five Chimneys: A Woman Survivor's True Story of Auschwitz*: 197-8.
[1307] Delbo, *Auschwitz and After*: 8.
[1308] Lengyel, *Five Chimneys: A Woman Survivor's True Story of Auschwitz*: 199.
[1309] Katz and Ringelheim, *Proceedings of the Conference Women Surviving the Holocaust*, 141-2.
[1310] Perl, *I was a Doctor in Auschwitz*: 182.
[1311] Poltawska, *And I Am Afraid Of My Dreams*: 160.
[1312] Grossmann, *Jews, Germans, and the Allies: Close Encounters in Occupied Germany*: 62-3.
[1313] Larry Orbach and Vivienne Orbach-Smith, *Soaring Underground; A young Fugitive's Life in Nazi Berlin* (Washington DC Compass Press, 1996.), 330-1.
[1314] Grossmann, *Jews, Germans, and the Allies: Close Encounters in Occupied Germany*: 63.
[1315] S Lillian Kremer, "Sexual Abuse in Holocaust Literature: Memoir and Fiction," in *Sexual Violence Against Jewish Women During the Holocaust*, ed. Sonja M Hedgepeth and Rochelle G Saidel (Waltham, Massachusetts: Brandeis University Press, 2010), 178.
[1316] Bendremer, *Women Surviving the Holocaust: In Spite of the Horror*: 40.
[1317] Rapoport, *Yesterdays and Then Tomorrows: Holocaust Anthology of Testimonies and Readings*, 120.
[1318] Des Pres, *The Survivor: An Anatomy of Life in the Death Camps*: 60.
[1319] Gitta Sereny, *Into that Darkness* (New York Mc Graw Hill, 1974), 101.
[1320] Levi, *The Drowned and the Saved*: 126.
[1321] Engelmann, *In Hitler's Germany: Everyday Life in the Third Reich*: 223.
[1322] Jennifer Rosenberg, "The Yellow Star," http://history1900s.about.com/od/holocaust/a/yellowstar.htm.
[1323] Chalmers, "The Influence of Theatre and Paratheatre on the Holocaust," 38.
[1324] Liza Chapnik, "The Grodno Ghetto and its Underground: A personal narrative," in *Women in the Holocaust*, ed. Dalia Ofer and Lenore J Weitzman (New Haven: Yale University Press, 1998), 113.
[1325] Raquel Hodara, "The Polish Jewish Woman: From the Beginning of the Occupation to the Deportation to the Ghettos," *Yad Vashem Studies* 32(2004): 10; Yahil, *The Holocaust: The Fate of European Jewry*: 149.

[1326] Dora Love, in *Massuah Institute for the Study of the Holocaust, Tel Aviv, 03/7504, 033c/3021*, 13.
[1327] Brigitte Halbmayr, "Sexualized Violence Against Women During Nazi "Racial" Persecution," in *Sexual Violence Against Jewish Women During the Holocaust*, ed. Rochelle G Saidel Sonja M Hedgepeth (Waltham, Massachusetts: Brandeis University Press, 2010), 36.
[1328] Tec, *Resilience and Courage: Women, Men and the Holocaust*: 125.
[1329] Hodara, "The Polish Jewish Woman: From the Beginning of the Occupation to the Deportation to the Ghettos," 11.
[1330] Hebermann, *The Blessed Abyss: Inmate #6582 in Ravensbrück Concentration Camp for Women*: 125.
[1331] Jeanne Bommezijn de Rochemont, "A memoir of dread," in *Imperial War Museum, London, 06/25/1* (1946 July), 1-2.
[1332] Myrna Goldenberg, "Memoirs of Auschwitz Survivors: The Burden of Gender," in *Women in the Holocaust*, ed. Dalia Ofer and Lenore J Weitzman (New Haven: Yale University Press, 1998), 331.
[1333] Pawlowicz, *I Will Survive*: 168.
[1334] Livia Bitton-Jackson, *I Have Lived a Thousand Years: Growing up in the Holocaust* (New York: Simon Pulse, 1999), 78.
[1335] Eichengreen and Chamberlain, *From Ashes to Life: My Memories of the Holocaust*: 93-4; Isabella Leitner, *Fragments of Isabella: A Memoir of Auschwitz* (New York: Laurel, 1978), 14; Nomberg-Przytyk, *Auschwitz: True Tales from a Grotesque Land*: 14; Pawlowicz, *I Will Survive*: 104; Reiser, "The Only Medicine was Charcoal," 75; Ibolya S, in *Survivors of the Shoah Visual History Foundation, Toronto, Canada, 18 June 1997* 52; Saidel, *The Jewish Women of Ravensbrück Concentration Camp*: 84; Tec, *Resilience and Courage: Women, Men and the Holocaust*: 238; Vago, "One Year in the Black Hole of Our Planet Earth: A Personal Narrative," 275.
[1336] Shik, *Sexual Abuse of Jewish Women in Auschwitz-Birkenau*, 229.
[1337] Gill, *The Journey Back From Hell: Conversations with Concentration Camp Survivors*: 29; ibid.
[1338] Nomberg-Przytyk, *Auschwitz: True Tales from a Grotesque Land*: 13-14.
[1339] Halbmayr, "Sexualized Violence Against Women During Nazi "Racial" Persecution," 37.
[1340] Moorhouse, *Killing Hitler: The Plots, the Assassins, and the Dictator Who Cheated Death*: 125.
[1341] Eichengreen and Chamberlain, *From Ashes to Life: My Memories of the Holocaust*: 103-4.
[1342] Morrison, *Ravensbrück: Everyday Life in a Women's Concentration Camp 1939-1945*: 33.
[1343] Monika J Flaschka, ""Only Pretty Women Were Raped": The Effect of Sexual Violence on Gender Identities in Concentration Camps," in *Sexual Violence Against Jewish Women During the Holocaust*, ed. Sonja M Hedgepeth and Rochelle G Saidel (Waltham, Massachusetts: Brandeis University Press, 2010), 80.
[1344] Fenelon, *Playing for Time*: 113.
[1345] Milton, "Women and the Holocaust: The Case of German and German-Jewish Women," 228.
[1346] Pawlowicz, *I Will Survive*: 104.
[1347] Nebel, "The Story of Ruth," 342.
[1348] Horowitz, "Women in Holocaust Literature: Engendering Trauma Memory," 375; Friedman, *Speaking the Unspeakable: Essays on Sexuality, Gender, and Holocaust Survivor Memory*: 42-43.
[1349] Berger, " " 3.
[1350] Zelda Moyal, in *Massuah Institute for the Study of the Holocaust, Tel Aviv, VT-842*, 4.
[1351] Yahil, *The Holocaust: The Fate of European Jewry*: 555.

[1352] Gerchik, "Massuah, Tel Aviv, 033c/3600," 3-4.
[1353] Venezia, *Inside the Gas Chambers: Eight Months in the Sonderkommando of Auschwitz*: 43.
[1354] Ludwig Eiber, Manfred Tremi, and Claus Grimm, eds., *The Dachau Concentration Camp 1933-1945* (Dachau: Dachau Concentration Camp, 2003), 147.
[1355] Horowitz, *In the Shadow of Death: Living Outside the Gates of Mauthausen*: 109.
[1356] Shmuel Gronner, 3 October 2011 2011.
[1357] Gill, *The Journey Back From Hell: Conversations with Concentration Camp Survivors*: 161-2.
[1358] Porter, *Kasztner's Train: The True Story of Rezsö Kasztner, Unknown Hero of the Holocaust*: 156-8, 85, 95; Sol Littman, *War Criminal on Trial: Rauca of Kaunas* (Toronto: Key Porter Books, 1993), 102; Berg, *The Diary of Mary Berg*: 37.
[1359] Hodara, "The Polish Jewish Woman: From the Beginning of the Occupation to the Deportation to the Ghettos," 11.
[1360] Ronald W. Zweig, *The Gold Train: The Destruction of the Jews and the Looting of Hungary* (New York: William Morrow, 2002), 58; Masters, *The Summer That Bled: The Biography of Hannah Senesh*: 206.
[1361] ———, *The Summer That Bled: The Biography of Hannah Senesh*: 206.
[1362] Porter, *Kasztner's Train: The True Story of Rezsö Kasztner, Unknown Hero of the Holocaust*: 170.
[1363] J Molnar, " Zsidósors 1944-ben az V. (szegedi) csendórkerületben.." (Budapest1995), 140-41.
[1364] Zweig, *The Gold Train: The Destruction of the Jews and the Looting of Hungary*: 58.
[1365] Dwork and Pelt, *Holocaust: A History*: 309.
[1366] Perl, *I was a Doctor in Auschwitz*: 18.
[1367] Goldenberg, "Lessons Learned from Gentle Heroism: Women's Holocaust Narratives," 85.
[1368] Tory, *Surviving the Holocaust: The Kovno Ghetto Diary*: 403.
[1369] Ibid., 414.
[1370] Gross-Martin, *Silvia*: 166-68.
[1371] Kremer, "Sexual Abuse in Holocaust Literature: Memoir and Fiction," 178.
[1372] Lengyel, *Five Chimneys: A Woman Survivor's True Story of Auschwitz*: 28.
[1373] Becker, 30.
[1374] Love, 20-21.
[1375] Morrison, *Ravensbrück: Everyday Life in a Women's Concentration Camp 1939-1945*: 334.
[1376] Smith, *Remembering: Voices of the Holocaust*: 161.
[1377] Shik, *Sexual Abuse of Jewish Women in Auschwitz-Birkenau*, 231.
[1378] Ibid.
[1379] Elias, *Triumph of Hope: From Theresienstadt and Auschwitz to Israel*: 130-31.
[1380] Steiner, *Treblinka*: 94; Chil Raichman, *The Last Jew of Treblinka* (New York: Pegasus Books, 2011), 64.
[1381] Dror and Linn, "The Shame is Always There," 275.
[1382] Leib Langfuss, "The Horrors of Murder," in *The Scrolls of Auschwitz*, ed. Ber Mark (Tel Aviv: Am Oves, 1985), 209; Shik, *Sexual Abuse of Jewish Women in Auschwitz-Birkenau*, 231.
[1383] Mendelsohn, *The Lost: A Search for Six of the Six Million*: 128.
[1384] Arad, *Belzec, Sobibor, Treblinka: The Operation Reinhard Death Camps*: 112.
[1385] Smith, *Remembering: Voices of the Holocaust*: 147.
[1386] Karay, *Death comes in Yellow: Skarżysko-Kamienna Slave Labor Camp.* : 39.
[1387] Kogon, *The Theory and Practice of Hell: The German Concentration Camps and the System Behind Them*: 67-8.
[1388] Pawlowicz, *I Will Survive*: 54.
[1389] Iranek-Osmecki, *He Who Saves One Life*: 28.

[1390] Levenkron, "Death and the Maidens: "Prostitution," Rape, and Sexual Slavery during World War II," 22; Vaisman, *A Jewish Doctor in Auschwitz: The Testimony of Sima Vaisman*: 56; Hebermann, *The Blessed Abyss: Inmate #6582 in Ravensbrück Concentration Camp for Women*: 110-1.
[1391] Perl, *I was a Doctor in Auschwitz*: 29-30.
[1392] Adelsberger, *Auschwitz: A Doctor's Story*: 86.
[1393] Shik, *Sexual Abuse of Jewish Women in Auschwitz-Birkenau*, 230.
[1394] Saidel, *The Jewish Women of Ravensbrück Concentration Camp*: 207.
[1395] Berger, " " 6.
[1396] Esther Reichmann, in *Massuah Institute for the Study of the Holocaust, Tel Aviv, 033c/4741* (8 May 1996), 22.
[1397] Halbmayr, "Sexualized Violence Against Women During Nazi "Racial" Persecution," 33-4.
[1398] Bruml, "I was a Nurse in Theresienstadt," 41; Steinhoff, Pechel, and Showalter, *Voices From the Third Reich: An Oral History*: 311.
[1399] Lengyel, *Five Chimneys: A Woman Survivor's True Story of Auschwitz*: 132.
[1400] Halbmayr, "Sexualized Violence Against Women During Nazi "Racial" Persecution," 33-4.
[1401] Pawlowicz, *I Will Survive*: 137.
[1402] Delbo, *Auschwitz and After*: 12; Venezia, *Inside the Gas Chambers: Eight Months in the Sonderkommando of Auschwitz*: 74; Saidel, *The Jewish Women of Ravensbrück Concentration Camp*: 207; Alexander Donat, *The Holocaust Kingdom: A Memoir* (New York: Holt, Rinehart and Winston, 1965), 299; Irith Dublon-Knebel, ""We're all well and hoping to hear the same from you soon..." The Story of a Group of Families.," in *Life, Death and Sacrifice: Women and Family in the Holocaust.*, ed. Esther Hertzog (Jerusalem: Gefen Publishing House, 2008), 78.
[1403] ———, ""We're all well and hoping to hear the same from you soon..." The Story of a Group of Families.," 78.
[1404] Venezia, *Inside the Gas Chambers: Eight Months in the Sonderkommando of Auschwitz*: 77.
[1405] Schwalbova, "They Were Murdered in the Infirmary," 161; Bergman.
[1406] Michael J. Neufeld and Michael Berenbaum, eds., *The Bombing of Auschwitz: Should The Allies Have Attempted It?* (New York: St Martin's Press, 2000), 247; Posner and Ware, *Mengele: The Complete Story*: 27; Magda Herzberger, "God Saved Me for a Purpose," in *Sisters in Sorrow: Voices of Care in the Holocaust*, ed. Roger A Ritvo and Diane M Plotkin (College Station, USA: Texas A &M University Press, 2000), 213; Nomberg-Przytyk, *Auschwitz: True Tales from a Grotesque Land*: 13; Fenelon, *Playing for Time*: 190.
[1407] Lengyel, *Five Chimneys: A Woman Survivor's True Story of Auschwitz*: 51,157; Hannelore Brenner, *The Girls of Room 28:Friendship, Hope, and Survival in Theresienstadt* (New York: Schocken Books, 2009), 265.
[1408] Interview with Jewish survivor Frau Dr Roth by Koonz, *Mothers in the Fatherland: Women, the Family and Nazi Politics*: 425; Lenji, 11; Morrison, *Ravensbrück: Everyday Life in a Women's Concentration Camp 1939-1945*: 173; Perl, *I was a Doctor in Auschwitz*: 43-44.
[1409] Laska, "Women in the Resistance and in the Holocaust," 264.
[1410] Shik, *Sexual Abuse of Jewish Women in Auschwitz-Birkenau*, 229.
[1411] Des Pres, *The Survivor: An Anatomy of Life in the Death Camps*: 51.
[1412] Gill, *The Journey Back From Hell: Conversations with Concentration Camp Survivors*: 35.
[1413] Des Pres, *The Survivor: An Anatomy of Life in the Death Camps*: 57.
[1414] Ibid., 58.
[1415] Adelson and Lapides, *Łódź Ghetto: Inside a Community Under Siege*, 27, 378-9.
[1416] Ibid., 27.

[1417] Lenji, 10.
[1418] Herzberger, "God Saved Me for a Purpose," 201-2.
[1419] Leitner, *Fragments of Isabella: A Memoir of Auschwitz*: 28.
[1420] Maria Ossowski, in *Imperial War Museum Sound Archive, London, 19794.*
[1421] Ibid; Smith, *Remembering: Voices of the Holocaust*: 158.
[1422] Alan S Rosenbaum, *Is the Holocaust Unique?* (Boulder, Colorado: Westview Press, 1996), 71.
[1423] Perl, *I was a Doctor in Auschwitz*: 32-33.
[1424] Halbmayr, "Sexualized Violence Against Women During Nazi "Racial" Persecution," 33-4.
[1425] Rochemont, "A memoir of dread," 10.
[1426] Halbmayr, "Sexualized Violence Against Women During Nazi "Racial" Persecution," 33-4.
[1427] Miriam Berger, in *Massuah Institute for the Study of the Holocaust, Tel Aviv, VD-1296* (15 August 1996), 13-14.
[1428] Levi, *The Drowned and the Saved*: 112.
[1429] Smith, *Remembering: Voices of the Holocaust*: 176.
[1430] Bergman.
[1431] Moorhouse, *Killing Hitler: The Plots, the Assassins, and the Dictator Who Cheated Death*: 125.
[1432] Perl, *I was a Doctor in Auschwitz*: 39.
[1433] Moorhouse, *Killing Hitler: The Plots, the Assassins, and the Dictator Who Cheated Death*: 125; Vago, "One Year in the Black Hole of Our Planet Earth: A Personal Narrative," 207.
[1434] Lengyel, *Five Chimneys: A Woman Survivor's True Story of Auschwitz*: 57.
[1435] Ellen Loeb, "Liebe Trude, Liebe Rudy [Dear Trudy, Dear Rudy]," in *Sisters in Sorrow: Voices of Care in the Holocaust*, ed. Roger A Ritvo and Diane M Plotkin (College Station, USA: Texas A&M University Press, 1998), 113.
[1436] Vrba, *I Escaped from Auschwitz*: 190-1.
[1437] Yahil, *The Holocaust: The Fate of European Jewry*: 361.
[1438] Saidel, *The Jewish Women of Ravensbrück Concentration Camp*: 123.
[1439] Smith, *Remembering: Voices of the Holocaust*: 249.
[1440] Gill, *The Journey Back From Hell: Conversations with Concentration Camp Survivors*: 35.
[1441] Bruml, "I was a Nurse in Theresienstadt," 47.
[1442] Fenelon, *Playing for Time*: 108.
[1443] Nebel, "The Story of Ruth," 340-41.
[1444] Inbar, *Spots of Light: To Be a Woman in the Holocaust*: 80.
[1445] Loeb, "Liebe Trude, Liebe Rudy [Dear Trudy, Dear Rudy]," 112.
[1446] Smith, *Remembering: Voices of the Holocaust*: 279.
[1447] Vago, "One Year in the Black Hole of Our Planet Earth: A Personal Narrative," 281.
[1448] Delbo, *Auschwitz and After*: 140.
[1449] Tec, *Resilience and Courage: Women, Men and the Holocaust*: 155.
[1450] Herz, *The Women's Camp in Moringen: A Memoir of Imprisonment in Germany, 1936-1937*: 66.
[1451] Love, 26.
[1452] Sereny Gitta, *Into that Darkness: An Examination of Conscience* (New York Viking, 1983), 237-38; Koonz, *Mothers in the Fatherland: Women, the Family and Nazi Politics*: 292.
[1453] Bondy, "Women in Theresienstadt and the Family Camp in Birkenau," 315.
[1454] Eichengreen and Chamberlain, *From Ashes to Life: My Memories of the Holocaust*: 107.
[1455] Judith Miller, *One By One By One: Facing the Holocaust* (New York: Simon and Schuster, 1990), 269; Vago, "One Year in the Black Hole of Our Planet Earth: A Personal Narrative," 277; Lengyel, *Five Chimneys: A Woman Survivor's True Story of*

Auschwitz: 98; Vaisman, *A Jewish Doctor in Auschwitz: The Testimony of Sima Vaisman*: 37; Becker, 59; Friedman, *Speaking the Unspeakable: Essays on Sexuality, Gender, and Holocaust Survivor Memory*: 50-51; Herzberger, "God Saved Me for a Purpose," 213; Herz, *The Women's Camp in Moringen: A Memoir of Imprisonment in Germany, 1936-1937*: 66; Gill, *The Journey Back From Hell: Conversations with Concentration Camp Survivors*: 35.

1456 Jean Jofen, "Long-Range Effects of Medical Experiments in Concentration Camps (The Effect of Administration of Estrogens to the Mother on the Intelligence of the Offspring)" (paper presented at the Fifth World Congress of Jewish Studies, Jerusalem, 1969), 55-71.

1457 Mitscherlich and Mielke, *Doctors of Infamy: The Story of the Nazi Medical Crimes*: 131-35.

1458 Schwertfeger, *Women of Theresienstadt: Voices from a Concentration Camp*: 60.

1459 Katz and Ringelheim, *Proceedings of the Conference Women Surviving the Holocaust*, 136; Morrison, *Ravensbrück: Everyday Life in a Women's Concentration Camp 1939-1945*: 173; Ritvo and Plotkin, *Sisters in Sorrow: Voices of Care in the Holocaust*: 15.

1460 Bitton-Jackson, *I Have Lived a Thousand Years: Growing up in the Holocaust*: 95; Tec, *Resilience and Courage: Women, Men and the Holocaust*: 168.

1461 Saidel, *The Jewish Women of Ravensbrück Concentration Camp*: 180-81; Susan Nowak, "Ruptured Lives and Shattered Beliefs: A Feminist Analysis of Tikkun Atzmi in Holocaust Literature.," in *Experience and Expression: Women, The Nazis, and the Holocaust*, ed. Elizabeth R Baer and Myrna Goldenberg (Detroit: Wayne State University Press, 2003), 186; Grossmann, *Jews, Germans, and the Allies: Close Encounters in Occupied Germany*: 189.

1462 Fenelon, *Playing for Time*: 94.

1463 Poltawska, *And I Am Afraid Of My Dreams*: 106.

1464 Perl, *I was a Doctor in Auschwitz*: 40-41.

1465 Rapoport, *Yesterdays and Then Tomorrows: Holocaust Anthology of Testimonies and Readings*, 148.

1466 Perl, *I was a Doctor in Auschwitz*: 75-76.

1467 Schiff, *Theresienstadt: The Town The Nazis Gave to The Jews*: 84,131.

1468 Lengyel, *Five Chimneys: A Woman Survivor's True Story of Auschwitz*: 30.

1469 Venezia, *Inside the Gas Chambers: Eight Months in the Sonderkommando of Auschwitz*: 133.

1470 Joseph Sargent, "Out of the Ashes," (USA: Showtime Netwoks, 2004); Schiff, *Hitler's Inferno: Eight Intimate and Personal Histories from the Holocaust*: vii; Viktor Frankl, *Man's Search for Meaning: An Introduction to Logotherapy* (New York: Washington Square Press, 1963), 13.

1471 Levi, *The Drowned and the Saved*: 82.

1472 Adelson and Lapides, *Łódź Ghetto: Inside a Community Under Siege*, 100, 06-07, 240-41, 368-69.

1473 Ibid., 100.

1474 Delbo, *Auschwitz and After*: 193; Saidel, *The Jewish Women of Ravensbrück Concentration Camp*: 208; Inbar, *Spots of Light: To Be a Woman in the Holocaust*: 121; Joan Ringelheim, "Women and the Holocaust: A Reconsideration of Research," *Signs* 10, no. 4 (1985): 747; Goldenberg, "Lessons Learned from Gentle Heroism: Women's Holocaust Narratives," 86-89; Tec, *Resilience and Courage: Women, Men and the Holocaust*: 186.

1475 Niewyk, *The Holocaust: Problems and Perspectives of Interpretation*: 64-65; Nutkiewicz, "Shame, Guilt, and Anguish in Holocaust Survivor Testimony," 9; Feinstein, "Absent Fathers, Present Mothers: Images of Parenthood in Holocaust Survivor Narratives," 171-72; Karay, *Death comes in Yellow: Skarżysko-Kamienna Slave Labor Camp.* : 196-97.

1476 Vrba, *I Escaped from Auschwitz*: 230.
1477 Tec, *Resilience and Courage: Women, Men and the Holocaust*: 188-89.
1478 Gill, *The Journey Back From Hell: Conversations with Concentration Camp Survivors*: 320.
1479 Gilbert, *The Boys: The Story of 732 Young Concentration Camp Survivors*: 142.
1480 Weiss.
1481 Shik, "Infinite Loneliness: Some Aspects of the Lives of Jewish Women in the Auschwitz Camps According to Testimonies and Autobiographies Written Between 1945 and 1948.," 138.
1482 Des Pres, *The Survivor: An Anatomy of Life in the Death Camps*: 97; Eli Weisel, *Night* (New York Avon, 1969), 52,122.
1483 Des Pres, *The Survivor: An Anatomy of Life in the Death Camps*: 99.
1484 Ringelheim, "Women and the Holocaust: A Reconsideration of Research.," 387-88.
1485 Mark Dworzecki, "To Ignore or To Tell the Truth," *Bein ha-betarim* (10 June 1945): 28-29.
1486 Boaz Cohen, "Setting the Agenda of Holocaust Research: Discord at Yad Vashem in the 1950's," in *Holocaust Historiography in Context: Emergence, Challenges, Polemics and Achievements*, ed. David Bankier and Dan Michman (Jerusalem: Yad Vashem and Berghahn Books, 2008), 270 note 44.
1487 Ibid., 270,60 note 11.
1488 Ibid., 270 note 44.
1489 Abraham Maslow, " A Theory of Human Motivation.," *Psychological Review* 50, no. 4 (1943): 370-96.
1490 Halbmayr, "Sexualized Violence Against Women During Nazi "Racial" Persecution," 31.
1491 Mühlhäuser, "Between 'Racial Awareness' and Fantasies of Potencies: Nazi Sexual Politics in the Occupied Territories of the Soviet Union, 1942-1945.," 199.
1492 Levenkron, "Death and the Maidens: "Prostitution," Rape, and Sexual Slavery during World War II," 14.
1493 Nick Squires, "Yazidi girl tells of horrific ordeal as Isil sex slave," *The Telegraph*, 7 September 2014.
1494 Sinnreich, "The Rape of Jewish Women During the Holocaust," 117; Friedman, "Togetherness and Isolation: Holocaust Survivor Memories of Intimacy and Sexuality in the Ghettos," 10.
1495 Nutkiewicz, "Shame, Guilt, and Anguish in Holocaust Survivor Testimony," 3-5.
1496 Zoe Waxman, "Rape and Sexual Abuse in HIding," in *Sexual Violence Against Jewish Women During the Holocaust*, ed. Sonja M Hedgepeth and Rochelle G Saidel (Waltham, Massachusetts: Brandeis University Press, 2010), 125; Friedman, "Togetherness and Isolation: Holocaust Survivor Memories of Intimacy and Sexuality in the Ghettos," 10.
1497 Pascale Rachel Bos, "Women and the Holocaust: Analyzing Gender Difference," in *Experience and Expression: Women, the Nazis, and the Holocaust*, ed. Elizabeth R Baer and Myrna Goldenberg (Detroit: Wayne State University Press, 2003), 33; Morrison, *Ravensbrück: Everyday Life in a Women's Concentration Camp 1939-1945*: 177-8.
1498 Heineman, "Sexuality and Nazism: The Doubly Unspeakable?," 60.
1499 Ibid.
1500 Desbois, *The Holocaust by Bullets:A Priest's Journey to Uncover the Truth Behind the Murder of 1.5 Million Jews*: 168.
1501 Sinnreich, "The Rape of Jewish Women During the Holocaust," 118.
1502 Waxman, "Rape and Sexual Abuse in HIding," 131.
1503 Sinnreich, "The Rape of Jewish Women During the Holocaust," 118; ibid; Donald Bloxham, "Jewish Witnesses in War Crimes Trials of the Postwar Era.," in *Holocaust Historiography in Context: Emergence, Challenges, Polemics and Achievements*, ed. David Bankier and Dan Michman (Jerusalem: 2008), 540.
1504 Sinnreich, "The Rape of Jewish Women During the Holocaust," 118; ibid.

1505 Sonja M Hedgepath and Rochelle G Saidel, "Introduction," in *Sexual Violence Against Jewish Women During the Holocaust*, ed. Sonja M Hedgepath and Rochelle G Saidel (Waltham, Massachusetts: Brandeis University Press, 2010), 1.

1506 Fogelman, "Sexual Abuse of Jewish Women During and After the Holocaust: A Psychological Perspective," 257.

1507 Ibid.

1508 Shik, *Sexual Abuse of Jewish Women in Auschwitz-Birkenau*, 237.

1509 Eugenia Fefer-Matz, in *Yad Vashem Archives, Jerusalem, 03/5199* (August 31, 1978), 17; Goldenberg, "Memoirs of Auschwitz Survivors: The Burden of Gender," 332, 35-6; Ringelheim, "Women and the Holocaust: A Reconsideration of Research.," 377.

1510 Judith Magyar Isaacson, *Seed of Sarah: Memoirs of a Survivor Chicago* (Illinois: University of Illinois Press, 1990), 10, 42,47,53.

1511 Goldenberg, "Memoirs of Auschwitz Survivors: The Burden of Gender," 332.

1512 Holliday, *Children in the Holocaust and World War II: Their Secret Diaries*: 123.

1513 Fefer-Matz; Lenji.

1514 Gill, *The Journey Back From Hell: Conversations with Concentration Camp Survivors*: 273.

1515 Tory, *Surviving the Holocaust: The Kovno Ghetto Diary*: 8, 23, 168; Littman, *War Criminal on Trial: Rauca of Kaunas*: 68.

1516 Katz and Ringelheim, *Proceedings of the Conference Women Surviving the Holocaust*, 48.

1517 Ringelheim, "Women and the Holocaust: A Reconsideration of Research.."; Martin Gray and Max Gallo, *For Those I Loved* (Boston: Little, Brown and Company, 1971), 104,09; Holliday, *Children in the Holocaust and World War II: Their Secret Diaries*: 224; Evans, *The Third Reich at War*: 51,53.

1518 Adelson and Lapides, *Łódź Ghetto: Inside a Community Under Siege*, 464; Smith, *Remembering: Voices of the Holocaust*: 263.

1519 Tec, *Resilience and Courage: Women, Men and the Holocaust*: 223-4.

1520 Sinnreich, "The Rape of Jewish Women During the Holocaust," 110.

1521 Friedman, *Speaking the Unspeakable: Essays on Sexuality, Gender, and Holocaust Survivor Memory*: 53.

1522 Pawlowicz, *I Will Survive*: 42.

1523 Friedman, *Speaking the Unspeakable: Essays on Sexuality, Gender, and Holocaust Survivor Memory*: 53.

1524 Ibid.

1525 Hanna Rothe Magid, in *Yad Vashem Archives, Jerusalem, 0.3/1570* (1960); Shik, *Sexual Abuse of Jewish Women in Auschwitz-Birkenau*, 243.

1526 Boris Zabarko, ed. *Holocaust in the Ukraine* (London: Valentine Mitchell, 2005), 51-2; Anatoly Podolsky, "The Tragic Fate of Ukrainian Jewish Women Under Nazi Occupation, 1941-1944.," in *Sexual Violence Against Jewish Women During the Holocaust*, ed. Sonja M Hedgepeth and Rochelle G Saidel (Waltham, Massachusetts: Brandeis University Press, 2010), 102.

1527 Chapnik, "The Grodno Ghetto and its Underground: A personal narrative," 113.

1528 Sinnreich, "The Rape of Jewish Women During the Holocaust," 120.

1529 Adelson and Lapides, *Łódź Ghetto: Inside a Community Under Siege*, 464.

1530 Sinnreich, "The Rape of Jewish Women During the Holocaust," 120.

1531 Ibid., 114.

1532 Schiff, *Hitler's Inferno: Eight Intimate and Personal Histories from the Holocaust*: 65-111.

1533 Sinnreich, "The Rape of Jewish Women During the Holocaust," 110.

1534 Podolsky, "The Tragic Fate of Ukrainian Jewish Women Under Nazi Occupation, 1941-1944.," 102; Zabarko, *Holocaust in the Ukraine*, 51-52.

1535 Podolsky, "The Tragic Fate of Ukrainian Jewish Women Under Nazi Occupation, 1941-1944.," 102; Zabarko, *Holocaust in the Ukraine*, 153-4.

[1536] Katz and Ringelheim, *Proceedings of the Conference Women Surviving the Holocaust*. 39-40.
[1537] Schiff, *Theresienstadt: The Town The Nazis Gave to The Jews*: 45.
[1538] Yehuda Bauer, *A History of the Holocaust*, 2nd ed. (Danbury, Connecticut: Franklin Watts, 2001), 198.
[1539] Berg, *The Diary of Mary Berg*: 60.
[1540] Sinnreich, "The Rape of Jewish Women During the Holocaust," 110.
[1541] Rubenstein and Altman, *The Unknown Black Book: The holocaust in the German-Occupied Soviet Territories*, 241.
[1542] Esther Hertzog, *Life, Death and Sacrifice: Women and Family in the Holocaust* (Jerusalem: Gefen Publishing House, 2008), 169.
[1543] Eichengreen and Chamberlain, *From Ashes to Life: My Memories of the Holocaust*: 84.
[1544] Friedman, "Togetherness and Isolation: Holocaust Survivor Memories of Intimacy and Sexuality in the Ghettos," 10-14.
[1545] Sinnreich, "The Rape of Jewish Women During the Holocaust," 112.
[1546] Friedman, "Togetherness and Isolation: Holocaust Survivor Memories of Intimacy and Sexuality in the Ghettos," 10-14.
[1547] Levenkron, "Death and the Maidens: "Prostitution," Rape, and Sexual Slavery during World War II," 17.
[1548] Ibid.
[1549] Dwork and Pelt, *Holocaust: A History*: 350.
[1550] Ibid.
[1551] Joan Ringelheim, "The Split Between Gender and the Holocaust," in *Women and the Holocaust*, ed. Dalia Ofer and Lenore Weitzman (New Haven: Yale University Press, 1998), 342.
[1552] Friedman, *Speaking the Unspeakable: Essays on Sexuality, Gender, and Holocaust Survivor Memory*: 60-1.
[1553] Selma Okrnt, in *Massuah Institute for the Study of the Holocaust, Tel Aviv, VD-1020*, 9.
[1554] Yehodit Zik Finkel, in *Yad Vashem Archives, Jerusalem, 0.3/12630* (2005).
[1555] Soria Schlomovitsch, in *Yad Vashem Archives, Jerusalem, 0.69/354* (1981); Shik, *Sexual Abuse of Jewish Women in Auschwitz-Birkenau*, 243.
[1556] Levenkron, "Death and the Maidens: "Prostitution," Rape, and Sexual Slavery during World War II," 27.
[1557] Carla Lessing, "Aging Child Holocaust Survivors of Sexual Abuse," in *Selfhelp Conference* (New York2012), 2-3.
[1558] Friedman, *Speaking the Unspeakable: Essays on Sexuality, Gender, and Holocaust Survivor Memory*: 63.
[1559] Fogelman, "Sexual Abuse of Jewish Women During and After the Holocaust: A Psychological Perspective," 271-2.
[1560] Aba Gefen, *Hope in Darkness: The Aba Gefen Holocaust Diaries* (New York: Holocaust Library, 1989), 29; Tec, *Resilience and Courage: Women, Men and the Holocaust*: 228,311-3.; ibid.
[1561] ———, *Resilience and Courage: Women, Men and the Holocaust*: 311-12.
[1562] Ibid., 313.
[1563] Edgar Hargreaves, "Imperial War Museum, London, 5378," (1981-11-23).
[1564] Rubenstein and Altman, *The Unknown Black Book: The holocaust in the German-Occupied Soviet Territories*, 152.
[1565] Ibid., 117.
[1566] Sinnreich, "The Rape of Jewish Women During the Holocaust," 110.
[1567] Ibid.
[1568] Waxman, "Rape and Sexual Abuse in HIding," 129.
[1569] Sinnreich, "The Rape of Jewish Women During the Holocaust," 110.
[1570] Ibid.
[1571] Ibid.

1572 Gilbert, *The Boys: The Story of 732 Young Concentration Camp Survivors*: 346.
1573 Black, *IBM and the Holocaust*: 179.
1574 Inbar, *Spots of Light: To Be a Woman in the Holocaust*: 77.
1575 Sinnreich, "The Rape of Jewish Women During the Holocaust," 110.
1576 Michael Kutz, *If, By Miracle* (Canada: the Azrieli Foundation, 2013), 24.
1577 Rubenstein and Altman, *The Unknown Black Book: The holocaust in the German-Occupied Soviet Territories*, 388,405.
1578 Ibid., 286,302,22,28.
1579 Levenkron, "Death and the Maidens: "Prostitution," Rape, and Sexual Slavery during World War II," 17.
1580 Liverpool, *The Scourge of the Swastika*: 132.
1581 Pawlowicz, *I Will Survive*: 42.
1582 Rubenstein and Altman, *The Unknown Black Book: The holocaust in the German-Occupied Soviet Territories*, 73.
1583 Gilbert, *The Boys: The Story of 732 Young Concentration Camp Survivors*: 259-60.
1584 Desbois, *The Holocaust by Bullets:A Priest's Journey to Uncover the Truth Behind the Murder of 1.5 Million Jews*: 167-8.
1585 Rubenstein and Altman, *The Unknown Black Book: The holocaust in the German-Occupied Soviet Territories*, 405.
1586 Owings, *Frauen: German Women Recall the Third Reich*: 162.
1587 Mazower, *Hitler's Empire: How the Nazis ruled Europe*: 334.
1588 Rubenstein and Altman, *The Unknown Black Book: The holocaust in the German-Occupied Soviet Territories*, 158.
1589 Podolsky, "The Tragic Fate of Ukrainian Jewish Women Under Nazi Occupation, 1941-1944.," 97.
1590 Ibid., 99.
1591 Ibid., 98-9.
1592 Rubenstein and Altman, *The Unknown Black Book: The holocaust in the German-Occupied Soviet Territories*, 73.
1593 Ibid., 126.
1594 Ibid., 186.
1595 Ibid., 275-6.
1596 Ibid., 245.
1597 Shik, *Sexual Abuse of Jewish Women in Auschwitz-Birkenau*, 243.
1598 Jan T Gross, *Neighbours: The Destruction of the Jewish Community in Jedwabne, Poland, 1941* (London: Random House, 2003), 19.
1599 Susan Zuccotti, *The Italians and the Holocaust: Persecution, Rescue, Survival* (New York: Basic Books, 1987), 9,199.
1600 Evans, *The Third Reich at War*: 159.
1601 Hogan and Aretha, *The Holocaust Chronicle*, 474.
1602 Karay, *Death comes in Yellow: Skarżysko-Kamienna Slave Labor Camp.* : 80-1,291.
1603 Sinnreich, "The Rape of Jewish Women During the Holocaust," 110-21.
1604 Ibid., 113.
1605 Ibid., 110-21.
1606 Pawlowicz, *I Will Survive*: 123-4, 51-3.
1607 Ibid.
1608 Sinnreich, "The Rape of Jewish Women During the Holocaust," 110-21.
1609 Ringelheim, "Women and the Holocaust: A Reconsideration of Research.," 745.
1610 Elias, *Triumph of Hope: From Theresienstadt and Auschwitz to Israel*: 120; Goldenberg, "Memoirs of Auschwitz Survivors: The Burden of Gender," 336; Ringelheim, "The Split Between Gender and the Holocaust," 341-2; Smith, *Remembering: Voices of the Holocaust*: 161; Arad, *Belzec, Sobibor, Treblinka: The Operation Reinhard Death Camps*: 115-7; Evans, *The Third Reich at War*: 291; Is, *U.B.B.: Unforgettable Bergen-Belsen*: 29; Saidel, *The Jewish Women of Ravensbrück Concentration Camp*:

212; Sinnreich, "The Rape of Jewish Women During the Holocaust."; Steiner, *Treblinka*: 106-7.

1611 ———, *Treblinka*: 106-7.

1612 Arad, *Belzec, Sobibor, Treblinka: The Operation Reinhard Death Camps*: 116-7.

1613 Sinnreich, "The Rape of Jewish Women During the Holocaust," 113.

1614 Elias, *Triumph of Hope: From Theresienstadt and Auschwitz to Israel*: 120.

1615 Sinnreich, "The Rape of Jewish Women During the Holocaust," 113; Levenkron, "Death and the Maidens: "Prostitution," Rape, and Sexual Slavery during World War II," 20.

1616 Flaschka, ""Only Pretty Women Were Raped": The Effect of Sexual Violence on Gender Identities in Concentration Camps," 77.

1617 Zofia Minc, in *Yad Vashem Archives, Jerusalem, M.49.E-Zih/2504* (1947); Shik, *Sexual Abuse of Jewish Women in Auschwitz-Birkenau*, 232.

1618 Goldenberg, "Memoirs of Auschwitz Survivors: The Burden of Gender," 336.

1619 Smith, *Remembering: Voices of the Holocaust*: 161; Roman Halter, in *Imperial War Museum Sound Archives, London, 17183.*

1620 Friedman, *Speaking the Unspeakable: Essays on Sexuality, Gender, and Holocaust Survivor Memory*: 57-8.

1621 Sinnreich, "The Rape of Jewish Women During the Holocaust," 113.

1622 Saidel, *The Jewish Women of Ravensbrück Concentration Camp*: 125-8.

1623 Ibid., 212.

1624 Mühlhäuser, "Between 'Racial Awareness' and Fantasies of Potencies: Nazi Sexual Politics in the Occupied Territories of the Soviet Union, 1942-1945.," 199.

1625 Richard Rhodes, *Masters of Death: The SS Einsatzgruppen and the Invention of the Holocaust* (New York: Alfred A. Knopf, 2002), 91, 248-9.

1626 Jack Kuper, *Child of the Holocaust* (Markham, Ontario: Paperjacks, 1978), 185-6.

1627 Mühlhäuser, "Between 'Racial Awareness' and Fantasies of Potencies: Nazi Sexual Politics in the Occupied Territories of the Soviet Union, 1942-1945.," 201.

1628 Helen Fremont, *After Long Silence: A Memoir* (New York: Delacorte Press, 1999), 153.

1629 Mühlhäuser, "Between 'Racial Awareness' and Fantasies of Potencies: Nazi Sexual Politics in the Occupied Territories of the Soviet Union, 1942-1945.," 199; Vyacheslav M. Molotov, "Molotov's Note on German Atrocities in Occupied Soviet Territory," http://www.ibiblio.org/pha/policy/1942/420106b.html.

1630 Jan Fleischhauer, "Nazi War Crimes as Described by German Soldiers," Spiegel Online International, www.spiegel.de/international/.../0.1518.755385-5.00/html.

1631 Ibid.

1632 Ibid.

1633 Ibid.

1634 Mühlhäuser, "Between 'Racial Awareness' and Fantasies of Potencies: Nazi Sexual Politics in the Occupied Territories of the Soviet Union, 1942-1945.," 201.

1635 Evans, *The Third Reich at War*: 502.

1636 Ibid., 193.

1637 David Raub Snyder, "The Prosecution and Punishment of Sex Offenders in the Wehrmacht, 1939-1945," (Nebraska: University of Nebraska, 2002), 219.

1638 Heineman, "Gender, Sexuality, and Coming to Terms with the Nazi Past," 48.

1639 Gross, *Neighbours: The Destruction of the Jewish Community in Jedwabne, Poland, 1941*: 145.

1640 Nutkiewicz, "Shame, Guilt, and Anguish in Holocaust Survivor Testimony," 1.

1641 Friedman, *Speaking the Unspeakable: Essays on Sexuality, Gender, and Holocaust Survivor Memory*: 59.

1642 Ibid.

1643 Tec, *Resilience and Courage: Women, Men and the Holocaust*: 311-3.

1644 Ibid.

1645 Barbara Stimler, in *Imperial War Museum Sound Archives, London, 17475* (1992 05 28).

1646 Friedman, *Speaking the Unspeakable: Essays on Sexuality, Gender, and Holocaust Survivor Memory*: 55.

1647 Nutkiewicz, "Shame, Guilt, and Anguish in Holocaust Survivor Testimony," 3-5.

1648 Inbar, *Spots of Light: To Be a Woman in the Holocaust*: 78.

1649 Feinstein, "Jewish Women in Time: The Challenge of Feminist Artistic Installations About the Holocaust," 263; Shik, "Infinite Loneliness: Some Aspects of the Lives of Jewish Women in the Auschwitz Camps According to Testimonies and Autobiographies Written Between 1945 and 1948.," 148.

1650 Ritvo and Plotkin, *Sisters in Sorrow: Voices of Care in the Holocaust*: 134.

1651 Berg, *The Diary of Mary Berg*: 13.

1652 Gray and Gallo, *For Those I Loved*: 204.

1653 Breitman, *The Architect of Genocide: Himmler and the Final Solution*: 200; Gilbert, *The Boys: The Story of 732 Young Concentration Camp Survivors*: 331; Hilberg, *The Destruction of the European Jews*: 199; Iranek-Osmecki, *He Who Saves One Life*: 77; Johnson and Reuband, *What We Knew: Terror, Mass Murder, and Everyday Life in Nazi Germany*: 232; Kogon, *The Theory and Practice of Hell: The German Concentration Camps and the System Behind Them*: 184-5; Koonz, *Mothers in the Fatherland: Women, the Family and Nazi Politics*: 427; Porter, *Kasztner's Train: The True Story of Rezsö Kasztner, Unknown Hero of the Holocaust*: 298; Daniel Asa Rose, *Hiding Places* (New York: Simon and Schuster, 2000), 22-3; Robert Rozett, "First-hand Accounts and Awareness of the Fate of the Jews under the Nazis: The Case of Hungarian Labor Service Men.," in *Holocaust Historiography in Context: Emergence, Challenges, Polemics an Achievements*, ed. Dan Michman David Bankier (Jerusalem: Yad Vashem and Berghahn Books, 2008), 465; Rubenstein and Altman, *The Unknown Black Book: The holocaust in the German-Occupied Soviet Territories*, 40,73,76,115,63,66,218,45,52,94,302; Stecknoll, *The Alderney Death Camp*: 33; Tory, *Surviving the Holocaust: The Kovno Ghetto Diary*: 41; Varon, 13; Guy Walters, *Hunting Evil* (New York: Broadway Books, 2009), 113.

1654 Yahil, *The Holocaust: The Fate of European Jewry*: 268.

1655 Gefen, *Hope in Darkness: The Aba Gefen Holocaust Diaries*: 2.

1656 Liza Chapnik, in *Massuah Institute for the Study of the Holocaust, Tel Aviv, VD-1058*, 6.

1657 Gefen, *Hope in Darkness: The Aba Gefen Holocaust Diaries*: 29.

1658 Schulman, *A Partisan's Memoir: Woman of the Holocaust*: 73.

1659 Ibid., 177-8.

1660 Dawidowicz, *The War Against the Jews 1933-1945*: 270.

1661 Hilberg, *The Destruction of the European Jews*: 146; Klee, Dressen, and Reiss, *The Good Old Days: The Holocaust As Seen By Its Perpetrators and Bystanders*, 179; Elena Kononenko, *Baby Killers* (Moscow: Foreign Language Publishing House, 1942), 8; Rhodes, *Masters of Death: The SS Einsatzgruppen and the Invention of the Holocaust*: 185-6.

1662 Kutz, *If, By Miracle*: 29.

1663 Desbois, *The Holocaust by Bullets:A Priest's Journey to Uncover the Truth Behind the Murder of 1.5 Million Jews*: 30,77,83,90,125,212-3.

1664 Rubenstein and Altman, *The Unknown Black Book: The holocaust in the German-Occupied Soviet Territories*, 162-3.

1665 Klee, Dressen, and Reiss, *The Good Old Days: The Holocaust As Seen By Its Perpetrators and Bystanders*, 197.

1666 Nicholas, *Cruel World: The Children of Europe in the Nazi Web*: 430.

1667 Ibid., 125.

1668 Rose, *Hiding Places*: 320-22.

1669 Ibid.

1670 Kaplan, *Between Dignity and Despair: Jewish Life in Nazi Germany*: 19-20.

1671 Spitz, *Doctors From Hell: The Horrific Accounts of Nazi Experiments on Humans*: 146.

[1672] Miller, *One By One By One: Facing the Holocaust*: 123.
[1673] Paris, *Unhealed Wounds: France and the Klaus Barbie Affair*: 94.
[1674] Tom Bower, *Klaus Barbie: Butcher of Lyons* (London: Corgi Books, 1984), 75.
[1675] Paris, *Unhealed Wounds: France and the Klaus Barbie Affair*: 94.
[1676] Karay, *Death comes in Yellow: Skarżysko-Kamienna Slave Labor Camp.* : 92; ———, "Women in the Forced-Labor Camps," 287.
[1677] Ingram, *The Hands of War*: 161-3; William Manchester, *The Arms of Krupp 1587-1968* (New York: Bantam Books, 1970), 613-23.
[1678] Hebermann, *The Blessed Abyss: Inmate #6582 in Ravensbrück Concentration Camp for Women*: 125; Cohen, *Human Behaviour in the Concentration Camp*: 81.
[1679] ———, *Human Behaviour in the Concentration Camp*: 81.
[1680] US Government, "Trial of the Major War Criminals before the International Military Tribunal. Official text in the English language. Published at Nuremberg, Vol X X I X" (1947), 329.
[1681] Hebermann, *The Blessed Abyss: Inmate #6582 in Ravensbrück Concentration Camp for Women*: 144.
[1682] Kogon, *The Theory and Practice of Hell: The German Concentration Camps and the System Behind Them*: 108.
[1683] Lifton, *The Nazi Doctors: Medical Killing and the Psychology of Genocide*: 344.
[1684] Becker, 71.
[1685] Lagnado and Dekel, *Children of the Flames: Dr Josef Mengele and The Untold Story of the Twins of Auschwitz*: 72.
[1686] Arad, *Belzec, Sobibor, Treblinka: The Operation Reinhard Death Camps*: 197.
[1687] Rozenberg, 6.
[1688] Steiner, *Treblinka*: 166.
[1689] Delbo, *Auschwitz and After*: 89.
[1690] Gill, *The Journey Back From Hell: Conversations with Concentration Camp Survivors*: 328.
[1691] Lengyel, *Five Chimneys: A Woman Survivor's True Story of Auschwitz*: 199.
[1692] Ritvo and Plotkin, *Sisters in Sorrow: Voices of Care in the Holocaust*: 141.
[1693] Moorehead, *A Train in Winter: A Story of Resistance, Friendship and Survival in Auschwitz*: 207.
[1694] Fenelon, *Playing for Time*: 173.
[1695] Greene, *Justice at Dachau: The Trials of an American Prosecutor*: 154.
[1696] Black, *IBM and the Holocaust*: 255-6.
[1697] Friedländer, *Nazi Germany and the Jews 1939-1945: The Years of Extermination*: 328-9.
[1698] Steiner, *Treblinka*: 383.
[1699] Moorehead, *A Train in Winter: A Story of Resistance, Friendship and Survival in Auschwitz*: 206-7.
[1700] David Matas and Susan Vharendoff, *Justice Delayed: Nazi War Criminals in Canada* (Toronto: Summerhill Press, 1987), 141.
[1701] Lengyel, *Five Chimneys: A Woman Survivor's True Story of Auschwitz*: 201-3.
[1702] Tec, *Resilience and Courage: Women, Men and the Holocaust*: 173.
[1703] Heger, *The Men with the Pink Triangle*: 84.
[1704] Haas, *The Doctor and the Damned*: 153.
[1705] Heger, *The Men with the Pink Triangle*: 41.
[1706] Ibid., 34,41,53-5,84; Gill, *The Journey Back From Hell: Conversations with Concentration Camp Survivors*: 33-4.
[1707] Evans, *The Third Reich in Power*: 534.
[1708] Perl, *I was a Doctor in Auschwitz*: 61-2.
[1709] Fenelon, *Playing for Time*: 88.
[1710] Laska, "Women in the Resistance and in the Holocaust," 266.
[1711] Symonowicz, *Beyond Human Endurance: The Ravensbrück Women tell Their Stories* 159.

1712 Laska, "Women in the Resistance and in the Holocaust." 266.
1713 Niewyk, *The Holocaust: Problems and Perspectives of Interpretation*: 92-94.
1714 Ibid., 92-4.
1715 Daniel Jonah Goldhagen, *Hitler's Willing Executioners: Ordinary Germans and the Holocaust* (New York: Vintage Books, 1997), 307.
1716 Steinhoff, Pechel, and Showalter, *Voices From the Third Reich: An Oral History*: 332.
1717 Heger, *The Men with the Pink Triangle*: 53-55.
1718 Steinhoff, Pechel, and Showalter, *Voices From the Third Reich: An Oral History*: 32.
1719 Roland, *Nazi Women: the Attraction of Evil*: 131-5.
1720 Evans, *The Third Reich at War*: 569, 643.
1721 Gill, *The Journey Back From Hell: Conversations with Concentration Camp Survivors*: 355.
1722 Smith, *Remembering: Voices of the Holocaust*: 229.
1723 Bar-On, *Legacy of Silence: Encounters with Children of the Third Reich*: 158.
1724 Dublon-Knebel, ""We're all well and hoping to hear the same from you soon..." The Story of a Group of Families.," 80.
1725 Daniel Mann, "Playing for Time." (Olive Films, 1980); Fenelon, *Playing for Time*: 247-50.
1726 Owings, *Frauen: German Women Recall the Third Reich*: 164.
1727 Sruoga, *Forest of the Gods*: 168.
1728 Evans, *The Third Reich at War*: 291.
1729 Delbo, *Auschwitz and After*: 177.
1730 Gideon Greif, "Between Sanity and Insanity: Spheres of Everyday Life in the *Sonderkommando* in Auschwitz-Birkenau.," in *Grey Zones: Ambiguity and Compromise in the Holocaust*, ed. Johnathon Petropoulos and John K Roth (New York: Berghahn Books, 2005), 33.
1731 Ibid.
1732 Herzog, "Hubris and Hypocrisy, Incitement and Disavowal: Sexuality and German Fascism.," 13-15.
1733 Heineman, "Sexuality and Nazism: The Doubly Unspeakable?," 57.
1734 Ibid., 64.
1735 Lifton, *The Nazi Doctors: Medical Killing and the Psychology of Genocide*: 211.
1736 Ibid., 310.
1737 Ibid., 151.
1738 Ibid., 319.
1739 Bar-On, *Legacy of Silence: Encounters with Children of the Third Reich*: 20.
1740 Christopher Browning, "Ordinary Germans or Ordinary Men? Another look at the perpetrators," in *Lessons and Legacies: Teaching the Holocaust in a Changing World*, ed. Donald G Schilling (Evanston, Illinois: Northwestern University Press, 1998), 42.
1741 Solomon Asch, " Opinions and social pressure.," *Scientific American* 193(1955): 31-35.
1742 T W Adorno et al., *The Authoritarian Personality* (Oxford, England: Harpers, 1950).
1743 Stanley Milgram, "Behavioral Study of Obedience" *Journal of Abnormal and Social Psychology* 67, no. 4 (1963): 371-8.
1744 Philip Zimbardo, *The politics of persuasion (O N R Technical Report: Z-06)*. (Washington DC: Office of Naval Research, 1971).
1745 Muzafer Sherif, *In common predicament: Social psychology of intergroup conflict and cooperation*. (Boston: Houghton-Mifflin, 1966).
1746 James Waller, *Becoming Evil: How Ordinary People Commit Genocide and Mass Killing* (Oxford and New York: Oxford University Press, 2002), 134.
1747 USA Government, *Nuremberg Medical Case, vol 1, pp 695.* : Vol 1, p 58ff; Cohen, *Human Behaviour in the Concentration Camp*: 266.
1748 ———, *Human Behaviour in the Concentration Camp*: 41, 232, 37, 51.
1749 Spitz, *Doctors From Hell: The Horrific Accounts of Nazi Experiments on Humans*: 266.
1750 Ibid.

[1751] Cohen, *Human Behaviour in the Concentration Camp*: 259.
[1752] USA Government, *Nuremberg Medical Case, vol 1, pp 695.* : 866.
[1753] Levi, *The Drowned and the Saved*: 47.
[1754] Friedman, *Speaking the Unspeakable: Essays on Sexuality, Gender, and Holocaust Survivor Memory*: 73.
[1755] Anne Frank, *The Diary of Anne Frank* (London: Pan Books Ltd, 1954).
[1756] Schiff, *Hitler's Inferno: Eight Intimate and Personal Histories from the Holocaust.*
[1757] Shulamit Imber, "The Educational Philosophy of the International School for Holocaust Studies," in *International Seminar for Educators* (Jerusalem2009): Vashem Yad. *Lesson 1 - The Educational Philosophy of the International School of Holocaust Studies* (Jerusalem: Yad Vashem, 2008).
[1758] Friedman, *Speaking the Unspeakable: Essays on Sexuality, Gender, and Holocaust Survivor Memory*: 73.
[1759] Lawrence Langer, *Admitting the Holocaust: Collected Essays* (Oxford: Oxford University Press, 1995), 5-6, 26-32.
[1760] Raul Hilberg, *Perpetrators Victims Bystanders: The Jewish Catastrophe 1933-1945* (New York: Harper Collins Publishers, 1992), 165.
[1761] Szwajger, *I Remember Nothing More: The Warsaw Children's Hospital and Jewish Resistance*: 55-8.
[1762] Langer, *Admitting the Holocaust: Collected Essays*: 32.
[1763] Levi, *The Drowned and the Saved*: 59.
[1764] Langer, *Admitting the Holocaust: Collected Essays*: 158.
[1765] Yael Danieli, "The Ageing Survivor of the Holocaust: On the Achievement of Integration in Aging Survivors of the Nazi Holocaust" *Journal of Geriatric Psychiatry* 14, no. 2 (1983): 209.
[1766] Desbois, *The Holocaust by Bullets:A Priest's Journey to Uncover the Truth Behind the Murder of 1.5 Million Jews*: 67.
[1767] Evans, *The Coming of the Third Reich*: 128-9, 375-6.
[1768] Dieter Kuntz, *Deadly Medicine: Creating the Master Race* (Washington: United States Holocaust Memorial Museum, 2008), 200.
[1769] Benedict, "Caring While Killing: Nursing in the "Euthanasia" Centers," 96.
[1770] Kuntz, *Deadly Medicine: Creating the Master Race*: 201.
[1771] Evans, *The Coming of the Third Reich*: 129.
[1772] Benedict, "Caring While Killing: Nursing in the "Euthanasia" Centers," 96.
[1773] Kuntz, *Deadly Medicine: Creating the Master Race*: 201.
[1774] Timm, "Sex with a Purpose: Venereal Disease, and Militarized Masculinity in the Third Reich," 234.
[1775] Hogan and Aretha, *The Holocaust Chronicle*, 61.
[1776] Milton, "Women and the Holocaust: The Case of German and German-Jewish Women," 220-21.
[1777] Kater, *Doctors Under Hitler*: 171.
[1778] Michalczyk, *Medicine, Ethics, and the Third Reich: Historical and Contemporary Issues*: 228.
[1779] Koonz, *Mothers in the Fatherland: Women, the Family and Nazi Politics*: 140-43, 66-67.
[1780] Hodann, *International Group for the Investigation of Contraception.* Cited byDavid, Fleischhacker, and Hohn, "Abortion and Eugenics in Nazi Germany" 89.
[1781] Evans, *The Coming of the Third Reich*: 375-6; Burleigh and Wipperman, *The Racial State: Germany 1933-1945*: 189-90.
[1782] Rittner and Roth, *Different Voices: Women and the Holocaust*, 22.
[1783] Ibid.
[1784] Bock, "Nazi Sterilization and Reproductive Policies," 82.
[1785] Ibid., 62.
[1786] Hogan and Aretha, *The Holocaust Chronicle*, 70.

[1787] Rittner and Roth, *Different Voices: Women and the Holocaust*, 22.
[1788] Bock, "Nazi Sterilization and Reproductive Policies," 85.
[1789] Spitz, *Doctors From Hell: The Horrific Accounts of Nazi Experiments on Humans*: 62.
[1790] Hillel and Henry, *Of Pure Blood*: 30; Burleigh and Wipperman, *The Racial State: Germany 1933-1945*: 249.
[1791] Rittner and Roth, *Different Voices: Women and the Holocaust*, 23.
[1792] Benedict, "Caring While Killing: Nursing in the "Euthanasia" Centers," 96.
[1793] Koonz, *Mothers in the Fatherland: Women, the Family and Nazi Politics*: 140-43, 66-67.
[1794] Rittner and Roth, *Different Voices: Women and the Holocaust*, 23.
[1795] Ibid.
[1796] Ibid.
[1797] Michalczyk, *Medicine, Ethics, and the Third Reich: Historical and Contemporary Issues*: 64; ibid.
[1798] Kuntz, *Deadly Medicine: Creating the Master Race*: 201.
[1799] Michalczyk, *Medicine, Ethics, and the Third Reich: Historical and Contemporary Issues*: 229.
[1800] Kuntz, *Deadly Medicine: Creating the Master Race*: 201.
[1801] Ibid.
[1802] Ibid.
[1803] Ibid., 202.
[1804] Pine, *Nazi Family Policy 1933-1945*: 16.
[1805] Bock, "Nazi Sterilization and Reproductive Policies," 85.
[1806] Kuntz, *Deadly Medicine: Creating the Master Race*: 201.
[1807] Ibid., 202.
[1808] Kater, *Doctors Under Hitler*: 22-23,140.
[1809] Bock, "Nazi Sterilization and Reproductive Policies," 72.
[1810] ———, "Racism and Sexism in Nazi Germany" 276; Evans, *The Third Reich in Power*: 518; David, Fleischhacker, and Hohn, "Abortion and Eugenics in Nazi Germany "93-94; Nicholas, *Cruel World: The Children of Europe in the Nazi Web*: 57.
[1811] Hogan and Aretha, *The Holocaust Chronicle*, 91.
[1812] Evans, *The Third Reich in Power*: 288.
[1813] Ibid; Benedict, "Caring While Killing: Nursing in the "Euthanasia" Centers," 96.
[1814] Michalczyk, *Medicine, Ethics, and the Third Reich: Historical and Contemporary Issues*: 229.
[1815] Bock, "Nazi Sterilization and Reproductive Policies," 82.
[1816] Timm, "Sex with a Purpose: Venereal Disease, and Militarized Masculinity in the Third Reich," 238.
[1817] Michalczyk, *Medicine, Ethics, and the Third Reich: Historical and Contemporary Issues*: 229.
[1818] Hogan and Aretha, *The Holocaust Chronicle*, 107.
[1819] Kuntz, *Deadly Medicine: Creating the Master Race*: 202.
[1820] Benedict, "Caring While Killing: Nursing in the "Euthanasia" Centers," 96; Michalczyk, *Medicine, Ethics, and the Third Reich: Historical and Contemporary Issues*: 64.
[1821] Kuntz, *Deadly Medicine: Creating the Master Race*: 202.
[1822] Grunberger, *A Social History of the Third Reich*: 588.
[1823] Hogan and Aretha, *The Holocaust Chronicle*, 118.
[1824] Kuntz, *Deadly Medicine: Creating the Master Race*: 202.
[1825] Rittner and Roth, *Different Voices: Women and the Holocaust*, 24.
[1826] Hogan and Aretha, *The Holocaust Chronicle*, 128.
[1827] Rittner and Roth, *Different Voices: Women and the Holocaust*, 24.
[1828] Hogan and Aretha, *The Holocaust Chronicle*, 133.
[1829] Rittner and Roth, *Different Voices: Women and the Holocaust*, 24.
[1830] Kuntz, *Deadly Medicine: Creating the Master Race*: 202.

[1831] Rittner and Roth, *Different Voices: Women and the Holocaust*, 24.
[1832] Ibid.
[1833] Ibid.
[1834] Evans, *The Third Reich in Power*: 520.
[1835] Ibid., 518.
[1836] Michalczyk, *Medicine, Ethics, and the Third Reich: Historical and Contemporary Issues*: 64; ibid.
[1837] Bock, "Nazi Sterilization and Reproductive Policies," 86; Thompson, "Lebensborn and the Eugenics Policy of the Reichsführer - SS," 73; Pine, *Nazi Family Policy 1933-1945*: 39-42; Burleigh and Wipperman, *The Racial State: Germany 1933-1945*: 65-66; Nicholas, *Cruel World: The Children of Europe in the Nazi Web*: 242.
[1838] Rittner and Roth, *Different Voices: Women and the Holocaust*, 25.
[1839] Weinberg, "Two Separate Issues? Historiography of World War II and the Holocaust," 383.
[1840] Michalczyk, *Medicine, Ethics, and the Third Reich: Historical and Contemporary Issues*: 230.
[1841] Evans, *The Third Reich at War*: 78; Lifton, *The Nazi Doctors: Medical Killing and the Psychology of Genocide*: 51-.
[1842] Rittner and Roth, *Different Voices: Women and the Holocaust*, 25.
[1843] Burleigh, "Nazi "Euthanasia" Programs," 133.
[1844] Kuntz, *Deadly Medicine: Creating the Master Race*: 202.
[1845] Rittner and Roth, *Different Voices: Women and the Holocaust*, 25.
[1846] Evans, *The Third Reich at War*: 79.
[1847] Kuntz, *Deadly Medicine: Creating the Master Race*: 202.
[1848] Sax and Kuntz, *Inside Hitler's Germany: A Documentary History of Life in the Third Reich*: 214-7.
[1849] Rittner and Roth, *Different Voices: Women and the Holocaust*, 25.
[1850] Timm, "Sex with a Purpose: Venereal Disease, and Militarized Masculinity in the Third Reich," 247.
[1851] Rittner and Roth, *Different Voices: Women and the Holocaust*, 25.
[1852] Kuntz, *Deadly Medicine: Creating the Master Race*: 202.
[1853] Ibid.
[1854] Timm, "Sex with a Purpose: Venereal Disease, and Militarized Masculinity in the Third Reich," 246.
[1855] Kuntz, *Deadly Medicine: Creating the Master Race*: 202.
[1856] Michalczyk, *Medicine, Ethics, and the Third Reich: Historical and Contemporary Issues*.
[1857] Friedländer, *Nazi Germany and the Jews 1939-1945: The Years of Extermination*: 38.
[1858] Kuntz, *Deadly Medicine: Creating the Master Race*: 202.
[1859] Ibid., 203.
[1860] Rittner and Roth, *Different Voices: Women and the Holocaust*, 25.
[1861] Kuntz, *Deadly Medicine: Creating the Master Race*: 203.
[1862] Rittner and Roth, *Different Voices: Women and the Holocaust*, 26.
[1863] Chalk and Jonassohn, *The History and Sociology of Genocide* 354-.
[1864] Rittner and Roth, *Different Voices: Women and the Holocaust*, 26.
[1865] Harlan, "Jud Süβ."
[1866] Hippler, "Der Ewige Jude."
[1867] Kuntz, *Deadly Medicine: Creating the Master Race*: 203.
[1868] Hogan and Aretha, *The Holocaust Chronicle*, 208.
[1869] Kuntz, *Deadly Medicine: Creating the Master Race*: 203.
[1870] Timm, "Sex with a Purpose: Venereal Disease, and Militarized Masculinity in the Third Reich," 231.
[1871] Rittner and Roth, *Different Voices: Women and the Holocaust*, 26.
[1872] Spitz, *Doctors From Hell: The Horrific Accounts of Nazi Experiments on Humans*: 191.

[1873] Kuntz, *Deadly Medicine: Creating the Master Race*: 203.
[1874] Michalczyk, *Medicine, Ethics, and the Third Reich: Historical and Contemporary Issues*: 230.
[1875] Mühlhäuser, "Between 'Racial Awareness' and Fantasies of Potencies: Nazi Sexual Politics in the Occupied Territories of the Soviet Union, 1942-1945.," 201.
[1876] Kuntz, *Deadly Medicine: Creating the Master Race*: 203.
[1877] Michalczyk, *Medicine, Ethics, and the Third Reich: Historical and Contemporary Issues*: 230.
[1878] Rittner and Roth, *Different Voices: Women and the Holocaust*, 26.
[1879] Kuntz, *Deadly Medicine: Creating the Master Race*: 203.
[1880] Ibid.
[1881] Chalk and Jonassohn, *The History and Sociology of Genocide* 355.
[1882] Rittner and Roth, *Different Voices: Women and the Holocaust*, 26.
[1883] Michalczyk, *Medicine, Ethics, and the Third Reich: Historical and Contemporary Issues*: 231.
[1884] Kuntz, *Deadly Medicine: Creating the Master Race*: 203.
[1885] Rittner and Roth, *Different Voices: Women and the Holocaust*, 27.
[1886] Ibid.
[1887] Ibid.
[1888] Kuntz, *Deadly Medicine: Creating the Master Race*: 203.
[1889] Rittner and Roth, *Different Voices: Women and the Holocaust*, 27.
[1890] Dror and Linn, "The Shame is Always There," 276, 90 (Notes).
[1891] Kuntz, *Deadly Medicine: Creating the Master Race*: 203.
[1892] Michalczyk, *Medicine, Ethics, and the Third Reich: Historical and Contemporary Issues*: 231.
[1893] Ritvo and Plotkin, *Sisters in Sorrow: Voices of Care in the Holocaust*: 12.
[1894] Rittner and Roth, *Different Voices: Women and the Holocaust*, 28.
[1895] Kuntz, *Deadly Medicine: Creating the Master Race*: 203.
[1896] Morrison, *Ravensbrück: Everyday Life in a Women's Concentration Camp 1939-1945*: 201-4; Saidel, *The Jewish Women of Ravensbrück Concentration Camp*: 213; Milton, "Women and the Holocaust: The Case of German and German-Jewish Women," 226; Haas, *The Doctor and the Damned*: 234-6.
[1897] Kogon, *The Theory and Practice of Hell: The German Concentration Camps and the System Behind Them*: 108.
[1898] Rittner and Roth, *Different Voices: Women and the Holocaust*, 27.
[1899] Rosenbaum, *The Holocaust and Halakhah*: 40-41.
[1900] Rittner and Roth, *Different Voices: Women and the Holocaust*, 28.
[1901] Michalczyk, *Medicine, Ethics, and the Third Reich: Historical and Contemporary Issues*: 231.
[1902] Arad, Gutman, and Margoliot, *Documents on the Holocaust*: 272-73.
[1903] Höss, *Death Dealer: The Memoirs of the SS Kommandant of Auschwitz*: 343.
[1904] Sommer, "Sexual Exploitation of Women in Nazi Concentration Camp Brothels," 45-47.
[1905] Rittner and Roth, *Different Voices: Women and the Holocaust*, 28.
[1906] Ibid., 29.
[1907] Arad, Gutman, and Margoliot, *Documents on the Holocaust*: 450-53.
[1908] Tory, *Surviving the Holocaust: The Kovno Ghetto Diary*: 114.
[1909] Rittner and Roth, *Different Voices: Women and the Holocaust*, 29.
[1910] Kuntz, *Deadly Medicine: Creating the Master Race*: 204.
[1911] Rosenbaum, *The Holocaust and Halakhah*: 41-42.
[1912] Evans, *The Third Reich at War*: 543; Noakes, *Nazism 1919-1945, IV: The German Home Front in World War II: A Documentary Reader* 374.
[1913] Tory, *Surviving the Holocaust: The Kovno Ghetto Diary*: 132.
[1914] Rittner and Roth, *Different Voices: Women and the Holocaust*, 29.
[1915] Ibid., 30.

1916 Chelouche, "Doctors, Pregnancy, Childbirth and Abortion during the Third Reich," 203.
1917 Rittner and Roth, *Different Voices: Women and the Holocaust*, 30.
1918 Ibid.
1919 Kuntz, *Deadly Medicine: Creating the Master Race*: 204.
1920 Rittner and Roth, *Different Voices: Women and the Holocaust*, 30.
1921 Ibid.
1922 Amesberger, "Reproduction Under the Swastika: The Other Side of the Nazi Glorification of Motherhood," 140-41; "*Erlass zum Verbot der Einweisung schwangerer Häftlinge in die Frauenkonzentrationslager Ravensbrück bzw. in die Frauenabteilungen der Konzentrationslager Auschwitz und Lublin* [Decree forbidding the admission of pregnant inmates into the women's concentration camp Ravensbrück or the women's section of the concentration camps Auschwitz and Lublin].".
1923 Kuntz, *Deadly Medicine: Creating the Master Race*: 204.
1924 Rittner and Roth, *Different Voices: Women and the Holocaust*, 30.
1925 Evans, *The Third Reich at War*.
1926 Lenore J Weitzman and Dalia Ofer, "Introduction," in *Women in the Holocaust*, ed. Dalia Ofer and Lenore J Weitzman (New Haven: Yale University Press, `1998), 7.
1927 Sommer, "Sexual Exploitation of Women in Nazi Concentration Camp Brothels," 45-47.
1928 Rittner and Roth, *Different Voices: Women and the Holocaust*, 31.
1929 Rosmus, "Involuntary Abortions for Polish Forced Labourers," 79.
1930 Sommer, "Sexual Exploitation of Women in Nazi Concentration Camp Brothels," 45-47.
1931 Rittner and Roth, *Different Voices: Women and the Holocaust*, 31.
1932 Ibid.
1933 Ibid.
1934 Sommer, "Sexual Exploitation of Women in Nazi Concentration Camp Brothels," 45-47.
1935 Ibid.
1936 Ibid.
1937 Kuntz, *Deadly Medicine: Creating the Master Race*: 204.
1938 Ibid.
1939 Sommer, "Sexual Exploitation of Women in Nazi Concentration Camp Brothels," 45-47.
1940 Rittner and Roth, *Different Voices: Women and the Holocaust*, 31.
1941 Ibid.
1942 Ibid., 32.
1943 Kuntz, *Deadly Medicine: Creating the Master Race*: 204.
1944 Sommer, "Sexual Exploitation of Women in Nazi Concentration Camp Brothels," 45-47.
1945 Kuntz, *Deadly Medicine: Creating the Master Race*: 204.
1946 Rittner and Roth, *Different Voices: Women and the Holocaust*, 32.
1947 Ibid.
1948 Ibid.
1949 Beevor, *The Fall of Berlin 1945.* : 326; ibid; Evans, *The Third Reich at War*: 710.
1950 Rittner and Roth, *Different Voices: Women and the Holocaust*, 32.
1951 Ibid.
1952 Ibid.
1953 Kuntz, *Deadly Medicine: Creating the Master Race*: 204.
1954 Brenner, *After The Holocaust: Rebuilding Jewish Lives in Postwar Germany*: 26.
1955 Hogan and Aretha, *The Holocaust Chronicle*, 659.
1956 Ben-Sefer, "Forced Sterilization and Abortion as Sexual Abuse," 160.

Bibliography

Adelsberger, Lucie. *Auschwitz: A Doctor's Story*. Boston: Northeastern University Press, 1995.

Adelson, Alan, and Robert Lapides, eds. Lódź *Ghetto: Inside a Community under Siege*. New York: Viking, 1989.

Adorno, T W, Else Frenkel-Brunswick, Daniel T Levinson, and Nevitt R Sanford. *The Authoritarian Personality*. Oxford, England: Harpers, 1950.

Alexander, Leo. "Public Mental Health Practices in Germany: Sterilization and Execution of Patients Suffering from Nervous and Mental Disease. Combined Intelligence Objectives Sub-Committee, Item No 24, File No Xxviii-50. Copy 41." 1-173. London: IWM, 19 August 1945.

Aly, Götz. *Hitler's Beneficiaries: Plunder, Racial War, and the Nazi Welfare State*. New York: Metropolitan Books, 2006.

Amesberger, Helga. "Reproduction under the Swastika: The Other Side of the Nazi Glorification of Motherhood." In *Sexual Violence against Jewish Women During the Holocaust*, edited by Sonja M Hedgepeth and Rochelle G Saidel, 139-55. Waltham, Massachusetts: Brandeis University Press, 2010.

Amesberger, Helga, and Brigitte Halbmayr. "Nazi Differentiations Mattered: Ideological Intersections of Sexualized Violence During National Socialist Persecution." In *Life, Death, and Sacrifice: Women and Family in the Holocaust*, edited by Esther Herzog, 181-96. Jerusalem: Gefen Publishing House, 2008.

Annas, George. "The Changing Landscape of Human Experimentation: Nuremberg, Helsinki and Beyond." In *Medicine, Ethics and the Third Reich: Historical and Contemporary Issues*, edited by John J Michalczyk, 106-14. Kansas City: Sheed and Wade, 1994.

Anonymous. "Woman Born in Nazi Concentration Camp Tells Remarkable Tale of Holocaust Survival to Linton Pupils." *Haverhill Echo*, 24 March 2012.

———. *A Woman in Berlin: Eight Weeks in the Conquered City*. New York: Picador, 2000.

Arad, Yitzakh, Israel Gutman, and Abraham Margoliot. *Documents on the Holocaust*. Edited by Yitzakh Arad, Israel Gutman and Abraham Margoliot. Lincoln, Nebraska, : University of Nebraska Press, 1999.

Arad, Yitzhak. *Belzec, Sobibor, Treblinka: The Operation Reinhard Death Camps*. Bloomington: Indiana University Press, 1987.

Arendt, Hannah. *Eichmann in Jerusalem*. New York: The Viking Press, 1963.

Asch, Solomon. "Opinions and Social Pressure. ." *Scientific American* 193 (1955): 31-35.

Baer, Hester, and Elizabeth Baer. "Introduction." In *The Blessed Abyss: Inmate #6582 in Ravensbrück Concentration Camp for Women*, edited by Hester Baer and Elizabeth Baer, 13-51. Detroit: Wayne State University Press, 2000.

Bankier, David, and Dan Michman. *Holocaust Historiography in Context: Emergence, Challenges, Polemics and Achievements*. Jerusalem: Yad Vashem and Berghahn Books, 2008.

Bar-On, Dan. *Legacy of Silence: Encounters with Children of the Third Reich*. Cambridge Massachusetts: Harvard University Press, 1989.

Bar-On, Dan, and Julia Chaitin. *Parenthood and the Holocaust*. Edited by Search and Research Lectures and Papers 1. Jerusalem: Yad Vashem, 2001.

Bauer, Yehuda. *A History of the Holocaust*. 2nd ed. Danbury, Connecticut: Franklin Watts, 2001.

Baumel, Judith. "Gender and Family Studies of the Holocaust: The Development of a Historical Discipline." In *Life, Death and Sacrifice: Women and Family in the Holocaust*, edited by Esther Hertzog, 21-40. Jeruslaem: Geffen, 2008.

Becker, Hadassah. In *Massuah Institute for the Study of the Holocaust, Tel Aviv, 033c/618*, 29 November 1987.

Beer, Edith Hahn, and Susan Dworkin. *The Nazi Officer's Wife: How One Jewish Woman Survived the Holocaust*. New York: Rob Weisbach Books, 1999.

Beevor, Antony. The Guardian, http://zhopa007.livejournal.com/

———. *The Fall of Berlin 1945*. . New York: Penguin Books, 2002.

———. "Introduction." In *A Woman in Berlin*, edited by Anonymous, xxiii-xxi. New York: Picador, 2000.

Ben-Sefer, Ellen. "Forced Sterilization and Abortion as Sexual Abuse." In *Sexual Violence against Jewish Women During the Holocaust*, edited by Sonja M Hedgepeth and Rochelle G Saidel, 156-73. Waltham, Massachusetts: Brandeis University Press, 2010.

Bendremer, Jutta T. *Women Surviving the Holocaust: In Spite of the Horror*. Symposium Series 43. Lewiston: The Edwin Mellen Press, 1997.

Benedek, Vera. In *Massuah Institute for the Study of the Holocaust, Tel Aviv, 033c/3450*, 1-33.

Benedict, Susan. "Caring While Killing: Nursing in the "Euthanasia" Centers." In *Experience and Expression: Women, the Nazis, and the Holocaust*, edited by Elizabeth R Baer and Myrna Goldenberg, 95-110. Detroit: Wayne State University Press, 2001.

Berg, Mary. *The Diary of Mary Berg*. Oxford: Oneworld, 1945, 2007.

Berger, Miriam. In *Massuah Institute for the Study of the Holocaust, Tel Aviv, VD-1296*, 1-21, 15 August 1996.

Berger, Tova. " " In *Massuah Institute for the Study of the Holocaust, Tel Aviv, VT-2007*

Bergman, Anna. In *Imperial War Museum Sound Archive, London, 26752.*

Berlin, Elliot, and Joe Fab. "Paper Clips." 1 hour 24 mins. Canada: Motion Picture Distribution, 2006.

Berlin, Gail Ivy. "The 'Canada' Commando as a Force for Resistance in Auschwitz: Redefining Heroism." http://www.theverylongview.com/WATH/essays/canada.htm.

Biale, Rachel. *Women and Jewish Law: The Essential Texts, Their History, and Their Relevance for Today.* New York: Schocken Books, 1984.

Binding, K, and A E Hoche. " Die Freigabe der Vernichtung Lebensunwerten Lebens. Ihr Maß und ihre Form. ." Leipzig, 1920.

Bitton-Jackson, Livia. *I Have Lived a Thousand Years: Growing up in the Holocaust.* New York: Simon Pulse, 1999.

Black, Edwin. *IBM and the Holocaust.* New York: Three Rivers Press, 2001.

———. *Nazi Nexus: America's Corporate Connections to Hitler's Holocaust.* Washington D C: Dialog Press, 2009.

Blackman, Shane. *Chilling Out: The Cultural Politics of Substance Consumption, Youth and Drug Policy.* Berkshire, England: Open University Press, McGraw Hill, 2004.

Bleuel, Hans Peter. *Sex and Society in Nazi Germany.* Philadelphia: J.B.Lipincott Company, 1971.

Bloxham, Donald. "Jewish Witnesses in War Crimes Trials of the Postwar Era. ." In *Holocaust Historiography in Context: Emergence, Challenges, Polemics and Achievements*, edited by David Bankier and Dan Michman, 539-53. Jerusalem, 2008.

Bluhm, H O. "How Did They Survive?" *American Journal of Psychotherapy* 11, no. 1 (1948): 3.

Bock, Gisela. "Nazi Sterilization and Reproductive Policies." In *Deadly Medicine: Creating the Master Race*, edited by Dieter Kuntz, 61-87. Washington: United States Holocaust Memorial Museum, 2008.

———. "Racism and Sexism in Nazi Germany" In *When Biology Becomes Destiny* edited by Renate Bridenthal, Atina Grossman and Marion Kaplan, 271-96. New York, 1984.

———. "Racism and Sexism in Nazi Society: Motherhood, Compulsory Sterilization, and the State." In *Different Voices: Women and the Holocaust*, edited by Carol Rittner and John K. Roth, 161-86. New York: Paragon House, 1993.

Boder, David P. "The Tale of Anna Kovitzka; a Logico-Systematic Analysis or an Essay in Experimental Reading." In *Collection 1238.* Los Angeles: Charles E Young Research Library, UCLA Undated.

Bondy, Ruth. "Women in Theresienstadt and the Family Camp in Birkenau." In *Women in the Holocaust*, edited by Dalia Ofer and Lenore J Weitzman, 310-26. New Haven: Yale University Press, 1998.

Bos, Pascale Rachel. "Women and the Holocaust: Analyzing Gender Difference." In *Experience and Expression: Women, the Nazis, and the*

Holocaust, edited by Elizabeth R Baer and Myrna Goldenberg, 23-50. Detroit: Wayne State University Press, 2003.

Botwinick, Rita Steinhardt, ed. *A Holocaust Reader*. New Jersey: Prentice Hall, 1998.

Bower, Tom. *Klaus Barbie: Butcher of Lyons*. London: Corgi Books, 1984.

———. *The Paperclip Conspiracy: The Hunt for Nazi Scientists*. Boston: Little, Brown and Company, 1987.

Breitman, Richard. *The Architect of Genocide: Himmler and the Final Solution*. New York: Alfred A Knopf, 1991.

Brenner, Hannelore. *The Girls of Room 28:Friendship, Hope, and Survival in Theresienstadt*. New York: Schocken Books, 2009.

Brenner, Michael. *After the Holocaust: Rebuilding Jewish Lives in Postwar Germany*. Princeton: Princeton University Press, 1997.

Bridenthal, Renate, Atina Grossmann, and Marion Kaplan, eds. *When Biology Became Destiny: Women in Weimar and Nazi Germany*. New York: Monthly Review Press, 1984.

British Intelligence Objectives Sub-Committee. "Interrogation Report No 518. Ref No Aiu/Pir/137. Target No: C24/744, Bwce/N/Int/"T"/1 162". London: Imperial War Museum, 12 June 1947.

Browning, Christopher. "Ordinary Germans or Ordinary Men? Another Look at the Perpetrators." In *Lessons and Legacies: Teaching the Holocaust in a Changing World*, edited by Donald G Schilling, 41-54. Evanston, Illinois: Northwestern University Press, 1998.

Bruml, Hana Muller. "I Was a Nurse in Theresienstadt." In *Sisters in Sorrow: Voices of Care in the Holocaust*, edited by Roger A Ritvo and Diane M Plotkin, 23-49. College Station: Texas A&M University Press, 1998.

Burleigh, Michael. "Nazi "Euthanasia" Programs." In *Deadly Medicine: Creating the Master Race*, edited by Dieter Kuntz, 127-53. Washington: United States Holocaust Memorial Museum, 2008.

Burleigh, Michael, and Wolfgang Wipperman. *The Racial State: Germany 1933-1945*. Cambridge: Cambridge University Press, 1991.

Caplan, Arthus. "The Relevance of the Holocaust in Bioethics Today." In *Medicine, Ethics, and the Third Reich: Historical and Contemporary Issues*, edited by John J Michalczyk, 3-12. Kansas City: Sheed and Ward, 1994.

Capra, Frank. "Prelude to War." In *Why We Fight Series*, 54 minutes. USA: Platinum, 1942.

Chalk, Frank, and Kurt Jonassohn. *The History and Sociology of Genocide* New Haven: Yale University Press, 1990.

Chalmers, Beverley. "Informed Choice for Women." In *ANDRIA Congress: 'The respected birth to choose for gaining health'*. Cesena, Italy 2007.

Chalmers, Dana Lori. "The Influence of Theatre and Paratheatre on the Holocaust." Masters Thesis, Concordia University, 2008.

Chapnik, Liza. In *Massuah Institute for the Study of the Holocaust, Tel Aviv, VD-1058*, 1-32.

———. "The Grodno Ghetto and Its Underground: A Personal Narrative." In *Women in the Holocaust*, edited by Dalia Ofer and Lenore J Weitzman, 109-19. New Haven: Yale University Press, 1998.

Chatwood, Kirsty. "Schillinger and the Dancer: Representing Agency and Sexual Violence in Holocaust Testimonies." In *Sexual Violence against Jewish Women During the Holocaust*, edited by Sonja M Hedgepeth and Rochelle G Saidel, 61-74. Waltham, Massachusetts: Brandeis University Press, 2010.

Chelouche, Tessa. "Doctors, Pregnancy, Childbirth and Abortion During the Third Reich." *IMAJ* 9 (2007): 202-06.

Clary, Robert. *From the Holocaust to Hogan's Heroes: The Autobiography of Robert Clary*. Lanham, Maryland: Madison Books, 2001.

Cohen, Boaz. "Setting the Agenda of Holocaust Research: Discord at Yad Vashem in the 1950's." In *Holocaust Historiography in Context: Emergence, Challenges, Polemics and Achievements*, edited by David Bankier and Dan Michman, 255-92. Jerusalem: Yad Vashem and Berghahn Books, 2008.

Cohen, Elie. *Human Behaviour in the Concentration Camp*. London: Free Association Books, 1988.

Cornwell, John. *Hitler's Scientists: Science, War and the Devil's Pact*. New York: Viking, 2003.

Czech, Danuta. *The Auschwitz Chronicle 1939-1945*. Translated by Barbara Harshav, Martha Humphreys and Stephen Shearier. New York: Henry Holt, 1990.

Danieli, Yael. "The Ageing Survivor of the Holocaust: On the Achievement of Integration in Aging Survivors of the Nazi Holocaust" *Journal of Geriatric Psychiatry* 14, no. 2 (1983): 209.

David, Henry, Jochen Fleischhacker, and Charlotte Hohn. "Abortion and Eugenics in Nazi Germany" *Population and Development Review* 14 no. 1 (March 1998): 81-112.

Dawidowicz, Lucy. *The Holocaust and the Historians*. Cambridge, Massachusetts: Harvard University Press, 1981.

———. *The War against the Jews 1933-1945*. New York: Bantam Books, 1975.

Delbo, Charlotte. *Auschwitz and After*. New Haven: Yale University Press, 1995.

Des Pres, Terrence. *The Survivor: An Anatomy of Life in the Death Camps*. New York: Oxford University Press, 1976.

Desbois, Father Patrick. *The Holocaust by Bullets:A Priest's Journey to Uncover the Truth Behind the Murder of 1.5 Million Jews*. New York: Palgrave, Macmillan, 2008.

Dietrich, Donald. "Nazi Eugenics: Adaptation and Resistance among German Catholic Intellectual Leaders." In *Medicine, Ethics and the Third Reich: Historical and Contemporary Issues* edited by John J Michalczyk, 50-63. Kansas City: Sheed and Ward, 1994.

Dobell, Byron. "Had She Lived." *The Nation* October 8 (2007): 19-20.

Dobrowolski, Irek. "The Portraitist." 52 minutes. Poland: Auschwitz Museum, 2005.

Donat, Alexander. *The Holocaust Kingdom: A Memoir*. New York: Holt, Rinehart and Winston, 1965.

Donet, Michelle. In *Massuah Institute for the Study of the Holocaust, Tel Aviv, 033c/3681*, 1-16.

Dror, Esther, and Ruth Linn. "The Shame Is Always There." In *Sexual Violence against Jewish Women During the Holocaust*, edited by Sonja M Hedgepeth and Rochelle G Saidel, 275-91. Waltham, Massachusetts: Brandeis University Press, 2010.

Dublon-Knebel, Irith. ""We're All Well and Hoping to Hear the Same from You Soon..." The Story of a Group of Families." In *Life, Death and Sacrifice: Women and Family in the Holocaust.*, edited by Esther Hertzog, 69-93. Jerusalem: Gefen Publishing House, 2008.

Dwork, Deborah, and Robert Jan van Pelt. *Holocaust: A History*. New York: W.W. Norton and Company, 2003.

Dworzecki, Mark. "To Ignore or to Tell the Truth." *Bein ha-betarim* (10 June 1945): 28-29.

Eber, Irene. *The Choice: Poland 1939-1945*. New York: Schocken Books, 2004.

Edsel, Robert M, and Bret Witter. *The Monuments Men*. New York: Center Street, 2009.

Eiber, Ludwig, Manfred Tremi, and Claus Grimm, eds. *The Dachau Concentration Camp 1933-1945*. Dachau: Dachau Concentration Camp, 2003.

Eichengreen, Lucille, and Harriet Hyman Chamberlain. *From Ashes to Life: My Memories of the Holocaust*. San Francisco: Mercury House, 1994.

Eisner, Jack. *The Survivor of the Holocaust*. New York: Kensington Books, 1980.

Elias, Ruth. *Triumph of Hope: From Theresienstadt and Auschwitz to Israel*. Translated by Margot Bettauer Dembo. New York: John Wiley and Sons, 1988.

Engelmann, Bernt. *In Hitler's Germany: Everyday Life in the Third Reich*. New York: Pantheon Books, 1986.

Enzenberger, Hans Magnus. "Introduction." In *A Woman in Berlin: Eight Weeks in the Conquered City: A Diary*, edited by Anonymous, ix-xi. New York: Picador, 2000.

Epstein, Helen. *Conversations with Sons and Daughters of the Holocaust*. New York: Penguin Books, 1988.

"*Erlass Zum Verbot der Einweisung Schwangerer Häftlinge in Die Frauenkonzentrationslager Ravensbrück bzw. in Die Frauenabteilungen der Konzentrationslager Auschwitz und Lublin* [Decree Forbidding the Admission of Pregnant Inmates into the Women's Concentration Camp Ravensbrück or the Women's Section of the Concentration Camps Auschwitz and Lublin].". Ravensbrück Memorial in Sammlungen, May 6 1943.

Evans, Richard J. *The Coming of the Third Reich*. USA: Penguin Books, 2005.
———. *The Third Reich at War*. New York: The Penguin Press, 2009.
———. *The Third Reich in Power*. USA: Penguin Books, 2006.
Fefer-Matz, Eugenia. In *Yad Vashem Archives, Jerusalem, 03/5199*, 1-22, August 31, 1978.
Feinstein, Margarete Myers. "Absent Fathers, Present Mothers: Images of Parenthood in Holocaust Survivor Narratives." *Nashim: A Journal of Jewish Women's Studies* Spring, no. 13 (2007): 155-82.
———. "Hear the Voices: The Need for Personal Narratives in Holocaust Studies." *CSW Update Newsletter* (2010): 27-33.
Feinstein, Stephen C. "Jewish Women in Time: The Challenge of Feminist Artistic Installations About the Holocaust." In *Experience and Expression: Women, the Nazis, and the Holocaust*, edited by Elizabeth R Baer and Myrna Goldenberg, 229-59. Detroit: Wayne State University Press, 2003.
Fenelon, Fania. *Playing for Time*. New York: Berkley Books, 1977.
Finkel, Yehodit Zik. In *Yad Vashem Archives, Jerusalem, 0.3/12630*, 2005.
Fitzherbert, Katrin. *True to Both My Selves: A Family Memoir of Germany and England in Two World Wars*. London: Virago Press, 1997.
Flaschka, Monika J. ""Only Pretty Women Were Raped": The Effect of Sexual Violence on Gender Identities in Concentration Camps." In *Sexual Violence against Jewish Women During the Holocaust*, edited by Sonja M Hedgepeth and Rochelle G Saidel, 77-93. Waltham, Massachusetts: Brandeis University Press, 2010.
Fleischhauer, Jan. "Nazi War Crimes as Described by German Soldiers." Spiegel Online International, www.spiegel.de/international/.../0.1518.755385-5.00/html.
Fogelman, Eva. "Sexual Abuse of Jewish Women During and after the Holocaust: A Psychological Perspective." In *Sexual Violence against Jewish Women During the Holocaust*, edited by Sonja M Hedgepeth and Rochelle G Saidel, 255-74. Waltham, Massachusetts: Brandeis University Press, 2010.
Frank, Anne. *The Diary of Anne Frank*. London: Pan Books Ltd, 1954.
Frankl, Viktor. *Man's Search for Meaning: An Introduction to Logotherapy*. New York: Washington Square Press, 1963.
Freidlander, Henry. "From "Euthanasia" to the "Final Solution"." In *Deadly Medicine*, edited by Dieter Kuntz, 155-83. Washington: United States Holocaust Memorial Museum, 2008.
Fremont, Helen. *After Long Silence: A Memoir*. New York: Delacorte Press, 1999.
Friedländer, Saul. *Nazi Germany and the Jews 1939-1945: The Years of Extermination*. New York: Harper Perennial, 2007.
———. *The Years of Persecution: Nazi Germany and the Jews 1933-1939*. London: Phoenix, 1997.
Friedman, Jonathan. *Speaking the Unspeakable: Essays on Sexuality, Gender, and Holocaust Survivor Memory*. Lanham: University Press of America, 2002.

———. "Togetherness and Isolation: Holocaust Survivor Memories of Intimacy and Sexuality in the Ghettos." *The Oral History Review* 28, no. 1 (2001): 1-16.

Galt, Eva. In *Yad Vashem Archives,Jerusalem,O.3/10275.1.12.1996.9.*

Gefen, Aba. *Hope in Darkness: The Aba Gefen Holocaust Diaries*. New York: Holocaust Library, 1989.

Gerchik, Miriam. "Massuah, Tel Aviv, 033c/3600." 1-24.

Gilbert, Martin. *The Boys: The Story of 732 Young Concentration Camp Survivors*. New York: Henry Holt and Company, 1997.

———. *Holocaust Journey: Travelling in Search of the Past.* Vancouver: Douglas and McIntyre, 1997

———. *The Holocaust: A Record of the Destruction of Jewish Life in Europe During the Dark Years of Nazi Rule*. London: Board of Deputies of British Jews, 1978.

———. *The Righteous: The Unsung Heroes of the Holocaust*. London: Black Swan, 2002.

Gill, Anton. *The Journey Back from Hell: Conversations with Concentration Camp Survivors*. London: Grafton Books, 1988.

Gillis-Carlebach, Miriam. *Each Child Is My Only One: Lotte Carlebach-Preuss, the Portrait of a Mother and Rabbi's Wife*. New York: Peter Lang, 2014.

Gitta, Sereny. *Into That Darkness: An Examination of Conscience* New York Viking, 1983.

Glass, James M. *Life Unworthy of Life: Racial Phobia and Mass Murder in Hitler's Germany*. New York: Basic Books, 1997.

Goldenberg, Myrna. "Lessons Learned from Gentle Heroism: Women's Holocaust Narratives." *Annals of the American Academy of Political and Social Sciences* 548 (1996): 78-93.

———. "Memoirs of Auschwitz Survivors: The Burden of Gender." In *Women in the Holocaust*, edited by Dalia Ofer and Lenore J Weitzman, 327-39. New Haven: Yale University Press, 1998.

Goldhagen, Daniel Jonah. *Hitler's Willing Executioners: Ordinary Germans and the Holocaust*. New York: Vintage Books, 1997.

Gordon, Sarah. *Hitler, Germans, and the "Jewish Question"*. Princeton: Princeton University Press, 1984.

Gottesman, Marion. In *USC Shoah Foundation Institute for Visual History and Education On-Line Archive,16163, (Accessed 14 February 2012).*

GottlieboGovernment, US. "Trial of the Major War Criminals before the International Military Tribunal. Official Text in the English Language. Published at Nuremberg, Vol X X I X", 1947.

Gray, Martin, and Max Gallo. *For Those I Loved*. Boston: Little, Brown and Company, 1971.

Greene, Joshua M. *Justice at Dachau: The Trials of an American Prosecutor*. New York: Broadway Books, 2003.

Greif, Gideon. "Between Sanity and Insanity: Spheres of Everyday Life in the *Sonderkommando* in Auschwitz-Birkenau." In *Grey Zones: Ambiguity and Compromise in the Holocaust*, edited by Johnathon Petropoulos and John K Roth, 37-60. New York: Berghahn Books, 2005.

Grodin, Michael. "Historical Origins of the Nuremberg Code." In *Medicine, Ethics and the Third Reich: Historical and Contemporary Issues*, edited by John J Michalczyk, 169-94. Kansas City: Sheed and Wade, 1994.

Grodin, Michael A, George J Annas, and Leonard H Glantz. "Medicine and Human Reich: A Proposal for International Action." In *Medicine, Ethics and the Third Reich:Historical and Contemporary Issues*, edited by John J Michalczyk, 199- 209. Kansas City: Sheed and Wade, 1994.

Gronner, Shmuel. Men's Beards in Camps. 3 October 2011 2011.

Gross-Martin, Silvia. *Silvia*. New York: Welcome Rain Publishers, 2000.

Gross, Jan T. *Neighbours: The Destruction of the Jewish Community in Jedwabne, Poland, 1941*. London: Random House, 2003.

Grossmann, Atina. "Feminist Debates About Women and National Socialism." *Gender and History* 3, no. 3 (1991): 350-58.

———. *Jews, Germans, and the Allies: Close Encounters in Occupied Germany*. Princeton: Princeton University Press, 2007.

———. "A Question of Silence: The Rape of German Women by Occupation Soldiers." *October* 72, no. Berlin 1945: War and Rape "Liberators take Liberties" (1995): 42-63.

Grunberger, Richard. *A Social History of the Third Reich*. Harmondsworth, UK: Penguin Books, 1974.

Gun, Nerin E. "Dachau, 1945." In *A Taste of War: Eyewitness Accounts of World War II*, edited by Harld Elk Straubing, 244-57. New York: Sterling Publishing Co, Inc., 1992.

Gupta, Charu. "Politics of Gender: Women in Nazi Germany." *Economic and Political Weekly* 26, no. 17 (April 27 1991): WS40-WS48.

Gutman, Israel, ed. *Encyclopedia of the Holocaust*. New York: Macmillan Publishing Company, 1990.

Haas, Albert. *The Doctor and the Damned*. New York: St Martin's Press, 1984.

Hájková, Dagmar, and Hana Housková. "The Stations of the Cross." In *Medicine, Ethics and the Third Reich* edited by John J Michalczyk, 129-42. Kansas City: Sheed and Wade, 1984.

Halbmayr, Brigitte. "Sexualized Violence against Women During Nazi "Racial" Persecution." In *Sexual Violence against Jewish Women During the Holocaust*, edited by Rochelle G Saidel Sonja M Hedgepeth, 29-44. Waltham, Massachusetts: Brandeis University Press, 2010.

Halter, Roman. In *Imperial War Museum Sound Archives, London, 17183*.

Hanauske-Abel, Hartmut M. "Not a Slippery Slope or Sudden Subversion: German Medicine and National Socialism in 1933." *BMJ: British Medical Journal* 313, no. 7070 (1996): 1453-63.

Hargreaves, Edgar. "Imperial War Museum, London, 5378." 1981-11-23.

Harlan, Veit. "Jud Süβ." 197 minutes. Germany: Terra-Filmkunst GmbH, 1934.

Harris, Victoria. *Selling Sex in the Reich: Prostitutes in German Society, 1914-1945*. Oxford: Oxford University Press, 2010.

Harris, Yehudit. In *Massuah Institute for the Study of the Holocaust, Tel Aviv, 033c/5515*, 1-55, 26 August 1997.

Hart, Kitty. *I Am Alive*. London: Abelard-Schuman, 1961.

———. *Return to Auschwitz*. London: Grafton Books, 1983.
Hausner, Gideon. *Justice in Jerusalem*. . New York: Schoken Books, 1968.
Hebermann, Nanda. *The Blessed Abyss: Inmate #6582 in Ravensbrück Concentration Camp for Women*. Detroit: Wayne State University press, 2000.
Heck, Alfons. *A Child of Hitler*. New York: Bantam Books 1986.
Hedgepath, Sonja M, and Rochelle G Saidel. "Introduction." In *Sexual Violence against Jewish Women During the Holocaust*, edited by Sonja M Hedgepath and Rochelle G Saidel. Waltham, Massachusetts: Brandeis University Press, 2010.
Heger, Heinz. *The Men with the Pink Triangle*. New York: Alyson Books, 1980.
Heineman, Elizabeth. "Gender, Sexuality, and Coming to Terms with the Nazi Past." *Central European History* 38, no. 1 (2–5): 41-74.
———. "Sexuality and Nazism: The Doubly Unspeakable?" *Journal of the History of Sexuality* 11, no. 1/2 (Jan-Apr 2002): 22-66.
Herf, Jeffrey. *Nazi Propaganda for the Arab World*. New Haven: Yale University Press, 2009.
Hertzog, Esther. *Life, Death and Sacrifice: Women and Family in the Holocaust*. Jerusalem: Gefen Publishing House, 2008.
Herz, Gabriele. *The Women's Camp in Moringen: A Memoir of Imprisonment in Germany, 1936-1937*. New York: Berghahn Books, 2006.
Herzberger, Magda. "God Saved Me for a Purpose." In *Sisters in Sorrow: Voices of Care in the Holocaust*, edited by Roger A Ritvo and Diane M Plotkin, 197-236. College Station, USA: Texas A &M University Press, 2000.
Herzog, Dagmar. "Hubris and Hypocrisy, Incitement and Disavowal: Sexuality and German Fascism." *Journal of the History of Sexuality* 11, no. 1/2 (2002): 3-21.
Hiemer, Ernst. *Der Giftpilz (the Poisonous Mushroom)*. Germany: Julies Streicher, 1938.
Hilberg, Raul. *The Destruction of the European Jews*. New York: Holmes and Meier, 1985.
———. *Perpetrators Victims Bystanders: The Jewish Catastrophe 1933-1945*. New York: Harper Collins Publishers, 1992.
———. *The Politics of Memory: The Journey of a Holocaust Historian*. Chicago: Ivan R Dee, 1996.
———. "Two Thousand Years of Jewish Appeasement." In *The Holocaust: Problems in European Civilization*, edited by Donald L Niewyk, 110-16. Boston, New York: Houghton, Mifflin Company, 1997.
Hilberg, Raul, Stanislaw Staron, and Josef Kermisz. *The Warsaw Diary of Adam Czerniakow: Prelude to Doom*. New York: Stein and Day, 1982.
Hill, Ronald Paul, and Elizabeth C Hirschman. "Human Rights Abuses by the Third Reich: New Evidence Form the Nazi Concentration Camp Buchenwald." *Human Rights Quarterly* 18, no. 4 (1996): 848-73.
Hillel, Marc, and Clarissa Henry. *Of Pure Blood*. New York: Pocket Books, 1975.

Hinton, Carla. "Israeli Sisters Visit Oklahoma City to Tell Their Parents' Holocaust Story." Newsok.com/article/3557742.

Hippler, Fritz. "Der Ewige Jude." 78 minutes. Germany: Deutsche Film Gesellschaft, 1940.

Hitler, Adolf. *Mein Kampf*. London: Hurst and Blackett, 1939.

Hodann, M. *International Group for the Investigation of Contraception*. London 1934.

Hodara, Raquel. "The Polish Jewish Woman: From the Beginning of the Occupation to the Deportation to the Ghettos." *Yad Vashem Studies* 32 (2004): 397-432.

Hogan, David, and David Aretha, eds. *The Holocaust Chronicle*. Illinois: Publications International, 2001.

Holliday, Laurel. *Children in the Holocaust and World War II: Their Secret Diaries*. New York: Pocket Books, 1995.

"Holocaust." 7 hr 29 min: Titus Productions, 1978.

Horowitz, Gordon J. *In the Shadow of Death: Living Outside the Gates of Mauthausen*. New York: The Free Press, 1990.

Horowitz, Sara R. "Women in Holocaust Literature: Engendering Trauma Memory." In *Women in the Holocaust* edited by Dalia Ofer and Lenore Weitzman, 364-77. New Haven: Yale University Press, 1998.

Horstman, Lalli. *Nothing for Tears*. London: Weidenfeld and Nicolson, 1953.

Höss, Rudolf. *Death Dealer: The Memoirs of the SS Kommandant of Auschwitz*. Edited by Steven Paskuly. New York: Da Capo Press, 1996.

Imber, Shulamit. "The Educational Philosophy of the International School for Holocaust Studies." In *International Seminar for Educators*. Jerusalem, 2009.

Inbar, Yehudit. *Spots of Light: To Be a Woman in the Holocaust*. Jerusalem: Yad Vashem, 2007.

Ingram, Marione. *The Hands of War*. New York: Skyhorse Publishing, 2013.

Iranek-Osmecki, Kazimierz. *He Who Saves One Life*. New York: Crown Publishers, 1971.

Is, Mo. *U.B.B.: Unforgettable Bergen-Belsen*. Montreal: A Emeth Publisher, 1993.

Isaacson, Judith Magyar. *Seed of Sarah: Memoirs of a Survivor Chicago*. Illinois: University of Illinois Press, 1990.

Jofen, Jean. "Long-Range Effects of Medical Experiments in Concentration Camps (the Effect of Administration of Estrogens to the Mother on the Intelligence of the Offspring)." Paper presented at the Fifth World Congress of Jewish Studies, Jerusalem, 1969.

Johnson, Eric A, and Karl-Heinz Reuband. *What We Knew: Terror, Mass Murder, and Everyday Life in Nazi Germany*: Basic Books, 2005.

Jones, Adam. *Genocide: A Comprehensive Introduction*. 2nd ed: Routledge/Taylor & Francis Publishers, 2010.

Ka-Tzetnik, 135633. *House of Dolls*. London: Granada, 1973.

———. *Piepel*. London: The New English Library, 1961.

Kaplan, Marion A. *Between Dignity and Despair: Jewish Life in Nazi Germany*. New York: Oxford University Press, 1998.

Karay, Felicja. *Death Comes in Yellow: Skarżysko-Kamienna Slave Labor Camp.* . London: Routledge, 1996.

———. "Women in the Forced-Labor Camps." In *Women in the Holocaust*, edited by Dalia Ofer and Lenore J Weitzman, 285-309. New Haven: Yale University Press, 1998.

Kater, Michael. *Doctors under Hitler*. Chapel Hill: The University of North Carolina Press, 1989.

———. "An Historical and Contemporary View of Jewish Doctors in Germany." In *Medicine, Ethics and the Third Reich*, edited by John J Michalczyk, 161-66. Kansas City: Sheed and Ward, 1944.

Katz, Esther, and Joan Miriam Ringelheim, eds. *Proceedings of the Conference Women Surviving the Holocaust*, Occasional Papers: The Institute for Research in History, 1983.

Katz, Jay. "The Concentration Camp Experiments: Their Relevance for Contemporary Research with Human Beings." In *Medicine, Ethics and the Third Reich* edited by John J Michalczyk, 73-86. Kansas City: Sheed and Ward, 1944.

Kellenbach, Katherina von. "Reproduction and Resistance During the Holocaust." In *Women and the Holocaust: Studies in the Shoah*, edited by Esther Fuchs, 19-32. Lanham, Maryland, 1999.

Kempner, Aviva. "Comment." Paper presented at the Women Surviving the Holocaust, 1983.

Kershaw, Ian. *Hitler: Profiles in Power*. Edited by Keith Robbins. London: Longman, 1991.

Klee, Ernst, Willi Dressen, and Volker Reiss, eds. *The Good Old Days: The Holocaust as Seen by Its Perpetrators and Bystanders*. Old Saybrook, Connecticut: Konecky and Konecky, 1991.

Klein, Matilda. In *USC Shoah Foundation Institute for Visual History and Education On-Line Archive, 6525 (Accessed 14 February 2012).*

Klemperer, Victor. *I Shall Bear Witness: The Diaries of Victor Klemperer 1933-1941*. London: Weidenfeld and Nicolson, 1998.

Knopp, Guido. *Hitler's Children*. Phoenix Mill, Gloucestershire: Sutton Publishing Limited, 2002.

Koehn, Ilse. *Mischling, Second Degree: My Childhood in Nazi Germany*. New York: Bantam Books, 1978.

Kogon, Eugen. *The Theory and Practice of Hell: The German Concentration Camps and the System Behind Them*. New York: Berkeley Books, 1950.

Kononenko, Elena. *Baby Killers*. Moscow: Foreign Language Publishing House, 1942.

Koonz, Claudia. "The Competition for a Women's Lebensraum 1928-1934." In *When Biology Becomes Destiny: Women in Weimar and Nazi Germany*, edited by Renate Bridenthal, Atina Grossmann and Marion Kaplan, 199-236. New York: Monthly Review Press, 1984.

———. *Mothers in the Fatherland: Women, the Family and Nazi Politics*. New York: St Martin's Press, 1987.

Kovacz, Olga. In *USC Shoah Foundation Institute for Visual History and Education On-Line Archive, 3012 (Accessed 14 February 2012).*

Kozlovsky-Golan, Yvonne. ""Public Property": Sexual Abuse of Women and Girls in Cinematic Memory." In *Sexual Violence against Jewish Women During the Holocaust*, edited by Sonja M Hedgepeth and Rochelle G Saidel, 234-51. Waltham, Massachusetts: Brandeis University Press, 2010.

Kremer, S Lillian. "Sexual Abuse in Holocaust Literature: Memoir and Fiction." In *Sexual Violence against Jewish Women During the Holocaust*, edited by Sonja M Hedgepeth and Rochelle G Saidel, 177-99. Waltham, Massachusetts: Brandeis University Press, 2010.

Kundrus, Birthe, and Patricia Szobar. "Forbidden Company: Romantic Relationships between Germans and Foreigners 1933-1945." *Journal of the History of Sexuality* 11, no. 1/2 (2002): 201-22.

Kuntz, Dieter. *Deadly Medicine: Creating the Master Race*. Washington: United States Holocaust Memorial Museum, 2008.

Kuper, Jack. *Child of the Holocaust*. Markham, Ontario: Paperjacks, 1978.

Kutz, Michael. *If, by Miracle*. Canada: the Azrieli Foundation, 2013.

Lagnado, Lucette Matalon, and Sheila Cohn Dekel. *Children of the Flames: Dr Josef Mengele and the Untold Story of the Twins of Auschwitz*. New York: William Morrow and Company, Inc, 1991.

Langbein, Hermann. *Menschen in Auschwitz* Vienna: Europe Verlag, 1972.

Langer, Lawrence. *Admitting the Holocaust: Collected Essays*. Oxford: Oxford University Press, 1995.

———. "Gendered Suffering? Women in Holocaust Testimonies." In *Women in the Holocaust*, edited by Dalia Ofer and Lenore Weitzman, 351-63. New Haven: Yale University Press, 1998.

———. *Versions of Survival: The Holocaust and the Human Spirit* New York: State University of New York Press, 1982.

Langfuss, Leib. "The Horrors of Murder." In *The Scrolls of Auschwitz*, edited by Ber Mark. Tel Aviv: Am Oves, 1985.

Laska, Vera. *Women in the Resistance and in the Holocaust*. Westport Connecticut: Greenwood Press, 1983.

———. "Women in the Resistance and in the Holocaust." In *Different Voices: Women and the Holocaust*, edited by Carol Rittner and John Roth, 250-69. New York: Paragon House, 1993.

Laughlin, Estelole. In *USC Shoah Foundation Institute for Visual History and Education On-Line Archive, 21582 (Accessed 14 February 2012)*.

Lebenswold, Ester. In *USC Shoah Foundation Institute for Visual History and Education On-Line Archive, 9230 (Accessed 14 February 2012)*.

Lee, Carol Ann. *The Hidden Life of Otto Frank*. New York: Harper Collins, 2002.

Leitner, Isabella. *Fragments of Isabella: A Memoir of Auschwitz*. New York: Laurel, 1978.

Lengyel, Olga. In *USC Shoah Foundation Institute for Visual History and Education On-Line Archive, 46138 (Accessed 14 February 2012)*.

———. *Five Chimneys: A Woman Survivor's True Story of Auschwitz*. First Academy Chicago edition, 1995 ed. Chicago: Ziff-Davis Publishing Company, 1947.

———. "Scientific Experiments." In *Women and the Holocaust: Different Voices*, edited by Carol Rittner and John K Roth, 119-29. New York: Paragon House, 1993.

Lenji, Anna. In *Massuah Institute for the Study of the Holocaust, Tel Aviv, 033c/4312.*

Lessing, Carla. "Aging Child Holocaust Survivors of Sexual Abuse." In *Selfhelp Conference*. New York, 2012.

Levenkron, Nomi. "Death and the Maidens: "Prostitution," Rape, and Sexual Slavery During World War II." In *Sexual Violence against Jewish Women During the Holocaust*, edited by Sonja M Hedgepeth and Rochelle G Saidel, 13-28. Waltham, Massachusetts: Brandeis University Press, 2010.

Levi, Primo. *The Drowned and the Saved.* New York: Vintage International, 1989.

Lewy, Guenter. *The Nazi Persecution of the Gypsies*. Oxford: Oxford University Press, 2000.

Library., Jewish Virtual. "Auschwitz-Birkenau Concentration Camp." http://www.jewishvirtuallibrary.org/jsource/Holocaust/auschbirk.html.

Lichtblau, Eric. "The Holocaust Just Got More Shocking." http://www.nytimes.com/2013/03/03/sunday-review/the-holocaust-just-got-more-shocking.html?pagewanted=all&_r=0.

Lifton, Robert Jay. *The Nazi Doctors: Medical Killing and the Psychology of Genocide*. New York: Basic Books, Inc, 1986.

Lipstadt, Deborah. "Introduction." In *Auschwitz: A Doctor's Story*, edited by Lucie Adelsberger. Boston: Northeastern University Press, 1995.

Littman, Sol. *War Criminal on Trial: Rauca of Kaunas*. Toronto: Key Porter Books, 1993.

Liverpool, Lord Russell of. *The Scourge of the Swastika*. London: The Military Book Club, 1954.

Loeb, Ellen. "Liebe Trude, Liebe Rudy [Dear Trudy, Dear Rudy]." In *Sisters in Sorrow: Voices of Care in the Holocaust*, edited by Roger A Ritvo and Diane M Plotkin, 106-25. College Station, USA: Texas A&M University Press, 1998.

Love, Dora. In *Massuah Institute for the Study of the Holocaust, Tel Aviv, 03/7504, 033c/3021*, 1-31.

Lower, Wendy. *Hitler's Furies: German Women in the Nazi Killing Fields*. New York: Houghton Mifflin, 2013.

MacPherson, Malcolm C. *The Blood of His Servants: The True Story of One Man's Search for His Family's Friend and Executioner*. New York: Times Books, 1984.

Magid, Hanna Rothe. In *Yad Vashem Archives, Jerusalem, 0.3/1570*, 1960.

Manchester, William. *The Arms of Krupp 1587-1968*. New York: Bantam Books, 1970.

Mann, Daniel. "Playing for Time." 150 minutes: Olive Films, 1980.

Marcus, Leo. "Notes of Leo Marcus Written in March 1943, During the Third Year of World War II in Holland, on the Occasion of the Birth of His Fourth Daughter, Leonie, While the Family Was in Hiding.". Tel Aviv, Israel, March 1943.

Martin, John Bartlow, and S L Sheiderman. "The Mother Who Lived a Miracle." *McCall's*, November 1957.

Maslow, Abraham. "A Theory of Human Motivation, ." *Psychological Review* 50, no. 4 (1943): 370-96.

Masters, Anthony. *The Summer That Bled: The Biography of Hannah Senesh.* London: Michael Joseph, 1972.

Matas, David, and Susan Vharendoff. *Justice Delayed: Nazi War Criminals in Canada.* Toronto: Summerhill Press, 1987.

Mazower, Mark. *Dark Continent: Europe's Twentieth Century*. New York: Vintage Books, 1998.

———. *Hitler's Empire: How the Nazis Ruled Europe*. New York: Penguin Books, 2008.

Mendelsohn, Daniel. *The Lost: A Search for Six of the Six Million.* New York: Harper Perennial, 2006.

Michalczyk, John J. *Medicine, Ethics, and the Third Reich: Historical and Contemporary Issues*. Kansas City: Sheed and Ward, 1994.

Milgram, Stanley. "Behavioral Study of Obedience" *Journal of Abnormal and Social Psychology* 67, no. 4 (1963): 371-8.

Miller, Judith. *One by One by One: Facing the Holocaust.* New York: Simon and Schuster, 1990.

Millu, Liana. *Smoke over Birkenau.* Evanston, Illinois: Northwestern University Press, 1986.

Milton, Sybil. "Women and the Holocaust: The Case of German and German-Jewish Women." In *Different Voices: Women and the Holocaust*, edited by Carol Rittner and John K Roth, 213-49. New York: Paragon House, 1993.

Minc, Zofia. In *Yad Vashem Archives, Jerusalem, M.49.E-Zih/2504*, 1947.

Mitscherlich, Alexander, and Fred Mielke. *Doctors of Infamy: The Story of the Nazi Medical Crimes*. New York: Henry Schuman Inc, 1949.

Molnar, J. " Zsidósors 1944-Ben Az V. (Szegedi) Csendórkerületben.", 140-41. Budapest, 1995.

Molotov, Vyacheslav M. "Molotov's Note on German Atrocities in Occupied Soviet Territory." http://www.ibiblio.org/pha/policy/1942/420106b.html.

Moorehead, Caroline. *A Train in Winter: A Story of Resistance, Friendship and Survival in Auschwitz*. London: Vintage Books, 2012.

Moorhouse, Roger. *Killing Hitler: The Plots, the Assassins, and the Dictator Who Cheated Death.* New York: Bantam Books, 2006.

Morrison, Jack G. *Ravensbrück: Everyday Life in a Women's Concentration Camp 1939-1945*. Princeton: Markus Weiner Publishers, 2000.

Moser, Brian. "The Search for Mengele." 80 minutes. USA: First Run Features, 1985.

Mosse, George. *The Image of Man: The Creation of Modern Masculinity*. New York1996.

———. *Nazi Culture: Intellectual, Cultural and Social Life in the Third Reich*. London1966.

Moyal, Zelda. In *Massuah Institute for the Study of the Holocaust, Tel Aviv, VT-842*, 1-26.

Mühlhäuser, Regina. "Between 'Racial Awareness' and Fantasies of Potencies: Nazi Sexual Politics in the Occupied Territories of the Soviet Union, 1942-1945." In *Brutality and Desire: War and Sexuality in Europe's Twentieth Century*, edited by Dagmar Herzog, 197-219. Houndmills, Basingstoke, Hampshire: Pelgrave Macmillan, 2009.

Müller, Charlotte. *Die Klempnerkolonne* Müller, Filip. *Eyewitness Auschwitz: Three Years in the Gas Chambers*. Chicago: Ivan R Dee, 1979.

Museum, United States Holocaust Memorial. "Homosexuals: Victims of the Nazi Era, 1933-1945." fcit.usf.edu/holocaust/people/USHMMHOM.HTM

Nadav, Daniel. "Sterilization, "Euthanasia", and the Holocaust – the Brutal Chain." In *Medicine, Ethics and the Third Reich: Historical and Contemporary Issues*, edited by John J Michalczyk, 42-49. Kansas City: Sheed and Ward, 1994.

Nebel, Ruth. "The Story of Ruth." In *When Biology Became Destiny: Women in Weimar and Nazi Germany*, edited by Renate Bridenthal, Atina Grossmann and Marion Kaplan, 334-48. New York: Monthly Review Press, 1984.

Nesaulle, Agate. *A Woman in Amber: Healing the Trauma of War and Exile*. New York: Penguin Books, 1995.

Neufeld, Michael J., and Michael Berenbaum, eds. *The Bombing of Auschwitz: Should the Allies Have Attempted It?* New York: St Martin's Press, 2000.

Nevins, Michael. "Moral Dilemmas Faced by Jewish Doctors During the Holocaust." www.jewishvirtuallibrary.org/jsource/Judaism/dilemma.html.

Nicholas, Lynn H. *Cruel World: The Children of Europe in the Nazi Web*. New York: Vintage Books, 2006.

Niederland, William G. *Folgen der Vervolgung: Das Überlebenden-Syndrom, Seelenmord.* : Suhrkamp, 1980.

Niewyk, Donald L. *The Holocaust: Problems and Perspectives of Interpretation*. Boston: Houghton Mifflin, 1997.

Noakes, Jeremy. *Nazism 1919-1945, IV: The German Home Front in World War II: A Documentary Reader* Exeter1998.

Nomberg-Przytyk, Sara. *Auschwitz: True Tales from a Grotesque Land.* Chapel Hill: University of North Carolina Press, 1985.

Norwood, Stephen H. *The Third Reich in the Ivory Tower: Complicity and Conflict on American Campuses*. Cambridge: Cambridge University Press, 2009.

Nowak, Susan. "Ruptured Lives and Shattered Beliefs: A Feminist Analysis of Tikkun Atzmi in Holocaust Literature." In *Experience and Expression: Women, the Nazis, and the Holocaust*, edited by Elizabeth R Baer and Myrna Goldenberg, 180-200. Detroit: Wayne State University Press, 2003.

Nutkiewicz, Michael. "Shame, Guilt, and Anguish in Holocaust Survivor Testimony." *The Oral History Review* 30, no. 1 (2003): 1-22.

Nyiszli, Miklos. *Auschwitz: A Doctor's Eyewitness Account*. New York: Arcade Publishing 1960.

O'Mathúna, Dónai P. "Human Dignity in the Nazi Era: Implications for Contemporary Bioethics." *MBC Medical Ethics*,no. 2 (2006), www.biomedcentral.com/1472-6939/7/2.

Ofer, Dalia. "Gender Issues in Diaries and Testimonies of the Ghetto: The Case of Warsaw." In *Women in the Holocaust*, edited by Dalia Ofer and Lenore J Weitzman, 143-67. New Haven: Yale University Press, 1998.

———. "Motherhood under Siege." In *Life, Death, and Sacrifice: Women and Family in the Holocaust*, 41-68. Jerusalem: Gefen Publishing House, 2008.

Okrnt, Selma. In *Massuah Institute for the Study of the Holocaust, Tel Aviv, VD-1020*, 1-37.

Orbach, Larry, and Vivienne Orbach-Smith. *Soaring Underground; a Young Fugitive's Life in Nazi Berlin*. Washington DC Compass Press, 1996.

Ossowski, Maria. In *Imperial War Museum Sound Archive, London, 19794*.

Owings, Alison. *Frauen: German Women Recall the Third Reich*. London: Penguin Books, 1993.

Oz, Amos. *A Tale of Love and Darkness*. London: Vintage Books, 2005.

Paris, Erna. *Unhealed Wounds: France and the Klaus Barbie Affair*. Toronto: Methuen, 1985.

Pawelka, Britta. "A Women in Concentration Camps Bergen-Belsen, Ravensbrück." In *Als Häftlinge Geboren – Kinder in Ravensbrück [Born as a Prisoner – Children in Ravensbrück.] in Frauen in Konzentrationslagern. Bergen-Belsen, Ravensbrück.*, edited by Klaus Füllberg-Stollberg et al. Bremen Edition Temmem, 1944.

Pawlowicz, Sala. *I Will Survive*. New York: W W Norton and Company, Inc, 1962.

Peled, Galia. "Pregnancy as Resistance in the Holocaust." 1-53. Jerusalem: Yad Vashem, 2005.

Peretz, Aharon. "The Trial of Adolf Eichmann." The Nizkor Project, http://www.nizkor.org/hweb/people/e/eichmann-adolf/transcripts/Sessions/Session-028-04.html.

Perl, Gisella. *I Was a Doctor in Auschwitz*. Reprint edition 2007 ed. North Stratford, NH: Ayer Company Publishers, 1948.

Pine, Lisa. *Nazi Family Policy 1933-1945*. Oxford: Berg, 1997.

Pini, Udo. *Leibeskult und Liebeskitsch. Erotik Im Dritten Reich*. Munich1992.

Pivnik, Sam. *Survivor: Auschwitz, the Death March and My Flight for Freedom*. London: Hodder and Stoughton, 2012.

Podolsky, Anatoly. "The Tragic Fate of Ukrainian Jewish Women under Nazi Occupation, 1941-1944." In *Sexual Violence against Jewish Women During the Holocaust*, edited by Sonja M Hedgepeth and Rochelle G Saidel, 94-107. Waltham, Massachusetts: Brandeis University Press, 2010.

Polgar, Edith. In *USC Shoah Foundation Institute for Visual History and Education On-Line Archive, 3994 (Accessed 14 February 2012)*.

Poliakov, L. *Harvest of Hate*. . Syracuse, New York1954.

Poltawska, Wanda. *And I Am Afraid of My Dreams*. London: Hodder and Stroughton, 1964.

Porter, Ana. *Kasztner's Train: The True Story of Rezsö Kasztner, Unknown Hero of the Holocaust*. Vancouver: Douglas & McIntyre, 2007.

Posner, Gerald L, and John Ware. *Mengele: The Complete Story*. New York: Cooper Square Press, 2000.

Preiss, Leah. "Women's Health in the Ghettos of Eastern Europe. Jewish Women: A Comprehensive Historical Encyclopedia " *Jewish Women's Archive* (1 March 2009), http://jwa.org/encyclopedia/article/womens-health-in-ghettos-of-eastern-europe.

Prochazka, Zsoka. In *USC Shoah Foundation Institute for Visual History and Education On-Line Archive, 39069, Accessed 14 February 2012.*

Proctor, Robert N. "Racial Hygiene: The Collaboration of Medicine and Nazism." In *Medicine, Ethics and the Third Reich: Historical and Contemporary Issues*, edited by John J Michalczyk, 35-41. Kansas City: Sheed and Ward, 1944.

Raichman, Chil. *The Last Jew of Treblinka*. New York: Pegasus Books, 2011.

Rapoport, Safira, ed. *Yesterdays and Then Tomorrows: Holocaust Anthology of Testimonies and Readings*. Jerusalem: The International School of Holocaust Studies Yad Vashem, 2002.

Rauschning, Hermann. "Testimony of Abrams Gerzovich Suzkever. Trail of the Major War Criminals before the International Military Tribunal. Nuremberg, November 14, 1945) October 1946. Vol 8. Proceedings February 20, 1946 – March 7 1946.". Nuremberg, 1947.

Reichmann, Esther. In *Massuah Institute for the Study of the Holocaust, Tel Aviv, 033c/4741*, 8 May 1996.

Reifer, Edith. In *USC Shoah Foundation Institute for Visual History and Education On-Line Archive, 36331 (Accessed 14 February 2012).*

Reiser, Ruth. "The Only Medicine Was Charcoal." In *Sisters in Sorrow: Voices of Care in the Holocaust*, edited by Roger A Ritvo and Diane M Plotkin, 61-92. College Station: Texas A&M University Press, 1998.

Rhodes, Richard. *Masters of Death: The SS Einsatzgruppen and the Invention of the Holocaust*. New York: Alfred A. Knopf, 2002.

Rich, Tracy. "Judaism 101: Life, Death and Mourning." http://www.jewfaq.org/death.htm.

Ringelblum, Emanuel. *Ringelblumyoman Ve-Reshimot Mitkufat, Ha-Milhama [Diary and Notes from the Warsaw Ghetto: Sept 1939-December 1942]*. Jerusalem: Yad Vashem, September 1939-December 1942.

Ringelheim, Joan. "The Split between Gender and the Holocaust." In *Women and the Holocaust*, edited by Dalia Ofer and Lenore Weitzman, 340-50. New Haven: Yale University Press, 1998.

———. "Women and the Holocaust: A Reconsideration of Research." *Signs* 10, no. 4 (1985): 741-61.

———. "Women and the Holocaust: A Reconsideration of Research." In *Different Voices: Women and the Holocaust*, edited by Carol Rittner and John K Roth, 373-418. New York, 1993.

Rittner, Carol, and John Roth, eds. *Different Voices: Women and the Holocaust*. New York: Paragon House, 1993.

Ritvo, Roger A., and Diane M Plotkin. *Sisters in Sorrow: Voices of Care in the Holocaust*. College Station: Texas A & M University Press, 1998.

Rochemont, Jeanne Bommezijn de. "A Memoir of Dread." In *Imperial War Museum, London, 06/25/1*, 1-18, 1946 July.

Roitman, Gina, and Jane Hawtin. "My Mother, the Nazi Midwife, and Me." 60 mins. Canada: JHL Productions, 2013.

Roland, Paul. *Nazi Women: The Attraction of Evil*. London: Arcturus, 2014.

Roos, Julia. "Backlash against Prostitutes' Rights: Origins and Dynamics of Nazi Prostitution Policies." *Journal of the History of Sexuality* 11, no. 1/2 (2002): 67-94.

Rose, Daniel Asa. *Hiding Places*. New York: Simon and Schuster, 2000.

Rosenbaum, Alan S. *Is the Holocaust Unique?* Boulder, Colorado: Westview Press, 1996.

Rosenbaum, Irving J. *The Holocaust and Halakhah*. USA: KTAV Publishing House, 1976.

Rosenberg, Jennifer. "The Yellow Star." http://history1900s.about.com/od/holocaust/a/yellowstar.htm.

Rosenroth, Masza. In *USC Shoah Foundation Institute for Visual History and Education On-Line Archive, 198 (Accessed 14 February 2012)*.

Rosenthal, Miriam. In *Yad Vashem Archives, Jeruslem, Tape 209A and 209, 069 209 209a, 3543503*, February 18, 1981.

Rosmus, Anna. "Involuntary Abortions for Polish Forced Labourers." In *Experience and Expression: Women, the Nazis, and the Holocaust*, edited by Elizabeth R Baer and Myrna Goldberg, 76-94. Detroit: Wayne State University, 2003.

Roth, John K. "Equality, Neutrality, Particularity: Perspectives on Women and the Holocaust." In *Experience and Expression*, edited by Elizabeth R Baer and Myrna Goldenberg, 5-22. Detroit: Wayne State University Press, 2003.

Rozenberg, Eli. In *Yad Vashem Archives, Jerusalem, 0-3/4039*.

Rozett, Robert. "First-Hand Accounts and Awareness of the Fate of the Jews under the Nazis: The Case of Hungarian Labor Service Men." In *Holocaust Historiography in Context: Emergence, Challenges, Polemics an Achievements*, edited by Dan Michman David Bankier, 461-74. Jerusalem: Yad Vashem and Berghahn Books, 2008.

Rubenstein, Joshua, and Ilya Altman, eds. *The Unknown Black Book: The Holocaust in the German-Occupied Soviet Territories*. Bloomington: Indiana University Press, 2010.

Rubenstein, Judith. In *USC Shoah Foundation Institute for Visual History and Education On-Line Archive, 747 (Accessed 14 February 2012)*.

Rubin, Susan. In *USC Shoah Foundation Institute for Visual History and Education On-Line Archive, 51522 (Accessed 14 February 2012)*.

Rubinek, Saul. *So Many Miracles*. Markham, Ontario: Viking, 1988.

Rupp, Leila J. "Mother of the 'Volk': The Image of Women in the Nazi Ideology" *Signs* 3, no. 2 (1977): 362-79.

S, Ibolya. In *Survivors of the Shoah Visual History Foundation, Toronto, Canada, 18 June 1997*

Sack, John. *An Eye for an Eye: The Untold Story of Jewish Revenge against Germans in 1945*. New York: Basic Books, 1993.

Saidel, Rochelle G. *The Jewish Women of Ravensbrück Concentration Camp*. Madison, Wisconsin: The University of Wisconsin Press, 2004.

Sargent, Joseph. "Out of the Ashes." USA: Showtime Netwoks, 2004.

Sathayamals, C. "Is Medicine Inherently Sexist?." *Socialist Health Review* 1, no. 2 (September 1984): 53-7.

Sax, Benjamin, and Dieter Kuntz. *Inside Hitler's Germany: A Documentary History of Life in the Third Reich*. Lexington, Massachusetts: D. C. Heath and Co., 1992.

Schäfer, Hans Dieter. *Das Gespaltene Bewußtsein:Über Deutsche Kultur und Lebenswirklichkeit, 1933-1945*. Munich1981.

Scheffer, Maria. In *USC Shoah Foundation Institute for Visual History and Education On-Line Archive, 4187 (Accessed 14 February 2012)*.

Scherr, Rebecca. "The Uses of Memory and Abuses of Fiction: Sexuality in Holocaust Film, Fiction and Memoir." In *Experience and Expression: Women, the Nazis, and the Holocaust*, edited by Elizabeth R Baer and Myrna Goldenberg, 278-98. Detroit: Wayne State University Press, 2003.

Schiff, Vera. *Hitler's Inferno: Eight Intimate and Personal Histories from the Holocaust*. Jacksonville, Florida: Raj Publishing Inc, 2002.

———. *Theresienstadt: The Town the Nazis Gave to the Jews*. Toronto: Lugus Publications, 1996.

Schlomovitsch, Soria. In *Yad Vashem Archives, Jerusalem, 0.69/354*, 1981.

Schlufman, Rachela. In *USC Shoah Foundation Institute for Visual History and Education On-Line Archive, 6076 (Accessed 14 February 2012)*.

Schulman, Faye. *A Partisan's Memoir: Woman of the Holocaust*. Toronto: Second Story Press, 1995.

Schwalbova, Margarita. "They Were Murdered in the Infirmary." In *Sisters in Sorrow: Voices of Care in the Holocaust*, edited by Roger A Ritvo and Diane M Plotkin, 158-69. College Station, USA: Texas A & M University Press, 1998.

Schwertfeger, Ruth. *Women of Theresienstadt: Voices from a Concentration Camp*. Oxford: Berg Publishers, 1989.

Seidelman, William E. "Medicine and Murder in the Third Reich." *Dimensions: A Journal of Holocaust Studies* 13, no. 1 (1999): 1-9.

Sereny, Gitta. *Into That Darkness*. New York Mc Graw Hill, 1974.

Serras, Edith. In *David P Boder Archive, Voices of the Holocaust, Spool 34.*, August 7 1946.

Shadowsky, R. "Organization of First Aid and Medical Help in the Vilna Ghetto (Yiddish)." *Bletter vegen Vilna* (1947): 31-37.

Shandler, Rhodea. *A Long Labour: A Dutch Mother's Holocaust Memoir*. Vancouver, Canada: Ronsdale Press, 2007.

Shelly, Lore. *Twenty Women Prisoner's Accounts*. San Francisco: Mellen Research University Press, 1991.

Sherif, Muzafer. *In Common Predicament: Social Psychology of Intergroup Conflict and Cooperation*. Boston: Houghton-Mifflin, 1966.

Shik, Na'ama. "Infinite Loneliness: Some Aspects of the Lives of Jewish Women in the Auschwitz Camps According to Testimonies and Autobiographies Written between 1945 and 1948." In *Lessons and Legacies Viii: From Generation to Generation*, edited by Doris L. Bergen, 125-56. Evanston, Illinois: Northwestern University Press, 2008.

———. "Mother-Daughter Relationships in Auschwitz-Birkenau, 1942-1945." In *Mutterliche Macht und Väterliche Autorität: Elternbilder Im Deutschen Diskurs*, edited by Josè Brunner, 108-27, 2008.

———, ed. *Sexual Abuse of Jewish Women in Auschwitz-Birkenau*. Edited by Dagmar Herzog, Brutality and Desire: War and Sexuality in Europe's Twentieth Century. Hounddsmills, Basingstoke, Hampshire: Palgrave Macmillan, 2009.

Sigmund, Anna Maria. *Women of the Third Reich*. Richmond Hill, Ontario, Canada: NDE Publishing, 2000.

Sinnreich, Helene J. "The Rape of Jewish Women During the Holocaust." In *Sexual Violence against Jewish Women During the Holocaust*, edited by Sonja M Hedgepeth and Rochelle G Saidel, 108-23. Waltham, Massachusetts: Brandeis University Press, 2010.

Sivan, Miryam. "Stoning the Messenger: Yehiel Dinur's House of Dolls and Piepel." In *Sexual Violence against Jewish Women During the Holocaust*, edited by Sonja M Hedgepeth and Rochelle G Saidel, 200-16. Waltham, Massachusetts: Brandeis University Press, 2010.

Smith, Bradley E, and Agnes F Peterson. *Heinrich Himmler: Geheimreden 1933 Bis 1945* Frankfort1974.

Smith, Lyn. *Remembering: Voices of the Holocaust*. New York: Carroll and Graf Publishers, 2005.

Smith, Michael. *Foley: The Spy Who Saved 10,000 Jews*. London: Hodder and Stoughton, 1999.

Snyder, David Raub. "The Prosecution and Punishment of Sex Offenders in the Wehrmacht, 1939-1945." Nebraska: University of Nebraska, 2002.

Sommer, Robert. *Das Kz-Bordell (the Concentration Camp Bordello; Sexual Forced Labor in National Socialist Concentration Camps).* . Paderborn Schoeningh Verlag, 2009.

———. "Sexual Exploitation of Women in Nazi Concentration Camp Brothels." In *Sexual Violence against Jewish Women During the Holocaust*, edited by Sonja M Hedgepeth and Rochelle G Saidel, 45-60. Waltham, Massachusetts: Brandeis University Press, 2010.

Spiegelman, Art. "Drawing the Holocaust." www.nybooks.com/blogs/nyr-blog/2011/oct/21/drawing-holocaust/?utm_m...

Spielberg, Steven. "Schindler's List." 3 hr.17 min, 1993.

Spitz, Vivien. *Doctors from Hell: The Horrific Accounts of Nazi Experiments on Humans*. Boulder: Sentient Publications, 2005.

Squires, Nick. "Yazidi Girl Tells of Horrific Ordeal as Isil Sex Slave." *The Telegraph*, 7 September 2014.

Sruoga, Balys. *Forest of the Gods*. Lithuania: Versus Aureus, 2005.

Stanislawa-Leszczynska. "Report of a Midwife from Auschwitz." In *Auschwitz-Birkenau Report #41335*, 188-89, 1965.

Stark, Handa. In *USC Shoah Foundation Institute for Visual History and Education On-Line Archive, 182 (Accessed 14 February 2012).*

Stauber, Mollie. In *USC Shoah Foundation Institute for Visual History and Education On-Line Archive, 512 (Accessed 14 February 2102).*

Stecknoll, Solomon H. *The Alderney Death Camp*. London: Grenada Publishing, 1982.

Steigman-Gall, Richard. *The Holy Reich: Nazi Conceptions of Christianity, 1919-1945*. Cambridge: Cambridge University Press, 2003.

Steinberg, Lillian. In *USC Shoah Foundation Institute for Visual History and Education On-Line Archive, 49918 (Accessed 14 February 2012).*

Steiner, Jean-Francois. *Treblinka*. New York: Simon and Schuster, 1967.

Steinhoff, Johannes, Peter Pechel, and Dennis Showalter. *Voices from the Third Reich: An Oral History*. Washington: Da Capo Press, 1989.

Stiffel, Frank. *The Tale of the Ring: A Kaddish*. New York: Bantam Books, 1984.

Stimler, Barbara. In *Imperial War Museum Sound Archives, London, 17475*, 1992 05 28.

Strnad, Halina. In *USC Shoah Foundation Institute for Visual History and Education On-Line Archive, 31815 (Accessed 14 February 2012).*

Symonowicz, Wanda, ed. *Beyond Human Endurance: The Ravensbrück Women Tell Their Stories* Warsaw, Poland: Interpress Publishers, 1970.

Szasz, Janos. "A Holocaust Szemei (Eyes of the Holocaust)." edited by Steven Spielberg and the Survivors of the Shoah Visual History Foundation. USA, 2002.

Szobar, Patricia. "Telling Sexual Stories in the Nazi Courts of Law: Race Defilement in Germany, 1933-1945." *Journal of the History of Sexuality* 11, no. 1/2 (2002): 131-63.

Szwajger, Adibna Blady. *I Remember Nothing More: The Warsaw Children's Hospital and Jewish Resistance*. New York: Simon and Schuster, 1988.

Taeuber, Conrad, and Irene B Taeuber. "German Fertility Trends." *The American Journal of Sociology* 46, no. 2 (1940): 150-67.

Tec, Nechama. *Resilience and Courage: Women, Men and the Holocaust*. New Haven: Yale University Press, 2003.

———. "Women among the Forest Partisans." In *Women in the Holocaust*, edited by Dalia Ofer and Lenore J Weitzman, 223-33. New Haven: Yale University Press, 1998.

Tedeschi, Giuliana. *There Is a Place on Earth: A Woman in Birkenau*. England: Random House, 1992.

Thompson, Larry V. "Lebensborn and the Eugenics Policy of the Reichsführer – SS." *Central European History* 4, no. 1 (1971): 54-77.

Tillion, Germaine. *Ravensbrück – an Eyewitness Account of a Woman's Concentration Camp*. New York: Anchor Press, 1975.

Timm, Annette F. "Sex with a Purpose: Venereal Disease, and Militarized Masculinity in the Third Reich." *Journal of the History of Sexuality* 11, no. 1/2 (2002): 223-55.

Tory, Avraham. *Surviving the Holocaust: The Kovno Ghetto Diary*. Cambridge Massachusetts: Harvard University Press, 1990.

Tracz, Wladyslawa. In *USC Shoah Foundation Institute for Visual History and Education On-Line Archive, 46621 (Accessed 14 February 2012).*

Trevor-Roper, H, ed. *The Bormann Letters. The Private Correspondence between Martin Bormann and His Wife from January 1943 to April 1945* London, 1954.

Troger, Annemarie. "Die Dolchstosslegende der Linken:" Frauen Haben Hitler En Die Macht Gebracht"." In *Frau und Wissenschaft: Beitrage Zur Berliner Sommeruniversitat Fur Frauen*, edited by Gruppe Berliner Dozentinnen. Berlin: Courage Verlag, 1976.

Tuszynska, Agata. *Vera Gran: The Accused*. New York Alfred A Knopf, 2013.

Unger, Michal. "The Status and Plight of Women in the Lodz Ghetto." In *Women in the Holocaust*, edited by Dalia Ofer and Lenore J Weitzman, 123-42. New Haven: Yale University Press, 1998.

United States Holocaust Memorial Museum. http://www.ushmm.org/research/center/encyclopedia/.

Uris, Leon. *Exodus: A Novel of Israel*. London: William Kimber, 1959.

USA, Government. "Case 1 Medical June 21-26. Official Transcript of the American Military Tribunal in the Matter of the USA against Karl Brandt yet Al, Defendants Sitting at Nurnberg, Germany." London: Imperial War Museum, 21 June 1947.

USA Government. *Nuremberg Medical Case, Vol 1, Pp 695.* . Washington.: U S Government Printing Office,.

Vago, Lidia Rosenfeld. "One Year in the Black Hole of Our Planet Earth: A Personal Narrative." In *Women in the Holocaust*, edited by Dalia Ofer and Lenore J Weitzman, 273-84. New Haven: Yale University Press, 1998.

Vaisman, Sima. *A Jewish Doctor in Auschwitz: The Testimony of Sima Vaisman*. New Jersey: Melville House Publishing, 2005.

Varon, Laura. In *Massuah Institute for the Study of the Holocaust, Tel Aviv, VD-1390*, 1-35, 14 November 1996.

Venezia, Shlomo. *Inside the Gas Chambers: Eight Months in the Sonderkommando of Auschwitz*. Malden, Massachusetts: Polity, 2009.

Vrba, Rudolf. *I Escaped from Auschwitz*. New Jersey: Barricade Books, 2002.

Waller, James. *Becoming Evil: How Ordinary People Commit Genocide and Mass Killing*. Oxford and New York: Oxford University Press, 2002.

Waller, John H. *The Devil's Doctor: Felix Kersten and the Secret Plot to Turn Himmler against Hitler*. New York: John Wiley and Sons, 2002.

Walters, Guy. *Hunting Evil*. New York: Broadway Books, 2009.

Waxman, Zoe. "Rape and Sexual Abuse in Hiding." In *Sexual Violence against Jewish Women During the Holocaust*, edited by Sonja M Hedgepeth and Rochelle G Saidel, 124-35. Waltham, Massachusetts: Brandeis University Press, 2010.

Weinberg, Gerhard L. "Two Separate Issues? Historiography of World War II and the Holocaust." In *Holocaust Historiography in Context: Emergence, Challenges, Polemics and Achievements.*, edited by David Bankier and Dan Michman, 379-401. Jerusalem: Yad Vashem-Berghahn Books, 2008.

Weindling, Paul. "The 'Sonderweg' of German Eugenics: Nationalism and Scientific Internationalism." *The British Journal for the History of Science* 22, no. 3 (1989): 321-33.

Weisel, Eli. *Night*. New York Avon, 1969.

Weiss, Ernest. Personal Communication. 24 November 2009

Weiss, Ernie. *Out of Vienna: Eight Years of Flight from the Nazis*. USA: Xlibris Corporation, 2008.

Weiss, Irene. In *USC Shoah Foundation Institute for Visual History and Education On-Line Archive, 393 (Accessed 14 February 2012)*.

Weiss, Sheila Faith. "German Eugenics, 1890-1933." In *Deadly Medicine: Creating the Master Race*, edited by Dieter Kuntz, 15-39. Washington: United States Holocaust Memorial Museum, 2008.

Weitzman, Lenore J, and Dalia Ofer. "Introduction." In *Women in the Holocaust*, edited by Dalia Ofer and Lenore J Weitzman, 1-18. New Haven: Yale University Press, '1998.

Wiesel, Elie. *Memoirs: All Rivers Run to the Sea*. Toronto: Alfred A Knopf, 1995.

Winter, Walter. *Winter Time: Memoirs of a German Sinto Who Survived Auschwitz*. Hertfrodshire: University of Hertfordshire Press, 2004.

Yad, Vashem. "The Implementation of the Final Solution: Auschwitz-Birkenau Extermination Camp." http://www1.yadvashem.org/yv/en/holocaust/about/05/auschwitz_birkenau.asp.

———. *Lesson 1 – the Educational Philosophy of the International School of Holocaust Studies*. Jerusalem: Yad Vashem, 2008.

Yahil, Leni. *The Holocaust: The Fate of European Jewry*. Oxford: Oxford University Press, 1990.

Yerushalmi, E. *Pinkas Shavli (Records of Shavli)*. Jerusalem1958.

Young, Phyllis. In *USC Shoah Foundation Institute for Visual History and Education On-Line Archive, 8359 (Accessed 14 February 2012)*.

Zabarko, Boris, ed. *Holocaust in the Ukraine*. London: Valentine Mitchell, 2005.

Zimbardo, Philip. *The Politics of Persuasion (O N R Technical Report: Z-06)*. . Washington DC: Office of Naval Research, 1971.

Zuccotti, Susan. *The Italians and the Holocaust: Persecution, Rescue, Survival*. New York: Basic Books, 1987.

Zweig, Ronald W. *The Gold Train: The Destruction of the Jews and the Looting of Hungary*. New York: William Morrow, 2002.

Index

CPSIA information can be obtained at www.ICGtesting.com
Printed in the USA
LVOW11s1026060516

487019LV00001B/81/P